Socio-Legal Approaches to International Economic Law

This collection explores the analytical, empirical and normative components that distinguish socio-legal approaches to international economic law both from each other, and from other approaches. It pays particular attention to the substantive focus (what) of socio-legal approaches, noting that they go beyond the text to consider context and, often, subtext. In the process of identifying the 'what' and the 'how' (analytical and empirical tools) of their own socio-legal approaches, contributors to this collection reveal why they or anyone else ought to bother – the many reasons why it is important, for theory and for practice, to take a social legal approach to international economic law.

Amanda Perry-Kessaris is Professor of International Economic Law at SOAS, University of London.

Socio-Legal Approaches to International Economic Law

Text, context, subtext

Edited by Amanda Perry-Kessaris

Routledge
Taylor & Francis Group
a GlassHouse Book

First published 2013
by Routledge
2 Park Square, Milton Park, Abingdon, Oxon OX14 4RN

Simultaneously published in the USA and Canada
by Routledge
711 Third Avenue, New York, NY 10017

A GlassHouse book

Routledge is an imprint of the Taylor & Francis Group, an informa business

British Library Cataloguing in Publication Data
A catalogue record for this book is available from the British Library

Library of Congress Cataloguing in Publication Data
A catalogue record for this book has been requested

ISBN: 978-0-415-51016-5 (hbk)
ISBN: 978-0-203-07575-3 (ebk)

Typeset in Baskerville
by Wearset Ltd, Boldon, Tyne and Wear

MIX
Paper from
responsible sources
FSC
www.fsc.org   FSC® C004839

Printed and bound by CPI Group (UK) Ltd, Croydon, CR0 4YY

Ten years, three wild things, countless wonders. One you.

Contents

Notes on contributors

Susan Block-Lieb is Cooper Family Chair of Urban Legal Studies at Fordham Law School, formerly chair of the American Bar Association subcommittee on International Insolvency Law, and has been a delegate from the ABA to UNCITRAL's Insolvency Working Group for over 10 years.

Roger Cotterrell is Anniversary Professor of Legal Theory at Queen Mary University of London, and a Fellow of the British Academy. His books include *Living Law* (2008), *Law, Culture and Society* (2006), *The Politics of Jurisprudence* (2003) and *Law's Community* (1995).

Ross C. Davis is a graduate of SOAS School of Law and has worked as a parliamentary intern in the office of The Rt Hon. David Lammy MP. He is currently a trainee Solicitor at Dundas & Wilson LLP.

Deval Desai is a Research Associate of the School of Law at SOAS. He was previously a justice and conflict specialist at the World Bank. He has published on justice reform and demand-side accountability in extractive industries in a range of academic and policy forums.

Cecilia Juliana Flores Elizondo is a PhD Candidate in Law at the University of Manchester. Her research addresses institutional and normative aspects of international economic institutions from a theoretical perspective.

Sabine Frerichs is Assistant Professor in Sociology of Law at the University of Helsinki and member of the Centre of Excellence 'Foundations of European Law and Polity' (funded by the Academy of Finland). She earned her doctorate in sociology.

Clair Gammage is a doctoral candidate at the University of Bristol. Her main research interest lies in international economic law and processes of regionalism, particularly in Africa.

Ioannis Glinavos is Lecturer in Law at the University of Reading. His research is on law and economics and he is the author of *Neoliberalism and the Law* (2010) and *Redefining the Market–State Relationship* (2013).

Terrence C. Halliday is Research Professor at the American Bar Foundation. His books include *Fates of Political Freedom: The Legal Complex in the British Post-Colony* (2011) with Lucien Karpik and Malcolm Feeley and *Bankrupt: Global Lawmaking and Systemic Financial Crisis* (2009) with Bruce Carruthers.

Amanda Perry-Kessaris is Professor of International Economic Law at SOAS, University of London. Her books include *Global Business, Local Law* (2008) and *Legal Systems as a Determinant of FDI* (2001).

David Schneiderman is Professor of Law and Political Science at the University of Toronto. His books include *Constitutionalizing Economic Globalization: Investment Rules and Democracy's Promise* (2008).

Kirsteen Shields is a Lecturer in Law at the University of Dundee. She was previously Fellow at the LSE Centre for the Study of Human Rights and undertook doctoral research as part of an QMUL/AHRC project on the Fairtrade Movement.

Celine Tan is Assistant Professor at the School of Law, University of Warwick, UK. She is author of *Governance through Development: Poverty Reduction Strategies, International Law and the Disciplining of Third World States* (2011).

Valentina Sara Vadi is a Marie Curie postdoctoral fellow at the Faculty of Law, Maastricht University, The Netherlands.

Aurora Voiculescu is an academic at Westminster University, specialising in Human Rights. She is Associate Research Fellow at the Centre for Socio-Legal Studies, Oxford University and Visiting Professor at the Institute for European Studies, Vrije Universiteit Brussel.

Sally Wheeler is Professor of Law, Business and Society at the School of Law, Queen's University Belfast. Her work focuses on corporate governance and its interface with environmental law, human rights and corporate social responsibility. She supports Aston Villa.

Ting Xu is a Research Fellow at London School of Economics and is soon to be a Lecturer in Law at Queen's University Belfast. Her main research interests include property law; law, governance and development; and socio-legal studies.

Ronnie R. F. Yearwood has previously lectured in law at Durham, Newcastle, UCL and SOAS, University of London, and worked for the Prime Minister's Office (Barbados). He is currently a trainee solicitor at Ashurst LLP.

Acknowledgements

Many thanks to the contributors to this volume for lending a hand and playing the game.

At SOAS my thanks go to Diamond Ashiagbor and Chandra Lekha Sriram without whom ... Also to the members of the Economic Sociology of Law Reading Group and my students (in particular of International Economic Law, Economic Approaches to Law and Sociological Approaches to Law) who have suffered from, and contributed to, my on-going obsession with the theme of approaching law.

There would be no time for flights of fancy such as this if not for the gracious Maria. Nor would I have any sense of perspective without those who love and are loved by me – most of all Nicos, Georgina, Leo and Alexia.

A.P.K.
London, June 2012

List of abbreviations

ACP states	African, Caribbean and Pacific states
ADB	Asian Development Bank
ADR	alternative dispute resolution
ANC	African National Congress
BIT	bilateral investment treaty
CARIFORUM	Forum of the Caribbean Group of African, Caribbean and Pacific (ACP) States
CDO	collateralised debt obligation
CEBS	EU Committee of European Banking Supervisors
CSR	corporate social responsibility
DG Trade	EU Directorate General for Trade
DSU	Dispute Settlement Understanding
DTI	Department of Trade and Industry
EBA	European Banking Authority
EBRD	European Bank for Reconstruction and Development
EPA	Economic Partnership Agreement
EU	European Union
FDI	foreign direct investment
FSA	UK Financial Services Authority
FSB	Financial Stability Board
GATT	General Agreement on Tariffs and Trade
IASB	International Accounting Standards Board
IBA	impact and benefit agreement
IBA	International Bar Association
ICANN	Internet Corporation for Assigned Names and Numbers
ICJ	International Court of Justice
ICSID	International Centre for the Settlement of Investment Disputes
IEL	international economic law
IETF	Internet Engineering Task Force
IFI	international financial institution
ILO	International Labour Organization

IMF	International Monetary Fund
IO	international organisation
IPE	international political economy
IPRs	intellectual property rights
L&E	law and economics
L&S	law and society
LURs	land use rights
MFN	most favoured nation
MNE	multinational enterprise
NAFTA	North American Free Trade Agreement
OECD	Organisation for Economic Cooperation and Development
RCRC	Rough Consensus and Running Code
SADC	Southern Africa Development Community
SEC	US Securities and Exchange Commission
SOE	state-owned enterprise
TNC	transnational corporation
TRIPS	Trade-Related Agreement on Intellectual Property
TWAIL	Third World Approaches to International Law
UN	United Nations
UNCITRAL	United Nations Commission on International Trade Law
UNCTAD	United Nations Conference on Trade and Development
UNDHR	United Nations Declaration on Human Rights
UNSRBHR	UN Special Representative for Business and Human Rights
WIPO	World Intellectual Property Organization
WTO	World Trade Organization

Part I

Approaching international economic law

Chapter 1

What does it mean to take a socio-legal approach to international economic law?

Amanda Perry-Kessaris[1]

Introduction

> Sure, it's a subject, and sure, it exists, but if it lacks theoretical and methodological underpinnings, it is not a *discipline* of inquiry.
>
> (Trachtman 2008: 45)

International economic law is not a discipline. It is a field of study. So it falls to each of us individually to decide how to approach it. International economic activities and their laws have positive, negative, variable and unknown implications at every level of social life – on our actions and interactions; on the regimes by which we govern and are governed; and on the rationalities that guide us (Frerichs 2011b: 68; Perry-Kessaris 2011a). It is possible to identify a number of 'approaches' to the field, each with its own distinctive analytical, normative and empirical tendencies (Twining 2000; Perry-Kessaris 2011a). There are, for example, doctrinal approaches which describe what adjudicators and legislators have written, and the public choice approaches which seek to uncover the 'desires' that law 'masks' (Trachtman 2008: 45–9; see also Shaffer 2008). But there exists no 'general theory of international economic law' (Charnovitz 2011: 3) by which to navigate.

Nor is it clear that any such grand narrative is needed. As sociologist Raymond Boudon has observed, theories are least useful to social inquiry when they attempt the 'hopeless and quixotic' tasks of identifying *the* 'overarching independent variable that would operate in all social processes', or '*essential* feature of the social structure', or even 'two, three, or four couples of concepts (e.g. *Gesellschaft/Gemeinschaft*) that would be sufficient to analyze all social phenomena.' Theories only become useful when they 'organize a set of hypotheses and relate them to selected observations ... which would otherwise appear segregated' (Boudon 1991: 519 and 520). Similarly, Joel Trachtman has argued that international economic law (IEL), like law generally, too often sets out 'to cover ground that has already been covered', and that such inefficiencies might be avoided if we focused some of our energies on acquiring '[g]reater understanding of, and agreement on, research methodology'. We might then 'form a consensus that certain issues are already known' and then turn to consider 'unknown issues' (2008: 43). What IEL really needs, then, are some of sociologist Robert K. Merton's (1957) 'theories' of the 'middle range' to enable us to consolidate, identify transferable lessons (analytical, empirical and normative), and then move more wisely onwards and upwards.

Among the array of currently discernable approaches to international economic law, the socio-legal appear to stand out as especially well placed to do the heavy lifting required of a middle-range approach, as well as the next, 'onwards and upwards', agenda-setting stage. The purpose of this chapter, and of the collection that it introduces, is to highlight some distinctive virtues and vices of these socio-legal approaches. Although some are reluctant to define 'socio-legal' work very precisely, beyond emphasising that it is interdisciplinary and sociologically attuned,[2] new comers are (and perhaps old timers ought to be) keen for some clarity.[3] This collection honours that tension by stopping short of a rigid definition of 'socio-legal' approaches. Instead it identifies three dimensions on which all 'approaches' to law vary (analytical, empirical, normative) and locates socio-legal approaches to international economic law along them.

Approaching law

> Disciplinary boundaries should be viewed pragmatically; indeed, with healthy suspicion. They should not be prisons of understanding.
>
> (Cotterrell 1998: 177)

Any approach to law has normative, analytical and empirical components that determine *what* is approached, as well as *how* and *why* it is approached (Figure 1.1). The 'analytical' components of an approach are the *concepts* and *relationships* it deploys to organise the field of study. The 'empirical' components of an approach are the *facts* and *methods* that may be used to confirm the real-life existence, or absence, of concepts and relationships. The normative components of an approach are the *values* and *interests* that it foregrounds or privileges.

For example, a 'legal' approach is an in-discipline approach. It involves the 'rationalisation of and speculation on the rules, principles, concepts and legal values considered to be explicitly or implicitly *present in* legal doctrine'; and it 'constitutes a major focus of past and present legal philosophy' (Cotterrell 1992: 3, my emphasis).[4] In other words, its substantive focus (what), analytical and empirical tools (how), and normative underpinnings (why) are all strictly legal. For those who adopt a black letter, positivist, strictly 'legal' approach, law comes first and is the substantive focus. There is no need to look any further.

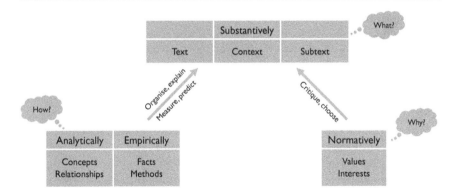

Figure 1.1 Approaching law.

Law has been travelling on (or returning to: see Frerichs, this volume) an interdisciplinary path for some time now. In fact, Gunther Teubner argues, 'we are faced with legal pluralism' not just in the sense of 'a plurality of local laws, of ethnic and religious rule-systems or of institutions and organisations', but also in the 'more radical sense' of a 'plurality of incompatible rationalities, all with a claim to universality in modern legal scholarship' (1997a: 157). Law has long been caught in a 'collision of discourses' – a post-modern 'polytheism' in which 'many Gods have even taken residence in the inner sanctum of law, *in legal theory and jurisprudence*' no less, as well as the bustling corridors of legal practice (Teubner 1997a: 149, original emphasis). Notable interlopers have been 'political theories of law' such as legal realism, the law and society movement, critical legal studies, feminist jurisprudence and critical race theories; and the more radical, even destructive, economic theories of law (Teubner 1997a: 152).

Law is not unusual in this respect. According to Klein, epistemologists are generally agreed that 'heterogeneity, hybridity, complexity and interdisciplinarity [have] become characterizing traits of knowledge' (Klein 1996: 4). Such 'boundary work' routinely crosses the 'demarcations' between disciplines, sub-disciplines, hybrid fields and 'clusters' of disciplines; between 'taxonomic categories' such as knowledge and research that are 'hard' and/or 'soft', 'basic' and/or 'applied', 'quantitative' and/or 'qualitative', 'objective' and/or 'subjective'; between 'sectors of society' such as 'industry, academe, government and the public' (Klein 1996: 4–5). For example, sociology has made inroads into (or back to) the substantive heartland of other disciplines. Examples are Economic Sociology[5] and its less developed cousin, Economic Sociology of Law. In the latter case, sociological approaches (empirical, normative, and analytical) are used to investigate relationships between law and economy (see Cotterrell, Frerichs, Gammage and Halliday and Block-Lieb in this volume; Ashiagbor *et al.* forthcoming 2013).

Furthermore, it is by now accepted from the radical fringes to the staid centre that we must reach beyond the discipline of law to economics, political science, cultural history, anthropology and geography if we are to understand international economic law (Jackson 1995: 599). In the main-stream *Journal of International Economic Law* and *American Journal of International Law* we find articles drawing on the analytical and empirical tools of history (Lowenfeld 2010), economics (Sykes 1998; Trachtman 2002), politics (Pauwelyn 2008) and political economy (Howse 2002; Slaughter *et al.* 1998 and Vandevelde 1998) to aid our understanding of international economic law. As Aurora Voiculescu puts it in this volume, 'the imagining of the new normative survival kit for the neoliberal programme, including IEL, necessitates a re-engagement with disciplines such as anthropology, sociology, moral philosophy and, of course, politics.'

So it is unsurprising that self-describing socio-legal scholars in the US and the UK have for some years been independently concerned with issues of relevance to international economic law, and have recently begun to move into the field in organised fashion.[6] The remainder of this chapter explores in greater detail how a 'socio-legal' approach distinguishes itself among other interdisciplinary approaches to international economic law. First, *what* is approached? Socio-legal approaches consider not only legal texts, but also the contexts in which they are formed, destroyed, used, abused, avoided and so on; and sometimes their subtexts. Second, *how* is socio-legal thinking and practice undertaken? It is interdisciplinary, drawing (analytically) on the concepts and relationships and (empirically) on the facts and methods of the social sciences, and sometimes the humanities. Third, *why* is socio-legal thinking and practice undertaken? Socio-legal approaches to international economic law aim to understand legal texts, contexts and subtexts, sometimes for the objective purpose of achieving clarity, sometimes with a view to changing them.

What is approached?

Socio-legal approaches consider not only legal texts, but also the contexts in which they are created, destroyed, used, abused, avoided and so on; and sometimes their subtexts. This substantive 'what' of socio-legal approaches is captured in the subtitle to this volume: text, context, subtext (Figure 1.1). I cannibalise this tripartite riff from the elegant phraseology of Sabine Frerichs:

> By *text* I mean the legal text, that is, the written rules and doctrines, or what can be considered black letter law. By *subtext* I refer to the moral subtext of a legal text, that is, its implied or deeper meaning. This includes the different notions of justice underlying a legal argument which make it necessary also to read between the lines. By *context* I

refer to the social context of a legal text, that is, its forceful link with reality. In this perspective, law is not a self-contained discourse but a powerful social institution.

(Frerichs 2012: 9, my emphasis)

Text

The most broadly recognised 'texts' of international economic law relate to international trade, and can be traced back to the negotiation of reciprocal trading agreements in the fifteenth century, through the development of the world trading system in the late 1940s, and forward through the negotiating agenda of the World Trade Organization (Charnovitz 2011: 6). But most would now agree that international economic law is much more than that.

It is 'economic' in the sense that it addresses the activities of production, distribution, exchange and consumption. It is 'international' in the classic understanding of international law is as of law among nations (inter nations), but also in the broader sense of being global. That is, the legal and/or the economic phenomena in question exist beyond national boundaries – whether regional, international, transnational and/or multinational. And, in keeping with broader 'glocalisational' trends, the field requires a consideration of local laws and economies. Indeed, 'perhaps the label "international" survives because of lawyers' attachment to traditional labels' (Valentina Vadi, personal communication 2012).

Many have tended towards a pragmatic and functional approach to defining the text of IEL, honouring the spirit of Roger Cotterrell's advice not to allow fields of study to become 'prisons of understanding' (Cotterrell 1998: 177). Their interest has been to 'correlate' laws with those actions and interactions 'which they purport to regulate or from which they spring'. They have felt free to identify and 'fructify' the laws and institutions of other 'specialized fields of public international law' – those directed primarily towards regulating ancillary fields such as 'culture, development, environment, public health, human rights, intellectual property, labor rights, monetary and currency issues, the sea, and telecom', without 'necessarily classifying ... as *part of*' international economic law (Charnovitz 2011: 4, my emphasis). The result is a field that is extensive yet not overwhelming, malleable but not shapeless.

The 'text' under consideration 'may take the form of hard law or soft, of conventions and best practices, of model laws or legislative guides, of prescriptive or diagnostic standards' (Halliday and Block Lieb this volume). In cases where the law in question is international in origin, it 'cannot be separated or compartmentalised' from general international law. Despite clearly identifiable trends towards fragmentation in the international law (Koskenniemi 2011: 265; Flores Elizondo, Schneiderman and

Yearwood in this volume), the interpretation and development of international economic law continues to affect, and be affected by, interpretations and developments in general international law (Jackson 1995: 599). International economic law is often distinguished from 'private' international commercial law governing particular transactions such as contracts (Charnovitz 2011: 7). But public and private actors and activities are in constant interaction, so it does not do to be too rigid on the matter (see Halliday and Carruthers 2009). Indeed, in this volume Roger Cotterrell specifically seeks to 'shift focus ... away from the idea of law as rooted in the governmental activity, agreements or relations of *nation states*' and 'towards a recognition that law is also rooted in the projects and aspirations of actors operating in *networks of community*', but at the same time to 'suggest that these contrasting perspectives are interdependent' (see also Xu in this volume).

Terrence Halliday and Susan Block-Lieb (in this volume) encourage us to pause a moment, to smell the ink, to 'confront[ ] who crafts the text, what form it takes, and how it is carried into global and national arenas of economic activity.' For the text is the result of decisive 'recursive' social processes that have all too often been 'left by sociolegal scholars to political scientists or jurists' (Halliday and Block-Lieb). Deval Desai answers the call with an examination of how 'the "text" of agreements between mining corporations and indigenous communities' is 'framed' through 'discourses of law, actors and the indigenous rights professional' (Desai in this volume). Likewise, Ioannis Glinavos charts the failed 'struggle towards text' to regulate the bonus culture in the banking industry (Glinavos in this volume).

Context

Whether or not they pay much attention to the text, those who take a socio-legal approach always set out to explore the actors, actions and interactions that form its context. This requires more than a legal analysis – more, for example, than simply tracking the, undoubtedly thrilling, evolution-by-interpretation of the US Alien Tort Statute from a 30-odd word side issue in 1789 to one of the greatest sources of hope for securing corporate liability for human rights abuses in the US Supreme Court case of *Kiobel v. Royal Dutch Petroleum, Co. (Shell)* on-going in 2012.[7] It requires an exploration of law's 'link with reality' (Frerichs 2012: 91).

It may not always be immediately obvious, but international economic actors (producers, distributors, exchangers, consumers, regulators, debtors – even, Actor Network Theorists would argue, objects: Cloatre 2008) both state and non-state (see Scheiderman and Shields, both this volume), their actions and their interactions, are always embedded in wider social life. Indeed, all actors are always engaged, to different degrees (from fleeting to stable), in multiple types (in the terms of Max Weber: traditional, instrumental, belief-based and affective) of social action, of which economic action and interaction are just one (instrumental) sub-type. For example, foreign direct investment creates and alters relations between many types of human actor – buyers and sellers, employers and employees, suppliers and retailers, consumers and producers, shareholders and company officials, regulators and regulatees – who may be located in the home states from which investments originate, the host states in which investments are made, and beyond. And these actors will at the same time be engaged in multiple, entangled, other forms and types of interactions. So, by applying Roger Cotterrell's socio-legal 'lens of community' to foreign investor–government–civil society relations in Bengaluru (Bangalore), I have been able to expose how the Indian 'legal system succeeds, and fails' to support actions and interactions of a 'broad range of actors, each with different motivations … but all requiring the support of the same facilitator for their productive interaction: mutual interpersonal trust' (Perry-Kessaris 2008). Likewise, in this volume, Roger Cotterrell and Ting Xu apply the lens of community to explore law in the contexts of internet developers and Chinese lineage-based communities respectively.

We may sometimes forget that 'economic' actions and interactions are part and parcel of wider 'social' life. In particular, our understandings of economy might sometimes become disembedded from wider social life, in the sense that the analytical and normative approaches (or rationalities) that are central to economic actions and interactions may be confused with, and privileged over, those that are central to non-economic actions and interactions. Sometimes that disembedding can even have a performative effect – we begin to 'think economics, do economics and feel economic' (Perry-Kessaris 2011b: 407. See also Xu in this volume). But the real world actions and interactions of individuals, and any networks of which they are part, remain firmly embedded in wider social life – in their context. As Roger Coterrell notes in this volume, when we remember that empirical embeddedness, we are more likely also to note and question 'the constituencies that IEL serves', the 'legitimacy of IEL', the 'moral distance' between IEL and the individuals and groups in whose lives it is intimately bound, and the 'regulatory hubris' implicit in proposing international action for 'local benefit'. Each of these 'issues may well be significant for the theoretical study of IEL'. Each of them also leads us to a direct confrontation with the subtext of IEL.

Subtext

Context is by now a reasonably well-mapped, fairly comfortable stomping ground for the sociologically inclined. But in the subtextual land of value and interests: There Be Dragons.

It is of deep concern to some in the field that '[s]ociology is not a good source of principled reflectiveness on the evaluation of values' (Krygier 2012: 277). For them, 'the vacant space marked out for a sociology of morals is ... a place of loss – a void that needs to be filled' (Cotterrell 2010: xiii; quoted in Krygier 2012: 318). But two fundamental questions remain unsettled and, for some, unsettling in the field of international economic law: Ought one to hunt for subtext? What ought one to do with it when one finds it?

The extent to which socio-legal work generally achieves a proper balance between theory, empiricism and moral appraisal has been the subject of much debate since at least the 1970s (see Travers 2001; Campbell and Wiles 1976). Some are not at all shy about hunting. For example, Celine Tan notes in this volume that 'socio-legal approaches allow a normative advance – the location of sites of domination and, conversely, of resistance which form the moral subtext of international economic law.' Paddy Hillyard has gone further, calling for socio-legal scholarship to be informed by 'an ethics which is not relativist, indeterminate and undecidable' and 'a vision of a just society which is informed by moral indignation' (Hillyard 2002: 656). Sally Wheeler answers that call twice over (in this volume) when she questions our tendency to pose to corporations the 'reassuringly familiar and conceptually near-vacuous request that they "respect" human rights.' She excavates the subtext of both the subject matter and the analytical approach, concluding that human rights are the wrong concepts for the job. Likewise, David Schneiderman uses the analytical tools of international political economy to unearth and critique subtextual continuities – such as the 'ideological tilt', omni-and-ever present (state and private) interests, 'universalistic pretensions' – that characterise what appears to others as a 'highly pluralistic and fragmented global [economic] scene'; and Valentina Vadi focuses specifically on the 'delicate and urgent subtext of cultural heritage' which she regards as 'dangerously exposed' to the 'highly differentiated bargaining power' at play in foreign investment arbitrations (both in this volume).

How is it approached?

Socio-legal approaches are interdisciplinary, drawing (analytically) on the concepts and relationships and (empirically) on the facts and methods of the social sciences, and sometimes the humanities. It requires 'little courage or originality ... to point out that a problem or issue can be addressed only in an interdisciplinary manner' – the 'more difficult proposition' is to realise the aspiration, especially in 'institutional settings' (Klein 1996: 209). Many of the early disciplines that were established in the nineteenth century such as psychology and economics were in reality 'pre-disciplinary' (Klein 1996: 8). So Sabine Frerichs has noted that in the first 'generation' of relations between sociology and law, which was populated by figures such as Émile Durkheim and Max Weber, 'legal and social theory were still closely connected', both because the fields were not yet fully 'differentiated', and because '[m]odern society was exemplified by the law which [was] ... thus a natural subject-matter of sociological enquiry' (Frerichs 2012: 11–12). There then followed a period of disciplinarity in which the 'surface structures' of academic institutions trended towards 'specialisation, professionalization, departmentalization, and fragmentation.' In this period 'cross-fertilizations, overlaps, and exchanges' between disciplines were often 'located in the "shadow structure"'' of academia (Klein 1996: 4). At this point law 'lost ground' in the second generation of sociology, whose leading figures[8] were 'less interested in formulating a theory of society as a whole than in understanding the partial perspectives of actors.' Indeed law came to be 'taken for granted (as "background knowledge")' by both practitioners and academics (Frerichs 2012: 11–12). In the latter half of the twentieth century, 'the balance of surface and shadow structure' began to change (Klein 1996: 4). At this point the third generation of socio-legal work was distinguished by the 'rediscovery' of law 'as a point of sociological interest'. Although those approaches entail 'considerable differences', they are all built on the premise that 'modern society is differentiated into a number of functional spheres' including politics, economics and, to a lesser extent, law 'each with distinctive ways of communication and forms of power' (Frerichs 2012: 12).[9]

The 'boundaries' between disciplinary 'neighbours' may themselves be 'overlapping' or 'disputed', 'maintained' or 'blurred' (Klein 1996: 19). Relations between neighbours may also 'shift over time'. For instance, citation analysis reveals that 'sociology's closest neighbors have shifted from anthropology in the 1940s to psychology and psychiatry in the 1950s, political science in the 1960s, economics in the 1970s, and history in the 1980s' to anthropology in the 1990s (Klein 1996: 71). Indeed contemporary academia has been described as 'a house in which the inhabitants are leaning out of the many open windows'. Some inhabitants are 'happily chatting', others 'are arguing with their neighbours' and still 'others have fallen out the windows'. Inside the building, '[m]any doors remain closed. Yet other doors have been broken down.' Moreover, 'in some cases entirely new buildings have been constructed' (Klein 1996: 19, citing John Higham).

As the borrowing and lending of approaches across boundaries becomes ever more involved, so it becomes harder – less meaningful or rewarding – to attempt to stake out distinctly 'socio-legal' territory. So while the Economic and Social Research Council has defined socio-legal studies as 'an area in which generic social science skills are predominantly employed as distinguished from doctrinal and arts based approaches to legal study' (ESRC 2005: F16), in fact those consciously drawing on the social sciences, even a self-describing 'socio-legal' scholar, may well find themselves, wittingly or otherwise, embracing elements of an arts-based approach in the process (see, for example, Desai's use of the Lacanian notion of intersubjectivity in this volume).

Sabine Frerichs (2012: 15–17) deftly fillets socially and legally informed scholarship into three conceptual tranches – law 'in', 'and', 'as'.[10] First are those who tend to think of 'law *in* society' – that is, as 'integral' to or 'embedded' in society. Second, are those who address 'law *and* society' that is, 'conventional legal scholarship (law)' complemented with 'an alternative, more sociological', critical (as opposed to normative) and empirical (as opposed to theoretical) 'perspective (society)'. Finally, there are those who address law as neither part of, nor ancillary to, but rather constructed by the social – 'that is, an "as if" reality'. Here 'the question is then not what law really is – if it is embedded or autonomous – but how it is conceived and performed' people (Frerichs 2012: 17).[11] Law 'and-in-as if' might safely seen as overlapping and mutually constitutive stages on a more-and-less socio-legal continuum. So for example, in attempting to demonstrate the merits of a 'Polanyi-meets-Cotterell economic sociology of law' I have touched on law's embeddedness *in* society, the theoretical and practical significance of law *and* economics, and the complicity of law and economics in the creation of an '*as if*' market for legal systems (Perry-Kessaris 2011a).

Two criteria do appear to be crucial to the 'how' of socio-legal approaches. First, '*like many other human practices* such as knitting or making a friend', all social sciences, including socio-legal work, 'should be about the world, which means it should attend to the world'. Second, they 'should also be something other than miscellaneous facts'. So, '[n]ot brute facts. And not mere theory' (McCloskey 2002: 39–40, original emphasis). Put another way, to take a socio-legal approach to international economic law is to 'consistently and permanently ... reinterpret' *both* economic activity and its law 'systematically and empirically' as 'social phenomen[a]' (Cotterrell 1998: 183). Analytically, this requires a conceptualisation of law 'as wholly concerned with the co-existence of individuals in social groups', and a commitment to assessing 'the significance of particularities in a wider perspective; to situat[ing] the richness of the unique in a broader theoretical context' so as to 'provide orientation for its interpretation'. Empirically, a socio-legal approach demands 'a detailed examination of variation and continuity in actual historical patterns of social co-existence, rather than in relation to idealized or abstractly imagined social conditions' (Cotterrell 1998: 183). These 'patterns' may be tracked in data collected from, for example, interviews, site visits, participant observation, conversation analysis, visual interpretation, surveys or archival research.

But fulfilment of these two criteria may be in peril. A report for the Nuffield Foundation suggested a lack of opportunities, enthusiasm and encouragement for legal scholars to undergo the necessary training in empirical methods that is often a key ingredient of socio-legal work (Genn *et al.* 2006). A second report commissioned by Nuffield argued that an 'engagement with theory' is also at risk, and that it is equally important as an engagement with facts:

> Because the facts do not speak for themselves, because concepts need to be constructed and because the process of concept construction needs to be ... informed [by] legal, political and social theory.
>
> (Adler 2007: 1)

In fact contemporary interdisciplinary work is most commonly *instrumental*, directed towards (demand side) applied objectives, such as solving social and technological problems and (supply side) 'breakthroughs in research, new scholarship, and new demands on the curriculum' (Klein 1996: 1). The result is some productive 'bridge-building' between disciplines (sometimes referred to as multi-disciplinarity). But these '[b]ridge builders do not tend to engage in critical reflection on problem choice, the epistemology of the disciplines being used, or the logic of disciplinary structure' (Klein 1996: 10). Such de-re-constructive work is left to the less common, and 'more radical' *epistemological* interdisciplinarity, which is directed towards 'restructuring' disciplines, often in response to an implicit or explicit critique of 'the prevailing structure of knowledge' (Klein 1996: 10–11). The concept of behavioural science is one example. Economic sociology of law is another. Rarer still is what I will call *integrative* interdisciplinarity (sometimes referred to as transdisciplinarity), which involves the creation of 'a paradigm or vision that transcends narrow disciplinary worldviews through overarching synthesis'. Marxism, general systems theory and structural theory are examples (Klein 1996: 10–11; see Flores Elizondo and Yearwood in this volume). To the extent that they seek to comprehensively rewrite the world, or our understanding it, grand integrative theories risk divisiveness and reductionism. More broadly useful are approaches, in particular interdisciplinary ones, which seek to facilitate an integrated consideration of diverse actors and perspectives – to put everyone on the same analytical page so that their similarities and differences are clearly visible (see Xu this volume).

Integrative studies specialist Julie Thompson Klein observes a tendency among commentators to claim that law and other predominantly 'applied' disciplines, such as management and public administration, are 'permeable' or 'inherently interdisciplinary'. Suggestions that such permeability is not necessarily a highly regarded trait are commonplace: while some disciplines, especially sciences, are described as 'hard, tight, restrictive, neat, narrow, compact, homogenous, and mature' and, therefore, impermeable, others, 'especially the humanities and some of the social sciences' (not, note well, economics) are described 'by the rhetorical foils of soft-ness and breadth' characterised by 'high degrees of differentiation and ... in a state of preparadigmatic development' (Klein 1996: 38–9). Such passive aggressive battles for authenticity abound across academia. For example, 'soft' ethnography contends that it is better able to face and accommodate the flexibility, breadth and complexity of life than 'hard' psychology, which buries its head in a rigid, narrow, simplistic unreality and wishes real life away (see Hammersley and Atkinson 1997). And socio-legal scholars, like ethnographers, would seek to distinguish themselves from 'doctrinal' or 'black letter' lawyers by arguing that there is nothing wrong with permeability – whatever it takes to get to reality.

Certainly some theoretical and practical danger lurks in disciplinary plurality – incompatibility, incommensurability, inconsistency and inco-herence to name but a few. For example, Valentina Vadi cautions in this volume against the risk of 'epistemological misappropriation' – that is interpreting other disciplines according to the criteria and 'culture' of international economic law. There is also the risk that those with an adven-turous intellectual disposition will throw themselves 'unreflexively' (see Cotterrell 1998; Nelken 1998) or even 'euphorically' (Klein 1996: 45, citing Eisel 1992) into treating a second discipline as a potential saviour. The dangers are perhaps at their worst when one discipline acts as a 'Trojan horse' for another (Teubner 1997a: 156; Fine 2010: 130).

Indeed Gunther Teubner argues that we must confront the babble of 'colliding rationalities' of different approaches head-on with a 'law of dis-course conflicts'. It would be crafted in the image of the conflict of laws system, by which is determined what court shall have jurisdiction over, and with what, equally respected, law they shall resolve private international disputes. Questions of legal significance could be systematically referred from one approach to another until a decision is made (even as the con-flicts between the approaches remain). The aim would be to 'calibrate[ ] law precisely to the plurality of social rationalities' so that attention might be focused on finding 'justice for the heterogeneous' (1997a: 159, 161 and 27). Of course, those who approach law are tangled in a 'politics of exper-tise', competing for control over 'expert spaces' (Nelken 2001a: 212). But the problems are surely not insurmountable. Perhaps the most important foundations for productive inter-disciplinarity are transparency, good will and common sense.

Finally, it is important to note that there are limits to what might be regarded as socio-legal, and modern mainstream 'law and economics' exceeds them (see also Frerichs in this volume). 'The field of *economics*, invented in the 18th century, did not discover a continent; instead, it built one from scratch, or, rather, organized one, conquered it, and colonized it' (Latour and Lépinay 2009). It has been 'organising' – acting as the normative, analytical and empirical frame for – ever-broader swathes of the intellectual terrain, whether by stealth or by invitation, ever since. For example, it is now commonplace to find law being explained as a response to market 'failure', measured as a transaction cost, chosen according to its relative efficiency. Economics thinks it is concerned with context, when in fact it is mostly concerned with text, in the form of theoretical modelling. 'The narrowness of the scientific concern of economists has of course a cost (which is itself an economist's point: the road not traveled is the opportunity cost). Prudence is the central ethical virtue of the bourgeoisie, but not the only one' (McCloskey 2002: 24). It also congratulates itself for eschewing the stickiness of moral subtext when in fact it is deeply normative – and some would argue, so it jolly well ought to be. We need to be aware of, and transparent about, the distinctive features of the approach we are taking, even if we are somewhat vague as to its boundaries – adopting a course somewhere between the rigidity promised by an *appelation d'origine contrôlée* and the promiscuity threatened by a mere flag of convenience.

Why is it approached?

Socio-legal approaches to international economic law aim to understand legal texts, contexts and subtexts, sometimes for the objective purpose of achieving clarity, sometimes with a view to changing them.

For some socio-legal scholars, the objective is to clarify the implications of taking a particular approach. This volume as a whole is one such example. Within it, for example, Clair Gammage explores the implications of a range of approaches to regional trade agreements (RTAs), even within economic sociology. For example, economic sociologists who take a structural-functional or systems theory approach 'tend to emphasize the constraining power of social structures on individual choices' and so would tend to view RTAs with 'suspicion and reluctance'; while those who take a symbolic-interactionist perspective focus instead on the capacity of individuals to 'resist, challenge and change social structures', and so would tend to regard RTAs as desirable to the extent that they are chosen and shaped 'from below' by individual states. Finally, those who adopt a social conflict perspective focus primarily on inequality and would be likely to regard RTAs as unwelcome manifestations of 'power asymmetries' between states (Hirsch 2008: 294–5). Ronnie Yearwood pushes the point further when he draws (via William Twining) on Italo Calvino's observation that whenever Marco Polo 'describe[d] a city' he was 'saying something about Venice', his home town (this volume). Our point of origin frames our approach, which in turn frames the (substantive, normative and analytical) terms of our engagement with a field.

Whether or not we can ever be objective, fully aware and able to counter our frame so that we are neutral and remote, ought we to try?

August Comte, Emile Durkheim and Max Weber shared the opinion that their talents were best directed towards describing, predicting and explaining rather than choosing. But early feminist sociologist Harriet Martineau (1802–1876) transformed her observations of nurseries, boudoirs and kitchens into activism on behalf of slaves and of women; beatnik contemporary C. Wright Mills (1916–1962) surely admired the revolutionary swirls of dust kicked up by his 'sociological imagination', as well as his motorcycle; and Karl Marx was all about activating the proletariat. In this volume, Ioannis Glinavos 'confronts the socio-economic context and moral subtext of an absence of legal text' to regulate compensation in the financial sector, and insists that we 'question the moral subtext of our decisions to allow bankers to determine their compensation structures, not as citizens ... at the mercy of market forces ... but as masters of the legislative process'; while Deval Desai asks that his analysis 'encourage those who advocate for legal empowerment of indigenous people to be reflexive, understanding themselves to be active participants in this process, rather than neutral tools to be deployed' (in this volume).

Conclusion

There is something inherently experimental in all interdisciplinary work, so it is often not a straightforward matter to know when it has been done well. While the 'conventional' measure of 'excellence ... rests on the assumption of a standard body of knowledge or a fixed body of content', interdisciplinary activities 'reconfigure', and in particular 'integrate', both 'knowledge and knowledge communities' (Klein 1996: 211). In 'selecting' and 'synthesising' the 'relevant fragments' – in particular the 'worldview or perspective' and 'underlying assumptions' – from other disciplines, 'tentativeness and reflexivity' are more valuable than 'absolute answers and solutions' (Klein 1996: 214). As Cecilia Flores Elizondo observes in this volume, 'efficiency should be understood as the capacity of a system to be responsive to the environment'. In academia as in, for example, the World Trade Organization, we must be both 'cognitively and normatively open' (see also Yearwood in this volume). Above all else, this requires a commitment to communication – decoding and rendering accessible one's own work and the work of others.

This collection aims to enable a sharpening of debate by focusing attention on the analytical, empirical and normative nuances that distinguish socio-legal approaches both from each other, and from other approaches. It is divided into three parts.

This Part (I: Approaching International Economic Law) is completed with two chapters. Chapter 2 is an assessment by Celine Tan of what she regards as the 'more substantial technical and theoretical arsenal' offered by socio-legal studies, and its transformative potential for international economic law. In Chapter 3 Sabine Frerichs presents a 'study guide' to 'Law, economy, and society in the global age', concluding with the observation that '[w]hat comes out when one mixes the legal and the social with the economic and the global is, obviously, no less than the world'.

The realities of that world are explored in detail in Part II: Context. Some contributors focus on a specific sphere of traditional international economic activity such as trade (Gammage, Halliday and Block-Lieb) or investment (Schneiderman), others turn our attention to less conventional focal points such as actor networks (Cotterrell) and systems (Yearwood and Flores Elizondo).

Finally the chapters in Part III: Subtext probe the moral meaning of international economic law, identifying and questioning the values and interests that inform its content, implementation and (non) reform. While some contributors focus on a specific sphere of traditional international economic activity such as investment (Vadi), banking (Glinavos) and corporate governance (Wheeler, Voiculescu), others address less conventional aspects of international economic law such as such as social movements (Shields), legal transplants (Xu) and community–investor discourse (Desai).

In the process of identifying the what and how of their own socio-legal approaches, contributors to this collection reveal why they or anyone else ought to bother – the many reasons why it is important, for theory and for practice, to take a social legal approach to international economic law.

Notes

1 Thanks to Roger Cotterrell, Sabine Frerichs, Martin Krygier, and Valentina Vadi for comments; and to Allison Lindner for research assistance on this chapter.
2 For example, the Socio-Legal Studies Association (SLSA) offers the strapline 'where law meets the social sciences and humanities', but chooses not to define socio-legal studies either in its constitution or in the rules governing its various competitions. See Thomas 1997 for examples of and reflections on a broad range of socio-legal work.
3 For example, the SLSA recently hosted two conferences 'Exploring' in turn the 'socio', and then the 'legal', of 'socio-legal studies'.
4 Cotterrell terms such an approach 'normative legal theory'.
5 Granovetter (1985) is widely regarded as the foundational text for the field. See Krippner *et al.* (2004) for a useful summary of developments thereafter.
6 SLSA annual conferences have seen themes of 'International economic law, justice and development' (2011), 'Socio-legal approaches to international economic law: text, context, subtext' (the origin of the present volume, 2011) and 'Exceptional states: international economic law in times of crisis and change'; while meetings of the Law and Society Association have seen individual papers, panels, and collaborative research networks on related themes.
7 For up-to-date information on this case see the Business and Human Rights Resource Centre page on the case: www.business-humanrights.org/Documents/SupremeCourtATCAReview.

8 Leading figures included sociologists George Herbert Mead, Alfred Schütz and Thomas P. Wilson: Frerichs 2012.
9 Leading figures include Talcott Parsons, Niklas Luhmann and Jürgen Habermas: Frerichs 2012.
10 Frerichs (2012) thereby rebrands the historical school of jurisprudence (together with classical sociology), realism (law and society together with legal sociology), and constructivism respectively.
11 A similar such continuum can be seen at the boundary between law and literature. 'Law *in* literature' turned to law as 'a kind of rhetorical and literary activity' (Klein 1996: 159, citing James Boyd White 1985).

Useful websites

Association for Integrative Studies: www.units.muohio.edu/aisorg/
Centre for the Study of Interdisciplinarity: http://csid.unt.edu/
International Sociological Association Research Committee on Sociology of Law RC12: www.isa-sociology.org/rc12.htm
Law and Social Sciences Research Network (LASSNet): www.lassnet.org
Law and Society Association: www.lawandsociety.org
SOAS Economic Sociology of Law Reading Group: www.soas.ac.uk/law/events/readinggroups/esol
Society for the Advancement of Socio-Economics: www.sase.org
Socio-Legal Studies Association: www.slsa.ac.uk

Chapter 2

Navigating new landscapes

Socio-legal mapping of plurality and power in international economic law

Celine Tan

Introduction

The evolution of international economic law[1] in the past three decades has been characterised by three notable developments: an expansion in the substantive areas governed by international law, the growth and diversification of international economic actors, and, crucially, the proliferation of multiple sites of international economic governance. These developments are manifestations both of the heterogeneity of contemporary international legal and economic engagements, and of the complex interplay of geopolitical and economic power that structure them.

International economic relations are constituted by international economic law. Law is instrumental in translating economic policy into practice, providing the normative framework for transnational economic activity, and narrating the contests and conflicts underlying international economic relations.

The challenge for international legal scholarship therefore rests in both mapping this web of multi-layered international economic governance and unmasking the power dynamics inherent in international economic relations. Locating and analysing these power relations is crucial to understanding how international economic law is constituted, and to unmasking the embedded discourses of international economic rules and the normative practices of international economic institutions.

Classical, formalistic accounts of international law cannot adequately capture the contextual complexity of contemporary international economic law and international economic relations. Socio-legal approaches may be able to overcome these epistemological limitations empirically, by supplying the methodologies to study international economic law beyond a focus on mere text (rules and institutions); and analytically, by supplying the critical theoretical lens to understand the power dynamics inherent in international legal relations. In this way socio-legal approaches allow a normative advance – the location of sites of domination and, conversely, of resistance which form the moral subtext of international economic law.

The objectives of this chapter are therefore twofold: first, it will seek to identify the challenges posed by the study of contemporary international economic law and the contributions of socio-legal approaches towards overcoming these challenges; and second, the chapter explores how socio-legal scholarship can provide an analytical and empirical framework to construct an understanding of contemporary international economic law, including its contextual and subtextual power dynamics.

Furthermore, the chapter argues that structural transformations in international economic law have been accompanied by a shift in its disciplinary force – the power of law to regulate the behaviour of economic actors – from one premised on hierarchical coercion and compliance, towards one that is reproductive in nature. In so doing the chapter demonstrates how a socio-legal approach to law can help us understand how geopolitical and economic power dynamics are channelled through legal instruments and other regulatory regimes.

Mapping international economic law

Moving from the periphery

One of the most striking features of the current landscape of international law and international economic relations has been the transformation of international economic law from a marginal subset of public international law into a highly specialised field of academic study and legal practice within a relatively short temporal space. The growing prominence of international economic law as a domain of professional specialism and academic study can be measured by the three indicative characteristics of contemporary international economic identified by Faundez: the increasing *volume* of new international economic rules; the expanding *scope* of such rules; and the increased *efficacy* of these rules in regulating the behaviour of international economic actors (Faundez 2010: 10–11).

Of these three measures, the latter characteristic has served most to shift international economic law from the periphery to the core of contemporary international law. The existence of mechanisms for the enforcement of rights and obligations has long been perceived of as a hallmark of a properly constituted legal system. The rapid development of formal frameworks dedicated to resolving international economic disputes – notably in the area of international trade and investment – and the correspondingly growing body of jurisprudence stemming from such tribunals have accordingly been instrumental to cementing its validity as a formal system for ordering relationships between its legal subjects.[2]

At the same time, the surge to prominence of international economic law in recent years is reflected not just in the proliferation of rules, institutions and jurisprudence but also in its heightened influence, even dominance, over both international law and relations generally, and the intersections between this international and domestic domains. It is this increased normative authority of international economic law not only over matters outside its immediate sphere of influence[3] but over those traditionally considered the preserve of 'the exclusive domestic jurisdiction of states' (Faundez 2010: 10–11) that exemplifies the preeminence of international economic law today.

The tentacular reach of international economic law into the domestic realm of nation states is both *expansive* and *intimate-expansive* in that international economic rules (broadly conceived, see discussion below) now extend to a broad range of economic and non-economic activities within the territorial jurisdiction of states; *intimate* in that they seek to reorganise fundamental aspects of the domestic social, economic and political constitution. For example, the regulatory scope of international trade law is no longer confined to border controls on imports and exports of goods and services, but includes a vast array of internal policies, including agricultural and industrial subsidies, intellectual property rights, competition policy and government procurement. Consequently, at the state level, this expansive, intimate international economic regulatory penetration reorders not only what economists term the 'policy space' (see Akyüz 2010; Chang 2005) within the domestic sphere but also the very political, socio-cultural and ecological landscape.

As will be discussed further below, the effect of these domestic penetrations of international economic law has been uneven. The susceptibility of states to the authority of international economic regulatory regimes – that is, their ability to influence and be influenced by the normative agenda of international economic law – depends on their relative power (see Braithwaite and Drahos 2000; also Faundez 2010). Those states, notably those from the third world, that have historically been marginalised from sites of global economic governance are more vulnerable to external legal and policy influences than more geopolitically or economically dominant states (see further discussion below; also Akyüz 2010; Faundez and Tan 2010). This marginalisation can be a *cause, effect* or *symptom* of a lack of power within institutions of global governance, rendering considerations of power dynamics crucial when evaluating the design, operation and implementation of international economic rules and legal institutions.

Systemic shifts

Accompanying the expansion in the scope of international economic law have been changes internal to the constitution of international economic law itself. This international economic legal 'revolution' has both contributed to and benefited from the evolving structure of the rules and institutions that shape its authority, many of which represent departures from the classical liberal model of international law. Most notably, the collapse of spatial and temporal boundaries brought on by processes of economic, cultural and technological globalisation has obscured traditional doctrinal boundaries of international law (see Boyle and Chinkin 2007: 19–24; Santos 2002: 178–187; Picciotto 2011: 26–30, 2006: 1–4).

Analytically, international legal scholarship and practice have progressively moved away from statist conceptualisations of regulation by states and of states, and towards the concept of 'transnational legal processes' in which a multiplicity of normative actors and regimes are aimed at regulating a diverse range of state and non-state actors (see, for example, Berman 2005; Cutler 2003; Koh 2006, 1996; Merry 1992; Picciotto 2011, 2006; Raustiala 2002; Slaughter and Zaring 2006; Wai 2005). The concept of transnational legal process – otherwise termed 'mutilayered regulatory regimes' or 'networked governance' – recognises the additional regulatory space that exists beyond the state and international organisations that comprises of a plethora of public and private entities, such as government agencies, non-governmental organisations (NGOs), multinational enterprises (Berman 2005; Cutler 2003; Koh 2006, 1996; Merry 1992; Picciotto 2011, 2006; Raustiala 2002; Slaughter and Zaring 2006; Wai 2005).

This change is most keenly felt in the conduct of international economic relations. Crucially, the import of external economic norms, many of which have the effect of constraining the aforementioned space for domestic governance, have occurred not through state practice in the classical liberal sense – such as accession to international agreements, acquiescence to principles of customary international law or adherence to judicial decisions – but have, instead, resulted from less hierarchical forms of regulation – rules of conduct and other regulatory devices collectively defined (for convenience inasmuch as for doctrinal classification) as 'soft law'.[4] Additionally, constraints on state activity have also been shaped by other informal external pressures – such as the discipline of credit ratings and development assistance – brought to bear on national authorities.

The framework of contemporary international economic law reflects this heterarchy of normative orders, resulting in a messy and often incongruent landscape of legal and non-legal regulatory regimes with disparate, sometimes competing, sites of normative authority. Formal legal and economic governance systems – such as multilateral and regional trade regimes of the World Trade Organization (WTO) and the North American Free Trade Agreement (NAFTA), the criss-crossing web of bilateral investment treaties (BITs) and the Bretton Woods institutions of the International Monetary Fund (IMF) and the World Bank – occupy the same regulatory realm as a raft of transgovernmental networks and private (including non-profit and non-governmental) ordering systems – such as the Financial Stability Board (FSB), the Basel Committee on Banking Supervision and the International Accounting Standards Board (IASB) –

many of which, exert far more influence on the behaviour of international economic actors than the former formal arrangements.

Rulemaking or, more precisely, norm creation in the sphere of international economic law thus transcends the traditional dichotomies of international law, notably between the domestic and the international, between public and private, and between 'hard' and 'soft' law[5] (see further below). In turn, this blurring of normative boundaries redefines the nature of coercion (and compliance) in international law and marks a shift in the disciplinary modalities of international economic law. As international economic norms are increasingly derived from informal and/or private institutions and non-binding instruments, and as regulatory authority is increasingly vested in non-traditional actors, such as networks of regulators or institutional bureaucrats, so the disciplinary force of these norms shifts away from legal supervision to non-legal, more instrumental forms of enforcement (see below).

Confronting the new landscape

Mooring the multiplicities

The movement from what Picciotto terms 'hierarchy to polyarchy' (Picciotto 2006: 2) in international economic law and governance raises two key analytical challenges for conventional international legal scholarship.

First, formalistic theories of international law pivot around the notion of a nation state and the primacy of territorial integrity and state sovereignty as its governing principles. This is manifested in two presumptive assertions of international legal scholarship: (a) the state holds the monopoly on 'making, interpreting and enforcing law' (Cotterrell 2002a: 641) so that states remain the chief architects of international law; and (b) international law is primarily concerned with constraining the exercise of state power, both at the international and domestic level.

This limited focus on the acts of nation states, as operationalised through governments and acts of government officials, discounts the significant changes to the constitution of the nation state in the wake of globalisation and international economic integration. Specifically, globalisation has resulted in the so-called 'decentering' of the state from its regulatory and functional roles. This transformation has taken place on two fronts. First, there has been a progressive decentralisation of national law-and-policymaking whereby the regulatory functions of the state have been either delegated downwards 'through principles of subsidiarity or devolution' or upwards to supranational or international organisations (Muchlinski 2003: 229–230) or dispersed to semi-autonomous public bodies (Picciotto 2011: 55, 2006: 13–15, 1998: 3–4). Second, there has been a move towards privatising regulation through the outsourcing of the state's prescriptive and enforcement functions to private entities or quasi-public regulatory authorities (see Stephan 2011; Picciotto 2011: 55, 2006: 13–15). The internationalisation of this disaggregation has contributed to the emergence of the aforementioned transnational sphere of governance with decentralised and privatised entities performing their legal and functional roles across territorial boundaries (Stephan 2011; Picciotto 2011: 55, 2006: 13–15).

The second analytical failing of the classical approach to international law is its doctrinal reliance on rigid normative categories and hierarchies of normative relationships. In particular, an emphasis on formalism leaves the classical approach unable to accommodate the diversity of normative authority in international economic law. Although much of international economic law is still derived from the traditional sources of law identified by Article 38 of the Statute of the International Court of Justice (ICJ) – treaties, custom, general principles of law and judicial decisions and writings of publicists – an increasing proportion of international economic norms, as discussed previously, originate from what international law conventionally terms 'soft law'.

These 'informal' regulatory norms are often considered peripheral to 'formal' sources of law and are often regarded as merely political norms that prescribe rules of conduct without having binding legal effect. As failure to comply with 'soft law' commitments do not incur a violation of international law per se, these norms are often discounted in formalist legal theory as sources of law. This approach conflicts with much of the reality of contemporary international economic law.

For example, transgovernmental networks – involving specialised domestic officials interacting directly with their counterparts in other states and collaborating on specific regulatory areas[6] through 'frequent interaction rather than formal [state-to-state] negotiations' (Raustiala 2002: 5) – create and implement a substantial portion of international economic law. Aside from developing discrete soft law instruments, transgovernmental networks also facilitate what is termed 'regulatory export' (Raustiala 2002: 7, 51–70) or 'modelling' (Braithwaite and Drahos 2000: 539) where regulatory rules and practices are reproduced in different jurisdictions through processes of regulatory imitation – for example, when states adopt US securities law because of market concerns (see Raustiala 2002: 28–35).

In this manner, what was national economic law comes to have an effect equivalent to that of international economic law but without involving the conventional mechanisms of treaty negotiation or supranationalism (direct effect of international as in the case of European Community law). Instead, regulatory change is effected through 'a decentralized, incremental process of interaction and emulation' (Raustiala 2002: 52).

The inability of formalist approaches to international law to accommodate these multiple systems of regulation in international economic law can be overcome with the application of a time-honoured socio-legal analytical framework: legal pluralism. First employed by legal anthropologists studying the relationship between so-called 'formal' state law and non-legal normative orders that guide individual and communal conduct, legal pluralism has provided a useful framework 'to identify hybrid legal spaces, where multiple normative systems occup[y] the same social field' (Berman 2009: 226). Borrowing from 'social systems', the approach of legal pluralism recognise the effect of principles and norms 'that are not and need not be incorporated into formal law-making processes, but still create normative standards and expectations of appropriate behaviour' (Chinkin 2003: 24–25).

The concept of non-state legal orders that coexist with, operate semi-autonomously from, and possess the same disciplinary clout over their subjects as, state legal orders can be similarly applied to international, including economic, law. So the analytical frame of 'global legal pluralism' is increasingly being used to capture this diversity of, and relationships between, formal international law, as constituted through official inter-state dialogue and negotiations, and informal law or 'soft law', as constituted through transgovernmental and private processes.

A legally pluralist approach to international economic law recognises that, despite globalisation, nation states remain the primary form of social and political organisation and that the inter-state system remains central to the constitution of international economic law. It does not discount the continuing relevance of territorial boundaries but rather allows for the mapping of the shifting contours of these boundaries and a changing conception of the state (see below). It also acknowledges that these political formations 'have become an inherently contested terrain', viewing 'the state and the interstate system as complex social fields in which state and non-state, local and global social relations interact, merge and conflict in dynamic and even volatile combinations' (Santos 2002: 94).

Adopting a legally pluralist perspective to the study of international economic law not only supplies the analytical lens through which to conceptualise the phenomenon of transgovernmental law, and analyse the privatisation of law itself, it also allows space for the conceptualisation of present and future difference and resistance.

Constituting globalisation

An important exercise in the mapping of contemporary international economic law is to examine the link between international economic law and economic globalisation and, relatedly, the contestation of power underlying this relationship. International economic law has played a significant role in facilitating the globalisation of economic relations by providing the regulatory framework for global economic integration. At the same time it has also been instrumental in validating the discourses of globalisation by sanctioning its normative narratives. Thus, a consideration of the power dynamics inherent in this process of translating economic policy into practice is pivotal to understanding how certain phenomena are sanctified within international economic law.

It has been no coincidence that the surge to prominence of international economic law has taken place at the same time as the globalising transformations in the international economy. The term 'globalisation' remains somewhat contested and a detailed discussion of these debates is beyond the scope of this chapter. However, it is important to note that the ongoing process of economic globalisation is driven primarily by an agenda for economic integration, in particular, one aimed 'at incorporating developing countries into the global economy' and that international economic law supplies the main mechanism through which the dominant principles of globalisation are translated into binding rules and policies (Akyüz 2010: 34–35; Faundez 2010: 10–11; Faundez and Tan 2010: 1).

The role played by international economic law in constituting globalised economic relations has been twofold: first, it has provided the regulatory mechanisms through which economic policies are globalised; and second, in doing so, it has legitimised these policies and their outcomes, thereby justifying the regulatory interventions of economic globalisation. International economic law thus fulfils two essential functions vis-à-vis the constitution of economic globalisation: *regulation* and *legitimation*, the former referring to 'its sanctioning and limiting role' and the latter referring to its 'culturally productive role' (Merry 1992: 362).

Once again, a doctrinal approach to international law cannot effectively deconstruct this constitutive role of international economic law and the discourses of economic globalisation. The self-referential lens of formalist legal theory focusing on purely textual and interpretative aspects of international rules and institutions fail to account for their contemporary context – what Berman describes as 'the multifaceted ways in which legal norms are disseminated, received, resisted and imbibed' (Berman 2005: 492). It is only with the aid of a socio-legal eye that we can capture this constitutive function of law, especially how law influences 'modes of thought', which in turn shape the conduct of legal actors (Berman 2005: 494). In this manner, we can deconstruct the organising rationalities behind contemporary international economic law and seek to understand how certain regulatory choices are privileged over others, including for geopolitical or ideological reasons. We can also seek to understand how a singular, universal construction of international economic law can have different applications for different state and non-state actors within the global economy.

Socio-legal theorists have long conceived of law and legal regimes as systems of symbols and signification, creating meaning and normalising or delegitimising images and presentations of social, political and economic relationships (see Berman 2005; Fitzpatrick 1992; Merry 1992; Rittich 2006; Tarullo 1985). Of particular relevance to the present context is Daniel Tarullo's depiction of international economic law as 'a set of myths' – legal texts that communicate 'facts about the world even as they purport to regulate it', the effect of which 'is to sanctify one way of knowing events in the world' (Tarullo 1985: 547–548). He argues that 'the myth of normalcy' is used to sanctify the image of what is 'normal' for states participating in the international economy, with the norm modelled on 'an industrialized nation with a capitalist, welfare-state economy' and departures from this norm seem aberrations that need to be corrected (Tarullo 1985: 547–552).

International economic law provides the means through which these differences – either of third world states which have not attained the normative model of economic organisation (the 'adolescence myth') or which are departing from the norm due to temporary crises (the 'sickness myth') – can be eradicated (Tarullo 1985: 547–552). This can be achieved through the conscription of affected states – developing countries or economies in financial crises – into respective disciplinary regimes, such as the liberalisation of domestic markets under international trade or investment law to facilitate the development of a free market economy or the adoption of fiscal austerity under IMF conditionality to facilitate return access to international capital markets. Normatively, international economic law sanctions external interventions into nation states in pursuit of the policies of globalisation, creating an imagery of economic relationships 'that seem natural and fair because they are endowed with the authority and legitimacy of the law' (Merry 1992: 361–362). Meanwhile, the ideological strands of neoliberalism, permeating global economic policymaking, provide the conceptual framework within which international rules are negotiated and implemented so that the choice of regulatory design is legitimised by the economic policies it supports.

The changes in the manner in which international economic law affects social and economic relations within states, particularly third world states, reflect the evolution international economic law's role and purpose over the past three decades. As Akyüz notes, the postwar international economic architecture was premised on the management of cross-border economic relations and on constraining domestic economic policies of states that may have ramifications outside their territory (Akyüz 2010: 39–40). However, contemporary international economic law has been driven primarily by 'a desire to achieve a deep and broad global economic integration' through policies of liberalisation and deregulation (Akyüz 2010: 40). The international economic legal system is, therefore, no longer premised on the facilitation of an orderly system with rules for multilateral cooperation in an era of economic interdependence but have, especially in the areas of trade and investment, increasingly been based on the need to facilitate access to global markets (Akyüz 2010: 40).

Additionally, a significant part of international economic law today is focused on the harmonisation and standardisation of domestic economic regulatory regimes, mainly to achieve the aforementioned global integration of markets. While some of this is achieved through independent and mutually negotiated norms, a significant portion is undertaken through the process of regulatory export (see above). This entails primarily the 'export of regulatory rules and practices from major powers to weaker states', thereby promoting global policy coherence and convergence based a regulatory model of major industrialised countries (Raustiala 2002: 7). Such convergence represents what Santos terms 'globalised localism' – the process by which a given phenomenon is successfully transplanted in another jurisdiction and 'develops the capacity to designate a rival social condition or entity as local'[7] (Santos 2002: 178–179). As discussed previously and further below, the 'diffusion of regulatory ideas, rules and practices' (Raustiala 2002: 7) in this manner, undertaken substantially through transgovernmental networks, alters the nature of international legal engagement, reconstituting not only the form of international norm creation (and consequently adjudication over norm conflicts) but also the forms of disciplinary power that structure these relationships between international economic actors.

Law and the contestation of power

A key theme emerging from the foregoing discussion on the nature and scope of contemporary international economic law is the relationship between regulatory regimes and the reality of geopolitical and economic power underpinning their design and implementation. The transformations that have occurred within the global economy and the changes in international economic law have largely been the outcomes of contests of power between international economic actors or, at the very least, reflect the exercise of power by these entities. With few exceptions, the choice of economic regulatory regimes and the substantive content of international economic law today is largely determined by those entities wielding the most geopolitical and economic power in a globalised world.

Yet the dynamics of power in international relations are marginalised, if not ignored, in traditional approaches to international law. Power here is viewed as 'external and opposed to law', as a means of constraining the exercise of state power – either domestically or internationally (Cotterrell 2002a: 643). For example, doctrinal international law places consent at the heart of the international legal system, focusing on the text of treaty signature and ratification as key indicators of the validity of international rules and the legitimacy of international organisations. It does not consider the context or subtext of the consent – whether it was secured in the course of an exercise of power by some states or other entity over another state or entity. By contrast, socio-legal scholarship places power at the heart of the study of law and legal institutions, paying close attention to the mechanisms by which power structures social and economic life.

According to Cotterrell:

> Most sociolegal work explores the power of law: how it is structured and organized, its consequences and sources, and the way people and organizations seek to harness it, have differential access to it or find themselves differentially affected by it ... Sociolegal scholarship ... has shown how law as institutionalized doctrine formalizes and channels power rather than controlling it, making its effects more predictable and precise and its exercise more orderly.
>
> (Cotterrell 2002a: 643)

An analysis of power is vital to understanding the causes and effects of international economic governance. The transnational web of multi-layered international economic law and its supporting institutions is laced with complex power dynamics that structure the legal and economic relations between the subjects of international economic law and other actors impacted by international legal rules and regulation. The capacity of international economic law to balance competing interests of international economic actors and other non-legal stakeholders[8] rests, in many respects, on the outcomes of 'contests of principles' between such actors (Braithwaite and Drahos 2000).

The central thesis of Braithwaite and Drahos' landmark study of global business regulation is that the globalisation of legal and non-legal norms is 'best conceptualised in terms of the relationships between actors, mechanisms and principles', with actors articulating, supporting and seeking to entrench principles in regulatory systems in different ways (Braithwaite and Drahos 2000: 15–19). They argue that international economic actors 'seek, through principles, to incorporate into regulatory systems and social practices changes that are consistent with their general values, goals and desires' (Braithwaite and Drahos 2000: 19). At the heart of this process of regulatory development is the relative power of each actor, whether manifested in the ability of actors to control 'webs of reward and coercion', or 'dialogic webs', or both (Braithwaite and Drahos 2000: 551).

Braithwaite and Drahos' empirical methodology enables us to locate sites of normative authority within international economic law through their establishment via contests of power between international economic actors. The ability of actors to effect compliance with regulatory change – such as reforms in international economic rules to facilitate globalisation – rests on their power to weave webs of reward and coercion (available only to states with the economic and military power to support compensation and/or threats) or the power to dominate dialogic webs or webs of persuasion (Braithwaite and Drahos 2000: 551–554). Thus, the ability of actors to influence the content of regulatory regimes as well as to determine which regime or forum is designated as the regulatory arena for a particular subject matter will rest on their power relative to other competing actors within and outside that regime.

Historically, geopolitically and economically powerful state actors have dominated the development of legal norms and determined the shape and content of normative orderings. In international economic law, as in other areas of international law, this has created a fairly clear demarcation between those states that constitute the rule-*makers* and those that constitute the rule-*takers* of the respective legal systems. The initial insertion of third world states into an international order outside their design and influence[9] and their continuing marginalisation from the sites of contemporary international economic governance mean that, for the most part, these countries have constituted the former and remained *objects* rather than *subjects* of the international legal system (see Faundez and Tan 2010: 2).

This marginalisation has been compounded by the processes of decentralisation and privatisation of regulatory regimes discussed above which have led to the emergence of powerful non-state actors, notably transnational corporations, in international economic law and global economic governance. Consequently, these actors, individually or collectively, significantly influence the direction of international economic regulation in a globalised economy. Braithwaite and Drahos argue that while weak states and non-governmental organisations (NGOs) 'can effectively tug at many of the strands of dialogic webs of influence', these regulatory coalitions remain dominated by hegemonic actors who have the capacity to 'escalate webs of reward and coercion' (Braithwaite and Drahos 2000: 551).

The dynamics of power relations can be illustrated by reference to two aspects of international economic law: the prevalence of forum-shifting; and the impact of transgovernmental networks. In the former, hegemonic actors seek to optimise their success in operationalising their regulatory principles by seeking out favourable regulatory regimes (Braithwaite and Drahos 2000: 564–565). Forum-shifting occurs via three strategies: 'moving an agenda from one organization to another; abandoning an organization and pursuing the same agenda in more than more than one organization' (Braithwaite and Drahos 2000: 564–565). For example, the United States, often at the behest of its pharmaceutical lobby, has shifted the global regulation of intellectual property rights (IPRs) from the World Intellectual Property Organization (WIPO) and back again as it suited their interests (Braithwaite and Drahos 2000: 564; see also Dutfield and Suthersanen 2008). Only 'the powerful and well-resourced' (Braithwaite and Drahos

2000: 564) can engage in this strategy but all states are affected by the regulatory shifts that result.

Moving to the second example of the influence of power dynamics, power is also deeply embedded within transgovernmental networks, which are a form of 'dialogic webs of influence' described by Braithwaite and Drahos (see above). There is no hierarchy of command within networks – regulatory change is instead effected through 'persuasion' (Raustiala 2002: 51) – but they have a propensity to be dominated by powerful actors and so are susceptible to the same power dynamics inherent in conventional forms of international lawmaking (Raustiala 2002: 7–8, 51–52). In fact, Raustiala's study of these networks demonstrates that 'power plays a critical role' in the export of 'regulatory ideas, rules and practices' from economically domi-nant states to weaker states, with 'economically weak jurisdictions' frequently embracing 'as substantial part of the regulatory models of the dominant powers' (Raustiala 2002: 51, 59–60). Of course there are a number of moti-vations for importing existing models – for example it can be more cost-effective than creating a new model from scratch, and there may pressures from market actors – but there is no doubt that in choosing to model them-selves on the United States and the European Union, poorer economies are often responding to the exercise of 'soft power' ('the power to attract' versus the 'hard power' to coerce) (Raustiala 2002).

In some cases dominant international economic actors insist on the use of transgovernmental networks and 'soft law' instruments over conven-tional modes of international economic rulemaking and adjudication. This insistence may be justified on the grounds that such informality allows for more efficacious responses to current events. However, it remains the case that such informality circumvents the democratic safe-guards of international law, enabling hegemonic actors to embed their preferred principles with little opposition.

An analysis of power here helps explain why soft law is preferred over hard law for some regulatory regimes but not others. It is also helpful in explaining why certain regulatory regimes are privileged over others and why some areas of the global economy are more regulated than others. For example, for Akyüz, the incoherent structure of international eco-nomic rules reflects the pursuit by dominant states of their individual interests (Akyüz 2010: 35). He points out that, while 'international trade is organised around a rules-based system with enforceable commitments', major industrialised countries have eschewed a binding multilateral regime to constrain their financial markets, opting instead to use less formal transgovernmental networks and non-binding standards and codes. So there 'are effectively no multilateral disciplines' over state level macr-oeconomic and exchange rate policies states – a gap that constitutes a significant source of instability for the international economic system (Akyüz 2010: 42–50).

Further incoherence is to be found in the substantive content of international economic rules, which, Akyüz argues, 'are not neutral' in their design nor in application. For example, international trade law promotes 'deep integration' in areas where advanced economies have comparative advantage such as 'free movement of industrial products, money and capital, and enterprises' and not in 'areas where liberalisation would generally benefit the developing world' such as 'agricultural goods, labour mobility and technology transfer' (Akyüz 2010: 40). A socio-legal approach to international economic regulation highlights law's role as constitutive and facilitative of social and economic relations – in this case, of highly asymmetrical international relations, motivated by economic considerations.

Towards a new cartography

The rapid expansion of international economic law over the past three decades has been matched by a proliferation of international legal scholarship on the subject, including a growing body of socio-legal scholarship focused on drawing out the contextual and subtextual complexities of contemporary international economic rules and institutional practice. These studies recognise, above all, and more than any other international legal field, that international economic law remains a contested terrain of policy, practice and scholarship. For example, even staying within the narrow confines of economic values and interests, scholars, regardless of orientation, have generally recognised that international economic law has to balance twin, conflicting, imperatives if it is to facilitate or, at least not impede, international economic transactions – the need for stability and predictability on the one hand, and responsiveness to an ever-changing global economy on the other.

Reconciling the tensions inherent in international economic law, as well as mapping its wider impact on social, economic and political relations requires the kind of contextualisation that can only be effectively achieved by using a socio-legal approach to law. A socio-legal approach to the study of international economic law enables us to both discern, and appreciate the significance of, two key related trends: first, the existence of emergent sites of normative authority for international economic rules and regulation outside the traditional inter-state system; and second, the shifting modalities of power in international economic governance that enable dominant actors to embed and globalise their models of economic organisation. Understanding the latter development is especially important to analysing the future directions of international economic law, including its reform and resistance.

Elsewhere I have argued that there has been a discernible shift in the disciplinary apparatus of international economic law, representing shifting modalities of power at the global level (Tan 2011: 218–220). The evolution of various structural aspects of international economic law – notably its movement away from hard coercive power as a mechanism of enforcing compliance towards a subtle, more reproductive form of persuasive power, as marked by the transition from hierarchical, inter-state law to plural, transnational law – signals a shift in the way that power is institutionalised within international economic law. This has occurred in tandem with the evolving rationality of international economic law, away from the imperative to secure transnational economic order and towards facilitating integration through harmonisation and standardisation of economic norms (see above). This transition requires a significant revision of the terms of engagement of weaker parties within the system, primarily third world states and their constituents but also, increasingly, communities from within decentred states in the industrialised north.

These developments within international economic law represent the beginnings of a transition from what Foucault terms the 'technologies of dominance' to 'technologies of self', the two poles from which 'the organisation of power of life' is deployed, or in other words, the movement from a disciplinary society' to a 'society of control' (Foucault 1991: 220–221, 1991: 261–263; Tan 2011: 14). Here, the movement is away from the disciplinary supervision of societies – that is, through establishing normative frameworks for behaviour and the exclusion/penalisation of departures from such norms – towards the establishment of a 'biopolitical' power in which the objects of power (societies or states) reproduce these norms and seek to insert themselves into the very relationship of power (ibid).

The previous sections have demonstrated that international economic discipline is no longer asserted through formal legal channels. Instead, enforcement of international economic rules has shifted from reliance on traditional modes of norm compliance – observance of treaty obligations and directives of international organisations – towards less legal, more instrumental but no less coercive forms of supervision – economic sanctions or incentives, socialisation, institutionalised habits, modelling, complex interdependency and normative commitments based on reputational concern (Djelic and Sahlin-Anderson 2008: 4–6; Braithwaite and Drahos 2000: 554–556; Koh 1996, 2006). International economic rules and regulatory practices are increasingly, in Raustiala's terms, 'diffused' around the world through the use of 'soft power' exerted by dominant states through 'persuasion rather than command' (Raustiala 2002: 51).

This analysis dovetails with Braithwaite and Drahos' analysis of the processual shifts in global business regulation today which sees the movement away from remunerative and coercive webs of influence towards the use of dialogic webs in securing both adoption and compliance with norms in the aforementioned contest of principles (Braithwaite and Drahos 2000: 563). A key component of this form of regulatory change is the constitutive function of international economic law discussed above. The mutually reinforcing roles of international economic law and the discourses of globalisation in sanctifying economic myths, particularly in legitimising policies of the Washington Consensus, reifies international economic rules. In this manner, states accept regulatory change not only because international law obliges them to, but because such adoption is necessary to demonstrate its eligibility for membership within the integrated, globalised economy.

Combining Braithwaite and Drahos' empirical methodology for mapping sites of global regulation with Foucault's critical conception thus enables us to critically evaluate not just the effects of power relations on the constitution of international economic law but also the changes in how these power dynamics are channelled through mechanisms of law. Adopting this approach to the study of international economic law will hopefully furnish us with a more substantial technical and theoretical arsenal in which to tackle the increasing complexity of international economic law and regulation and more effectively map the landscape of international economic law in this globalised era.

Notes

1 The term international economic law is used extensively to refer to a vast array of regulatory subject matter incorporating both public and private international legal relations, including international trade law, international law of finance and investment, international commercial law and the regulation of intellectual property rights and transnational business (see, for example, Loibl 2006). Borrowing from the definition by Ortino and Ortino (2008), I use the term international economic law to denote broadly the rules and institutions regulating economic relations 'that cross or have impacts across the boundaries of a single legal and economic system' and that 'operate in or impact the global economic system' (Ortino and Ortino 2008: 89).

2 See for example the Dispute Settlement Gateway website of the World Trade Organization (WTO) and the case law section of the International Centre for the Settlement of Investment Disputes (ICSID) at: http://icsid.worldbank.org/ICSID/FrontServlet.

3 The impact of international economic law on other areas of international law, such as human rights and environmental law, is largely manifested through conflicts between states' obligations under international economic regimes and their obligations under other international legal orders.

4 See note 5 below.

5 The terms 'hard' and 'soft' law are often used more as heuristic devices than as reflections of the normative nature of the legal principles subject to such categorisations. 'Hard' law is often used to refer to legally binding obligations that are precise (or can be made precise through judicial interpretation and executive directives) and that are justiciable in an appropriate adjudicatory tribunal while 'soft law is used to denote commitments that are not legally justiciable but which may possess normative force due to the attraction of non-legal sanctions for failure of compliance.

6 For example, banking regulation, money laundering, or environmental cooperation (see Raustiala 2002).
7 The counterpart of a globalised localism is that of a 'localised globalism' – the alterations in local conditions to accommodate the transplanted entity or concept (Santos 2002: 178–179).
8 By other stakeholders I mean actors who are not formally constituted in status as international legal subjects for the purposes of international economic law but who are nonetheless affected by international economic rulemaking, including individuals and groups of individuals, such as indigenous peoples, as well as the environment.
9 The nature of the incorporation of third world states into the postcolonial international legal order has been examined by numerous scholars of international law, notably Anghie 2004, Balakrishnan 2003, and more, recently, Pahuja 2011.

Useful websites

Institute for International Law and Justice, New York University School of Law: www.iilj.org/
International Centre for the Settlement of Investment Disputes: http://icsid.worldbank.org/ICSID/Index.jsp
South Centre: www.southcentre.org/
Third World Network: www.twnside.org.sg/
World Trade Organization Dispute Settlement Gateway: www.wto.org/english/tratop_e/dispu_e/dispu_e.htm

Chapter 3

Law, economy and society in the global age

A study guide

Sabine Frerichs

Introduction: 'sociologizing' international economic law

I will begin with a personal remark. I am sociologist at the University of Helsinki. The institute I am affiliated with is called *Kansainvälinen talousoikeuden instituutti* – Institute of International Economic Law. But almost four years had to pass before I came to think about socio-legal studies in international economic law. The present book provides the occasion. In her introductory chapter, Amanda Perry-Kessaris (in this volume) carefully defines 'socio-legal studies' and 'international economic law' in ways that would not include or exclude too much. As to the latter, my working definition is also a 'functional' one. Eventually, I start not with a legal, but with a sociological understanding of international economic law, which is derived from the work of Karl Polanyi (1886–1964).

While Polanyi started his career as a doctor of law, he is much better known as an economic historian and economic sociologist. He owes his rise to prominence, first and foremost, to his treatise *The Great Transformation* (1957 [1944]), which was published at the height of the Second World War. In this book, Polanyi describes the institutional and ideological foundations of the 'market society', which emerged in the nineteenth century and which ended in a catastrophe: two world wars and a world-economic crisis. How Polanyi's historical account of the market society is linked to today's international economic law is, hence, the first thing I would like to explain (Frerichs forthcoming).

Historically, Polanyi's focus is on the 'long' nineteenth century and, notably, 'the rise and fall of market economy'. At the very beginning of his book, he claims that 'nineteenth century civilization rested on four institutions', namely, the 'balance-of-power system', the 'gold standard', the 'self-regulating market', and the 'liberal state' (1957 [1944]: 3). Within this institutional framework, he emphasizes the role of the self-regulating market. Accordingly, '[t]he key to the institutional system of the nineteenth century lay in the laws governing market economy' (Polanyi 1957

[1944]: 3). In the main part of his book, Polanyi then explains how the market economy was itself instituted with the help of legal and economic fictions, notably, the 'fictitious commodities' of 'labour', 'land', and 'money' (Polanyi 1957 [1944]: 71–72). He points out that these so-called production factors cannot be separated from the substance of human, natural, and social life itself, which is put at risk when it is subjected to the laws of the market. Accordingly, the birth of the modern market society is owed to the 'philosophy of economic liberalism' (Polanyi 1957 [1944]: 269), which results in 'running society as an adjunct to the market' (Polanyi 1957 [1944]: 57).

After the Second World War, this 'utopian experiment' (Polanyi 1957 [1944]: 89) was continued, albeit with different political and legal means, in the form of the *social* market economy. The 'rise and fall' of the social market economy is the story of the twentieth century, which links Polanyi's study to the present (Streeck 2009). The connection to international economic law is implied by Polanyi's initial emphasis on the 'organization' of the world which he defines less in terms of 'centrally directed bodies acting through functionaries of their own' than of the 'universally accepted principles' and the 'factual elements' on which the international order rests (Streeck 2009: 18). Obviously, the gold standard, and its political 'superstructure', the balance-of-power system (Streeck 2009: 3) form part of the 'principles' and 'facts' of international economic law in the nineteenth century, which is today also characterized by 'central organizations', such as International Monetary Fund or the World Trade Organization.

In this respect, we can claim that the laws of the market society are, in its global extension, reflected in international economic law. In David Kennedy's terms (1999: 38), this is 'the law, of whatever origin, which governs international economic transaction'. As such, '[i]t mixes national and international law', and, while it is 'rooted in private law' (Kennedy 1999: 38), it is also shaped by public law. In the remainder of this chapter, I will give an introduction into 'socio-legal studies' in this field, first focusing on its general elements and then on exemplary agendas.

General elements

If a student wanted to enrol in 'socio-legal studies of international economic law' what guidance would I give her? How to provide a first orientation in a field that is probably still better qualified as 'emerging' than well 'established'? Sure enough, I would recommend her this book, which I consider representative of the kind of studies undertaken and exemplary in giving a structured overview. Within this book, I would, notably, point to the chapters that go deep into the material – which analyse data and discourses, policies and practices – and, in doing so, 'reconstruct' the contents of international economic law in 'socio-legal' terms. This is the work to be done, and there are plenty of things to do, both from a non-legal and a non-economic perspective (or from non-dogmatic legal and economic perspectives). My own contribution falls behind all this empirical work. In fact, it can best be understood as reflections from the armchair. If this comfortable position has anything to add to the present collection, and to offer to students (and researchers) of this field, it is possibly to link the ongoing activity in the field to some larger projects that shaped and shape our 'socio-legal' thinking. Let us begin with some systematic enquiries concerning the 'legal' element in society and the 'social' element in the law as well as 'economic' and 'global' aspects in socio-legal studies.

The legal element in sociology

As a sociologist, I feel bound to start with classical sociology (Frerichs 2012). My first question is, thus, what the 'sociological founding fathers' thought about the law. And why did they think about the law at all? In fact, they considered law a constitutive part of society and, in analysing society, they could, hence, not ignore the law. Moreover, some of them had even studied jurisprudence. Max Weber (1864–1920) is most prominent in this respect, as he completed both his first, doctoral dissertation and his second, postdoctoral dissertation in the legal discipline. Karl Marx (1818–1883) began as a law student but ended up as a doctor of philosophy, and Emile Durkheim (1858–1917) started as a teacher of philosophy but soon became acquainted with legal scholarship as well. (Even Polanyi, the above-mentioned analyst of the market society, was a doctor of law.) However, it was not so much black-letter law that formed their thinking than a historical concept of law – and of law in its social context – which was also influential in legal scholarship at that time (notably, in the historical school of jurisprudence).

Now what *is* the legal element in society, which the sociological classics found so intriguing? By and large, they were all preoccupied with the emergence of modern society (or the 'market society', in Polanyi's terms): how it was brought about in a process of massive social transformations – including the industrial revolution, with all its consequences for work and family life – and how it differed from more traditional forms of society. Key terms in this respect are: differentiation and specialization, secularization and rationalization, liberalization and individualization – attributes that have come to stand for the modernization process, more generally. And part and parcel of this modernization is a changing role – and form – of the law. Let us illustrate this with a distinction that a sociologist, Ferdinand Tönnies (1855–1936), once borrowed from a legal scholar, Henry James Sumner Maine (1822–1888), and which he enriched sociologically.

Accordingly, the transition from traditional to modern societies can be depicted as a movement 'from status to contract' (Maine 1983 [1861]; Tönnies 2001 [1887]). In simplified terms, status is attributed to the family one is born into, whereas contract is a free agreement between individuals.

The idea that the modern society is structured, or even constituted, by modern forms of law can also be found in the works of Marx, Durkheim and Weber. Marx (1859) famously distinguished between the economic structure of society and its legal and political superstructure. Legal categories would thus both reflect and mask unjust economic realities. Marx (1842) illustrates this with the invalidation of customary rights of the poor (collecting fallen wood in the forests) in favour of property rights of the rich (turning wood into an industrial commodity). Durkheim (1893) argued, instead, that the law is a symbol of social solidarity, or of the moral consciousness of a given society. Accordingly, modern societies build on different patterns of solidarity (organic solidarity) than traditional societies (mechanical solidarity). And these different forms of solidarity are expressed in different forms of law (restitutive versus repressive law). Weber (1978 [1922]) worked, in turn, with a series of ideal-types that capture the rationalization of modern society and its law. In his view, the main driving force of modernity is a purposive (means-ends) rationality. Within the legal field, this means that irrational forms of law are replaced with rational ones and that the instrumental qualities of the law trump its idealistic contents.

The social element in jurisprudence

All in all, the law was thus central to sociology from its very beginnings, even though it was somewhat lost sight of later on. Now, what about the social (or sociological) interests of lawyers? Two major schools of legal thought are worth mentioning in this respect: the historical school of jurisprudence, which was most influential in the nineteenth century, and legal realist scholarship, which rose to prominence in the twentieth century. The historical school of jurisprudence competed, at its time, with the positivist school of law, on the one hand, and the natural law school, on the other. In this contest of schools, different concepts of law were at stake. This can be illustrated as follows. For the positivist school, law is 'essentially a political instrument, a body of rules promulgated and enforced by official authorities, representing the will, the policy, of the lawmakers' (Berman 2005: 13). Law is thus conceived as a 'text' given by the legislator. For the natural law school, law is 'essentially a moral instrument, an embodiment of principles of reason and conscience implicit in human nature' (Berman 2005: 13). In this case, emphasis is put on the 'subtext' of the law, which is subject to moral reasoning. For the historical school of jurisprudence, law is 'essentially a manifestation of the group memory, the historically developing ethos, of the society whose law it is' (Berman 2005: 13). Accordingly, law cannot be understood without its historical, cultural, and social 'context'. Comparing these different conceptions, historical jurisprudence was clearly the most sociological school of thought in the nineteenth century – at least in principle (Frerichs 2012). In practice, the historical school turned towards conceptualist jurisprudence and, thereby, lost its references to social reality.

In response to massive social problems, economic crises, and two world wars, 'the social' was given much more weight in twentieth century legal thinking. As Duncan Kennedy (2006) argues, a social orientation of the law becomes even paradigmatic under these circumstances. For the concept of law, this means that law is increasingly understood 'as a purposive activity, as a regulatory mechanism that could and should facilitate the evolution of social life in accordance with ever greater perceived social interdependence at every level, from the family to the world of nations' (Kennedy 2006: 22). In this social engineering perspective, law is thus conceived as a means to social ends. Even though the general shift towards 'the social' did not mean that everybody would become a legal realist now, legal realism was a central driving force in this respect – including its beginnings in 'sociological jurisprudence' and also its offspring, the 'law and society' movement (Simon 1999). What unites the different fractions of legal realism is – obviously – 'a critical, detached stance as to all the schools and approaches to law with a non-realistic bent' (Siltala 2011: 149). These, notably, include 'legal idealism as proffered by the natural law philosophy' (that is, the above mentioned natural law school), 'analytical legal positivism with its emphasis on the historical will of the sovereign and the original intentions of the legislator under legal exegesis' (that is, the above mentioned positivist school of law), and 'legal formalism under the German or American constructivism' (or what was referred to above as conceptualist jurisprudence) (Siltala 2011: 149). Within legal scholarship, an orientation towards the social context of the law can thus, first and foremost, be found in the twentieth century tradition of legal realism, which, notably, furthers the encounter between law and the (other) social sciences.

The economic element in socio-legal studies

In the present chapter, I understand socio-legal studies as part of the movement that opens law to the social sciences in order to better understand its context. Within the realist heritage, this includes not only sociology but also economics. In this regard, the term 'socio-legal studies' seems preferable to what is known, within the American context, as 'law and society' (L&S) movement. The reason can be found in the big 'other' of the L&S movement, which emerged at the same time, namely, the 'law and economics' (L&E) movement. When L&S spokesman Lawrence Fried-man (2005: 8–9) wonders: 'Why is the [L&S] movement unattractive to economics?', the answer is that there is a more attractive movement for economists – and a more successful one, too, as L&E spearhead Richard Posner proudly states (1995: 275). Hence, while both movements inherited the 'scientific outlook' and the 'consequentialist' (means-end oriented) concept of law from legal realism (Galanter and Edwards 1997: 377), they have taken different turns as regards their preferred approaches (e.g. structuralism or constructivism vs rational choice) and their respective ancillary sciences (sociology vs economics).

This might look like a reasonable division of labour: L&E for law and economics, L&S for the rest. However, in highlighting the economic element *in* socio-legal studies, I want to counter the impression that economic questions can simply be delegated to another 'law-and' discipline. Instead, socio-legal scholars should include these matters in their own agenda and address them in their own terminology and theoretical frameworks. To the same effect one can claim that the sociology of law needs to include an *economic* sociology of law (just as economic sociology needs to include an economic sociology of *law*). This describes my own project (Frerichs 2009; Frerichs 2011b), which draws on Richard Swedberg's pioneering work (2003, 2006) and which, notably, builds on the sociological classics, who were still general sociologists, economic sociologists, and legal sociologists, at the same time. However, to illustrate this point I will draw, in the following, not on the related discourse in sociology but in L&S scholarship (which is itself informed by sociological arguments).

In her 2004 Presidential Address to the Law and Society Association, Lauren Edelman (2004) discusses the relationship between L&S and L&E scholarship and the 'contested terrain' between the two. As to L&E, she argues that this movement 'has been extremely influential in the policy realm, so much so that concepts of law and justice are increasingly *defined* in economic terms and understood through the lens of market efficiency' (Edelman 2004: 182; original emphasis). The political impact of L&E calls, in her view, for critical commentary on the part of L&S, whose perspectives are said to have 'important, if largely unexplored, implications for the nexus of market rationality and justice' (Edelman 2004: 182). What she refers to here is, notably, the concept of economic rationality, which is an unproblematic assumption in L&E scholarship (at least in its 'mainstream') but regarded as a highly contingent social phenomenon in L&S scholarship. In other words, 'L&S scholars would call attention to the social, political, and legal construction of rational economic behavior' (Edelman 2004: 184; emphasis omitted) and not simply take it as given, that is, as an exogenous variable. Edelman's argument can, accordingly, be summarized in terms of the 'endogeneity' (or embeddedness, to speak with Polanyi) of the economic element in the law, and of the legal element in the economy. In a genuine socio-legal perspective law and economy are thus considered as mutually constitutive.

The global element in socio-legal studies

Having thus addressed the main elements of our imaginary study pro-gramme – the legal, social, and economic – we still have to define its scope. And, since we are living in 'the global age' (Albrow 1996), this is no less than global. To be sure, notions of 'globalization' are used in an infla-tionary way, thus concealing continuities in transnational interdependen-cies and exchange, which go well beyond the recent decades. However, references to 'the global' also help to overcome the 'methodological nationalism' that was long prevalent in the social sciences: a preoccupa-tion with 'the national' in economics, sociology, and the law. To focus on law, economy, and society in the global age thus means to take the dynamic of the modernization process seriously (differentiation and specialization, secularization and rationalization, liberalization and indi-vidualization), which does not end at national borders but brings about a highly interdependent 'world society' (Krücken and Drori 2009). Also, criticisms of this trend, and related counter-movements are, in many ways, globalized. Even though it can be questioned if economic, legal, and social practices are *really* global today (the bulk of it is not), the effects of global-ization – or of a global frame of reference – can be perceived (almost) everywhere, and long before we are all 'going global'.

As to the sociology of law, 'the globalization of law' has already made it into the textbooks (e.g. Deflem 2008, chapter 12). As to the wider field of socio-legal studies, and of L&S scholarship, I would like to point to the concept of 'global legal pluralism', which combines something old (legal pluralism) with something new (the global). One can also speak, of 'the globalization of legal pluralism' (Michaels 2009: 245), or of a double move from 'past to present' and 'from local to global' in this respect (Tamanaha 2008). What is interesting about legal pluralism is that what was long per-ceived as a marginal, sociological or anthropological, discourse (which deals not only with official but also unofficial law) has now – in the global age – found its way into the centre of legal thought. The reason is simple:

> The irreducible plurality of legal orders in the world, the coexistence of domestic state law with other legal orders, the absence of a hier-archically superior position transcending the differences – all of these topics of legal pluralism reappear on the global sphere.
>
> (Michaels 2009: 244)

We should thus take a quick look at how the global dimension is included in socio-legal pluralism – without neglecting the economic element either. In this respect, Tamanaha's account (2008) appears to be helpful. He distinguishes between six systems, or categories, of 'normative ordering', which are 'commonly discussed in studies of legal pluralism' (Tamanaha 2008: 397). These include, besides official legal systems, various cultural normative systems, namely, customary systems (made up by shared customs, norms, and institutions), religious systems (often merged with customary systems), and community systems ('imagined communities' of any scale, be it local, national, or global). In addition, Tamanaha mentions functional normative systems (which regulate specific social spheres or sectors) and singles out economic normative systems (namely the capitalist market economy) (Tamanaha 2008: 377–399). He thus lists a number of normative orders that do interact or – conflict with – official law but are themselves not confined to state borders. One of his claims, which brings us back to globalization and the economy, is, notably, 'that, riding on the tidal wave of economic globalisation, the most powerful contemporary impetus, momentum, and penetration of new norms is taking place through the economic/capitalist normative system' (Tamanaha 2008: 406).

Exemplary agendas

At this point, the prospective student would already know what ingredients the chosen field of studies is made up from. And she would certainly also have an idea of how, or why, it is different to study international economic law from a socio-legal perspective rather than from the perspective of single-issue disciplines, such as law or economics. Even law *and* economics is generally reduced to the economic analysis of law, and can thus be subsumed to the perspective of economics. But now that we have combined the legal with the social, the economic, and the global, what to do with this colourful cocktail? In order to explore possible – or exemplary – agendas of socio-legal studies in international economic law, let us come back to our sociological understanding of the latter as the law of the (globalized) market society. This idea is also behind the book *Karl Polanyi, Globalisation and the Potential of Law in Transnational Markets* (Joerges and Falke 2011), which is closely linked to a collaborative research project on 'trade liberalization and social regulation' – hence, to international economic law. In this collection, the contributions are loosely organized around Polanyi's fictitious commodities, that is, land, labour and money. To recap, it is the 'commodity fiction' which helps to constitute markets even where the laws of the market put the substance of human, natural and social life at risk. In this context, 'trade liberalization' means the deregulation of markets and, thus, a strengthening of the market logic, on a global scale. In contrast, 'social regulation' stands for the protection of society, which is, in this case, more about global sustainability than national protectionism. In the following, I will further elaborate on this theoretical framework and link it to exemplary studies in the field.

Land: turning nature into property rights

Polanyi considers both 'man and nature' in need of protection from the market forces, that is, of social regulation (1957 [1944]). Due to his frequent references to nature, which takes the commodified form of land, Polanyi is sometimes seen as a pioneer of the environmental movement. Even though this only took shape a generation later, it can easily be recognized as one of the social counter-movements that Polanyi described – and advocated – in his book. This prophecy notwithstanding, Polanyi discusses nature always in its relation to man or, rather, man in his relation to nature. While he thus acknowledges that 'production is interaction of man and nature' (Polanyi 1957 [1944]: 130), he sharply criticizes the 'utopian' project of economic liberalism, which subjects both man and nature to the self-regulating mechanism of the market. At the same time, Polanyi's understanding of nature, or land, is quite comprehensive. Besides its 'economic function' he therefore also points to the 'vital functions' of land: 'It invests man's life with stability; it is the site of his habitation; it is a condition of his physical safety; it is the landscape and the seasons' (Polanyi 1957 [1944]: 178). Moreover, when listing 'the conditions of safety and security attached to the integrity of the soil and its resources', he includes, amongst others, 'the vigor and stamina of the population, the abundance of food supplies, [...] even the climate of the country which might suffer from the denudation of forests, from erosions and dust bowls' (Polanyi 1957 [1944]: 184).

Historically, the commodification of nature – with all its consequences for the livelihood of a given population – provoked a strong social reaction. This includes the (re-)introduction of 'land laws and agrarian tariffs', which Polanyi explains 'by the necessity of protecting natural resources and the culture of the countryside against the implications of the commodity fiction in respect to them' (Polanyi 1957 [1944]: 132). Today, the countryside is often found in the so-called developing world, in which the primary sector (including agriculture, fishing and forestry, mining, and oil and gas production) is still relatively strong. The commodification of the natural resources of these countries is pushed forward by the highly industrialized countries, which are themselves increasingly specialized on the service sector. The missing link can be found in transnational corporations, which typically have their headquarters in one of the leading economies but own, fertilize, and exploit land all over the globe (both literally and figuratively). The ownership of land, or natural resources, has meanwhile even been extended to include genetic resources. In other words, nature can not only be owned materially but also intellectually. As with any other property regime, the respective owners, or holders of intellectual property rights, can then exclude others from the use of their patents (notably, their commercial use).

In order to illustrate what kind of conflicts arise and what kind of studies are undertaken in this field, I want to give but three examples that I have recently come across at conferences (including the one leading to the present collection). Deval Desai (in this volume) illuminates the 'narratives' of law that he found in mining agreements between transnational corporations and indigenous communities. Emilie Cloatre (2008) analyses the effects of trade-related property rights – namely, pharmaceutical patents – on healthcare in a 'least developed country' from the viewpoint of actor-network theory. Mizanur Rahaman (2010) studies the effects of the agrobiotechnological 'knowledge economy' on food sovereignty in developing countries. All three are thus concerned with the intersection of 'market and nature' (Polanyi 1957 [1944]: 178), and, interestingly, all three employ post-realist research perspectives.

Labour: turning human activity into services

While all production is defined by man's interaction with nature, Polanyi makes sure that neither of them belongs to the market sphere. Labour is for him 'only another name for a human activity which goes with life itself, which in its turn is not produced for sale but for entirely different reasons, nor can that activity be detached from the rest of life, be stored or mobilized' (Polanyi 1957 [1944]: 72) Hence, if labour is treated as a commodity, this brings about risks for 'the human individual who happens to be the bearer of this peculiar commodity', 'the physical, psychological, and moral entity "man" attached to that tag' (Polanyi 1957 [1944]: 73) – and for society at large. The organization of markets for labour services – which are 'demanded' by a minority of entrepreneurs and 'supplied' by the majority of workers – deeply affects 'the forms of life of the common people' (Polanyi 1957 [1944]: 75). Historically, the exploitation of labour in the liberal market economy was supported by a laissez-faire policy of the state, that is, the absence, or rather, abolishment, of social regulation. For the workers, the flexibility of wages, which resulted from 'the laws of supply and demand in respect to human labor' (Polanyi 1957 [1944]: 177), implied an 'extreme instability of earnings, utter absence of professional standards, abject readiness to be shoved and pushed about indiscriminately, complete dependence on the whims of the market' (Polanyi 1957 [1944]: 176).

In order 'to protect industrial man from the implications of the commodity fiction in regard to labor power' (Polanyi 1957 [1944]: 132), social institutions were needed, which became crucial for the containment of the market economy in the twentieth century – including 'social legislation, factory laws, unemployment insurance, and, above all, trade unions', which would, by necessity, interfere 'with the mobility of labor and the flexibility of wages' (Polanyi 1957 [1944]: 177). While this is the core of Polanyi's argument with regard to human life, I want to add another aspect here, which is less about man's abilities, or productivity, than his life-sustaining needs. Modern humans not only have to sell their labour for a living but also have to buy – besides food and clothing and basic household equipment – a number of services, including water, electricity, healthcare, transport and telecommunication. Next to labour, these 'services of general interest' are a test case for how today's market economies design the interface of 'market and man' (Polanyi 1957 [1944]: 163). The liberalization of services, which entails the economic restructuring of (often monopolistic) network industries, draws on the 'principle of freedom of contract', which Polanyi considers 'an atomistic and individualistic' form of social organization (Polanyi 1957 [1944]: 163). Accordingly, everyone should be able to choose her own service contract from one of the (ideally competing) delivering companies.

To conclude, I will, again, give some examples of research undertaken in this field, which illustrate the conflicts arising from the commodification of man both as a supplier and a recipient of services that are, to a certain extent, existential to him. David Nelken (2010) deals with a drastic example of the mobility of labour – namely, human trafficking – which can, however, also be 'framed' in different terms. Diamond Ashiagbor (forthcoming) studies the effects that European market integration has on labour law, both with regard to the member states and with regard to third countries (notably of the global South). Markus Krajewski (2011) analyses the (de-)regulation of 'services of general interest', taking the liberalization of healthcare in European Union and World Trade Organization as an example. All three, thus, address the vulnerability of human life, and the viability of protective institutions in a highly interconnected world economy.

Money: turning investment into exuberance

Money is, certainly, the trickiest among Polanyi's fictitious commodities. If the substance of land is nature and the substance of labour is man, what is the substance of money then? Is not money always fictitious in that it symbolizes a certain value but is not an end, or value, in itself? In fact, since money has taken the form of cheap metal coins and paper bills, or, more recently, digital representations, all of its value seems nothing but a social convention which crumbles in times of crisis. For Polanyi, the question was, on the one hand, who is in control of the money: the state or the market. As long as governments could manage the money supply according to the needs of the national economy, it was mainly a political instrument.

However, already under the gold standard, currency exchange became predictable, 'world commodity markets, world capital markets, and world currency markets' evolved (Polanyi 1957 [1944]: 76), and a 'self-regulating mechanism of supplying credit' came into being (Polanyi 1957 [1944]: 195). Money thus became a matter of the market. On the other hand, Polanyi relates money to the substance of economy, namely, 'productive organization' (Polanyi 1957 [1944]: 130) or 'capitalistic production' (Polanyi 1957 [1944]: 132). He thus seems to replicate the distinction between real capital (or productive investment) and money capital (or speculative investment). At any rate, he could not predict the degree to which today's 'finance capitalism' would have come to rely on the latter, virtual function of money.

Nevertheless, Polanyi clearly identified the 'powerful social instrumentality' which international finance already developed in the late nineteenth and early twentieth century (Polanyi 1957 [1944]: 9) and the effects it had on the lives of the people:

> By the fourth quarter of the nineteenth century, world commodity prices were the central reality in the lives of millions of Continental peasants; the repercussions of the London money market were daily noted by businessmen all over the world; and governments discussed plans for the future in light of the situation on the world capital markets.
>
> (Polanyi 1957 [1944]: 18)

At the beginning of the twenty-first century it seems that recurrent financial crises with international repercussions challenge not only the remaining network of stabilizing institutions but also economic theory. In response to the perceived failures of neoclassical models (notably, the efficient-market hypothesis), alternative interpretations make their way into politics, including behavioural economics, or behavioural finance. The emphasis is here more on individual biases and human failure (namely, of boundedly rational actors) than on institutional shortcomings and system failure (Frerichs 2011a). When behaviouralists speak of 'irrational exuberance' (Shiller 2000) they thus tend to neglect the 'political economy' behind it (Krippner 2010).

How socio-legal scholars address this overall complex – from the attraction of foreign direct investment to the restriction of financial speculation – can be illustrated with the following works: Amanda Perry-Kessaris (2008) studies the effects of investment climate discourse on the legal system in India, finding that the latter's instrumentalization also jeopardizes its integrative functions. Ioannis Glinavos (this volume) analyses economic, legal, and moral justifications of the 'bonus culture' in the international banking sector, which fuelled the 2008–2011 financial crisis.

Mitchel Abolafia (2010) explains 'why speculative bubbles still occur', focusing on the role of academic economics, the political discourse, and regulatory structures. All these accounts have in common that they go beyond – or behind – economic 'truths' and point to the cultural and discursive constructedness and performativity of these realities.

Law: turning communities into commodities

At this point, our 'Polanyi-inspired' account (Randles 2003) of socio-legal studies in international economic law could end. However, there is a certain paradox, or tension, in putting 'economic law' in a 'socio-legal' perspective, and this we can also reflect upon in a Polanyian way. My argument is here that under the premises of economic liberalism, law may itself turn into a commodity (Frerichs forthcoming; Frerichs 2011b). In order to make this point, let us first recall the three stages of 'law's great transformation'. In the first stage, market exchange is still embedded in law, and law is embedded in society, or rather, the collective conscience. Polanyi speaks of an (undifferentiated) complex of 'custom and law, magic and religion', in this respect, which keeps the gain motive in check (1957 [1944]: 55). In the second stage, market exchange is released from social constraints. In other words, it is no longer restricted by 'human laws' (Polanyi 1957 [1944]: 125) but, instead, left to 'the laws of Nature' (Polanyi 1957 [1944]: 114). In practice, the principle of laissez-faire means that man-made law starts mimicking quasi-natural law. Just as the market, it thereby becomes disembedded. In the third stage, the market is reembedded in a framework of social regulation, which would, again, be a legal framework. However, law would now be understood as a social instrument rather than as the (in)visible hand of the market. We may equate the latter position with legal realism.

With regard to the fictitious commodities of land, labour and money, the second stage implies their commodification, which includes the enablement and enforcement of the market logic by legal means, and the third stage their decommodification, which includes legal interference with the market logic. Law can, hence, act both as a commodifier and a decommodifier. And it can itself become subject to the commodity fiction. This is, at least, the case when regulatory competition between different polities – or legal communities – allows a 'law market' to arise (O'Hara and Ribstein). One may then choose between different regulations according to one's personal preferences – or, for economic rather than political reasons. In this way, the logic of the self-regulating market is also applied to the law. Now, if this is the commodity form of the law, what is its original substance? We may suppose that Polanyi would have answered this question (which he never posed, though) in a Durkheimian way. For Durkheim (1893: 54), as sketched out above, law was a symbol of social solidarity. As such, it is embedded in a community of interdependent and mutually committed individuals. This argument is taken up by Roger Cotterrell (in this volume), who has gone a long way to find 'law's community' (1995; cf. 1997), also in transnational networks of a more instrumental – or economic – kind. However, in the latter case, social solidarity seems to take a rather reduced form (say, of abiding by contracts).

Conclusion: labouring on a new (economic) world order?

I will, however, end with another account of law's inherent conflict, which points to the big 'other' of today's socio-legal studies (if this is not legal doctrine). Nourse and Shaffer (2009) identify 'varieties of new legal realism' which are, notably, directed against a 'new legal formalism'. The two camps, thus labelled, are, by and large, identical with today's representatives of the law and society movement, on the one hand, and of the law and economics (L&E) movement, on the other. And just as 'old' legal realism included an economic outlook on the law (Hovenkamp 2009), 'new' legal realism seems to have invited behavioural L&E in. Be this as it may, Nourse and Shaffer's argument is, in a nutshell, that neoclassical L&E – or what can be equated with mainstream L&E – has brought about a 'new' legal formalism which replaces legal principles with economic assumptions but is, otherwise, as axiomatic or dogmatic as the 'old' legal formalism. In contrast, the 'new' legal realism is sustained by 'behaviorist', 'institutionalist' and 'contextualists' strands of thinking which address

> the re-triumphalism of market laissez-faire (now chagrined), a cynicism toward an unresponsive state, and the hollowing out of traditional conceptions of law in light of new governance challenges from below and the challenges of new global and transnational institutions from above – in sum, the new world order before us.
>
> (Polanyi 1957 [1944]: 128–129)

This is a big agenda and should suffice to illustrate the challenges lying ahead of students (and researchers) who decide to enter this field – but also the significance of their work. What comes out when one mixes the legal and the social with the economic and the global is, obviously, no less than the world.

Part II

Context

Chapter 4

How World Trade Organization law makes itself possible

'Every time I describe a city, I am saying something about Venice'

Ronnie R. F. Yearwood with Ross C. Davis[1]

(Polo) 'Sire, now I have told you about all the cities I know.'
(Khan) 'There is still one of which you never speak.'
Marco Polo bowed his head.
'Venice,' the Khan said.
Marco Polo smiled. 'What else do you believe I have been talking to you about?'

(Calvino 1997)

Introduction

International law is 'fragmented' into a number of specialised systems such as trade, environment and human rights (see Koskenniemi 2006; Pauwelyn 2003). Each system has developed its own analytical framework (concepts and relationships), normative concerns (values and interests) and institutions to understand itself and the world around it. This makes the systems appear as autonomous from both the broader system of general international law and each other (Koskenniemi 2006 at paras 53–4). However, these separate systems are often applied to the same substantive issues and situations. With no single system able to claim analytical or normative superiority, there appears no method for commensuration. In the context of World Trade Organization (WTO) law it is possible to identify three common responses to the systemic fragmentation of international law. The first is 'openness': arguing that external international law can be used in particular as a defense against the violation of WTO law, but also generally to emphasise the holistic nature of the international legal system (Pauwelyn 2003, 2001: 536). The second common response is 'closure': arguing that the WTO can only use WTO law, beyond which WTO law should not reach (see Trachtman 1999: 855–61).

Openness and closure therefore appear to be mutually exclusive propositions on how the WTO should respond to fragmentation in its application of external international law. Proponents of openness criticise closure for not seeing the vast jurisdiction and norms available to the WTO adjudicating bodies in using external international law to come to a decision in WTO law. Proponents of closure counter that proponents of openness see too vast a jurisdiction and the corresponding norms available to the WTO adjudicating bodies in their decision-making process. Each proposition appears to contain its equal and justifiable counter-argument. In fact the propositions of openness and closure are what can be termed 'nested oppositions' (Balkin 1990: 1671–7, 1683–6, 1994: 396–8), that is while appearing contradictory, they start from a shared premise. I argue that neither the openness nor the closure of WTO law can be maintained simultaneously because there is constant oscillation between the two propositions.

The third common response is to attempt to reconcile openness and closure by claiming that WTO law overrides external international law because of a conflicts clause inferred in WTO law (for example, Bartels 2001). But this middle ground is untenable, because at any given moment the view of WTO law takes on the characteristics of either 'closure' or 'openness'. Rather than adhere to openness or closure, I argue that it is more productive to build upon the concept of 'operational closure' originated by Gunther Teubner (1987a and 1993), and Julia Black (1996). The approach informs the conceptual framework of constrained openness that I put forward to understand WTO law and its interaction with external international law. I explain and supplement the framework of constrained openness by reference to Italo Calvino's (1997) *Le città invisibili* (*Invisible Cities*). The analysis provides the basis for a re-examination of the existing propositions on the interaction between WTO law and external law. In conclusion, I posit that constrained openness would provide a more nuanced understanding of the interaction between WTO law and external international law.

'Every time I describe a city, I am saying something about Venice'

Invisible Cities is an imaginary dialogue between Kublai Khan and Marco Polo. The young Polo is an ambassador and 'obliging narrator at the service of the Khan' (Springer 1985: 290). Calvino's interest is epistemological – he is concerned with the reliability or unreliability of Marco Polo's accounts of the cities he visits to the Khan. As William Twining (2000: 137) has suggested, Calvino's writing can be used to map law. In the excerpt below, 'all' of Polo's descriptions rely on Venice as a reference point. As such they are an exercise in operational closure:

(Polo) 'Sire, now I have told you about all the cities I know.'
(Khan) 'There is still one of which you never speak.'

Marco Polo bowed his head.

'Venice,' the Khan said.

Marco Polo smiled. 'What else do you believe I have been talking to you about?'

The emperor did not turn a hair. 'And yet I have never heard you mention that name.'

And Polo said: 'Every time I describe a city I am saying something about Venice.'

(Khan) 'When I ask about other cities, I want to hear about them. And about Venice. When I ask you about Venice.'

(Polo) 'To distinguish the other cities' qualities, I must speak of a first that remains implicit. For me it is Venice.'

(Calvino 1997: 86)

This dialogue underlines the relevance of *Invisible Cities* as a tool for mapping WTO law through the conceptual framework of constrained openness. Systems can apprehend new data, but in order to do so, they draw on existing data or frameworks of thought to make practical use of the new data. In describing the cities, Polo is employing a methodological and a conceptual framework in Venice to select the data he observes, and the way in which that data will make sense. Systems use their internal point of view to make sense of things around them. We are embedded in our practices or our assessments proceed from our particular (internal) point of view. For Polo the account of every city proceeds from Venice. Therefore, Polo accounts for fifty-five different cities but every city is only made intelligible by reference to Venice. Venice is his 'model city' to distinguish his external environment, and 'deduce' all other cities (Calvino 1972 [1997]: 69). Polo does not seek to escape this operational closure. Moreover, no view or proposition is universal in the sense of being able to capture the past, present or future situations. The subsequent analysis of the current discourse will reveal the contradictions and inadequacies amongst all of the existing propositions. It is my contention that such flaws in current thought can be alleviated if the relationship between WTO law and external law is viewed with an awareness of this internal point of view, its operational closure. Does the WTO not have its own Venice?

The journey to Venice: 'openness' and 'closure' to 'operational closure'

Nested oppositions

The propositions of openness and closure described as 'nested oppositions' means that conceptually the propositions contain each other. Openness has a conceptual dependence upon closure, and vice versa. This does not mean that there is no difference in the propositions of openness and closure. Of course there is a difference, otherwise they would not be opposites. While proposing opposing views the propositions consider and apply the same evidence, cases or practice of WTO law (Lindross and Mehling 2005: 862). Furthermore, because of the general legal principle that the 'counsel of the unsuccessful litigant is not discredited' (Twining 1973: 205), opposites appear as the modus operandi of legal argument. This is bolstered by the fact that the change from the General Agreement on Trade and Tariffs (GATT), the forerunner to the WTO, met a change from diplomats to the rule of law and the rule of lawyers, resulting in the manifestation of legal argument in the form of opposites (Weiler 2001: 197–8). Therefore, nested oppositions in the context of WTO law are ineliminable.

The fact that nested oppositions characterise discourse surrounding WTO law has various implications. First, the points of contention between openness and closure can be viewed as functional and perhaps even complimentary, because they both retain a fundamental commitment to the idea of WTO law having gaps or lacunae (Trachtman 1999: 338 and Pauwelyn). This is what makes them conceptually dependent on each other. A gap here means that WTO law is not capable of producing a complete legal answer without the application of external international law.

Openness proposes that where there are gaps, the adjudicating bodies should apply external international law to the WTO legal system to produce a complete legal answer. Its proponents argue that general international law and the rules of state responsibility (Crawford 2002) operate as fallbacks, which can remedy the gaps in WTO law, except where WTO law has specifically 'contracted out' of these rules. Thus, through the lens openness, gaps in WTO law seem to offer an opportunity to build a unitary and holistic international legal system (see Lindross and Mehling 2005 and Pauwelyn 2003: 200–21).

By contrast, closure posits that the domain of WTO law should be limited to the application of WTO law. This means that the adjudicating bodies can address all disputes under existing WTO law. In this view, international law cannot be a defense against a violation of WTO law. The adjudicating bodies in only applying existing WTO law do not make new WTO law in their interpretation and application of WTO law, even when there is a gap in existing WTO law (Trachtman 1999: 343, 2004: 137).

The propositions of openness and closure may appear as somewhat one-sided appropriations of the practice and facts of WTO law in that they do not see a world outside themselves. Openness shows no consideration for closure, and vice versa. It is therefore important to formulate a more adequate and nuanced proposition of how WTO law interacts with external law that takes us beyond the nested opposites of openness and closure.

'Resolving conflict by superficial means'[2]

The third proposition, spearheaded by Bartels, is that WTO law is privileged over external international law in the event of a conflict, through the operation of a conflicts clause inferred from Articles 3.2 and 19.2 of the Dispute Settlement Understanding (DSU). Bartels (2001: 499) claims that this proposition is different from that of closure, which he believes is 'too restrictive', 'unduly positivistic' and 'not reflecting the actual practice' of the adjudicating bodies. It is important to place Bartels's proposition in the context of openness and closure, as it appears to be an attempt to reconcile the two. While WTO norms interact with external norms (openness), this interaction is regulated (closed) through the WTO, which means the prioritising of WTO norms above external norms to create a hierarchy. Whilst I agree with the goal of reconciliation, I think that the means of reconciliation that Bartels proposes is flawed.

There are several problems with the inference of a conflicts clause. Primarily, I am doubtful as to whether the texts of Articles 3.2 and 19.2 constitute a conflicts clause in that the Articles do not specify that the WTO is to prevail over external law. In addition, the Articles do not direct members in their future negotiations that they cannot change, overrule or in essence derogate, from WTO law. Even if the Articles were a conflicts clause, the WTO could always clarify or change the relationship with external law, through authoritative interpretations of the treaty, waivers, amendments or, more generally, the adoption of guidelines by the Ministerial Council (Pauwelyn 2003: 344 and 354; Marrakesh Agreement nd: Arts: IV, X, XI). Furthermore, the conflicts clause could turn out ineffective in regulating a conflict between WTO law and external international law, given that the *lex posterior* rule of general international law – under which a newer treaty prevails over an older in the event of a conflict – is not deactivated. Bartels himself has admitted to having changed his mind. For him, the 'question of applicability' is 'decided in accordance with the secondary rules of public international law', such as rules on treaty conflicts (Andenas and Ortino 2005: 517–18). However, such rules may also not be able to sustain a wholly satisfactory understanding of the interaction between WTO law and external law. Take, for example, *lex posterior* as discussed above which directs that the treaty that was created later in time will prevail. VCLT Articles 30(3) and 30(4) can be considered as embodying the *lex posterior* principle (Mus 1998: 219–20; Borgen 2005: 603). The determining factor for the applicability of Articles 30(3) and 30(4), according to Article 30(1), is that the conflicting treaties cover the 'same subject-matter'.[3] However, consider that an issue 'related' to trade is not the equivalent of covering the 'same' subject matter, which is necessary to activate *lex posterior* under Article 30(4) (Wold 1996: 911). Given the potential overlap of trade with many other areas of international law, it is quickly realised that the practical use of *lex posterior* is wide to the point of being ineffectual, because everything can be somewhat trade related in the context of the globalised trading system.

Furthermore, a conflicts clause would be ineffectual in reconciling openness and closure in that it assumes that one proposition has to take precedence over the other. However, this normative hierarchy that Bartels appears to propose would lead to quite arbitrary practice as the meaning of fragmentation as discussed earlier suggests that there is nothing inherent or naturally occurring in the propositions that would explain why one proposition would take precedence over the other. The nested opposites of openness and closure cannot be reconciled to be the total elimination of one in favour of the other, as the proposition of privilege appears to suggest. Not only is such an idea out of synch with socio-legal reality (norms cannot simply be erased by a court or organisation), but this proposition also overlooks the possibility of operational closure being in play, in a similar manner to how the Khan presumed that Polo had overlooked Venice in his account.

I now wish to use the concept of operational closure to allow me to re-examine the current propositions so that I can advance a new conceptual framework for understanding WTO law. Through this new approach, I think we can take the discourse beyond openness and closure, the shortcomings of which have previously been highlighted and indeed, beyond Bartel's unstable middle ground. My approach, unlike Bartel's, explains the interaction in socio-legal terms, which fully appreciate the nature of norms and the true extent of the possibilities that normative interaction exposes any legal system to. This is something that has been missed by all three propositions.

Venice is key: 'operational closure' as an analytical solution

The concept of 'operational closure' takes its cue from Niklas Luhmann's autopoiesis or *Systemtheorie* (systems theory), which proposes that law is best thought of as a system of communications (Luhmann 2004; Teubner 1989: 739 and 742). Like other systems, law produces its own 'constructs of reality' that are based on binary codes, for example, illegal/legal in law, profit/loss in economy, or true/false in science (Beckett 2007: 310).

Law, as Julia Black has put it, is 'cognitively open' – in the sense of being able to 'observe other systems and their environment' and to be 'indirectly affected by them'; but 'normatively [operationally] closed' in the sense that it will not 'recognise' as 'valid' any 'norms' that it has not itself produced (Black 1996: 44; 2002: 5). Furthermore, law exhibits a recursive quality: law is law because it is law.

The 'internal environment' of a system provides a space through which it can respond to the 'noise' posed by another system. In the case of the

WTO, the law of systems external to the WTO are not simply imported, but rather are (re)constructed, so that WTO law can make sense of it, into a new hybrid that is WTO law (Teubner 1989: 749). The result is that the decisions of the WTO are decisions of the WTO; its own original interpretation of the external 'noise' in question.

The constrained openness of WTO law

The analytical frame of systems theory, including the concept of operational closure, reveals what I call the 'constrained openness' of WTO law. That revelation calls for a bold break from a focus on WTO law as part of either a unitary (Pauwelyn/openness) *or* a differentiated (Trachtman/closure) system. The focus is instead on how WTO law makes itself possible, and how it interacts with external systems, given that it is at once 'open' and 'closed' (Teubner 1989: 739–40). Of course, adjudicating bodies apply rules of general international law, general rules of treaty interpretation and general rules of treaty law (see Lindross and Mehling 2005: 857–77). The point is that adjudicating bodies in the application of WTO law also make use of (are 'open' to) general international law. Together, the technical rules of treaty interpretation and the general rules of international law are necessary for a legal system to function (Lindross and Mehling 2005: 875–6). However, the application by the WTO of general international law does not, nor should it, limit consideration of the WTO legal system as creating and existing within its own normative space as an operationally closed system (Cover 1983).

It is true that 'no regime can be created outside the scope of general international law' (Lindross and Mehling 2005; Koskenniemi 2006: para 172); however, WTO law, like any other special system of international law, remains a differentiated system of international law. Fragmentation of international law is not the result of some failing of reason but is a realisation, or perhaps more correctly, an actualisation of the fact that multiple values and interests form international law. The emergence of these differing laws is not of itself important but it is important to recognise the fact that each of these laws has arisen individually and each operates within its own operationally closed system that reflects its own interpretation and understanding of international law (Koskenniemi 2007: 4–8; Koskenniemi 2006: paras. 8–9, 15). Fragmentation then is a process of differentiation or a 'division of labour' in international law that manifests technical specialisations in varying areas of legal regulation. The technical competence of the different systems results in the rise of a group of specialised professionals and the requisite community to approve and restrict behaviour. We can expect that judicial officials of a system will give effect and purpose to their system (Cover 1983: 102–5). Fragmentation, as a process of differentiation means that for WTO law there is the emergence of a 'new specialised international bar' which is comprised of 'specialists in WTO law and litigation' (Sacerdoti 2005: 131). In other words, WTO law has established a culture or normative order amongst its actors, so quite simply; *trade lawyers will act and think like trade lawyers.*

In WTO disputes, measures are assessed first and foremost as potential violations of WTO law. So every question to the adjudicating bodies is the basic form of 'Was WTO law violated?'. The possibility that an exception might apply is only addressed secondarily. The standard recommendation in the reports of the WTO adjudicating bodies is that the Member State concerned brings the measure into conformity with the relevant covered WTO agreement. The WTO is 'open' in the sense that it can observe anything external to it, including other legal systems. But that openness is 'constrained' in that external law can only be understood by reference to the primary law of the WTO, namely, the 'covered agreements', which direct its purpose and operations to prohibit trade restrictions.

Constrained openness allows us to re-examine the propositions of openness and closure. Consider Pauwelyn's proposition of openness, especially his notion that the WTO should defer to a higher epistemic authority (Pauwelyn 2003: 119–20; Mavrodis 2003: 244). The WTO would not be 'directly' able to seek external advice as Pauwelyn proposes since as a constrained opened system, the WTO would only understand such advice on its own terms and by reference to its operation to prohibit restrictions on trade. The only way the WTO could seek advice would be to turn the case over to the other legal authority. If the judgment of the case returns to the WTO, the adjudicating bodies would then only understand it through a (re)construction of the ruling based on the WTO's operational closure.

Equally, the idea of a completely closed WTO faces criticisms of being 'narrowly focused' (Wai 2003), 'myopic' (Nicholas 1996), and singularly focused on trade (Guzaman 2004; Stiglitz 2002: 216) with a likelihood of hostile responses (Kelly 2006: 86). Hence, Trachtman's desire for a limited jurisdiction and to limit the law that is deemed applicable to that of the covered agreements as response to the fragmentation of international law would seem inadequate. In his view, the proposition of closure appears to have the 'better of the textual arguments' (Dunoff 2001: 998). However, closure seems self-defeating in its attempt to contain the influence of external law in the WTO by narrowly sticking to the texts of the WTO treaty to produce the single right answer (Howse 2002: 106; Lindross and Mehling 2005: 863). Moreover, this could perhaps re-ignite the opinion of the WTO as 'ignorant' to international law (see Kuyper 1994; Marceau 1999: 95). Thus, each proposition is an unsatisfactory explanation of the complex epistemological issue of how the adjudicating bodies apply external international law.

By contrast, constrained openness considers that external law is not simply incorporated into WTO law or exists within the WTO legal system.

The WTO would likely pass over the different constituents and agendas that represent external law, and homogenise it. In doing this, the fragmentation of international law remains. It is hidden as coherence in Pauwelyn's idea of systemic interpretation, where the WTO applies external law since the WTO is just another system of international law. The other result could be that the fragmented systems are potentially rendered impotent by WTO hegemony, in that it (re)constructs external law as variables of WTO law. This makes an ironic mockery of Pauwelyn's political justification for pursuit of WTO 'openness' to 'see more to life than money [and the] money-making exercise [of trade]', and to embed WTO law as part of international law (Pauwelyn 2003: xi).

Conclusion

WTO law explained as constrained openness does not provide Pauwelyn's complete legal answer or Trachtman's single right answer. Furthermore, as Calvino suggests in that Polo's 'cities neither interact nor refer to one another', so there is no direct access to reality (James 1982: 150). Polo does not deny that other cities exist but suggests that his description of them only occurs through referring to himself, that being, his own operation in the account of Venice. Each city is a reference of itself. Hence, *Invisible Cities* illustrates why constrained openness replaces the current propositions of closure, openness and privilege. In that, there is 'nothing inherent' in a proposition that 'makes its existence ontologically necessary' as 'all' propositions are 'ontologically aleatory' (Rasulov 2006: 810).

Therefore, though we argue that the proposition of constrained openness appears more satisfactory than the propositions of closure, openness or privilege have proved to be, *Invisible Cities* demonstrates that revisability is possible, even if based on the approach of operational closure. The purpose of this chapter is to demonstrate how socio-legal analysis can begin to enrich and enliven our understanding of relationship between WTO law and general international law.

Having noted the limitations of current thinking in the area, four main observations can be made based on the proposition of WTO law as constrained openness. First, no proposition is an epistemic hegemony, or in fact, is even necessary. The value of a new proposition is in its power to offer a more adequate explanation than the old versions. Second, the new proposition illuminates the old propositions by being able to recast past premises based on present situations. Third, constrained openness is revisable because it does not claim universality. Fourth, instead of imposing an account of WTO law in the manner of the former propositions, constrained openness sets up a way from which we think about WTO law as a self-creating and operating legal system. I therefore advance that constrained openness is a more desirable way to think about WTO law in that it does not purport to reconcile openness and closure. Rather than attempting to somehow remedy the deficiencies within the propositions, constrained openness creates a functional theory out of the fact that the two cannot be reconciled. It accepts the flaws in the status quo and tries to use this to aid our understanding.

The point is that WTO opponents are perhaps correct to think that the interaction between different external laws in the WTO occurs according to WTO law. However, what may disappoint them is that this is not a negative presumption. The institutional nature of the WTO, as it would be in reverse for say an international environmental law institution, is to function based on its operational goals, which explain and define on what basis and how that system will relate to external law. The WTO interprets external law, rather than external law being adopted wholesale without modification. No matter what demands are placed on the WTO by a fragmented system, the WTO will tackle them by reference to its own overarching principles: *'Venice' is never marginalised.*

Hence, the WTO's internal environment consists of guiding and omnipresent norms that have two critical characteristics: they are in constant interaction with other external norms and this interaction determines how WTO law develops, as it results in the (re)construction of new (hybrid) WTO norms. Constrained openness describes the mechanism behind the process that the WTO legal system uses in order to develop. It describes the manner in which WTO and external norms interact, the crux of which is as follows: the WTO can only ever apply external norms on its own terms. It will only ever interact within the confines of its internal environment. What is fundamental here is the notion that norms by nature will interact. Hence, an external norm will only be accepted to the extent that it can be reconciled with the WTO's internal environment.

To conclude, if we think about WTO law as based on constrained openness, then we realise that WTO law is 'open in a closed sort of way' (Kennealy 1988). It interacts with the fragmented systems but within its own limits. These limits are determined by its guiding ethos, embedded in its internal environment. This does not mean that interaction between WTO law and external law is one-sided. What it does mean is that constrained openness can provide a basis from which we can further inquire into what the WTO rules provide and how the adjudicating bodies apply those rules when faced with external law. We do this bearing in mind that the adjudicating bodies only ask and answer one question: *Has WTO law been violated?*

Notes

1 The views expressed in this chapter are those of the authors and not the firms mentioned in the Notes on Contributors. Reliance should not be placed on the content and independent legal advice should be taken if necessary.

2 This heading is borrowed from the artwork of Mark Titchner, See Yearwood 2012.
3 VCLT Article 30 (1) states that 'Subject to Article 103 of the Charter of the United Nations, [T]he rights and obligations of States parties to successive treaties relating to the *same subject-matter* shall be determined in accordance with the following paragraphs [that is Articles 30 (2) – (5)].'

Chapter 5

(Re)conceptualising international economic law

A socio-legal approach to regionalism

Clair Gammage

Introduction

This chapter confronts what Björn Hettne (2005) has described as the 'ontological problem' of dominant approaches to regionalism and international economic law. These theories tend to be mono-disciplinary, focusing on one mode of knowledge production, such as economics or politics, and thereby privilege certain research questions at the expense of others (Hettne, 2005: 543). They provide atomised accounts of economic action, in which the international legal system appears as fixed and determinable. By contrast, this chapter draws on economic sociology to reconceptualise economic activity, and its laws, as embedded in social life. It does so using the example of the inter-regional agreement between the European Union (EU) and the Southern Africa Development Community (SADC), known as the EU–SADC Economic Partnership Agreement, and its interaction with provisions of a multilateral agreement, in particular Article XXIV of the General Agreement on Tariffs and Trade (GATT) administered through the World Trade Organization (WTO).

Regions in international economic law

Regions are commonly understood to be groups of geographically proximate countries (Mansfield and Milner, 1999: 50), but the reality is often more complicated. The term 'region' may also refer to the cultural, political or linguistic commonalities between countries. Regions may come into existence where the inhabitants of different spaces have a shared or common sense of identity (Söderbaum, 2004). So a region can be understood not only as a geographical area but also as a fluid space with politically contested boundaries capable of change. Region-building can refer to both policy cooperation and/or coordination between countries based on some cultural, social, economic or common interest and, more specifically, the grouping of countries on the basis of economic flows (Mansfield and Milner, 1999: 591). Regionalism may, therefore, be non-geographical and it can take the form of trading blocs, security arrangements or monetary arrangements, to name but a few.

This complexity is reflected in International Economic Law in so far as Article XXIV GATT provides that free-trade areas or customs unions may be created between WTO member states irrespective of their geographic location. Over time, this has resulted in a shift towards the negotiation of regional arrangements not only *among* developed countries in the global 'North' such as the European Union (EU), and *among* developing countries in the global 'South' such as Southern Africa Development Community (SADC), but also *between* those two groups – such as the EU–SADC Economic Partnership Agreement.

Economists seeking to understand the causes and effects of regionalisation tend to begin with Viner's (1950) customs union theory, which focuses on potential welfare gains (trade creation) and losses (trade diversion) to members and non-members of unions. Also referred to as 'static impact effect', this theory proposes that preferential trade is generally welfare-enhancing for member states but may be detrimental to global welfare.

It is with this balance in mind that Article XXIV GATT 1947 permits Member States to derogate from the Most Favoured Nation principle in order to create 'preferential trade agreements', in the form of either customs unions or free trade agreements. The substantive requirements of Article XXIV have an internal and external dimension. Internally, the members of a preferential arrangement must liberalise 'substantially all trade', within a 'reasonable period of time'. While the requirement to liberalise 'substantially all trade' has yet to be conclusively defined, according to the WTO Appellate Body it is 'not the same as *all* the trade' but 'something considerably more than merely *some* of the trade' (*Turkey-Restrictions on Imports of Textile and Clothing Products* WT/DS34/AB/R, 22 October 1999 para 48). It was expected that incorporating the internal requirement into Article XXIV GATT would minimise the use of preferential arrangements for sector specific, partial liberalisation (Das, 2004: 99).

Meanwhile the external dimension of Article XXIV addresses Vinerian concerns about the diversionary effects of preferential trade by requiring that access to products from third countries must not be prohibited or made impossible. In fact most preferential arrangements are free trade areas, because they require only the removal of tariffs among members (not the negotiation of a common external tariff) and so offer the benefits of 'speed, flexibility and selectivity' (Fiorentino *et al.* 2009: 42).[1]

Economic Partnership Agreements

Until the end of 2007, the EU enjoyed a 'special relationship' with the African, Caribbean and Pacific states (ACP) trading under *non-reciprocal* preferential trade agreements known as the Lomé (1975–1999) and

Cotonou (2000) framework agreements. As part of the Cotonou regime, the non-reciprocal preferences granted to the ACP expired at the end of 2007. Thereafter a new system of *reciprocal* trade agreements, known as Economic Partnership Agreements, was negotiated in order to protect the 'special relationship' between the EU and ACP countries. In a revolutionary move, the ACP will no longer trade as one unified regional bloc but rather as six separate regional configurations: the Pacific, the Caribbean (CARIFORUM), West Africa, Central Africa, Eastern and Southern Africa, and southern Africa (SADC). This chapter focuses on the Economic Partnership Agreement between the European Union and the Southern Africa Development Community (EU–SADC Agreement).

Economic Partnership Agreements have been designed to restructure ACP–EU trade relations into progressive, reciprocal North–South trade and development agreements. A primary motivation for this transformation was to avoid 'hub-and-spoke' regionalism – that is, to promote regional integration among the ACP countries while also promoting integration of ACP states into the global economy (Hinkle and Schiff, 2004: 1325). The EU argues that:

> the EPA will support the ambitious regional integration process that is already underway, helping to maximise its benefits. The EPA will build in flexibility to reflect the socio-economic constraints of SADC countries. It will ensure flexibility because it will comply with WTO rules and prevent other WTO members from challenging the trade preferences by the SADC region.
>
> (European Commission, 2005: 9)

Negotiations for the EU–SADC Agreements began in Namibia in 2004 and were expected to conclude in 2008. However, states have so far failed to agree on the proposed scope of liberalisation and at present there exists only an interim agreement signed by Botswana, Lesotho, Mozambique and Swaziland in 2007–2009 (European Commission, 2009). Namibia also reluctantly initialled the agreement but only on the understanding that its concerns about the scope of liberalisation would be comprehensively addressed during the negotiations towards a full Economic Partnership Agreement (EPA) (Julian, 2010). Angola and South Africa have not signed or initialled the interim Agreement, preferring instead to continue to trade with the EU through alternative agreements (Angola under the Everything But Arms Initiative, South Africa under the Trade and Development Cooperation Agreement). This fragmentation is especially problematic in the wider context of sub-Saharan Africa's 'spaghetti bowl' of uncoordinated, overlapping and weak regional initiatives. It is only because they are not properly implemented that the various initiatives can coexist, and it is for that reason that lack of implementation is tolerated.

There is concern that the proposed Economic Partnership Agreements will do little to improve, and may worsen, the situation (Stevens, 2006).

The EU's approach to regionalism reflects the legal formalism of the WTO system, which privileges economic values and interests, and in doing so it fails to challenge the ambiguous nature of WTO obligations. The following section of this chapter explores alternative, sociologically informed, approaches to regionalism in order to highlight the problems associated with traditional analyses of economic action.

Socio-legal approaches to regionalism

To take a socio-legal approach to regionalism is to (re)conceptualise regionalism as a social phenomenon. In so doing we not only challenge the *status quo* but broaden our understanding of the diverse processes that may influence regionalism at the formal and informal level.

Law and economy as social interaction

Perhaps the most significant difference between the various disciplinary approaches to IEL is the importance given to agency, or the role of actors. Whereas traditional legal and economic conceptualisations of IEL are generally state-centric, perceiving actors as rational and self-interested, socio-cultural analyses place greater emphasis on the roles of actors coexisting across different spatial levels and the interaction of these actors is also an important consideration when analysing the (re/de)construction of regional space. Moving away from the notion of the Westphalian state, these socio-cultural theories offer an alternative model of regionalism that conceptualise trade as a social phenomenon.

Economic sociologist Moshe Hirsch proposes that we must 'recast the global/regional debate in a different light', by conceptualising international trade as a specific type of 'social interaction'. He argues that sociological analyses of IEL allow us not only to develop multiple conceptualisations of IEL, depending on which social theory we use, but also to discern different interpretations of the legal provisions governing regionalism (Hirsch, 2008: 299).

Economic sociology of the type developed by Mark Granovetter considers economic activity as 'embedded' in social life and social structure. It is an explicit response to the 'over-socialised' or 'under-socialised' accounts of economic action provided by other approaches (Granovetter, 1985: 283). Neoclassical economics envisages economic actors as individual rational utility maximisers, but for economic sociologists:

> Actors do not behave or decide as atoms outside a social context, nor do they adhere slavishly to a script written for them by the particular

intersection of social categories that they happen to occupy. Their attempts at purposive action are instead embedded in concrete, ongoing systems of social relations.

(Granovetter, 1985: 487)

Of particular significance to economic sociologists is the role of interpersonal trust between parties involved in economic transactions. Granovetter proposes that the trust that facilitates economic activity is found in social relations and not in institutional arrangements or generalised morality (Granovetter, 1985: 491). Since social relations penetrate different sectors of economic life in different ways and to different degrees, this allows room for distrust, opportunism and disorder. So, economic sociology highlights the ways in which economic activity is coordinated by groups, such as firms, rather than rational, self-interested actors (Granovetter, 1992: 4).

Andrew Lang applies such a sociological lens to the question of interpretation, noting that the very 'content and effect of WTO law is determined not just by the processes through which texts are negotiated but also by the manner of their interpretation and application' (Lang, 2011: 165). This 'interpretive dimension' is overlooked because the WTO system is built on the notion that the legal texts reflect the interests and objectives of the members. The law may appear to be certain and predictable, but only because of the lack of legal interpretation undertaken at the WTO level. Actors involved in trade negotiations across the different spatial levels are not mere automatons – they are active participants who develop a 'feel for the game' that guides and influences their policy choices. It is through their social interactions that government officials and trade professionals co-construct IEL. Their interpretations of the text give meaning to its provisions (Lang, 2011: 164–5, 172 and 175). In other words:

All law, whether generated by state or non-state actors, arises at the macro-level of regimes (state or non-state) but is used, abused and avoided in the social actions and interactions that take place at the micro and meso levels.

(Perry-Kessaris, 2011c: 14)

The vague drafting of Article XXIV leaves plenty of room for interpretation. First, although it states that external barriers to trade must not be increased following the creation of a preferential arrangement, it does not specify how external trade barriers will be measured – an extremely difficult task involving the analysis of thousands of commodity tariff lines. Second, the application of Article XXIV has gradually loosened over time such that the political cost of creating a preferential arrangement is now perceived as being relatively low (cf. Snape, 2007: 84). Indeed, it is not uncommon for states to create regional arrangements specifically to protect certain industries (Grossman and Helpman, 1999: 319). Members of regional arrangements are able to protect vulnerable industries from liberalisation by listing these as 'sensitive products' in the legal document. The legality of failing to liberalise 'sensitive products' and excluding sectors could be challenged under Article XXIV, but the fact no disputes have been brought through the WTO dispute settlement system to date implies a reluctance to do so. Finally, there are a vast array of non-tariff barriers to trade that are not considered to fall within the scope of Article XXIV such as import licences, sanitary and phytosanitary measures, technical barriers to trade and anti-dumping measures (McMillan, 1993: 14). Non-tariff barriers to trade are often extremely restrictive and can have significant trade distorting effects. Failure to concisely define the boundaries of the legal obligations therefore leaves the text open to interpretation and abuse by dominant members.

Social conflict

Social conflict theorists such as Karl Marx propose that society is stratified according to the unequal distribution of wealth. As each group seeks to advance their own interest against rival groups, a social structure begins to emerge distinguishing a dominant class from the subordinate class (Hirsch, 2008: 294). The dominant class seeks to protect its position and will even use the law to ensure the social stratification remains intact (Hunt, 1976):

> The social conflict conception of IEL is conscious of economic and social stratification in the international system and it is poised to unveil parallel inequalities in IEL ... the exposure of the international system's hidden priorities sheds light on the 'dark side' of IEL and may trigger a legal form. Such a reform should promote equality and redistributive policies that would be implemented, inter alia, through the allocation of differential legal obligations to different states according to their level of economic development.
>
> (Hirsch, 2008: 294–5)

From a social conflict perspective, the WTO privileges the dominant class in the international economic order – richer states. Under the auspices of the WTO, regional arrangements are seen to reinforce the structural inequality between regional partners, with the dominant member able to protect its interests at the expense of weaker members and non-members.

There is concern that the EPAs will destabilise and deconstruct existing regional processes in southern Africa by creating four separate trade arrangements with the EU, each with different schedules of liberalisation and market access commitments. Since all countries are members of the Southern Africa Development Community, a free trade area of fifteen southern African countries, it will be necessary for the region to implement appropriate customs administrative measures to avoid trade deflection.

Another issue stems from the differing levels of commitment on new trade issues, such as investment and services, which ultimately may create unavoidable long-term policy divisions within the region. While EU rhetoric supports regional integration in southern Africa and encourages the SADC–EPA countries to deepen their regional commitments before engaging with the EU, this is simply not feasible under the existing timeframe. Creating four separate EPAs will only hamper efforts to build a stronger, more unified intra-regional market among African countries. In this sense the process of regional deconstruction and reconstruction seems to run counter to the spirit of the European regional experience 'where regional rules, regional market opening and integration among EU Member States takes precedence over market openings to non-EU partners' (ANSA, 2009: 2). So it is understandable that many countries in the region are resistant to EU pressure on them to sign an interim EPA contrary to their existing regional policy goals.

Furthermore, as the EPA negotiating configurations do not align with existing regional initiatives, the parties do not have formal legal status. So, it is not clear, *legally* speaking, with whom the EU is signing the EPAs or how the agreement will be administered (Draper, 2007: 19), whether the EPAs will be complementary to existing trade frameworks and whether it will be more difficult to make changes to the regime in the future (ANSA, 2009: 3). Civil society groups have argued that by pressuring the ACP countries to negotiate a broad liberalisation package the EU is pre-empting regional integration decisions (Mambara, 2007), thereby shaping ACP regionalism in its own vision. The neoliberal values and interests appear to have become embedded in the EU–ACP relationship as reflected not only within the EU's policy orientation, but also in the EU's development policy with the ACP (Hurt, 2003: 162).

The vague nature of Article XXIV noted above leaves it vulnerable to abuse, and that vulnerability has been worsened by its interpretation in practice. It is argued that the exceptions permitted so far 'have set a dangerous precedent for further special deals, fragmentation of the trading system, and damage to the trade interest of non-participants' (Leutweiler, cited in McMillan, 1993: 9). In order to preserve the integrity of the multilateral trading system, the GATT rules should therefore be redesigned and strictly adhered to by the members.

The EPA, as an inter-regional North–South trade agreement, appears to be a vehicle for the exploitation of fragile ACP markets by the EU.

Demanding extensive liberalisation on an unprecedented scale, the EPA highlights the structural inequalities of the EU–ACP relationship. The EPA also serves as an example of how dominant members can use regional arrangements to protect their position: the EU excludes most of its agricultural products from liberalisation by listing them as 'sensitive products' to preserve its controversial subsidised Common Agricultural Policy, while pushing developing countries to liberalise beyond trade in goods. By participating in discrete and discriminatory regional trading arrangements with the EU, the ACP is at risk of becoming ever more dependent on the EU:

> The risk to the group remains that of perpetuating the unhealthy postcolonial dependence on Europe for developmental aid and fiscal support, which unfortunately authors further neo-liberal market integration, trade liberalisation and privatisation of state-owned-enterprises.
>
> (Kamidza, 2007: 5)

Social conflict theorists regard such 'hegemonic preferential trade agreements' as an attempt to circumvent rule-making at the multilateral level and instead seek to create a new system of rules at the regional or bilateral level (Hirsch, 2008: 295). The EPA framework asks developing ACP countries to make greater concessions through regional arrangements than they have been required to make at the multilateral level. The EPAs are being negotiated in line with WTO policy and with the EU's controversial Common Agricultural Policy in mind, for the EU is heavily reliant on developing country markets for its own development (van Reisen, 2007: 43). Arguably, the EPAs are little more than a strategic instrument for the EU to penetrate and further exploit developing country markets. The provisions of Lomé have certainly encouraged a relationship of dependency between the EU and ACP countries and it has been suggested that the asymmetrical relationship has done little more than reinforce pre-existing structural inequalities in the developing nations (Kwarteng, 1993). The Euro–African relationship has always been asymmetrical, and has now become so entrenched that it has been said that 'each time the European economies sneeze, the African economies catch pneumonia' (Adedeji, cited in Kwarteng, 1997: 52).

New regionalism

New Regionalism theorists such as Frederik Söderbaum criticise the rationalist, positivistic tendencies of traditional regionalism for being both 'overly concerned' with methodology and 'under-concerned' with 'the socio-economic circumstances and historical context of regionalism' (Söderbaum,

2004: 193). They encourage a focus on 'by whom, for whom and for what purpose various forms of regionalism occur and how these are connected', and they take care to distinguish regionalism from regionalisation – the processes involved in 'creating a regional space'. Regionalism, they argue, is a multidimensional process in which regions are constructed, deconstructed and reconstructed; intentionally and/or unintentionally; for negative and/ or positive purposes, by formal and informal actors (Söderbaum, 2004: 2–3 and 7). It is a constructivist approach which emphasises the importance of 'shared knowledge, learning, ideational forces and normative and institutional structures' (Hettne and Söderbaum, 2000: 460).

New regionalism theory does not prioritise either formal or informal regionalism. Rather, it seeks to highlight the involvement of *all* actors that may influence the construction, deconstruction and reconstruction of a regional space. It is not only important to identify all the actors involved, but we must also acknowledge that they do not operate in a mutually exclusive way. Sociological analyses, such as economic sociology, social conflict theory and new regionalism theory, conceptualise the international economic order as spreading:

> knowledge, norms, and values through traders who often cross boundaries and settle into new communities and by the content of the products or services purchased by the members of different communities. Socio-cultural factors do not necessarily support international economic relations, and resistance to the expansion of global economic integration is often based on socio-economic concerns.
>
> (Hirsch, 2008: 281)

Frederik Söderbaum, who has developed a specifically reflectivist New Regionalism account of southern Africa, discusses how the regional space has been shaped across different spatial levels by social, cultural and economic motivations. For example, the migration of the Bantu and Zulu-Nguni were important in the spread of culture and ethnicity across southern African borders that gradually created a more homogenous regional space. Another significant turning point for the region was the discovery of gold and diamonds, which led to the construction of a unified economic regional space. However, in South Africa, regional space was not only carved out by economic motivations but also as a result of racialisation during the Apartheid era. The region was built on the basis of a shared identity according to racial classification (Söderbaum, 2004: 55–8). This analysis of southern Africa shows that there may be overlapping processes of regionalisation during the construction and subsequent reconstructions of a region.

Agency is given a broad interpretation with a regional actor being defined as someone who 'takes part – consciously or unconsciously – in activities on a regionally defined area' (Söderbaum, 2004: 196). New regionalism theory proposes that agents are reflective:

> The reflectivist-constructivist stance is that interest formation should neither be separated from ideas, identities, the process or interaction, nor from contextual conditions. This, in turn, implies that a region is seen as a social construct and that 'regionalism is what regional actors make of it' to paraphrase Wendt.
>
> (Söderbaum, 2004: 198)

The purpose of new regionalism theory is therefore to adopt a holistic approach to understanding regionalism. Applied to analyse the processes of regionalism and regionalisation on a macro- and micro-level, it reveals the influence of both state and non-state actors in shaping regional integration. It challenges the assumption of the international economic system that the same countries experience the same level of economic development. Using a multidimensional approach to analyse the role of various actors, considering institutional and non-institutional factors, and referring to globalisation as an exogenous factor in the process of regionalism, the new regionalism theory certainly offers an alternative view of conceptualising regionalism (Warleigh-Lack, 2006: 755).

From a New Regionalism perspective, Article XXIV overlooks both formal and informal processes that may influence macro-regional processes. By only recognising regionalism at the macro-level it precludes any consideration of regional processes occurring across other spatial levels. In fact, the ongoing EPA negotiations between the EU and southern Africa are an interesting example of trade agreements as constructing, deconstructing and reconstructing regional space between non-geographically proximate North–South partners. At a macro-level, the EPAs represent a phase of regional deconstruction and simultaneous reconstruction. Conceptualising trade as a social phenomenon necessitates analysis of the interaction between actors. We must therefore ask for whom, by whom and for what purpose are regional spaces being constructed, deconstructed and reconstructed? In the context of the Economic Partnership Agreements, who is driving the negotiations and why?

Many mainstream theoretical approaches to regionalism focus on state-centric models of trade with the state assuming the role of dominant actor. While the state and other international organisations are extremely important actors, particularly in relation to macro-regionalism, they are not the *only* actors. New regionalism theory places emphasis on the role of various types of state and non-state actors operating within the regional framework. Non-state actors shape the interests pursued at the state level and therefore the focus should be on both state actors operating within the formal interstate framework and also the non-state actors acting in a more informal capacity participating in what is broadly referred to as 'non-state' or informal regionalism (Hettne, 2005: 554). So, from the perspective of new regionalism theory, the region itself can be both an arena in which actors engage in processes of regionalisation and an actor participating in regional activity.

There are various actors involved in the EPA negotiations at both the formal and informal level, from EU and government ministers to small non-state organisations. Importantly, we must question what motivates actors to behave in a particular way. The construction of an inter-regional EU–SADC space has been contested across different spatial levels. At the EU level, ministers express clear economic motivation rather than a political, social or cultural desire to forge links with their former colonial territories. Although the rhetoric may be couched in political terms to preserve the 'special' relationship enjoyed by the ACP, the negotiations are very much geared towards the construction of an economic inter-regional space.

At the formal negotiating level the Namibian Minister for Trade and Industry, Hage Geingob, has been particularly outspoken about the EPA process:

> A partnership means that all partners are equal. Why else would you include the word partnership in the EPA? It also means transparency … We're talking about Africans standing together. Namibia places a high premium on that.
>
> (Duddy, 2009)

It is interesting to note that Geingob has not always been so critical of the neoliberal institutions or indeed liberal trade models. For some time, he worked on the World Bank's African development scheme, known as the 'Global Coalition for Africa', so it is perhaps surprising that he now rallies against the liberal trade model of the EPA. Perhaps the motivation behind Geingob's stance on the EPAs could be purely for personal political gain in the hope that his radical approach will win him the next presidential vote in Namibia. On the other hand, perhaps he is truly trying to ensure that the construction of a new inter-regional space between the EU and southern Africa is founded on principles of equity and fairness. In any case, the Namibian minister's reaction has acted as a platform for many informal actors to contest the creation of the EU–SADC inter-regional space under the proposed terms.

The Cotonou Agreement envisaged stakeholder participation in the negotiation process and recognises 'the complementary role of and potential for contributions by non-state actors to the development process' (Article 4). In particular, the Cotonou Agreement provides a more significant role for private actors in the trade negotiation process. Article 21 outlines the importance of ensuring that 'cooperation' leads to a 'favourable environment for private investment and the development of a dynamic, viable and competitive private sector'. Furthermore, 'cooperation' should support implementation of 'structural policies designed to reinforce the role of the different actors, especially the private sector' (Article 22 Cotonou Agreement).

For industries that already have comparative advantage or who wish to expand their influence on the global market, preferential trade agreements are an important market tool. Since preferential arrangements are by their very nature discriminatory, they provide a means for industries to protect their market share by pushing out third party competitors through a legal trading arrangement. The private sector is often extremely influential in lobbying the national government to pursue particular terms of trade (Mansfield and Milner, 1999: 602). In some cases, the decision as to whether or not a state will enter into a preferential arrangement may very much depend on the pressure exerted by non-state actors (Grossman and Helpman, 1995: 681).

Non-state actor participation would be an integral part of the consultation leading to the adoption of National Indicative Programmes for the EPAs. However, Hurt suggests that the increasing role of democratically unaccountable parties, such as non-state actors and private firms, could weaken the process of democratisation in ACP countries (2003: 172). Kwarteng acknowledges the importance of non-governmental forces in shaping regional processes:

> It will be important that African leaders encourage social groups, such as journalists, trade unions, marketing and industrial groups, students and non-governmental organisations, to play a role in Africa's regional integration ... Like Europe, private sector development should be the linchpin of the strategy to integrate African economies ... In an effective regional market, the private sector becomes the principal actor, while the public sector plays the role of formulator and regulator of policies.
>
> (Kwarteng, 1997: 43–4)

At the informal level, non-state actors have mobilised to raise their concerns about the ongoing trade negotiations with civil society networks across southern Africa have accusing the EU of adopting 'bullying, arm-twisting tactics' (COSATU, 2009).

The Corporate Observatory Europe has accused the EU Directorate General for Trade (DG Trade) of not only bullying ACP countries into negotiating the EPAs but also of orchestrating support for the trade framework from phantom private sector lobby groups (Corporate Observatory Europe, 2009). A forum was created by the former DG Trade lead EPA negotiator, Ivano Casella, to facilitate discussion between businesses about the EU–SADC EPA. It later transpired that the Business Trade Forum EU–Southern Africa was in fact a figment of DG Trade's imagination allowing the EU to falsely promote its position with respect to the EPA. The Corporate Observatory Europe argues that DG Trade's motivation for pursuing the EPA framework with the ACP countries is purely economic, with the EU seeking to construct an inter-regional space with southern Africa for the purpose of:

> opening markets for large EU corporations ... securing access to raw materials, protecting their intellectual property rights and limiting opportunities for ACP countries to regulate their economies in the interest of their people and the environment.
>
> (Corporate Observatory Europe, 2009: 3)

Overall, the EPA negotiations have been criticised for failing to integrate non-state actors into the consultative process (Kamidza, 2007; ACTSA, 2010). While the international 'Stop the EPA' campaign has gathered momentum internationally, visible non-state actor participation in the negotiations is lacking. It is certainly the case that there is relatively little information available about non-state actor involvement in the negotiation process or details of their work at the grass-roots level. This lack of transparency erodes the consultative process envisaged by the Cotonou Agreement.

Conclusion

Why and how are regional agreements formed? What makes regionalism successful or unsuccessful, as compared, for example, to multilateralism or isolationism? Who tends to benefit from regionalism, how and why? An important first step in answering these questions is to understand how regions are constructed, deconstructed and reconstructed. We can only begin to understand the complexities and contours of those processes if we accept that they are the result of social interactions, embedded in social life. It seems unlikely that Article XXIV will be revised in any meaningful way in the near future. But in the meantime we can best begin to highlight its effects and defects by conceptualising them as social phenomena.

Note

1 The provisions of Article XXIV are likely to cause trade diversion since states creating a preferential trade agreement are only obliged to freeze, not lower, external tariffs. In this way it encourages a culture of discriminatory trade practices which can become increasingly distortive over time. McMillan (1999: 15) argues that Article XXIV could be improved by focusing on volumes of trade rather than tariff levels.

Chapter 6

Global duelists

The recursive politics of the text in international trade law

Terence C. Halliday and Susan Block-Lieb

Introduction

The intellectual turn that produced the law and society movement in the United States, the law in context movement in the United Kingdom, and sociolegal scholarship internationally may be characterized as an escape *from* the text. Whereas legal scholarship centred on the legal text and its normative meanings, sociolegal scholarship insisted that it was necessary to see past the text, whether a statute, case or regulation, to practice and behaviour. Invariably a gap lay between the text and action and that gap warranted empirical investigation and theoretical explanation. Inquiry into how the text got onto the books and normative distinctions between one sort of text versus another for the most part was left by sociolegal scholars to political scientists or jurists, a legacy that still constrains sociolegal scholarship to the present, whether on national or international terrains.

In recent years, the sociolegal neglect of getting *to* the text has been challenged. Although important exceptions can be seen in national law-making, a growing interest in international law, global regulation and governance has brought new attention to the politics of global standard-setting which, in effect, amounts to a politics of the text (Braithwaite and Drahos 2000; Canan and Reichman 2001). Here 'text' may take the form of hard law or soft, of conventions and best practices, of model laws or legislative guides, of prescriptive or diagnostic standards. Sociolegal scholars have asked, whose texts are these and whose interests do they reflect (Jensen and Santos 2000)?

In the world of global affairs, not least in international economic law, neither of these moves – from law on the books or *to* law on the books – can be divorced from the other. In the world of scholarship, good social theory requires that each move be held in tension with the other since each constrains and shapes the other and indeed they unfold through time in dynamic engagement. A theoretical move to systematize the creative tension that produces legal change in a global context is captured by the concept of the recursivity of law (Halliday 2009; Halliday and Carruthers 2007; Halliday and Carruthers 2009). Developed originally to explain how global economic normmaking engages with national lawmaking and the local practices that emerge, the recursivity framework also offers a distinctively inter-disciplinary orientation for assessing the process through which these texts are crafted. Does the process result in texts that mesh with practice, or compete with it? If a text is in competition with behaviours and practices, recursivity theory predicts that pressures will form to press for its revision, whether at a national or international level.

We argue that a politics of the text sits at the centre of global governance over the making of international trade law and, indeed, of global economic normmaking more generally. This is a recursive politics. It confronts who crafts the text, what form it takes, and how it is carried into global and national arenas of economic activity. To exemplify the argument we focus on a duel between two international organizations (IOs) over which would emerge as the pre-eminent global authority on the norms for corporate bankruptcy law. On the one side was the United Nations Commission on International Trade Law (UNCITRAL), a multilateral body that develops a variety of trade laws for national and international markets. On the other side was the World Bank, an international financial institution that has reached increasingly in the last two decades to economic lawmaking for the world. Between 1999 and 2005 these two IOs fought behind the facades of global institutions for primacy over which would promulgate the 'gold standard' for corporate bankruptcy systems.

This chapter is based on ten years of participant observation of deliberations by UNCITRAL's Working Group V on Insolvency, hundreds of informal and formal interviews with delegates, the UNCITRAL Secretariat, and World Bank officials, and close analysis of all draft and final texts of UNCITRAL and the World Bank on insolvency (see further Block-Lieb and Halliday 2006, 2007a, 2007b and 2011; Halliday 2009 and 2011; Block-Lieb and Halliday 2011; and Halliday *et al.* 2009).

We proceed in four steps. First, we encapsulate the theory of the recursivity of law for the making of international economic law and note how its *sociolegal* sensibilities add to general political or economic or sociological theories of globalization. Second, we describe the duel between UNCITRAL and the World Bank and show how its broader context shaped the institutional reputations and legitimacy of the combatants, the struggles over the substantive scope and form of the text they produced, and the probability of its adoption in practice. Third, we refract the drama of the duel through the theory of the recursivity of law, simultaneously showing how the empirical materials refine the theory as the theory amplifies the meaning of the events. Finally, we conclude with extrapolations of this single case to the making of international economic law of any kind.

The recursivity of law

The recursivity of law offers a systematic theoretical approach to the explanation of legal change in a global context. The framework generates hypotheses about global normmaking, national lawmaking, local practices, and the relationships among each of them both to explain why new episodes of legal change begin and the conditions under which change settles in a new form or level. It emphasizes historical contingency and the dynamics of temporality. Concomitantly it is also a comparative theory in both the senses of place and fields of law. Since the formulation of the theory itself has been extensively elaborated elsewhere (Halliday 2009; Halliday and Carruthers 2007, 2009), we summarize here its main terms.

Legal change in a global context occurs through three intersecting sets of cycles. First, there are cycles of national lawmaking, where actors bring issues to lawmaking bodies that produce legal texts. Two influential instances in the insolvency field were the 1978 US Bankruptcy Code and the 1986 English Insolvency Act (Carruthers and Halliday 1998). Each of these led to subsequent cycles of regulations, statutory amendments and court rulings. Those texts were intended to change existing behavioural norms and practices and to create or modify social organizations. These cycles simultaneously emerge from practice, in response to perceived problems or gaps or limitations in the extant state of affairs, and they seek to alter practice. At once they are moves from law on the books to law in action and vice versa.

Second, there are iterations of transnational, international and global normmaking among IOs. In any issue area, such as trade law or conflicts of laws or international commercial law, there are international bodies, or states with aspirations for international influence, that may produce complementary or competing texts that claim authority to regulate or govern economic activity among and within nation-states. The competition between the World Bank and UNCITRAL over the 'gold standard' for corporate bankruptcy norms followed scattered efforts by IOs to generate norms through the 1990s. The European Bank for Reconstruction and Development (EBRD) produced a diagnostic instrument to evaluate the insolvency laws that had been adopted quickly after the Soviet Union dissolved (Ramasastry et al. 2002). The EU spent 30 years drafting a convention to address the need for cross-border recognition of insolvency proceedings within Europe (EU Regulation 1999). UNCITRAL produced its own model law in 1996 on cross-border insolvency (UNCITRAL 1999). The International Bar Association (IBA) worked in the 1990s on a model law to handle corporate liquidations. INSOL International, a peak association of national insolvency associations, produced a set of norms and practices for bank work-outs of distressed companies. Ideas, drafts and drafters flowed back and forth amongst these institutions.

Third, there are cycles of engagement between the national and the global.[1] In emergency times, the IMF and World Bank pressed their norms upon nations, as we have shown for Indonesia and Korea during the Asian Financial Crisis. In strained times, nations reach out to adopt global norms to forestall the prospect of crisis, as we have shown for China. In ordinary times, global lawmakers produce texts, such as UNCITRAL's *Legislative Guide on Insolvency* (UNCITRAL 2004) or the World Bank's principles on creditor law and insolvency (World Bank/UNCITRAL 2005), which they may seek to institutionalize as an international standard by encouraging national enactment. These global texts variously seek to unify or harmonize or modernize economic law (Block-Lieb and Halliday 2007b). Flows of influence come from 'below,' when states influence IOs, and from 'above', often simultaneously. For example, France concomitantly shaped UNCITRAL's *Legislative Guide* and integrated the *Guide* into its own law.

Cycles of change in economic law have beginnings and endings. Long periods of quiescence or minor incrementalism or unquestioned compliance occur in between episodes. Recursivity theory seeks to explain when unsettling occurs (i.e. the beginning of a new reform episode) and when settling (i.e. the conclusion of a reform episode) can be observed in legal texts and practices.

Beginnings are facilitated by growing economic or political pressures to create or reform a regulatory order, by industry changes, inventions, shifting patterns of trade or sources of capital, among others. The long episode of creating corporate bankruptcy norms for the world began with facilitating conditions, such as the US and UK reforms, the growth of multinational corporations, a retreat by governments from hard budget constraints and the economic integration of the EU. With these in the background a new episode may be precipitated by a sharp jolt to regional and international financial systems, such as the Asian Financial Crisis, by geopolitical seismic shifts, such as the collapse of Eastern Europe's command economies, by important technological or market paradigm shifts, such as the shift from bank to market sources of finance, or by political conflict, such as the 9/11 attacks in the United States.

Episodes of legal change also have endings. Cycles of reforms invariably settle on the meanings of legal texts and on practices. Sometimes episodes end because reforms are adopted (e.g. the comprehensive bankruptcy law of Korea in 2006), sometimes because the agents of reform are exhausted (e.g. Indonesia in the later 2000s), and sometimes because attention shifts elsewhere. In all cases, however, cycles of interaction between the global and local, or lawmakers and law-takers, tend to settle, usually in normative understandings and accompanying behaviours that are perceptibly different from those that existed before the onset of an episode of legal change.

Cycles of change within an episode are driven by at least four mechanisms. Each mechanism increases or decreases the probability that legal texts or practices will settle.

In economic and political contexts populated by actors with material and ideal interests, legal change invariably involves *diagnostic struggles*. Actors seek to name and frame a particular problem in ways that will produce a lawmaking response to their liking. Mistaken diagnosis may enable norm and lawmaking in the short term, but falter when it confronts realities of practice. Lawmakers may be compelled to press forward further cycles of reform to adjust to the hard lessons of practice. In corporate bankruptcy law these struggles are well exemplified by implicit and sometimes open rifts between bankers and company directors. If the problem of failed companies is considered to be the moral or business failings of company directors, then bankruptcy laws may sanction directors and remove company reorganizations from their control (i.e. the former UK practice). If the problem of business collapse, however, is thought to be more a result of the business cycle, then law reform may enable current directors to rescue their companies by other means (e.g. the generic US approach). Directors clearly have a much stronger interest in the latter than the former approach, whereas bankers may prefer the former to the latter.

These diagnostic struggles can, in turn, result in *actor mismatch* within the lawmaking process. Actor mismatch occurs when the actors engaged in economic activities are not fully represented amongst those who formulate the rules that structure economies. When the European Bank for Reconstruction and Development (EBRD), Asian Development Bank (ADB) and International Monetary Fund (IMF) formulated their bankruptcy norms in the 1990s, they did so with a handful of in-house lawyers in consultation with a tiny number of consultants. No representatives of industry or banking, labour or tax authorities, were invited to participate, nor were delegates from states. Said one leading lawyer on the global insolvency stage: 'there really is no debtor's lobby. There's a bank lobby, there is a regulatory lobby, but there's no organization that speaks for the debtors of the world' (Int 2052B).[2] Severe actor mismatch can delegitimate global normmaking and incite excluded actors in domestic politics to veto in practice what they could not accommodate in drafting.

Sometimes cycles of reform fail to settle because *contradictions* are drawn inside legal texts and the institutions that implement them. *Substantive contradictions* can occur when political settlements between seemingly irreconcilable interests remain incomplete and the legal texts themselves import unstable compromises that require later rounds of negotiations, administrative clarifications and court rulings for resolution. In corporate bankruptcy law, at least three such contradictions might have subverted global lawmaking. One pitted legal systems that prioritized the right of banks to liquidate failing companies versus those that permitted rehabilitation of companies while restraining unilateral creditor actions. Another concerned the relative primacy of accountants as the profession designated to preside over corporate failures versus lawyers. A third pitted those states and interests that held that courts must be integral to the liquidation or rehabilitation of companies versus those that favoured either administrative agencies or private agreements. Regional and global normmaking in the late 1990s and early 2000s managed to resolve each of these contradictions. *Institutional contradictions*, however, were another matter. These can occur when competing IOs struggle for normative supremacy on the international stage, such as the duel between UNCITRAL and the Bank, or when rival branches of governments within states produce instability in legal meanings and practices because they disagree with each other.

Finally, economic norms and laws may fail to settle to settle when the law itself or the source of law is *indeterminate*, inconsistent, ambiguous or unduly complex. The introduction of new concepts into global norms or national statutes may require years of regulatory and judicial clarification. Inconsistencies can drive further rounds of statutory amendments. The swift cycles of statutory amendments in Korea following the Asian Financial Crisis well exemplify the consequences of quick and diagnostically questionable reforms (Oh 2003; Oh and Halliday 2009). Legal indeterminacy undermines settling and promotes further rounds of recursive legal reform; so, too, can institutional indeterminacy when new IOs emerge, when an IO broadens its mission or purpose and enlarges its intended scope of authority, existing jurisdictional clarity can get muddied.

Ultimately, a theory of legal change should be able to explain when settling will occur, both in the legal texts and the practices they purport to guide.

Recursivity theory focuses attention on four distinctive problems that political scientists and sociologists conventionally ignore. First, it attends closely to the politics of the legal complex – that variety of configuration of occupations that are trained in law and continue to practice it, whether in government agencies, private firms, courts or prosecutorial offices (Halliday Forthcoming; Karpik and Halliday 2011). Second, it takes seriously the constitutive components of legal concepts, the invention of new legal terms and the suppleness of law as a regulatory option (McBarnet and Whelan 1997). Third, it presumes that legal institutions, whether international trade law regimes or national regulatory agencies and courts, have their own interests, resources and capacities. Fourth, law's formal properties, including the rhetorical structure of global norms and national texts, require inter-disciplinary examination, not least because they frequently have distributive consequences for configurations of power in international and national social organization of markets (Halliday *et al.* 2009).

The duel: World Bank v. UNCITRAL

In the urbane world of international diplomacy, not least that of international trade law, the imagery of pistols at dawn seems misplaced. Nonetheless global economic normmaking in general, and trade lawmaking in particular, occurs in 'ecologies' where IOs struggle to remain in a space that has too few resources to accommodate them all (Block-Lieb and Halliday 2011. See also Abbott 2005; Hannan 2005; Popielarz and Neal 2007). Scarce resources beget competition between some, and cooperation among others.

Against the backdrop of norm-drafting in the 1990s by international financial institutions, professional associations and the EU, the legal departments of the World Bank and IMF had expanded beyond their bread and butter transactional lawyering to become legal institution-builders. In the 1990s Bank and Fund personnel were drawn into law reform efforts to resolve national debt crises in Ecuador and Mexico and to erect preventive institutions. But it was the Asian Financial Crisis that propelled legal departments at both international financial institutions (IFIs) into the business of constructing corporate bankruptcy regimes, a shift that impelled both to seek a systematic and ordered approach to doing so.[3] It was no small triumph for lawyers in the Bank's legal department to be included for the first time in the initial intervention team that flew into Seoul as Korea's financial crisis came to a head (Int 2040). The Assistant General Counsel of the IMF similarly spent weeks of intensive drafting in Jakarta as Indonesia was pressed to erect a functioning corporate bankruptcy system in the fraught days of early 1998. But these organizational breakthroughs proceeded without coherent templates and formulae for global reconstruction of corporate insolvency systems, not to mention plans for reshaping the 'architecture of the state'. And this was the enterprise in which the IFIs ultimately were engaged (Halliday 2011; Shaffer Forthcoming).

Shaken by the threat to regional and global financial stability by the Asian Financial Crisis, the G-7 and later the G-22 encouraged the Bank and Fund to produce sets of norms on corporate insolvency law in an effort to forestall future financial meltdowns (G-22 1998b). Indeed, the G-22 caucused with INSOL to produce a set of insolvency norms to guide the IFIs in their more extensive normmaking (G-22 1998a). The IMF was quick to produce a small book on insolvency procedures (IMF 1999). So, the ADB took its own steps to develop standards that it used to appraise the insolvency laws of eleven Asian countries (Asian Development Bank 2000).

The response of the World Bank to the G-22 was more deliberative. With the support of US Treasury, the World Bank created an insolvency initiative within its Legal Vice-Presidency and charged it to respond to the G-7 and G-22 mandates. It hired an experienced US bankruptcy lawyer,

Gordon Johnson, to lead its insolvency programme. With some involvement in efforts by the IBA and INSOL, and post-graduate training in comparative law at the London School of Economics, Johnson's practice
experience was slim but his agenda was expansive (Int 2004C). On the one
hand, he intended that the Bank develop principles that would cover not
only substantive law for corporate creditors and debtors but also the institutional and regulatory frameworks that implement the principles. On the
other hand, he wanted to link the principles to diagnostic instruments and
a template that could be used for national reform programmes.

The diagnostic approach was entirely consistent with World Bank and IMF
practices to appraise the financial systems of nations through its Reports on
the Observance of Standards and Codes (ROSCs), a joint global effort that
eventually expanded to twelve extensive diagnostic instruments that peer
into most corners of a national financial system.[4] Lying behind these pragmatic texts there typically was a scholarly technical report, possibly in the
form of a comparative lawyers' brief, which demonstrated how programmatic
documents fitted with extant national laws and institutions.

The Bank deployed its singular advantage by heavily funding its insolvency initiative. It leveraged this funding to create an extensive infrastructure for development of its insolvency norms, both prescriptive and
diagnostic. Its expansive claims to expert legitimation and global consultation are best encapsulated in its own words:

> The ad hoc committee that served as an advisory panel comprised rep-
> resentatives from the African Development Bank, Asian Development
> Bank, European Bank for Reconstruction and Development, Inter-
> American Development Bank, International Finance Corporation,
> International Monetary Fund, Organisation for Economic Co-
> operation and Development, United Nations Commission on Interna-
> tional Trade Law, INSOL International, and the International Bar
> Association (Committee J). In addition, over 70 leading experts from
> countries around the world participated in the Task Force and
> Working Groups.
>
> (World Bank 2005)

The Bank hosted a series of global forums, beginning with a conference in
Sydney in December 1999, where it rolled out its first draft. It thereafter
'vetted' iterations of the *Principles* 'in a series of five regional conferences,
involving officials and experts from some 75 countries', culminating in a
major conference in 2003, the Global Forum on Insolvency Risk Management where the Bank's principals reviewed

> the experience with and lessons from the application of the *Principles*
> in the assessment program. The forum convened over 200 experts

from 31 countries to discuss the lessons from this application and to discuss further refinements to the *Principles* themselves.

(World Bank 2005: 1)

This massive Bank enterprise, which purported to integrate not only all the relevant regional development banks and the key professional associations, and to draw into its deliberations well-known academics and practitioners from many countries, would seem to have pre-empted global debate and to have seized the high ground of normative supremacy. The Bank's point person had a clear 'mental ecology' of how his enterprise differentiated itself from potential rivals. Compared to the IMF's effort, which was strong on its legal framework but weak on institutions, and seemed focused more on short-term and emergency situations, the Bank saw its role 'as a longer infrastructure project' with a long-term developmental perspective (Interview 2004C). Compared to the ADB product, which was also more attentive to substantive law than institutions, the Bank took a 'more systems-oriented approach' that required 'adequate institutions, regulatory institutions, commercial institutions' and a 'more holistic view of commercial relationships from the beginning of the credit relationship' (Int 2004C). The EBRD at that point had no formal prescriptive text; Johnson thus presumed they could be ignored. Johnson also believed he had support from INSOL and 'advisory' input from the IBA, not least because he had had some personal involvement in both.

It came as a shock to the World Bank, therefore, when UNCITRAL announced in 1999 that it was considering development of a definitive text of its own. UNCITRAL's Secretariat had been pleasantly surprised by the expeditious effort of its Insolvency Working Group to produce a global consensus in its 1996 Model Law on Cross-Border Insolvency. Official and observer delegations from scores of countries and key non-state organizations, most notably the INSOL and IBA, had broken through what seemed to be the deadlocked impasse of any wide-ranging international normmaking in bankruptcy law. Buoyed by this success, Australia proposed that UNCITRAL take on bigger game and consider the prospect of creating an entire corporate bankruptcy set of norms for all countries, but particularly for lawmakers in developing and transitional economies.

UNCITRAL's Commission authorized its Insolvency Working Group to reconvene for exploratory consideration of Australia's proposal, which it did in late 1999. While there was some scepticism about overreach, there was also concern that the World Bank had pre-empted UNCITRAL, and the US and other governments were reluctant for UNCITRAL to move until the Bank had showed its hand. UNCITRAL's Secretariat, in consultation with its inner core of Working Group delegates, decided to host a Colloquium in late 2000 to appraise prospects. Many delegates, even optimists, were doubtful that UNCITRAL's venture had any realistic prospects, given that this area of law was at once deeply embedded in local culture and generally resistant to unification or harmonization. Moreover, delegates felt UNCITRAL might be too late – what was left for them to say that hadn't already been said?

But UNCITRAL's Secretary, Jernej Sekolec, told the 200 or so participants in his opening remarks to the 2000 Colloquium, that UNCITRAL had three strong claims to its involvement in global normmaking. It had a track record of completing a prior set of norms, the Model Law, in this fractious area of trade law, and this momentum, carried along by an already functioning community of global crafters of norms, should not be squandered. By virtue of its status as a UN body, and in view of its recent success in bringing together a wide array of nations with industry interests, UNCITRAL had a claim to representative authority that existed in no other international institution. Moreover, UNCITRAL could boast the technical legitimacy it obtained from integral involvement of the two key expert professions of accountants and lawyers, many law professors who were also state and non-state delegates, and delegates themselves who were lawmakers on bankruptcy law in their own countries. Behind the scenes, the Secretariat would also point out that UNCITRAL had nothing of the odium attached to it that was widely believed to result from the IMF's and World Bank's coercive use of conditionality in dealing with nations in financial distress. At least one regional development bank official expressed what others thought, namely, an 'ambivalence about what game is being played' and the 'heavy-handed and culturally insensitive insistence on reforms' that had been pushed by the Bank and Fund through their unpopular policies of conditionality (Int 2101).

Delegates left the 2000 Colloquium perceptably buoyed by an unexpected level of consensus on high-level goals of bankruptcy systems and the topics that might be addressed. Block-Lieb had prepared a careful comparative document showing that ADB, IMF and draft Bank norms converged substantially.[5] A sense of optimism and considerable vigor therefore put UNCITRAL on a potential collision course with the World Bank. Said one close observer, the World Bank was 'blindsided'. It thought it would have the stage to itself but 'now has to fit in and adapt' (Interview 2101). With a fear of being 'upstaged', the Bank had to consider how to proceed, whether competitively or cooperatively.

When UNCITRAL's Commission authorized the Working Group to proceed on new bankruptcy project in 2001, it appeared the World Bank had decided on some combination of cooperation and a division of labour. The Bank attended UNCITRAL Working Group sessions as an observer delegation; it simultaneously proceeded to develop its diagnostic ROSC, something that UNCITRAL never aspired to do.

From 2001 until 2003, a quiet political settlement seemed to prevail. Several regional development banks and professional associations joined the IMF and World Bank as participating delegations in the twice-yearly Working Group meetings. The World Bank Principles, drafted in 1999 and revised in 2001, would inform UNCITRAL's deliberations; the technical capacity and resources of the Bank would be directed to national assessments against a benchmark and technical assistance.

This illusion was shattered at an international forum hosted at Bank headquarters in January 2003. The world learned that the World Bank had quietly continued to develop its principles, with the assistance of a small group of distinguished consulting scholars, and it intended to establish them out as a global standard by obtaining the endorsement of the World Bank/IMF Boards as the ultimate stamp of multi-lateral authority.

Reactions ranged from mild characterizations of the conflict as a 'scrap' to outright anger at the World Bank's 'pure power play' (Int 2055B). From UNCITRAL's Secretariate's vantage point, an incipient 'air of conflict' with the Bank in 2002 now turned into outright 'turf war' (Int 4003). The US delegation to UNCITRAL was thrown into confusion, in part because its leader, Hal Burman, and an advocate of UNCITRAL's endeavor, was a diplomat in the commercial section of the State Department. It seemed that the Bank had convinced US Treasury that it should be preferred over UNCITRAL. But this put the State Department at odds with Treasury. Other leading state delegations shared the view of UNCITRAL's Secretariat that the 'weakness' of the World Bank approach was that 'they are not fully enough consultative or participatory to draw in such a diversity of nations to consider national variation' (Int 1947). The IMF delegation was 'not in favor of two competing products' and thought that 'the US could never go along with a product that is so secretive and private, as the World Bank approach has been' (Int 1950). The IMF didn't want the World Bank 'going it alone'; neither did the professional associations involved in the UNCITRAL project (Int 1951).

Some delegates saw quickly that the conflict might be resolved in any combination of three ways. First, the IOs could divide the normative domain between a focus by the Bank on a text with high level principles and an UNCITRAL product that provided more precise rules for statutory adoption by national legislators. Second, they could reach a jurisdictional settlement in which the Bank focused on institutions, consistent with its 'systemic' approach, and UNCITRAL focused on legal substance. Third, they could divide the normative territory along a different line of demarcation: UNCITRAL could provide the prescriptive norms, whether as principles or rules, and the Bank could integrate these into diagnostic instruments that informed technical assistance and directed legal change inside nation states.

However, the Bank opted for the zero-sum strategy of 'winner takes all'. It had material resources, global reach, and extensive networks of specialists and IOs. It had proximity and the apparent confidence of US

Treasury. Why should it capitulate to a small, relatively poor, technical deliberative body far away in Vienna?

Through 2003 intense negotiations criss-crossed the Atlantic, between UNCITRAL and Bank lawyers. Two extremes defined the most drastic option: either UNICTRAL or the World Bank would withdraw from norm-making. Less drastically, the Bank proposed that perhaps it could keep its principles and UNCITRAL's emerging legislative guide would be styled as the 'methodology' that operationalized the principles. Or, the Bank suggested, it might add to its principles a comparative analysis of bankruptcy regimes in various countries and the Bank's appraisal of those experiences. Alternatively, the Bank might produce some sort of 'technical paper'.

UNCITRAL's Secretariat, and those delegates heavily invested in its program, resisted any marginalization or dilution of a draft legislative guide at an advanced stage of completion. By 2003, UNCITRAL's draft guide comprised hundreds of pages of principles and goals, organized in the form of chapters of a potential statute, together with close on 200 recommendations which were often in statutory form, together with commentary to justify the recommendations (Int 4002). Moreover, UNCITRAL feared that if the World Bank could sweep in to a global normmaking process late in the day, it would 'render superfluous' UNCITRAL's heavy reliance on volunteers. Who would volunteer to work on an UNCITRAL project if the Bank could seize the initiative at the penultimate moment? Ultimately the UN process itself would be undermined and a key resource – extensive volunteer goodwill and effort – squandered.

Bank officials drafted the first of many iterations of a 'Points of Understanding,' which might produce a concordat between the Bank and UNCITRAL. When UNCITRAL's Working Group convened at its mid-year meeting in New York, many delegates remained 'agitated and angry' with the proposed settlement (Int 1970). UNCITRAL's Secretary produced his own draft agreement. UNCITRAL could live with the Bank *Principles*, since they were largely consistent with UNCITRAL's Legislative Guide, but UNCITRAL's recommendations and extensive text should be recognized as specifying the principles.

Suspicion remained about the so-called Technical Paper to be prepared by the Bank, because it might conflict with the commentary in the Legislative Guide. Furthermore, UNCITRAL's lawyers believed that one reason that the key professional associations had thrown their weight behind UNCITRAL was precisely because 'they wanted a product *not* developed by the Bank' (Int 1970). Yet to alienate the Bank entirely might rob UNCITRAL of the capacity to disseminate its product: 'UNCITRAL', said one of its officials, 'doesn't have the resources to go out and sell. If you can get an aid organization to essentially promote the product, then in theory that is good' for UNCITRAL (Int 1970). Ironically, while UNCITRAL's officials also feared dominance by the US, the very strong presence of the US delegation and many senior North American participants provided some degree of protection for UNCITRAL.

Meanwhile, officials at the Bank had been effective in obtaining support from US Treasury and the New York Federal Reserve on the dubious grounds, alleged Bank critics, that the World Bank was 'the only game in town' (Int 1971). When an UNCITRAL delegate, and leading US bankruptcy lawyer, eventually briefed Treasury in mid-2003 on the extensive output of the Working Group and the advanced state of its draft, this gave Treasury pause, even as an American Bar Association delegate was similarly briefing the General Counsel of the US Federal Reserve Bank (Int 1958).

Leaders of both competitive IOs appealed up the chain of command of their own huge organizations. UNCITRAL's officials called upon the UN Vice-President for Legal Affairs to intervene; the acting general counsel of the World Bank was drawn by his own officials and the UN general counsel into negotiations to resolve the dispute. In July 2003, the UN general counsel convened a meeting of the IMF Deputy General Counsel, a Bank official, and the UNCITRAL Secretariat and Working Group Secretary. They set a timetable and an outline for agreement: the Bank would produce a document identifying points of divergence and a joint expert group would seek to ensure consistency between the IOs; the Bank would complete its principles and a comparison of those with UNCITRAL's product would be discussed at a September 2003 UNCITRAL Working Group meeting; the Bank would provide a commentary to its own principles; the UNCITRAL Secretariat would respond; the Bank would take appropriately revised principles to its Board in late 2003.

The IMF favoured reliance on the UNCITRAL product, but its close association with the Bank required a gentle touch. The Fund was keen to get a 'consensual instrument' because the Fund itself 'got so much criticism for heavy-handedness' (JS, Int 1973). It applauded UNCITRAL's widely participatory, open, deliberative process. Whatever product the IMF pushes, said one official, 'must be legitimate'. Said a close observer of the Fund, 'they have been burnt politically' in the past and, if they are to use global standards as 'a stick', that stick must be the product of a legitimate process. Indeed, the sensitivity of the Fund on this account led to its euphemistic description of its own effort as 'a staff paper' (Int 4008). Moreover, its own lawmaking interventions in countries required precise UNCITRAL-style recommendations rather than the Banks' *Principles*, which were 'so vague and general' (Int 2351B).

A three-way agreement between the World Bank, IMF and UNCITRAL, with concord between US Treasury and the State Department, became the *sine qua non* of a settled outcome on a single text, something the US government strongly advocated for its own trade interests. Already countries 'are being whiplashed by different IFIs – the EBRD and World Bank' – and a third text from UNCITRAL would compound confusion (Int 4004B).

By early 2004, with no clear resolution, a senior official at the IMF 'got fed up and twisted arms and got a deal done' (Int 2100B). The unified standard would take the form of a single text that incorporated (a) the World Bank's Principles, with no technical paper or comparative commentary, but with some amplification on institutions integral to an insolvency system; and (b) UNCITRAL's Legislative Guide; with (c) some complementary material from the Bank on issues not treated by the UNCITRAL Guide, and (d) a ROSC diagnostic instrument that would be keyed into UNCITRAL's recommendations (Int 2100B, 4008B; confidential memo, 25 March 2004).

Still, matters did not end there. The so-called merging of the documents took until the end of 2005 to complete, as each IO fought rear guard battles over the specific form of a 'unified standard' (Int 5503). The final settlement didn't resolve itself until a change of leadership and personnel at the Bank brought a 'change in tone', a 'giant shift in attitude' and the prospect of a 'framework that preserves the integrity of both documents' (Int 5504).

The compromise document, released and posted to the World Bank website on 21 December 2005, was entitled: *Creditor Rights and Insolvency Standards, based on The World Bank Principles for Effective Creditor Rights and Insolvency Systems and UNCITRAL Legislative Guide on Insolvency Law.* The text itself, presented as a 'unified standard', nevertheless rhetorically valorizes the World Bank. It has placement priority before UNCITRAL at every point, from the title page forward. The text repeats the quasi-representativeness of Bank deliberations from earlier Bank drafts of its *Principles*. The pattern of presentation always places Bank principles first and then follows them, with the overall result that the Bank appears ascendant presentationally and rhetorically and the document as a whole is a confusing jumble. National legislators will need to go back to UNCITRAL's Legislative Guide to find its commentary on its recommendations. And the World Bank has its diagnostic instrument, its ROSC on insolvency, purportedly mapped onto UNCITRAL's specific recommendations but nowhere in sight for public inspection.[6]

A theoretical reading

As in law, a single case can amplify social science and sociolegal theory of legal change in the international economic order. The struggle between UNCITRAL and the World Bank for normative supremacy opens a window into a much longer and more variegated politics of the text that come into sharp focus through the lens of the recursivity of law.

The climactic conflict between UNCITRAL and the World Bank must be positioned temporally at the end of three to four decades of efforts to produce global texts and practices regulating cross-border corporate failures and guiding national lawmaking to protect domestic businesses, jobs and financial stability. The reform episode began with wide-ranging national law reforms in the United States (1978), Britain (1986) and Germany (1999), quickened with the legal reconstruction of command economies, and gained urgency with a succession of national debt crises in major regional economies. But it was the Asian Financial Crisis that precipitated wholesale global normmaking to ensure a new international architecture for global and national markets. The etiology of the global reform enterprise explains why the Bank and the Fund, together with regional development banks, were inserted onto center stage. From their ad hoc rescue and reform efforts, they were charged by the G-7 and G-22 to become methodical, systematic, and comprehensive in their normmaking prescriptions and applications.

Already, in the years of accelerating reform efforts during the 1980s and 1990s, instances of recursivity appear between local, national and global actors. A leading Australian bankruptcy law reformer influenced the Asian Development Bank's normmaking and national assessments. The shifting jurisprudence of US and English law reforms towards rehabilitation rather than liquidation of companies influenced EBRD, IMF and Bank practices in the early and mid 1990s. The EBRD, Bank and Fund in turn pressed national lawmakers to implement ad hoc transnational norms. And local actors, most notably, major law firms and eminent lawyers, aligned themselves as consultants to IOs in the reconstruction of bankruptcy regimes across the world.

The three cycles of relationships between transnational, national and local actors speed up significantly and display a richly nuanced complexity after Thailand, Malaysia, Indonesia and South Korea suffered financial collapse and threatened to turn a regional financial crisis into a global economic calamity. The recursive framework requires examination of multiple cycles, often occurring simultaneously.

First, iterations of normmaking occur among international and global normmakers. Each crafts its own texts with an eye on the others. The EBRD's diagnostic tools in the mid-1990s are attuned to the underlying normative consensus that seemed to be emerging from IMF and Bank emergency interventions and the reconstruction of Central and Eastern European economies. The Bank and Fund are accustomed to working together in national interventions and their respective texts in 1999 deviate little from each other in their substantive fundamentals. Neither the Fund nor Bank seemed to take much notice of the ADB's standard-producing exercise, but when UNCITRAL entered the fray it gave the ADB equal standing to the Bank and Fund as it acknowledged the shoulders of the giants on which it stood. UNCITRAL's declaration of interest in creating its own text for global norms on national bankruptcy laws illustrates how an IO, from 1994 onward, propagated first a modest, then a more ambitious, then a highly ambitious global text that purported to reach into most corners of corporate insolvency practice. And when UNCITRAL and the Bank clashed openly in 2003, rapid iterations of observation, adaptation and revisions of each other's texts punctuated the road to final settlement.

Second, recursivity theory directs attention to the intense engagement between certain IOs and states in the drafting of their respective texts. In some degree, the global texts came from 'below', as they reflected national reforms in the US, France, Germany, the UK, and other nations. More generally, UNCITRAL's legitimacy rested heavily on broad and variegated representation of states (Halliday *et al.* 2011). Since its text was primarily produced by state delegates, leading delegations had a powerful interest concomitantly in building into global standards key aspects of their own laws and defending the primacy of norms developed by representatives of states themselves. It was the singular relationship of UNCITRAL's Secretariat and working methods to a wide range of states that underwrote its principal claim to legitimacy. Our case shows, however, that states themselves may be fractious and fractured internally, and that one state agency, such as US Treasury, might favor the IO with which it has closest links, while another, the US State Department, might be invested in another IO. Here the 'vertical' cycles of engagement between the state and IOs depends on a 'horizontal' settlement of relations between competing state agencies.

Third, recursivity theory points to the salience of local actors in the global politics of legal texts. Sometimes they are invisible, as they influence the negotiating positions to be taken by their governments. But here we have shown they manifest themselves in several ways that escape the scrutiny of much IO research. For the Fund and Bank, local experts, whether practitioners or professors, comprised the deliberative enterprise, effectively bypassing states. For UNCITRAL, local experts were drawn into delegations, including those of industry groups such as the American Bar Association, but also more subtly into direct informal expert advice to the Secretariat. Here lawyers, judges and professors from France, US, Mexico, UK, Australia, among other countries, convened in expert groups as learned and practiced individuals, and they advised, drafted, revised and consulted broadly with the Working Group Secretary. Indeed, detailed empirical analysis of UNCITRAL's own proceedings shows that small clusters of individuals operated at the heart of its various trade lawmaking enterprises (Halliday *et al.* 2011). Local actors, therefore, function recursively in two types of cycles: engaging with their own governments, as US lawyers did in their efforts to break the Bank/UNCITRAL impasse with

Treasury and State, and engaging directly with the IOs, which in turn endowed the individuals and their industry groups with a panoply of distinction.

Since recursivity theory aims to explain why cycles persist and when settling occurs, it points to four mechanisms that repeatedly drive lawmaking from the beginning to end of episodes. Settlement requires resolution of the impetus for further reform cycles within each mechanism.

Actor mismatch occurs when national or industry actors are missing from the international text-writing enterprise, and when local actors are missing from national lawmaking. Since our case concerns an international setting, we must ask – does the presence or absence of actors in either IO explain the dueling that occurred between the Bank and UNCITRAL? In fact, much of the ground of the entire dispute turns on particular actors and their involvement in the dueling IOs. UNCITRAL's principal claim to normative primacy rested on its UN auspices as the only IO that drew all states into parliamentary-like deliberative lawmaking. Equally as important, UNCITRAL could boast that its deliberations also systematically included industry interests, as well as the professions that would interpret any global text and implement it in practice. Even if detailed research shows that neither of these claims is actually vindicated entirely in practice, the perception of its inclusiveness sets UNCITRAL apart from the Bank. The Bank looked to characterize itself as representative, but sought only to build a quasi- or pseudo-representativeness by multiplying the numbers of experts it included from various regions. None of these experts had been anointed as delegates from their state of origin. UNCITRAL's effort to minimize mismatch between the variety of the world's nations and the production of its global norms ultimately proved a decisive basis for agreement in the US, France and the IMF that UNCITRAL's text must triumph. The politics of legitimation at the heart of the UNCITRAL/Bank conflict emerge from institutional awareness of the costs of actor mismatch for dissemination and adoption of a global text.

Little of the Bank/UNCITRAL conflict can be explained by differences over the diagnosis of the underlying problem. Both institutions agreed that very many countries lacked any law or institutions to rescue businesses or save jobs through bankruptcy proceedings. Too often countries either circumvented law on the books, or the law itself was inflexible and even punitive, destroying businesses that could have thrived if given a chance to reorganize while being protected from their creditors. There may have been some differences of emphasis but it was not diagnostic differences that fuelled the conflict.

Neither were the IOs in conflict over ideology. Both IOs proceeded on the assumptions that every country needed a comprehensive corporate bankruptcy system of substantive laws and supporting institutions. They agreed that this system should not prioritize liquidation of failing companies but rather protect creditors while permitting managers to rescue businesses that had some hope of rehabilitation. The Bank did adhere more closely to the US line in the early drafts of its principles, and UNCITRAL did provide more alternatives to US ways of constructing bankruptcy systems, but these differences amounted only to details on the edges.

No, the principal contradiction was institutional, a rivalry over institutional primacy, over which deliberative methods, which forms of power, which experts would emerge triumphant. Similarly, the principal indeterminacy was institutional, not so much as to what the text should say but which institution should be charged with drafting the text.

A fourth mechanism that can drive cycles of legal change, indeterminacy or ambiguity, comes most closely to the politics of the *text*. Here the form of the text itself was both part of the problem and the solution. The Bank championed high-level principles that might be flexibly applied and adapted across the world. While in theory these might give sovereign states the ability to adapt and apply broad principles to the exigencies of their local circumstances, in practice critics argued that the text was so abstract that it would provide little guidance to lawmakers struggling to enact a complex statute in any area of law invariably thought to be obscure or technical. UNCITRAL championed a legislative guide, which organized its norms in a hierarchy of abstraction and specificity. The form of the guide and the recommendations it promulgated came much closer in form to a statute than the Bank's principles; in addition to recommendations, the accompanying commentary provided legislators with reasoning for why they might prefer one variant of a statutory provision to another. UNCITRAL's guide assisted more than national legislators. From the recommendations in the Legislative Guide, the Bank subsequently forged a very precise diagnostic instrument, a ROSC on insolvency law, something neither the Bank nor the Fund had been able to craft from their broadly phrased principles.

While this conflict between principles and rules refracts in practice a long-standing academic debate over the relative merits of either in regulation (Braithwaite 2002; Braithwaite and Drahos 2000; Schwarz 1995; Scott 1994), it also provided grounds for compromise. We have seen that a 'pyramidal' notion of transnational norms, with abstract principles at its peak and detailed rules at its base, permitted a settlement in which one institution could claim the high ground of the principles and the other the precision of the rules. Further, the organizational mandate of UNCITRAL restricted its text to prescriptive norms while the mandate of the Bank authorized its diagnostic instrument, another division of labour which made settlement between the two IOs possible.

We show elsewhere that settlement of episodes of legal change in a global context requires stabilization both of norms and practice. Resolving that the actor mismatch problem was best managed by UNCITRAL, that the institutional contradictions should not be allowed to perpetuate global normative confusion, and that ambiguity in the transnational legal order could be reduced by differentiating the texts of the Bank from that of UNCITRAL, by early 2006 it could be concluded that normative settlement, at least at the global level, had been achieved. In fact, since many states also found UNCITRAL's *Legislative Guide* consistent with their own actual or intended reforms, settling began to occur between global and state actors.

Settlement in behavior and practices, however, is another matter. It is not known how precisely the Bank has incorporated the particulars of UNCITRAL's *Legislative Guide* in the diagnoses and technical assistance it undertakes in various countries. Nor is it yet known to what extent lawyers and accountants, owners and bankers, state regulators and lenders, are conforming their behaviour to the norms adopted by UNCITRAL and the Bank, and the statutes and institutions adopted by states to change behaviour.

The sociolegal edge

In the haste to differentiate their revisionist turn from traditional legal scholarship, the sociolegal and law in context movements turned away from either the form and content of the text or the processes that placed law on the books. Intensified focus on international law and global governance by social scientists is drawing sociolegal scholarship back to the text. A new *problematique* confronts inter-disciplinary scholars – how does the text emerge, what form does it take, and what are its impacts?

We have argued that that this turn back *to* the text – in this case, international economic law as a sociolegal problem – can create new comity between legal and sociolegal scholarship when both are drawn systematically inside the framework of the recursivity of law. At once, a recursive analysis points both to actions that put international law on the books and to effects of that law as they unfold over multiple cycles between the onset and completion of reform episodes. Put another way, transnational recursivity theory (Shaffer 2011) assimilates the politics of the text inside a systematic theory of globalization and law and transnational legal orders. In this theory, politics influences the text and the text shapes politics.

The positioning of a sociolegal perspective on international economic law situates this politics of the text not only in relation to legal scholarship but also to the social science of globalization. Recursivity theory insists upon a new sensitivity to law by social scientists who conventionally assume or neglect it.

Theories of international economic law must investigate the politics of the legal complex. We observe in international bankruptcy lawmaking not only coalitions of law professors, international lawyer-civil servants, private lawyers, and judges, but the form and content of the law itself presupposes certain divisions of labour in practice that elevate or minimize the involvement of domestic legislatures, which give more or less discretion to judges and practitioners in the implementation of law, which enable scholars more or less authority to shape legal doctrine or justify legal practice.

Legal and sociolegal scholarship can join in common cause to convince social science that legal creativity, the invention and creative extension of legal concepts, are integral to the politics of international economic law. UNCITRAL's Working Groups invented terms that transcended the partiality of national legal concepts (Block-Lieb and Halliday 2006), created new concepts to deal with emerging problems in cross-border trade (COMI), and enabled compromises when deadlock seemed inevitable (ST).

Sociolegal scholarship also insists that social science scholarship on international law and globalization must draw both transnational and national institutions more integrally into research and theory. Recursivity theory affirms that cycles of change invariably involve courts and regulatory agencies as well as legislatures. Transnational recursivity theory insists that transnational reform enterprises very frequently are directed to the architecture of states where the powers of legal institutions become a fundamental point of negotiation in the balance of power among state institutions (Halliday 2011; Shaffer Forthcoming).

And, finally, sociolegal scholarship informed by recursivity theory heeds Stinchcombe's (Stinchcombe 2001) call for sociologists to re-consider their dismissal of the formal properties of law and organizations as worthy objects of inquiry. This essay has shown that principles versus rules, prescriptive versus diagnostic instruments, substantive versus institutional norms, can at once be the object of intensive political manoeuvring and offer prospects for political settlement (Braithwaite 2002; Schwartz and Scott 1995). Transnational economic law cannot be divorced from a recursive politics of the text.

Notes

1 Here and elsewhere we will use the shorthand 'global' to refer to any sets of norms or organizations that transcend the nation-state. These may be regional, international, or global in aspirations or actuality.
2 For protection of the privacy of subjects and interviewees, all interviews are given arbitrary identifying numbers.
3 The fully rounded model of a national bankruptcy system included (1) substantive and (2) procedural law; (3) a government bankruptcy agency; (4) a bankruptcy court of division of a court; (5) an out-of-court resolution body; and (6) expert professions.
4 See www.worldbank.org/ifa/rosc.html and www.imf.org/external/NP/rosc/rosc.aspx (accessed 6 January 2012).
5 Available online at http://law.fordham.edu/assets/Faculty/uncitral.pdf

6 Matters didn't end there. As tense as relations between these IOs had become between 2003 and 2005, since that time the World Bank and UNCITRAL have coordinated closely with each another. The World Bank continues to sit as an observer at UNCITRAL Insolvency Working Group meetings; UNCITRAL staff are invited to attend certain World Bank meetings. UNICTRAL's Working Group moved on to develop recommendations on the insolvency treatment of corporate groups. In 2009, the Commission approved these as well as a Practice Guide on Cross-Border Insolvency Cooperation, which arose out of several judicial colloquia hosted jointly by UNCITRAL and INSOL. In 2011, UNCITRAL released a report regarding 'judges' perspectives' on its Model Law on Cross-Border Insolvency, while its Insolvency Working Group continued to deliberate on two ongoing projects: (i) the interpretation and application of selected concepts in the Model Law, as well as (ii) directors' responsibilities and liabilities in insolvency and pre-insolvency cases. In 2011, the World Bank held two Insolvency and Creditor/Debtor Regimes Task Force Meetings. Its background documents refer copiously to the consistency of the World Bank *Principles* and the UNCITRAL Legislative Guide, and to a desire to continue these cooperative efforts into the future.

Chapter 7

Power and production in global legal pluralism

An international political economy approach

David Schneiderman[1]

Introduction

Legal pluralism has been described as being at the core of debates in the sociology and anthropology of law (Santos 2002: 91–2). Researchers in the field principally have been on the lookout for the presence one of more legal orders within a given social field (Griffiths 1986) outside of officially state-sanctioned law. Issuing out of this cluster of research were closely described practices and highly contextualized accounts of plural legal practices operating within a variety of locales, including within settler-states (Llwellyn and Hoebel 1941; Arthurs 1985), developing states (Santos 2002), and colonial settings (Chanock 1985; Moore 2000).[2] These studies carefully attended to the relationship between 'official' and 'unofficial' law. They were not so much about denigrating state law as accommodating it to the 'inescapable framework' that is legal pluralism (Merry 1988: 879). Research in the area 'increasingly emphasized the dialectic, mutually con-stitutive relation between state law and other normative orders,' observed Merry (Merry 1988: 880).

Following upon the decentering of states and the transfer of authority to newer legal regimes, we are likely to see a proliferation of new norm-ative orders. In contrast to state legal fields, there might not be any obvious hierarchy and each might be contending for supremacy within their fields of operation. This is how some have characterized con-temporary international law – as being fragmented (Koskenniemi and Leino 2002) – but it captures well the phenomenon of global legal plur-alism. Scholars have been extending insights drawn from nation-state focused legal pluralism into transnational domains. There is, indeed, great merit to this sort of move. Researchers are rendered free to find law and legal processes occurring in all variety of domains, ones that may be oper-ating at some distance from state law. With international economic regula-tion dispersed amongst an array of functional norm-developing and dispute-resolving institutions, we are in a better position to observe the transference, evolution and uptake of legal processes and norms at various levels. By decentering national states as the principal locus of law making and opening up the question about what 'law' is, we are enabled empirically, analytically and normatively to better understand change occurring within contemporary global processes.

If early pluralist accounts were about taking stock of the complex relationship between state and other normative orders that look like law, in its contemporary guise legal pluralism is about excising states altogether (Wai 2008). Global legal pluralist scholarship typically displays a 'cosmopolitan style,' a spirit of unabashed internationalism (Kennedy 1994: 13). While abandoning an exclusively state-centric focus may be appropriate, how helpful is an account that envisages 'global law without the state'? (Teubner 1997b). In this chapter I question the utility of global legal pluralism in the absence of an accompanying account of power currently being exercised in global legal domains principally, but not exclusively, via state agency. There is a danger in bracketing the ways in which power relations define and then configure legal norms and institutions that regulate economic life at multiple levels. Not only is there a naiveté about power that infects the global legal pluralist account, one also loses sight of the partiality and ideological tilt of the contemporary global scene. As a corrective, I supplement the pluralist account with insights drawn from the critical branch of international political economy (IPE). Critical IPE aims to bring both politics and economics to bear on the study of international politics. The aspiration of this chapter is to bring law into dialogue with this branch of IPE with a view to better ascertaining the political stakes involved in analyzing the rise of international economic law.

I propose doing so by focusing on a particular sub-discipline, namely, international investment law and arbitration (the 'investment law regime'). This is a distinct, post-1989, field of law (with ties to customary international law and the constitutional law of capital-exporting states) that has arisen to promote and protect foreign investment abroad. States commit to high standards of protection for investors via bilateral investment treaties (BITs), which investors then are entitled to enforce before international investment tribunals.

It would be uncontroversial to say that this sub-discipline of international economic law looks like 'law'[3] and is a good example of global legal pluralism in action. A stylized account of the investment law regime resonating in pluralist terms has been offered by U.S. property law theorist Marc Poirier. The virtues and limitations of this analytic are on full display in Poirier's account, which I discuss in the second part of this chapter. Such an account requires a supplement that is better attuned to the production of legal power in international economic law. I turn, then, to a discussion of critical IPE in order to offer a corrective to the global legal pluralist account. I turn, first, to a brief review of legal pluralism's early instantiations and its contemporary global variant.

Pluralism's abundance

Some suggest that the origins of legal pluralism can be traced back to medieval European times (Michaels 2009: 245; Pospisil 1967: 13; Tamanaha 2008: 377–81). It undoubtedly is correct to say that its twentieth-century variant had its kick start with medievalism of a sort: the translation and introduction by Frederic W. Maitland of Otto Gierke's *Political Theories of the Middle Age* (1900) (Runciman 1997: 64). Gierke's account of the medieval theory of groups (a fragment of a much larger book) appealed to Maitland's conception of the British state as composed of many 'group wills' operating beyond and without the authority of the English Crown. The law of German fellowship contemplated associational life as autonomous in its will formation, without the imprimatur of some central state authority. The corporate legal form contemplated associational life in all of its dimensions and so was the preferred vehicle though which group accommodation could be pursued. English law, by contrast, failed miserably in accounting for associational existence beyond that conceded by the Crown – what Maitland famously described as that 'supralegal, suprajural plenitude of power concentrated in a single point at Westminster' (Maitland 1900: xliii). Maitland ridiculed the English legal system's failure to reconcile the 'manyness of the members' with the 'oneness of the body' (Maitland 1900: xxvii). '[I]njustice will continue to be done,' he advised, 'unless corporateness is treated as a matter of fact' (Maitland 1900: xxxviii). English law failed to reconcile legal norm with legal fact.

This was no mere descriptive account. Maitland set his sights on the reigning Austinian paradigm so as to refocus a legal lens on those places where law actually was being lived and experienced: 'It has often struck me that morally there is most personality where legally there is none,' Maitland wryly observed (1911: 383). His project was enthusiastically taken up by the group of writers associated with British political pluralism in the early twentieth century, thinkers such as Figgis (1913), Cole (1920a, 1920b) and Laski (1919; 1922) (Nicholls 1994; Runciman 1997). 'We must learn to think of railways and mines, cotton and agriculture, as areas of government just as real as London and Lancashire,' Laski maintained (Laski 1922: 12, 1948: 272). A sort of '[f]ederalistic feeling' was 'curiously widespread' in this period (Barker 1947: 158).

If a decentered leviathan state was normatively desirable in the early twentieth century, British political pluralism largely fell off the radar screen as its adherents moved on to other political projects. A version of political pluralism did get taken up by U.S. political scientists in the mid-twentieth century. This was not for reasons having to do with the promotion of group life, however, but to explain the functioning of a political system that responded to the inputs of a plurality of political actors (Dahl 1961). It would be left to a future generation of scholars, preferring sociological and anthropological methods, to revive thinking about legal pluralism. Sally Falk Moore's oft-cited paper on the 'semi-autonomous social field' (1973), which forms part of her book-length study concerning the Chagga of Mount Kilimanjaro (Moore 2000), described interactions between official state law and local forms of social regulation. Similarly, Santos' fieldwork on Pasagarda law carefully analyzed dispute resolution in a Brazilian *favela*, attending to questions of power and authority that arise in the encounter between official and unofficial *favela* law. Though not self-identifying as a legal pluralist, Robert Cover described the 'proliferation of legal meaning' in multiple interpretive communities that was inevitable and impossible to suppress. For Cover 'insular communities' contributed to the creation of constitutional meaning in the United States, creating law 'as fully as does the judge' (1983: 28). Official law, however, had the effect of inhibiting legal production by such communities, what Cover associated with the 'violence' of 'jurispathic' courts (Cover 1983: 53).[4]

If it is correct to claim that legal pluralism is inscribed into legal DNA (Cover 1983: 15), then multiple, overlapping legal orders will be found everywhere. We should expect legal pluralism to be thriving, then, under conditions of globalization (Michaels 2009: 255). The literature on global legal pluralism, for this reason, continues to grow as numerous lines of inquiry are being pursued. My aim here is modest: merely to highlight a feature that is common to this body of work, namely, the erasure of states in this evolving narrative.

Building on the pioneering work of Neil MacCormick in the European context, Nico Krisch helpfully distinguishes between 'systemic' and 'institutional' pluralism (2010: 72–3). The latter aims to tame the diversity of plural legal orders under common frameworks but without unifying mechanisms for reconciling conflict. The former assumes not even a common legal framework, rather, there is a reigning disorder that mostly is tolerated. Along these more 'radical' lines, McCormick characterized the European situation as one of 'overlapping legalities,' 'where differing systems can overlap and interact without the necessarily requiring that one be subordinate or heirarchically inferior to the other or to some third system' (MacCormick 1993: 10, 8).

Paul Berman rejects both the state-centrism of the methodological nationalism and international law's claims to universality in favor of 'messy' and hybrid global legal spaces that reveal no consensus around any specific set of norms (2007: 1164). He describes a de-territorialized world in which multiple and overlapping communities seek to impress their law upon others. The task at hand, he argues, is to devise procedural mechanisms for managing this messy hybridity (2007: 1236). Such mechanisms are envisaged by Robert Ahdieh, who identifies dialogic patterns of voluntary institutional learning that result in what he calls 'dialectical regulation' (Ahdieh 2006; Berman 2007).[5] A more institutional response to the transnational legal ordering is suggested by Christian Joerges who has proposed a 'conflict of laws' approach so as to better manage the disconnect between European legal norms and national legal ordering. The diversity of 'conflict constellations,' Joerges writes, 'militates against any hierarchical reconstruction of the European polity' (2010: 14). Instead, a spirit of openness to diversity and a concern with democratic legitimation underscores his 'conflicts' approach (Everson 2011).

The radical variant of transnational legal ordering aims to capture myriad, functionally-differentiated, transboundary legal orders operating in the contemporary world. State law has always had a fragile existence, Zumbansen maintains, and this has been laid bare by the dynamic expansion of regulatory spaces in the context of a world society (Zumbansen 2010: 151). Gunther Teubner explores this radically decentred legal order through a systems-theoretic lens, inspired not by McCormick but by Niklas Luhmann (Luhmann 2004; Fischer-Lescano and Teubner 2004).[6] Teubner's formulation regarding 'societal constitutionalism' (2004a) describes the emergence of autonomous legal orders proliferating at the global level that are 'emerging in relative isolation from politics' (1997b: 6). Teubner's account of *lex mercatoria*, or the 'law merchant' that is product of international commercial practice, is a paradigmatic instance, he claims, of 'global law without the state' (1997b: 8; Sweet 2006: 627). As in many of these accounts, there is no hierarchical relationship amongst autonomous legal orders, rather, each responds to their external environment by devising appropriate strategies of self-regulation and self-limitation.

Rather than calling on states to reorganize so as to account for these new normative orders (as with the British political pluralists), or carefully attending to the interaction between official and unofficial law (as in late twentieth-century socio-legal work), contemporary trends appear to excise the state altogether. What we then get is heterarchy without heirarchy. Though not everyone writing in the global legal pluralist vein stands so accused,[7] the tendency is to elide these relationships despite the lessons of earlier pluralist work. I turn next to a discussion of one realm of transnational legality where a state presence largely is being displaced, at least in theory, by pluralist conceptions of the global legal order.

Global legal pluralism and international investment law

International investment law and arbitration is a distinctly new legal order that is the product of global realignment in the aftermath of the Cold War. With the disintegration of the Soviet Union in 1989, states all over the world were expected to fall into line with edicts promoted by powerful capital-exporting states and issuing out of international financial institutions (Amsden 2007; Streeck 2011). Constituted by over 2,800 BITS and some bilateral and regional trade agreements (UNCTAD 2011: 100), international investment disciplines discourage a wide range of state behavior that may have the effect of substantially depriving investors of the value of their investment. Measures equivalent to an expropriation (in whole or in part), measures preferring local nationals over foreign ones, or measures that deny to investors 'fair and equitable treatment,' amongst other disciplines, provide grounds for investors to seek damages against host states for extraordinary sums of money (from tens of millions to hundred of millions of dollars).

There are innumerable remarkable features of this regime – I mention only a few here. Though its disciplines are drawn from the legal traditions of dominant capital-exporting states, the regime imposes restraints that do not represent well the historical experiences of those states. That is, the path to development that is being promoted by the investment regime, and touted by international financial institutions like the International Monetary Fund and the World Bank, are largely mythical ones that these states never themselves encountered in the course of developing their own economic muscularity (Chang 2002; Schneiderman 2008: 225–30). Nor would these sorts of disciplines have been tolerated then or even now – in some respects, they reach further in breadth and depth than do the current national legal systems of many capital-exporting states (i.e., in the U.S. context see Been and Beauvais 2003). Put differently, the regime is intended to establish thresholds concerning what would reasonably, at least prior to the ascendance of neoliberalism, have been construed as legitimate exercises of public authority. Today these are thresholds beyond which states and citizens are expected never to step (Van Harten 2007).

Of utmost significance is the investment regime's departure from international law practice, previously the exclusive reserve of states via 'diplomatic espousal,' by entitling investors to enforce treaty terms before investment arbitration tribunals. The regime purports to have the effect of removing disputes from local courts and 'elevating' them to a 'depoliticized' forum of dispute resolution staffed with lawyers having almost exclusively expertise in commercial and investment arbitration (Schneiderman 2011). I have described the regime elsewhere as 'constitution-like' (Schneiderman 2008), and so not fully constitutional, understanding that there are plural constitutional orders and norms vying for supremacy in the contemporary world. I have been advancing, in other words, a version of constitutional pluralism that is transnational in context. Neil Walker helpfully theorizes this possibility by drawing on the European experience. '[W]e can only begin to account adequately for what is going on within the European constitutional configuration,' Walker writes, 'if we posit a framework which identifies multiple sites of constitutional discourse and authority' (2002: 337, 2008). Weiler contends that the signal moment in the constitutionalization of the European Union was the rendering of individuals, and not just member states, as 'subjects of law' (1999: 222).[8] This too is an achievement secured by the investment rules regime. Understanding that international investment law and arbitration is a constituent element of the global legal scene invites further opportunity to theorize global legal pluralism. Though not well know in international law circles, Marc Poirier has taken up this task in the context of theorizing about property rights in a North American context, in particular, in thinking about the North American Free Trade Agreement's (NAFTA) investment chapter (Chapter 11) (Poirier 2003).[9]

Chapter 11 of NAFTA is in some measure the prototype of the modern bilateral investment treaty, with a comprehensive set of disciplines and an accompanying investor–state dispute mechanism. The problem with NAFTA's investment chapter, Poirier claims, is that its standards are being invoked 'broadly to attack perfectly standard exercises of the police power that purport to protect public health, safety, welfare and the environment' (2003: 852–53).[10] In this passage, Poirier invokes U.S. Supreme Court doctrine concerning 'police powers': the jurisdictional room to enact laws for the advancement of public peace, order, welfare and morals, which are the exclusive reserve of public authority, principally state governments, under the U.S. Constitution. These are laws that, by definition, do not attract the requirement of 'just compensation' under the Fifth and Fourteenth Amendments. According to this interpretation, NAFTA is depriving the national (or sub-national) state parties from enacting laws that properly fall beyond the purview of the rule of just compensation. In U.S. constitutional parlance, outside of instances of outright expropriation (the exercise of 'eminent domain'), permanent physical occupation or complete loss of economic value, measures that attract compensation will amount to a 'regulatory taking' (Dana and Merrill 2002). Chapter 11 turns out to be serving, then, functions similar to an expansive regulatory takings doctrine (Poirier 2003: 856).

The problem is that U.S. regulatory takings doctrine has been described as 'haphazard' (Sax 1964), 'highly uncertain' (Dana and Merrill 2002: 163–4), and 'hugely vague' (Poirier 2002: 138). This is because it often is hard to predict when a government measure will attract the payment of just compensation. Typically U.S. courts will apply a multi-factor balancing test outlined in the U.S. Supreme Court's *Penn Central* case (1978). Unpredictability may not be such a good thing, however. Elsewhere, Poirier described the virtues of doctrinal murkiness in the law of regulatory takings that resonated in particular 'republicanist' themes (Sunstein 1993; Michelman 1988). The virtue of U.S.-style property rules and its doctrine of regulatory takings, Poirier argued, is that its vagueness slows down political processes while enabling communities to work out disagreement between contending approaches to regulation (Poirier 2002: 190). Regulatory takings doctrine reinforces a sense of political community, he maintained, by facilitating 'the generation and acceptance over time of property practices and regulatory practices that are appropriate to a community's circumstances' (Poirier 2003: 859). A murky regulatory takings doctrine, in other words, entitles citizens to demand that fellow citizens take them seriously, thereby generating a sense of political community – 'muddy rules force them to put on their civic republican thinking caps and work together as citizens' (Poirier 2002: 152). It amounts to a 'beacon of reassurance to those who feel on the verge of exile' (2002: 178).

This is the particular way in which regulatory transitions get justified in U.S. constitutional law, Poirier maintains. It does not necessarily represent, however, the way in which regulatory transitions get worked out in international investment law. Poirier rightly recognizes that the origins of standard investment treaty language will mirror, in important respects, the takings doctrine of the Fifth and Fourteenth Amendments to the U.S. constitution. He also recognizes that relevant U.S. actors have purposely sought to promote U.S. constitutional law abroad via international investment treaties (2003: 898). Poirier, nevertheless, prefers to theorize the differences between national and global regulatory space along pluralist lines. He does so by invoking Cover's account of 'nomos' (1983). It will be recalled that Cover understood legal meaning as the product of multiple interpretive communities that engage in law making and interpreting. These communities are capable of creating an entire nomos: the 'common script' from which a community will comprehend the world (Cover 1983: 10). For Poirier, the tension between property rules worked out within the geographic boundaries of national states and those emerging out international investment disciplines are best represented as a conflict between two different communities of meaning – the first nomos balances property rights with police powers, the second nomos generates bright-line rules intended to establish the highest available standards of property protection. This results in what he calls a 'split-nomos problem.' There is, on the one hand, an international community of foreign investors who wish 'clear and portable' property rules (Poirier 2003: 877) – these will be the rules that reflect the standards of capital exporting states associated with the rules of 'civilized justice.' On the other hand, are 'equally legitimate' local political communities who wish to 'renegotiate property practices piecemeal, in appropriate circumstances, without undue constraint' (Poirier 2003: 860, 877) – these will be local rules that are more attentive to the problems associated with regulatory transitions.

For Poirier, foreign investors deserve this heightened protection because they cannot be considered members of the relevant national political community (2003: 894); this, presumably, because they are not 'represented' (Schneiderman 2010). The split-nomos problem results, he writes,

in 'two interpretive communities ... at loggerheads,' each vying to determine the content of international investment law in the realm of regulatory takings (Poirier 2003: 928). The problem, according to Poirier, is that
there has arisen a competing political community, outside of any particular national community, desirous of establishing non-national rules
that act as a prophylactic in the face of regulatory transitions in which they
will have no voice. This complements well Teubner's conception of global
law as a-national; that is, developed in relative insulation from states. This
also is an account that is congenial to investors' understandings of political community, unmoored from the inter-state system, which diminishes
the coordinating functions played by states host to foreign investment.

While appreciating the distinctive policy outcomes that issue out of
democratic processes operating within local legal spaces, Poirier's pluralism ends up siding with the constraints on policy options posed by international investment law. This is because he believes that, as in the U.S.
analogue, the regime's takings rule has the virtue of being sufficiently
vague so as to provide reassurance to investors that their investment interests will remain stable across time. This approach responds well to purported 'demoralization costs' that may be incurred in a political regime
without a regulatory takings rule (Michelman 1967).[11] All of which, Poirier
admits, amounts to a defense of the *status quo*: it brings him precisely to
the place 'where international law currently stands' (2003: 907). Following
the logic of Poirier's account, are global legal pluralists consigned to being
mere apologists for the status quo? Is it a genus of what Cox calls 'problem-
solving theory,' which 'takes the world as it finds it, with the prevailing
social and power relationships and the institutions into which they are
organized, as the given framework for action'? (Cox 1981: 88). This is in
contrast to a 'critical theory' that calls into question the taken-for-granted
premises of problem solvers. In order to avoid such an outcome, I recommend taking up an international political economy approach. This provides both a normative critique and a methodological corrective
generating a better account of how global law is being produced.

A critical corrective

The field of international political economy (IPE) in the English-speaking
world is described as divided between two schools (Cohen 2008; cf. Ravenhill 2008). A U.S.-based version emphasizes the testing of scientific models
via empirical methods generating 'middle-level' theory (Cohen 2008: 3–4;
Strange 1995: 164). This is the model that is described as the 'prevailing
orthodoxy' (Cohen 2008: 4). A more ambitious British version aims be
more qualitative and normative (Cohen 2008: 44), with an emphasis on
society, power, and history (Gill and Law 1988: xviii). It is a more interpretive method of political economy, asking what values get promoted and

who benefits from particular institutional arrangements (Strange 1988: 18). For some, there is an emphasis on historical materialism, eschewing the economic determinism of orthodox Marxism (Cox 1992a: 176) while cultivating a transformative and emancipatory ethic (Cutler 2000: 162). Susan Strange, one of the founders of the British school, defined the branch of IPE as concerning:

> the social, political and economic arrangements affecting the global systems of production, exchange and distribution and the mix of values reflected therein. Those arrangements are not divinely ordained, nor are they the fortuitous outcome of blind chance. Rather they are the result of human decisions taken in the context of man-made institutions and sets of self-set rules and customs.
>
> (Strange 1988: 18)

This is a mode of analysis that will be familiar to critical scholars working in many disciplines, but an IPE approach has the advantage of thinking about contemporary global problems on multiple scales. Critical IPE is ontologically inclined, in other words, to theorize about a global society interacting with actors operating at various levels (Gill and Law 1988: 19). It looks, Cox maintains, to the 'complex whole rather than to the separate parts' (Cox 1981: 89). I turn now to six lessons to be drawn from a critical IPE account that may prove fruitful for thinking about global legal pluralism.

Ideological tilt

For those working within IPE, the global economy is fuelled by the globalization of both (i) production and (ii) finance (Cox 1992b: 300). The globalization of (i) production is made possible by mobile production techniques coupled with innovative technological strategies. States, in turn, seek to attract mobile facilities by reducing the costs of production resulting in intense competition for capital (Cerny 1997). Seeking to attract new inward investment and the support of international financial institutions, states become the 'suitors' of transnational capital (Stopford and Strange 1991: 56). These strategies weaken states' bargaining power as competition intensifies, correspondingly weakening their ability to deliver on national policy objectives (Stopford and Strange 1991: 215). The globalization of (ii) finance has rendered the availability of credit critical to the successful globalization of production, in which case, the accessibility and spread of financing becomes a principal objective of state policy (Cox 1992b: 301). It is for this reason that Wall Street in the early twenty-first century can be described as the 'new American oligarchy – a group that gains political power because of its economic power, and then uses that power for its own benefit' (Johnson and Kwak 2010: 6). The tepid response of the U.S. Congress to the financial debacle of 2008–09 (Nocera 2010) speaks to the continuing power of financial markets to turn political fortunes in their favor despite ongoing global financial instability.

The global economic field similarly is tilted in such a way as to favor interests allied with powerful capital-exporting states with goods and services desired by consumers the world over. Nor is public authority merely about facilitating market freedoms, rather, the state itself is expected to succumb to the logic of economic rationality (Foucault 2008: 240). Market logic is generalized into all of the domains of human activity, most especially political and social life – an ideological agenda associated with a continually reconfiguring neo-liberalism (Peck 2010). All public policy is limited internally and subject to constant critical evaluation by the criterion of efficiency, flexibility and individuality – a sort of 'permanent economic tribunal confronting government' (Foucault 2008: 247). Economic success, efficiency, and individual self-maximization emerge as the new Gramscian 'common sense' (Cox 2002b: 176) but now operating on a global scale (Bourdieu and Wacquant 2005: 179). These neo-liberal suppositions, observes Jodi Dean, 'have become part of the air we breathe' (Dean 2009: 73).

Scholars therefore need to be attentive to the presence of an ideological tilt in this highly pluralistic and fragmented global scene. Seemingly alerted to the problem, global legal pluralists nevertheless pay too little attention to the revealed patterns of global law, particularly in its economic realms. Berman, for instance, describes international investment law as merely one of plural sources of authority 'without an official hierarchical relationship based on coercive power' (2007: 1997). If it is correct to claim that the regime is highly protective of investors, contains expansive disciplines that exceed analogous norms drawn from legal systems of principal capital-exporting states, enforceable by investors and resulting in substantial damage awards, this hardly appears to be an accurate portrayal. Instead of attending to such power relations, the literature often exhibits a celebratory tone rather than one of circumspection and caution. Berman, again, describes global legal pluralism as preserving 'spaces of opportunity for contestation and local variation that legal pluralists have long documented' (2007: 1165). Teubner envisages global legal orders as functional sub-systems that normatively self-reproduce in relative isolation from each other. They are expected to 'maximize' their partial rationalities while internalizing self-limitation strategies so as to curb irritations felt by competing global sub-systems (2011c: 224). With states out of the picture, only modest means are contemplated that attend to the power asymmetries prevailing in international economic law.

False universality

A critical IPE account is attentive to historical contingency: to the fact that contemporary practices are the product of past (and even ongoing) conflict. An ethic of historicity enables us to appreciate how what we label as 'global' and 'universal' is the product of past choices between different and contending views of how to live together. The emergence of a neo-liberal universal common sense, however, implies the collective forgetting of the conditions that gave rise to the universal in the first place (Bourdieu and Wacquant 2005: 179). So as the mantra of economic globalization gets repeated, the past recedes in the collective minds of the citizenry. Yet history is a prerequisite for ascertaining what is going on – where power is and how it is being exercised. It provides 'the means to criticise and evaluate the practises and ways of thinking to which we are subject by comparing and contrasting them with possible alternatives' (Tully 2002: 25).

International political economists have turned to a 'civilizational' discourse so as to better comprehend the contingency of the contemporary global world. Susan Strange, for instance, refers to 'international business civilization' to describe the ideological predilection for free markets and constrained states, organized around 'securing of property rights, for individuals and for firms', that is promoted on a global scale (Strange 1990: 260, 263). The disciplinary features of economic globalization (i.e. the 'new constitutionalism,' discussed below) facilitate what Gill calls 'market civilization' (Gill 2008: 124). Market civilization refers to the successful spread of the ideology of neo-liberalism, reinforced by institutional manifestations that are configured by powerful economic actors, resulting in patterns of social disintegration: 'ahistorical, economistic and materialistic, me-oriented, short term and ecologically myopic' (Gill 2008: 125). Aiming to break away from a single, universalistic conception of 'civilization,' Cox proposes that we think of them instead as operating in the plural. If civilization is represented by the correspondence between 'material conditions' and 'inter-subjective meanings' (Cox 2002a: 4), then we can envisage multiple civilizations that have been evolving over time, as material conditions change and technological innovations spread information (Cox 2002a: 7). This suggests that there are alternative paths to economic success that are not defined solely by a 'one-civilization' approach (Cox 2002b: 43).

Global legal pluralists similarly should aim to historicize contemporary claims and uncover the universalistic pretensions of global law. They should be attentive to the unequal conditions of access to naming what qualifies for the moniker 'universal' (Bourdieu 2000: 70). Santos captures this process well in his description of the phenomenon of 'globalized localism,' whereby local rules successfully get taken up as global rules (Santos 2002: 179). Yet these conceits get continually overlooked. Writing in a way entirely congenial to the pluralist point of view, Ratner describes the myriad international institutions that cumulatively have contributed to the making of a global 'regulatory takings' doctrine. Sifting through the fragmented domains of regulatory takings law in the international context, including international investment law, Ratner concludes that there exists a non-national 'overlapping consensus' on regulatory takings (Ratner 2008: 483). He arrives at this conclusion even while acknowledging the 'seeming similarity' of that revealed global consensus to U.S. constitutional law doctrine on the subject (Ratner 2008: 483, fn. 30).

Persistence of states

Nor does the state merely fade away, according to a critical IPE account. Even if altered, the state has a continuing role to play in the global political economy. This changed role was not very well captured, however, in Cox's initial formulation:

> The domestic-oriented agencies of the state are now more and more to be seen as transmission belts from world-economy trends and decision making into the domestic economy, as agencies to promote the carrying out of tasks they had no part in deciding.
>
> (Cox 1991: 193, 1992b: 302)

The transmission-belt analogy was perhaps too unidirectional a description of the role of states – states are active agents shaping, sometimes resisting, the rules and institutions of global law. Cox has since resiled from this formulation.[12] What the metaphor underscores, however, is the continuing role of states in the structuration of economic globalization – what Sassen likens to 'state-work' (2006: 232) – even as states precommit to behave certain ways via transnational legal tethers.

Inspired by the account provided by Karl Polanyi in *The Great Transformation* (1944), critical IPE scholars have been better equipped than most to understand that, in the era of economic globalization, the spread of markets is not spontaneous and unplanned but requires the deliberate planning by and intervention of states. Markets were the outcome, Polanyi wrote of the nineteenth and twentieth centuries, 'of a conscious and often violent intervention on the part of government which imposed the market organization for non-economic ends' (Polanyi 1944: 250). Polanyi described a spontaneous counter movement arising in response to the deleterious effects of seemingly unregulated markets 'using protective legislation, restrictive associations, and other instruments of intervention' (Polanyi 1944: 138–9). In the contemporary world, rather than receding, the state is reconfigured so as to generate profitable conditions for private economic power, one of the principal indicators by which state success is measured (Block 1987). From this angle, *lex mercatoria* turns out not to be a pristine form of global law without the state but operating with the state's 'full support' (Cutler 2003: 190).[13] According to Cutler, the 'privileging of private commercial regulation is being promoted and enforced by states, which function in alliance with corporate actors as a part of a broader mercotocracy' (Cutler 2003: 190). Even at its origins, *lex mercatoria* was less the product of uniform custom than the product of specific contract and local legislation. 'It is highly improbable,' Emily Kadens writes, 'that medieval merchants could have created, transmitted, and maintained a body of commercial customs that remained uniform from place to place' (2012: 1158–9).

All of which should give rise to the suspicion that states play a critical role in the construction and maintenance of plural global legal orders. The 'state organizes its own decentring,' Santos rightly observes (Santos 2002: 94). This insight gets lost, however, in many global pluralist accounts. Poirier, for instance, describes a community of like-minded denationalized investors who aim to supplant local rules for stricter transnational ones. In this account, the state, presumably, vindicates only local rules, in which case, the ambivalent role of states in the structuration of transnational legality is missed. A continuing state presence is more apparent in the GATT/WTO regime, as states are pivotal to the operation and surveillance of global trading rules. In international investment law, likewise, states are critical both to the construction and ongoing maintenance of the regime, though this is less apparent. States nevertheless are both authors of the regime and parties to the disputes that inevitably arise (Roberts 2010). Their continued presence, I have argued elsewhere, is critical to the regime's modest success to date (Schneiderman 2006). Given that global law arises out of the global take-up of local law, we should expect states to be championing global regimes that mimic rules drawn from their own national legal systems. From this angle, we should understand that many of the disciplines enforced by investment arbitration tribunals are drawn from, or complement well, the national legal orders of powerful capital exporting states (Schneiderman 2008).

Absence of state unity

Global legal pluralists assume a unity of purpose in states. Global legal pluralists assume this unity even when the formal unity and coherence of state law precisely was the target of political and legal pluralism in times past. A critical IPE approach, informed by a sociological insights, eschews this unity in favor of an understanding of states as fractured, and less cohesive, entities. The critical account distinguishes between the formal unity of state law and its '*substantive* operational unity' (Jessop 1990: 261), thereby bringing into view 'political struggles within and between state apparatuses' (Jessop 1982: 223). The state can then be understood, observes Jessop, as representing a 'form-determined condensation' of the balance of class forces at a particular juncture (1990: 256) or, in Bourdieu's phrasing, the 'trace in reality of social conquest' (1998: 33). States thereby exhibit a 'strategic selectivity,' making the state more accessible and available to some interests and less available to others (Jessop 1990: 260). The reconfigured state also prefers certain state agencies, such as ministries of finance, 'which are key points in the adjustment of domestic to international economic policy' (Cox 1981: 109). Other ministries, such as those associated with industrial development, labor, and social welfare, often end up being side-lined by the exigencies of economic globalization (Stopford and Strange 1991: 56). Along these lines, Bourdieu contrasts the 'left-hand of the state,' represented by the 'spending ministries,' with its 'right hand,' represented by the technocrats in economic and finance departments (Bourdieu 1998: 2).

The balance of social forces within states, however, may be rendering neo-liberal 'success' somewhat vulnerable. The 'right arm' of the state is being expected to better manage relations with its 'left arm.' By way of illustration, let me refer to two such instances. In the Republic of South Africa, officers in the Department of Trade and Industry (DTI) have been adjusting South Africa's model treaty so as to buffer threats to the program of 'black economic empowerment' (Schneiderman 2009). Having signed bilateral investment treaties based on a U.K. model, the DTI decided that a capital-exporting friendly model threatened the few programs that the African National Congress (ANC) government had established to redistribute wealth to South Africans dispossessed by apartheid (South Africa 2009). Elsewhere, heated conflict erupted in South Korea after the ruling party unilaterally ratified the US–Korea free trade and investment agreement in November 2011 (US–Korea FTA). Opposition was fuelled by concerns about allowing investors to initiate disputes for breach of investor protections in the FTA. Senior provincial district court Judge Choi Eunbae was denied reappointment for posting a message on Facebook critical of the President for enacting the FTA (Jeong-pil 2011; Hyo-sik 2011). A second district court judge received a six-month suspension for making similar remarks over an internal judicial intranet (Hee-jin 2012) while dozens of judges expressed similar opinions (Rahn 2011). These reports suggest that agents acting within or having access to state authority are threatening the presumed local (and seeming global) unanimity over investment rules.

Blurring of the public and private

A plurality of actors is promoting the neoliberal version of global law associated with the failing Westphalian system (Strange 1999). They include not only state actors but also private economic actors who stand to profit by the global promotion of neo-liberal law and institutions. Cox theorizes that there exists a 'transnational managerial class' (Cox 1987: 359–60) of global elites who converge around a global common sense and merge into a 'common structural force' even as they compete amongst themselves for global supremacy (Cox 1992c: 516. See also Sklair 2002: 99 and Robinson 2008: 30–33). We should not make the mistake of assuming a unity in the class that aspires to govern globally only that, for our purposes, it is constituted of both public and private actors.

There remains a great deal at stake in choosing to emphasize the public or private dimensions in the production of transnational law (Zumbansen 2010: 179). Privatizing transnational legal domains portrays as inexorable, seemingly beyond the reach of accountability, that which is closely intertwined with public authority. It also empowers private authority in ways that stiffen its resolve, rendering it difficult, perhaps, for public authority to reverse course. Some IPE scholars, nevertheless, hypothesize that it should be easier to reverse delegations of public authority to private actors (what Bierstecker and Hall call 'institutional market authority') than to roll back the institutionalization of neo-liberal rationality within public institutions (what they call 'normative market authority') (2002: 215). The resistance of financial markets to new rules curtailing the exercises of private authority in order to avoid a repeat of the 2008–09 global financial crisis suggests otherwise (measures that might be characterized as reversing institutional market authority). The public catterwalling by the banking industry to modest restrictions on proprietary trading by banks (the so-called 'Volcker rule') in the Dodd-Frank Wall Street Reform and Consumer Protection Act and modest capital reserve requirements proposed by the Basel Committee on Banking Supervision at the Bank for International Settlements (Basel III) indicates that institutional authority is closely connected to normative authority (Masters and Braithwaite 2011). Both institutional and market normative authority may be difficult to reverse in the current age.

The persistent role of states in global law should make pluralists attentive to how public authority channels private interests in the construction and maintenance of global law. In the domains of the GATT/WTO, Greg Shaffer has shown how private economic actors shape the direction of U.S. policy in the GATT – a phenomenon he also has observed in the EU (Shaffer 2003). This is more than the claim that home states will protect national champions, rather, it speaks to the existence of a legal transmission belt (of a sort) between powerful economic actors and the U.S. trade representative's office in determining what disputes get lodged at the WTO. Susan Sell documents how, in the run-up to negotiation of the Trade-Related Agreement on Intellectual Property (TRIPS), enforced by the WTO, powerful American pharmaceutical companies promoted specific policy prescriptions that would get taken up by U.S. negotiators in the global arena. She concludes that 'TRIPS is a stunning triumph of the private sector in making global IP [intellectual property] rules and in enlisting states and international organizations to enforce them' (Sell 2003: 163). Indeed, public and private legal ordering may not be in as much collision as global legal pluralists intimate (Wai 2008: 109). Tamanaha observes that the multiple domains of global law 'do not necessarily lead to a clash' of normative systems. Instead, inconsistent operative regimes may wish to bury, even preserve, these inconsistencies (Tamanaha 2008: 405). To the extent that international investment law is the product of capital-exporting state legal aspirations, both harmony and dissonance will continue to be experienced.

'New constitutionalism'

With an emphasis on non-state global law, global legal pluralists seem to be less interested in identifying the mechanisms of constraint posed by transnational legal orders on the exercise of state authority. Stephen Gill has been developing the idea of the 'new constitutionalism' so as to better capture these developments (Gill 2008). New constitutionalism refers to the institutionalization of so-called 'best practices' associated with the rise of 'global governance' (Freidrichs 2008). These are practices that privilege market efficiency via disciplinary mechanisms over other models of development. They are intended to insulate 'key aspects of the economy from the influence of politicians or the mass of citizens by imposing, internally and externally, "binding constraints" on the conduct of fiscal, monetary and trade and investment policies' (Gill 2008: 139). While many of these practices incorporate elements of the old constitutionalism, with an emphasis on justiciable rights and constitution-like limits on state capacity, the new constitutionalism elevates these operations to a global scale. International investment law performs precisely these sorts of functions, insulating markets from domestic politics so as to guarantee returns on investments free from the exigencies of disorderly domestic politics. There will be no escaping these disciplines as footloose capital can easily relocate in order to exploit investment law's dampening effects (Aguas del Tunari 2005: para. 332).

We should expect the institutions of global law to mimic patterns of classical liberal constitutionalism insofar as they seek to shield markets from unruly politics (Polanyi 1944: 205, 255). We are likely to see, in other words, global legal orders exhibiting some of the features associated with the 'new constitutionalism.' Their object will be to 'lock-in' gains secured in the post-1989 environment and to successfully disperse a version of neo-liberal institutional design worldwide. The aim of institutionalizing constitution-like constraints corresponds well with contemporary diagnoses of global legal pluralism as being irreversible. A 'reversal or return to a co-ordinating form of international law,' observe Fischer-Lescano and Teubner, is 'foreclosed' (2004: 1007). Hardt and Negri endorse Teubner's pluralistic account (these 'legal theorists fit so closely with our analyses,' they write) and so characterize the legal construction of what they call 'empire' as the irreversible product of non-state actors (2009: 374). Not only does this misdiagnose the persistent role of states, it narrows the rules of engagement for those seeking to roll back gains secured by economically powerful private actors and their state surrogates. It makes more difficult attempts at unlocking states and peoples from the shackles of unwise restraints associated with the current global legal order.

Not all scholars working under the rubric of IPE are attentive to these concerns and the role of law and legal institutions in the construction of global neoliberal law. Philip Cerny, for instance, declares that the emergence of what he calls 'global governmentality' (associated with neoliberal governing), derived from state practices 'learned' in domestic spheres, 'is not embodied in institutions as such' (2008: 223–4). The hypothesis that practices learned at the local level now are expanding to global environs, complements well the 'new constitutionalist' account. It does not accurately describe, however, the institutionalization of such practices via regimes associated with global legal pluralism. The international investment regime is designed precisely to lock-in particular practices learned within national states, namely capital-exporting ones, making them all the harder to dislodge.

Conclusion

The body of work associated with global legal pluralism has vastly improved our capacity to diagnose the current global legal scene. Adopting the legal pluralist insight that states are not necessarily the creator of all legal meaning, freed from the constraints of a state-centered paradigm, global legal pluralists have enabled the identification of a rich repertoire of locales of legal production. Despite an enthusiasm for seeking out law everywhere, however, much of this work has elided important linkages between states, private economic power, and global law. My aim in this chapter has been to better elucidate these connections by bringing the habits of critical international political economy to the endeavor. By bringing to the surface these linkages, we render global legal pluralism less complicit with extant power relations and are better able to critique transnational economic legal edicts.

There admittedly are other ways of achieving this objective other than conceptualizing the pluralism of international economic law through a critical IPE lens. We might gain a critical foothold, for instance, by measuring the legitimacy of transnational legal ordering by the degree to which it is authorized by democratic and accountable public authority (Krisch 2010; Joerges and Rödl 2012). Taking note of democratic legitimacy has the benefit of attending to power relations and to decentring the primacy of economic rationality – the organizing logic of many transnational legal orders – rendering it subordinate to the dictates of public law (Van Harten 2007). International investment law might not fare so well according to this standard. Particularly if we appreciate the informational and bargaining asymmetries between state parties to such treaties (Poulsen 2010), the democratic deficit looms very large indeed. Even in operative democracies, processes giving rise to investment policy, like many other policy domains, are inaccessible, lacking in transparency and democratic inputs. There are some instances where states have begun opening up this authority, ordinarily within the prerogative of the executive, by consulting more widely about its exercise (i.e. United States and South Africa). Yet, investment law scholars are quick to point out that the network of bilateral investment treaties are the product of duly authorized state officials (relying on the 'voluntary acquiescence' of government 'elites,' admits Alvarez) (2009: 971). Investment arbitration conducted pursuant to these international instruments, moreover, is contemplated by an Convention on the Settlement of Investment Disputes between States and Nationals of Other States to which most states in the world are by now signatories. Legitimacy is not a problem, according to these analysts (Paulsson 2005: 263).

I do not propose to resolve this debate here. Rather than settling this question on proceduralist terrain, I have proposed adopting the normative stance associated with critical IPE. Operating on the presumption that power is being exercised in most places, it is less focused on problem solving and more about sniffing out its real-world manifestations. It aims to inquire, in Susan Strange's words, into the 'fundamentals of how the multiple authorities in the world market economy allocate values among classes, generations, genders, and other social groups' (Strange 1995: 157). It has its sights fixed on the nature and exercise of power and its 'cui bono' effects (Strange 1988: 136). With this problematic in mind, we are better situated to understand the world and, if need be, to change it.

Notes

1 I am grateful to Amanda Perry-Kessaris and Peer Zumbansen for comments.
2 Admittedly a short, even idiosyncratic, list but these are authors whose work I greatly admire.
3 There has been some controversy, spurred on by Tamanaha (2000), about the expansive notion of law as understood by legal pluralist scholars rendering it difficult to distinguish between legal and other social norms. As international investment law has multiple markers associated with the traditional concept of law, this is not an issue that needs to be addressed here. If it were an issue, I would follow Twining's less anxiety-inducing criteria for identifying law in the transnational field (2009: 369–71).

4 Cover, though not a prototypical legal pluralist, exhibited 'very marked pluralistic tendencies' (Melissaris 2009: 40), prompted theoretical interventions of the sort undertaken by Poirier, discussed in the next section.

5 Ahdieh deliberately connects this process to Berman's notion of 'cosmopolitan pluralism' (Berman 2002: 321–22) – referring neither to the local nor the universal, but to the intermediate world of plural and intersecting affiliations (Ahdieh 2006: 884).

6 Though Teubner does not self-identify as a legal pluralist (Teubner 1992).

7 For accounts that are more attentive to a state presence, see Anderson (2005), Krisch (2010) Michaels (2009), Tamanaha (2008) and Zumbansen (2010).

8 The European debt crisis has precipitated the contemplation of even deeper levels of integration via constitutionalism, according to German Chancellor Angela Merkel, who contemplates moving beyond the economic to an expressly 'political union' (Peel 2012).

9 Poirier promotes a conception of investor rights under NAFTA drawn from principles of property theory more generally. Indeed, others have offered accounts of U.S. property rights, premised upon republican conceptions, which are congenial to Poirier's own account (i.e. Rose 2000; Alexander 2000).

10 He might also have admitted that investors do not win in every instance – the system would quickly lose its legitimacy in the eyes of state parties if this were otherwise.

11 For Michelman, demoralization costs represent the sum total of the costs of '(1) the dollar value necessary to offset utilities which accrue to losers and their sympathizers specifically from the realization that no compensation is offered, and (2) the present capitalized dollar value of lost future production (reflecting either impaired incentives or social unrest) caused by demoralization of uncompensated losers, their sympathizers, and other observers disturbed by the thought that they themselves may be subjected to similar treatment on some other occasion' (1967: 1214).

12 'I hereby withdraw this misleading metaphor,' Cox wrote (2002b: 33).

13 Santos regrettably succumbs to the allure of lex mercatoria, severing its ties to particular state locales (2002: 208–12). According to Wai (2008: 109–10), Santos fails to situate this form of global law 'within the broad array of state public and private laws that regulate business law.'

Chapter 8

Reflexive international economic law

Balancing economic and social goals in the construction of law

Cecilia Juliana Flores Elizondo[1]

Introduction

Economics has provided much of the analytical and normative foundations for international economic law. For example, analytically, concepts
such as cost-benefit analysis, and normatively, values such as efficiency
have tended to dominate the discourse. This dominance has raised concerns, in particular regarding the ability of economics to take account of
wider social – non-economic – goals. This chapter argues that a reflexive
approach to law facilitates the construction of international economic law
that is responsive to social reality. Specifically, the values and interests that
are usually categorised as non-economic and, therefore, external to international economic law – such as access to health, education, labour and
development – are translated and reconstructed as integral to international economic law. After a brief account of reflexive law theory, the
chapter explores the internal dynamics by which social values and interests
could be translated into international economic law and the implications
for 'justice'.

Reflexive law theory

Gunther Teubner proposes reflexive law theory as a third way to the social
systems theory of Niklas Luhmann and the discourse theory of Jürgen
Habermas (1983). Drawing from both systems and discourse theories,
which perceive society as a system of communications (Teubner 1983),
reflexive law theory focuses on processes and is concerned with the structures and mechanisms in which communication develops (Calliess 2002:
190–1; Teubner 1983).

Reflexive law theory is based on two key premises. First, society is fragmented into 'functionally' as opposed to territorially 'differentiated subsystems' (Luhmann 1985: 158–60). Hence, society is divided into, *inter
alia*, law, politics, economics and education as functionally differentiated
subsystems. So a reflexive approach to international economic law would

recognise those functional boundaries in subsystems such as trade, investment, financial and monetary issues.

Second, the subsystems of, *inter alia*, law, politics and economics are 'autopoietic' – that is, capable of producing their own elements, boundaries and internal processes by means of recursive references to themselves – and are, therefore, 'autonomous' (Luhmann 2004: 79–84; Teubner 1993: 25–36). Subsystems are 'normatively closed' – that is, they only recognise and validate the components that are produced within the subsystem, thus distinguishing a subsystem from the environment. In so doing, they use a specific code. In the case of law, this code differentiates between legal and illegal (Luhmann 2004: 173–210, specifically 183; Teubner 1993: 33–6). The first distinction involves descriptions about legal concepts, elements and processes (Teubner 1993: 39–42). Reflexive law further maintains that this distinction is used in the regulation of 'legal communications', that is, when criteria are applied in decision-making processes (Teubner 1993: 39–42). In sum, autopoiesis in the legal system means that law is validated by its own components without any external intervention from other subsystems such as politics, economy, morality or natural law (Teubner 1987b: 19–20). Nevertheless, 'interferences' between subsystems are possible because, although subsystems are 'normatively closed', they remain 'cognitively open' – that is, capable of observing communications developing within other subsystems (external environment) (Teubner 1993: 33–6).

So, closure should not be seen as the incapacity of subsystems to interrelate. Rather, it establishes limits to subsystems preventing a 'regulatory trilemma': (a) the incongruence of law and society, that is, the incapacity of law to produce behavioural changes; (b) the over-legalisation of society characterised by the 'colonisation' of subsystems by virtue of the direct intervention of law; or, (c) the over-socialisation of law in which law is 'captured' by demands from subsystems thus becoming, for instance, politicised or economised (Teubner 1986: 309–13, 1987b: 19–27). Indeed, the interdependence between subsystems becomes more entrenched as subsystems increase their autonomy (Teubner 1987b: 20). In this vein, interrelation allows the co-evolution of subsystems in which law can recreate an image of the economy and vice-versa (Teubner 1993: 75–82).

Reflexive law also entails the act of applying a process to itself. In this sense, a system would be capable of creating laws about decision-making or regulation of self-regulation (Teubner 1993: 36–42). It involves the delimitation of processes by means of which society communicates and thereby constitutes and regulates itself (Calliess 2002: 191). Hence, it recognises that subsystems have the capacity to engage in their social constitution, i.e. the establishment of principles according to their own rationality (Calliess 2002: 191; Teubner 2010, 2011a). Reflexive law departs from command and control mechanisms (Teubner 1983: 254–6).

It promotes changes in organisational structures and procedures by which subsystems are responsive to the environment without direct control, thus inducing action (Black 1996: 44–6; Teubner 1983: 254–6). However, reflexive law theory also deals with a substantive element. This is related to the concept of rationality. This means that the system is able to observe itself and thus make selections as a result of reasoning (Calliess 2002: 191–2).

Law is hence a system of communications (Teubner 1989: 739). This assertion has been misunderstood in the sense that reflexive law disregards the individual and thereby, its ideas (Beck 1994). Indeed, the interrelation of individuals within the system requires a different perception. This does not necessarily mean that the system is indifferent to their ideas. Reflexive law theory is concerned with the structures and processes by which these ideas (values and interests) are communicated. As a system of actions, the legal system consists of legal communications not only about norms – or actions – but also of legal expectations deriving from individuals (Luhmann 1981, cited in Teubner 1984: 294). It has been stated that reflexive law theory is more concerned with processes than with substantive issues; nevertheless, the latter are supported by recognising the autonomy of different social functions (Teubner 1984: 297). Therefore, a reflexive approach to law would facilitate the substantive development of international economic law based upon the creation of processes that allow the establishment of connections to diverse social functions, particularly with the values and interests communicated therefrom.

Changing the structure of meaning: economic goals in a social context

What does the construction of international economic law within a social context imply? Answering this question is not straightforward. The international economic system is fragmented and thus has evolved in specialised autonomous bodies that, by following their own rationality, engage in the attainment of specific objectives (Koskenniemi and Leino 2002: 578; Koskenniemi 2007: 9). This is epitomised in the clear distinction of the functions attributed to each international economic institution, for example, trade, finance, monetary and investment issues. However, fragmentation has not only generated collisions between specialised autonomous bodies and their laws, but more concretely between the values upon which they develop (Fischer-Lescano and Teubner 2004: 1004). Consequently, specialisation has complicated the interrelation of diverse areas of international economic law. Further, it has caused a clear distinction between areas of international law that are considered economic in nature – trade, finance and investment – and those comprising a wider social perspective such as human rights, development and labour.

In this respect, international economic institutions have attempted to interpret economic issues in a wider social context (Leebron 2002: 26–7). For example, the WTO has explored environmental (Dixon and McCorquodale 2003: 503–4) and health 'linkages' with trade (Leebron 2002: 26–7). This approach seems inadequate, not only because it has been unduly legalistic but also because it implies a very limited notion of the social context, i.e. the roots from which social values and interests generate, develop and are thereby communicated. Andrew Lang argues that characterising values as trade or non-trade is counterproductive because it fosters the expansion and entrenchment of the trade regime. Indeed, this distinction produces a natural exclusion of 'non-trade' values inhibiting their advancement (2007: 537–8). Hence, 'linkages' forestall the development of international economic law that is adequately responsive to the environment. Achieving this involves acknowledging and thus internalising the meaning conveyed by external factors and the values therewith (Yearwood 2011: 86–90, 208–9). Therefore, it seems that the distinction between economic and non-economic factors hinders the construction of an international economic law that is more sensitive to social claims.

A transformation of international economic law requires changing the structure of meaning, i.e. re-evaluating its contents (Lang 2007). This re-evaluation should entail not only an economic appraisal but also methodological tools that could be of use to unravel the social context of international economic law. In this sense, a socio-legal approach, namely reflexive law, could provide this tool aiding to integrate divergent social values developing in functionally differentiated subsystems (Black 1996: 48). This would involve the multiplicity of stakeholders in international economic relationships.

The social context

Reflexive law supports the view that every subsystem of society – including law, economics and politics – is composed of communications (Teubner 1993: 89). In this regard, subsystems have their own coding structure by which distinctions within its internal operations are made. While law distinguishes between legal/illegal, economics would code efficient/inefficient or in terms of payment transactions (payment/no payment), and politics would code powerful/not powerful (Luhmann 1992: 1435–6; Teubner 2011a: 18). Subsystems can establish interferences (connections) to each other, despite their operational closure, because they develop and are constituted from the same material, that is, communications and 'meaning'. Indeed, their specialised actions – legal, economic or political – are at the same time social acts of communication (Teubner 1993: 86–9). This means that, although sharing a common external environment (society), subsystems have their own internal environment and rationality (values) (Luhmann 1977: 31). Following this logic, international economic law would develop in the external environment concurrently with an array of social rationalities with which interferences would be produced. Interferences with the legal system would not be restricted to economics and politics. They would involve a multiplicity of rationalities *inter alia* health, labour, environment, science, technology and fundamental rights (Paterson 2003; Teubner 2006, 2008). What does this social context comprise and how is it to be acknowledged and internalised by international economic law?

Law is the result of social reality at a particular period of time. It must constitute the values and interests, as well as the expectations, of society, together with the necessary conditions to improve social reality (Koskenniemi 1989: 422). This constitutes the social context that should be recognised by law and thereby it should establish connections to the ideas emerging from society (Koskenniemi 1989: 422).

Reflexive law theory emphasises that the social context should not be confused merely with 'fundamental' rights deriving from the relationship between individuals and the State by which the former are protected from state power (Teubner 2008: 331–2). Society comprises a diversity of social sectors (spaces) that constitute and develop autonomously upon their own rationality (Teubner 2004b). Law should reflect the diversity of social perspectives that emerge from these spaces (Teubner 2007). Law therefore must observe and establish contact to social subsystems as 'communicative centres of reflection' from which social values and interests generate (Teubner 1993: 86–90; 2011b). For example, a range of rules – from eco-labelling to corporate governance – have been observed without following a formal legislative process (Calliess 2002; Calliess and Zumbansen 2010; Teubner 1997c. See also Cotterrell in this volume). This reflects the intricate nature in which the social context develops in the international economic system. Although international economic law usually derives from intergovernmental institutions, the development of values and interests is not restricted to the State, but can also derive from diverse, transnational, international or multinational bodies involving a private or public element (Black 1996: 51–5). Functional systems constitute and acquire autonomy, therefore creating their own organisational structures, rules and decision-making processes, comprising the expectations from actors therein. These have repercussions on their external relations. The Internet Corporation for Assigned Names and Numbers (ICANN) is a case in point (Calliess 2002: 201–6; Teubner 2010: 16–17). Generally, these constitute the values (and expectations) that may be communicated and observed by the legal system. The importance of this lies in the fact that specialised autonomous bodies may generate external pressures that, ultimately, initiate the internal dynamic of the legal system. Law cannot remain indifferent to these pressures. However, it needs to engage in couplings that prevent its colonisation (Teubner 2011a: 9–10). In this vein, the importance of a reflexive law approach is not only the emphasis in values and interests constituted within these subsystems but also in the communication techniques that are deemed necessary as a *limitation* to the system (Black 1996: 55).

Communication of values and meanings

The diverse social subsystems that comprise the international economic system are informed by different underlying rationales (Fischer-Lescano and Teubner 2004). Each subsystem of society claims a distinctive expertise and specialised knowledge about, for example, labour, health or technological issues, and these often collide (Fischer-Lescano and Teubner 2004). Some of these constitute norms that are generally accepted by international law, for instance, those deriving from the United Nations Systems such as the International Labour Organization or the World Health Organization (Teubner 2010: 17). Other autonomous or semi-autonomous bodies, such as NGOs, trade unions, social movements, academia and so forth, produce external pressures that may initiate the internal logic of the law (Teubner 2010: 20–1). When law is cognitively open, these claims may be recognised and, thereby, translated into international economic law. In a reflexive law approach, the internalisation of the external world of meaning (social claims) would not be an intervention of one system into another. It represents the manner in which law could establish connections to the multiplicity of spaces from which values and interests develop, thus acting as a limitation of the choices available to the legal system (Teubner 2010: 20). If it is to remain normatively closed, and thereby prevent the colonisation of the system by specialised bodies or social spaces (Teubner 2011a: 9–11), the legal system must establish a clear mechanism by which selection, variation and retention of values and interests are made. The creation of these mechanisms is paramount to balance economic and social goals in the construction of international economic law.

The process of internalisation: a communication technique

The rationale of reflexive law theory is that law cannot be responsive to social reality by direct intervention because specialised knowledge about the internal operations of other subsystems remains unknown to it (Teubner 1987b: 20; 2001: 2). Therefore, law needs to establish connections to these subsystems and the process of internalisation provides this opportunity. Cognitive openness allows the establishment of communications (connections) through which international economic law could reflect on divergent social perspectives deriving from a multiplicity of spaces. However, law would remain normatively closed, so only it would be capable of reconstructing social values and interests, thus providing a different meaning according to its legal rationality. Changing the structure of meaning would allow the overcoming of the entrenched division between economic and non-economic factors. As such, it may be a step forward in the construction of international economic law with a wider social perspective.

In this context, the process of internalisation is a communication technique that develops in three stages: irritation, re-entry and reconstruction. The first stage, irritation, refers to the external pressures emanating from social spaces from which values and interests emerge. For example, civil society, trade unions and diverse organisations may generate such strong forces that initiate the internal logic and transformation of law, ultimately, encouraging innovation (Teubner 1993: 58–9).

Re-entry is the key element of the process by which law can internalise rationalities developing within other subsystems, and hence transcends boundaries (Skordas 2009; Teubner 2001: 180), Therefore, re-entry compensates for operational closure as it endows law with the capacity to recreate its own image of social reality (Teubner 1993: 97; 2001: 3, 9–10). External factors observed by law cannot be directly incorporated to it. This prohibition – that is more analytical than practical – implies that law should reconstruct these factors into legal constructs – that is, it should apply the legal/illegal distinction and thereby provide a different meaning (Black 1996: 46). For example, economy would develop notions of the market, sustainability and competition upon cost-benefit rationales (Teubner 2011a: 24–6). Law would be capable of translating and reconstructing these into legal rules that regulate the market, sustainability and competition. However, these new rules would now confer a meaning based upon notions of legality. Balance of payments, for instance, is an economic term referring to the accounting record of transactions between residents of a country and the rest of the world (Stein 2008). Nevertheless, when the IMF reconstructs the economic nature of balance of payments into legal terms, it validates this, thereby involving a legal rationale with regard to lineaments, processes and conditions to access the IMF resources (Article V, Articles of Agreement, 20 December 2011).This implies the creation of legal rules about economic activities. Despite this transformation, hitherto there is not in place a truly reflexive construction of international economic law. This is because this transformation does not seem responsive to the values and interests of the social subsystems to which these legal rules are directed, i.e. states.

Certainly, the process of irritation, re-entry and reconstruction would allow different discourses and rationalities to become part of international economic law. Facts entered into the legal subsystem, would be reconstructed as new law, and proceed to have consequences in the external world (Teubner 1989: 745–52; 2001: 2–4). However, this internalisation should not be limited to mere 'linkages' or the introduction of external factors into decision-making processes (Teubner 2001: 6–8). This practice has indeed already been taking place in some international organisations. Ronnie Yearwood argues that the WTO dispute settlement mechanism has further made use of external law by reconstructing this to legitimise and fulfil the purposes of the institution. Nevertheless, this is ineffectual to substantive issues within external social rationalities (2011). This seems insufficient. International economic law ought to be reflexive in the sense that is capable of responding to social claims, in particular, to the intricate values emerging from them. Responsiveness to the environment could only be achieved in a higher degree of autopoiesis in which subsystems have both a 'constitutive and a limitative function' (Teubner 2011a: 18; Yearwood 2011: 208–9). Subsystems have a constitutive function because they construct themselves according to their rationality, for instance, power (politics) and payment transactions (economy). Moreover, they have a limitative function because they establish their own boundaries; thus acting as a limitation to other subsystems (Teubner 2011a: 17–19). This implies a broader understanding of social constitutions, i.e. the capacity of subsystems to establish their own principles, organisation and fundamental rights based upon their rationality (Teubner 2010: 7). However, social constitutions would need the reflexivity of law to stabilise expectations by reconstructing them as legal rules. Likewise, law would engage in a relation to politics by which it would stabilise operations with regard to the attribution and exercise of power (Teubner 2011a: 23). Therefore, law would have a limiting function in the self-regulation of social rationalities such as economy or politics. Nevertheless, these too would have a limiting function. The fundamental principles, and thus values inherent to diverse social rationalities, would constitute options and discourses from which law would select to construct new law (Black 1996: 50; Teubner 2011b).

The constitution of social rationalities implies subjecting subsystems – economy, law and politics – to a further code distinguishing between constitutional/unconstitutional, i.e. questions about the adequacy of a system to the constitutional values and principles of the social rationality and responsibilities therein (Teubner 2011a: 25–8). In the case of economy and law, re-entry of the constitutional distinction into this relationship would bring about the reconstruction of principles of economy as legal rules of constitutional law. The introduction of economic principles and values into law would inhibit the direct implementation of these as natural law (Teubner 2011a: 25–8). Reflexive processes between economy and law would engage in a permanent co-existence of constant irritation producing two separate but interrelated autonomous subsystems (Teubner 2011a: 21–7). In this sense, the constitution of principles and values inherent to *inter alia* health, labour and human rights could have a limiting function in the construction of international economic law. The key lies in the irritation these social constitutions produce to the legal system.

The crucial process of re-entry upon irritation, by which self-constituted principles of social rationalities could be translated into international economic law, cannot be exclusive of judicial processes (Teubner 2011a: 26). This should also develop within other decision-making mechanisms such as legislative processes. In this sense, access to information and structures allowing public discussions to a multiplicity of social spaces could be an important element in the internalisation of wider social perspectives (Teubner 2011a: 30; 2011b). This would imply permitting interactions (communication) amongst subsystems as a means of securing a variety of options, discourses and opinions that would limit the selectivity of law (Black 1996: 50). However, the irritation of subsystems would not necessarily derive only from external social rationalities. Gunther Teubner identifies 'more abstract and open space for new social differentiation' epitomised in diversity of discourses (2011b). This could provide scope for the application of re-entry by irritation amongst decision-making procedures within international economic organisations. For example, the internalisation of external factors within judicial processes could further irritate legislative processes, thus it could be involved in the creation of constitutional rights within international economic institutions.

The role of individuals in reflexive law systems

Irritation is necessary to initiate the transformation of law. The irritation of the legal system is produced usually by conflict, and thereby represents the opportunity to internalise external constituencies to legal argumentation (Teubner 2001: 3). Therefore, these irritations or conflicts should be brought to legislative and judicial processes (Teubner 2002: 164–5). However, one of the main concerns is how or by whom these (external) communications are to be introduced into legal argumentation and, ultimately, into judicial and legislative processes.

In the context of reflexive law, individuals are merely a means of communication, constructs by which social subsystems confer an attribution of action and communicate expectations therein (Paterson 1995: 224–5; Teubner 1989: 739–41, 2001: 10–11). The attribution of action and communication occurs once a social construct has irritated the legal system and so acquires recognition. Multinational enterprises, for example, are the result of communications of the market (Teubner 2001: 11). Moreover, international organisations are a legal construct that produces communications that have a fundamental role in creating inter-systemic linkages with divergent social rationalities (Black 1996: 46). In this regard, attribution of action is provided to individuals – claimants, defendants, judges and legislators – who act as irritators to the legal system by communicating about the environment in which they develop (Teubner 1989: 741). This attribution of action is concerned with the execution of roles in which individuals act independently from their personal views (Teubner 1993: 44–6; 2011a: 5). The division between the attribution of action and the individual's consciousness should not be misunderstood as a displacement of individuals in the construction of law. It only means that individuals have the attribution to execute a role and thereby are restricted to the selection of options provided by the legal systems itself – that is, the application of previous decisions, law, doctrine and legal argumentation (Teubner 2001: 4–6).

In the context of the WTO dispute settlement mechanism, disputes brought to the institution are subjected to the Dispute Settlement Understanding (DSU), which under Article 3.2 limits the Dispute Settlement Body to customary rules of interpretations and wherein it 'cannot add to or diminish the rights and obligations provided in the covered agreements' (2010). In this sense, individuals execute their conferred action independently of their views. The possibility to use customary rules of interpretation would endow legal persons with the capacity to act as a linkage between diverse social rationalities. This does not mean that there would be an incorporation of consciousness – personal inclination to human rights or environmental issues – because it would still be limited to the covered agreements. Two different systems would co-exist: the individual and the WTO. The problem is that the WTO decisions might not respond to expectations entailing a wider social perspective, i.e. actual protection of the environment or fundamental rights. This could only be attained where there is a higher degree of autonomy in the process of law creation, thus involving the constitution of rights. The role of individuals would be to irritate the legal system, introducing these rights into legal reasoning and ultimately, to legal argumentation within legislative and judicial processes (Teubner 1989: 740). This would imply a change within intergovernmental organisations such as the WTO, allowing the interaction of legal actors to produce linkages with the external world without directly intervening in the direction of the institution. Indeed, the introduction of these rights into legal argumentation within judicial branches, may act as an irritator to legislative processes. This may ultimately produce a change in the structure of meaning by which social perspectives would thereby be reconstructed as international economic law values. It could further involve the construction of constitutional rights.

The opportunity for justice: balancing economic and social goals in reflexive international economic law

Balancing economic and wider social – non-economic – values and interests requires that we no longer naturally exclude the latter from our conceptions of international economic law, that we re-evaluate the values inherent to international economic law (Lang 2007: 538). Indeed, Debra Steger suggests that there is a need to redefine the shared values and norms among WTO members (2002a: 144–5). Justice, in this sense, is not merely a balance of tensions between two or more areas of law (Yearwood 2011: 132–3), it involves changing the structure of meaning of international economic law, with due regard of both economic values and the fundamental principles and rights (values) of other social rationalities.

In this context, the rationale of reflexive law is that direct intervention in other subsystems does not solve conflicts, it impinges on the adequate regulation of social rationalities. This is because they lack specialised knowledge of the internal dynamic of other subsystems (Teubner 2001: 2). Law needs to create mechanisms allowing the acquisition of information that is then reconstructed and validated by law itself. The issue at stake is how to construct international economic law cognisant of social reality that is thus translated and reconstructed into the legal system while respecting the rationality of both the legal and other social subsystems. Can a reflexive law approach facilitate the construction of an international economic law that is just, in the sense that it balances economic and wider social interests and values?

Reflexive law accepts that cognitive closure does not mean an absolute denial of the external environment, and this provides scope for speculation that there is an actual possibility to develop international economic law with a social context. Furthermore, law is capable of producing new law and hence evolving by means of the irritation, re-entry and reconstruction process. In this vein, social factors developing in diverse social spaces may generate strong forces that have the capacity to irritate the legal system towards an internal reconstruction (Teubner 2010: 20–1). These irritations could be initiated as a result of conflicts between diverse legal actors (Teubner 2001: 5–8). Conflict has indeed been important in the attainment of some changes in institutions such as the WTO and the IMF. However, these have generally been single external interventions, insufficient to produce strong external pressures towards the self-limitation of these institutions. It might have led to some adjustments, but these have not yet resulted in a change to the structure of meaning, in which constitutional principles and values developed within social rationalities are reflected by the reflexivity of international economic law.

Reflexive law theory recognises that legal actors – including individuals (lawyers, judges and claimants), states, international organisations, multinational enterprises and NGOs are capable of alienating justice, i.e. searching for justice by bringing about their own conflicts into the international economic law system (Teubner 2001: 4–6, 10–12). Hence, it is important to recognise the duality of individuals – that they can develop a conscious autonomous process independently from the attribution of action (role) conferred by law and that they may simultaneously be involved in, and communicate the values of, multiple social rationalities (Teubner 2011a: 5). So individuals or legal actors can themselves act as an irritant to the legal system, bearing the social communications internalised by Law and hence, allowing the construction of law that is sensitive to social claims emanating from social spaces (Teubner 1989: 740–1, 2006: 344–6).

However, reflexive law recognises that each social subsystem has a different rationality, i.e. values and interests. In this context, a social act may have different values depending on the rationality to which it is exposed. The *Hazel Tau v Glaxo and Boehringer* case is a clear example of conflicting values in which antiretrovirals (ARV) necessary for the treatment of HIV/AIDS have a different value if exposed as an intellectual property right involving pricing policies or a human right entailing access to health (Teubner 2006: 327–8). The range of functionally differentiated subsystems present within society is increasing, threatening to generate insurmountable collisions of social expectations that will interfere with the legal system (Fischer-Lescano and Teubner 2004). Justice in this sense is fragmented too: an act regarded as just in one social rationality may transgress the values and social expectations of another (Teubner 2009: 5–6). So, can justice be granted by reflexive international economic law?

The process of irritation, re-entry and reconstruction offer the potential for an international economic law that integrates the values and interests of wider – not merely economic – social life. This potential to internalise and reconstruct social rationalities into legal constructs emerges from conflict – that is, when external social pressures produce irritation to the system. In this sense, the search for justice may commence when legal actors perceive a situation to be unjust (Teubner 2009: 20) – that is, they lack a sense of belonging (Steger 2002a: 140–1), feel excluded from the benefits of a system (Skordas 2009), or consider a right has been neglected (Teubner 2006). Law thus engages in the removal of injustice (Teubner 2006: 346). Paradoxically, the removal of one injustice may create another, as law will have to decide between divergent external rationalities that emerge and are communicated from society (Teubner 2009: 14). Gunther Teubner exemplifies this in the abovementioned *Hazel Tau v. Glaxo and Boehringer* case, in which a trade decision would imply favouring either the pharmaceuticals' property rights or the right to have access to health (2006).

Despite this, conflict provides law with the capacity to internalise external factors to its rationality. It is in the 'role interferences' of those legal actors who have been granted an attribution of action that the law finds opportunity to reconstruct reflexively communications of social reality (Teubner 1993: 99). So, it is important to re-structure international economic institutions (processes), providing scope for interactions between subsystems by means of legal actors, thus increasing access to information, discourse and participation of those constituencies affected by the international economic system (Black 1996: 47–9; Blecher 2009: 11–12; Teubner 2011b). Concerns about imbalances in bargaining powers may arise; therefore, transparency and capacity building are important (Steger 2002a: 140–1). Indeed, increasing access to institutions within legislative and judicial processes could grant the possibility to introduce social conflicts into the rationality of law (Teubner 2011a: 28–31) Nevertheless, the internalisation of external factors does not guarantee the attainment of justice. International economic discourse already includes some linkages to technical, scientific, environmental and health issues, but these are usually individual cases not yet changing the structure of meaning of international economic law. Just international economic law ought to be reflexive in the sense that once external factors are internalised to the system, they transcend the notion of conflict between legal actors, thus emerging as conflicts amongst colliding social rationalities (Teubner 2006: 344). Therefore, it implies a higher degree of autonomy not only from law but also from diverse social rationalities – in other words, their capacity to constitute fundamental rights and principles (Teubner 2011a: 19–24). Justice, in the sense of balancing economic and wider social goals, would involve directing international economic law towards questions about the constitutionality of law with regard to the consequences it produces to the external world (Teubner 2009: 18–20, 2011a: 25–8). Therefore, just international economic law entails not only recognising the self-constitution (rights) of other social rationalities, but also internalising them as a limitation to the system (Teubner 2006: 345). Only then will international economic law transcend the boundaries of conflict between legal actors, for example, deciding between pharmaceutical or human rights in the case of *Hazel Tau v. Glaxo and Boehringer*, thereby moving towards a justice in which the internal economic rationality of international economic law is balanced with the intrinsic rights of other social rationalities (Teubner 2006: 334). The internalisation of these principles (constitutional rights) into international economic law would allow for reassessing its values, therefore, providing the opportunity to change the structure of meaning in which wider social perspectives are reconstructed as internal to international economic law.

Conclusion

This chapter has proposed using a reflexive law approach to construct an international economic law that balances the values and interests associated with wider – not merely economic – social life. Reflexive theory acknowledges that recognition of social values and interests is only possible with the development of communication techniques. Specifically, the irritation, re-entry and reconstruction process is a crucial tool for the internalisation of social external factors into the rationality of international economic law. Legal actors have an important role as bearers of communications which irritate the system, thus introducing social values and interests into legal reasoning, and ultimately, to legal argumentation within judicial and legislative processes. Therefore, decision-making mechanisms (executive, legislative and judicial) within international economic institutions should be restructured to create connections to diverse social spaces by means of legal actors. Increasing access to information and opening spaces for participation and deliberation could be of utmost importance in generating those connections to reconstruct reflexively communications of social reality. However, the internalisation process is not sufficient to construct just international economic law. Only when international economic law recognises the constituting function of social rationalities, and introduces the fundamental values inherent to them – not merely concepts – into the construction of new law, will it substantively develop from merely deciding between two colliding individual interests, to changing the structure of it meaning.

The internalisation process should not be applied merely to introduce external factors into the rationality of international economic law. The application of the irritation, re-entry and reconstruction process to the internal operation of international economic institutions could produce strong forces within internal structures, involving in the construction of constitutional rights. Indeed one of the main criticisms that some international organisations such as the WTO face nowadays is that law mainly develops within judicial branches lacking the approval from the whole membership. The internalisation of social factors into legal reasoning within judicial bodies may act as an irritator to legislative processes. Upon this rationale it could be possible to further engage in the creation of international economic rights.

International economic law has mainly developed based upon an economic rationale, including efficiency. However, efficiency should be understood as the capacity of a system to be responsive to the environment. Responsiveness can only be achieved when international economic law evaluates the constitutionality of law with regard to the consequences it produces in the external world. Therefore, efficiency in this sense is related to notions of justice. A reflexive law approach would provide opportunity to establish communication processes with diverse social spaces, internalising the values inherent to them, thus allowing the construction of international economic law that is 'just' in the sense that it balances economic values with the intrinsic rights and principles of wider social perspectives.

Note

1 I would like to thank Professor Asif Qureshi and Amanda Perry-Kessaris for their valuable comments. This paper has been written with the support of the School of Law Scholarship of the University of Manchester and the governmental grants of the Consejo Nacional de Ciencia y Tecnología (CONACYT) and the Education Ministry in Mexico. The responsibility remains my own.

Chapter 9

Transnational networks of community and international economic law

Roger Cotterrell

Introduction

This chapter can be regarded as a sociological footnote to debates about the authority and effectiveness of international economic law.[1] It is intended to shift focus to some extent from the 'international' in international economic law (IEL) towards the 'transnational' character of economic legal relations: that is, away from the idea of law as rooted in the governmental activity, agreements or relations of *nation states* towards a recognition that law is also rooted in the projects and aspirations of actors operating in *networks of community* – which may be national, intra-national or transnational in scope. But I shall suggest that these contrasting perspectives are interdependent.

International law, despite its extensive concerns with non-state actors, builds from a heritage of thought that focuses on nation states as legal actors, and on treaties and conventions as key instruments of legal regulation. A concept of *transnational* law might, however, leave open, or put into contention, the question of the dominant sources of creation, interpretation and enforcement of law – noting that these are sometimes national sources, sometimes international and sometimes only indeterminately connected with the 'national' as a category, reflecting a complex mix of regulatory authority and of political and cultural legitimacy. The idea of the transnational insists only that regulatory reach and regulated social relations can stretch beyond national boundaries (Jessup 1956). The broadest conceptions of IEL already encompass the diversity of kinds of regulation that this suggests (Tietje and Nowrot 2006; Charnovitz 2011). But they leave open vast questions: What counts as 'law' in this field? What is the nature of the social relations this law should regulate?

These questions are too large to address directly here. But they can be commented on indirectly, from a particular perspective, by considering a third question which is this chapter's central focus: What follows if we think of IEL as existing ultimately to satisfy the regulatory needs of transnational economic networks of community?[2] This would be to consider

IEL in relation to social networks that create their own regulatory expectations and practices. It would be to confront a 'top-down' idea of law created by states, treaties, conventions and international institutions supported by states, with a more 'bottom-up' production of normative understandings and aspirations in many diverse communal networks (see also Xu in this volume).

IEL might indeed be seen as *ultimately* existing to address the transnational economic relations of private actors. If this law is often seen as mainly concerned with large-scale regulatory structures linking nations in their economic relations and validated by the high authority of states, it might also be seen in more radical terms as needing to find ultimate justification for its existence in its contribution to the welfare of *individuals* and specifically in the quality of their everyday economic interactions. If its form is public, its arena of ultimate effect is private. As with all law, it can be argued that what matters finally is what it contributes to the life of people in their personal social relations with others.

An important strand of sociology of law has for a century (since the writings of the pioneer legal sociologist Eugen Ehrlich) developed a kind of *constructive subversion* in considering state law. Today this can also be relevant to international economic law. Ehrlich's (1936) concept of 'living law' – that is, social norms that mirror or substitute in experience for the categories and functions of state law – was his vehicle for this constructive subversion. When he contrasted living law with the official juristic law of the state (which could be sometimes ineffective and ignored – and so, 'dead') his aim was not to destroy the idea of law as lawyers understand it, but to illuminate and strengthen this law by bringing to light its permanent need for cultural as well as political relevance and grounding.

Ehrlich's writings argue that, however powerful the modern nation state might be, the legitimacy of its law (that is, its active recognition as operational and authoritative) requires not only the support of political authority but also a rootedness in relations of community – in what he terms 'social associations' (Ehrlich 1936). Hence state law must reflect or address living law. In important respects state law's social significance depends on its relation to living law. A similar argument can be made that IEL needs firm rooting in the living law of transnational and national networks of economic relations.[3]

The 'public' and the 'private' in regulation

Today, widespread popular ideas about economic regulation oscillate between opposing poles: on the one hand, the legitimacy and necessity of much of this regulation (despite its long history and extensive scope) is questioned as an 'interference' with private economic enterprise; on the other, in times of economic crisis sudden demands are made for regulatory security, oversight and retribution for perceived wrongdoing (exploitation, corruption) in fields thought to be insufficiently controlled in the public interest. And different constituencies may tend naturally to gravitate to one or other of these poles of opinion.

International economic regulation seems powerful, firmly established and ever-expanding; yet also subject to ongoing debates about its legitimacy, proper scope and sources of recognition and support (e.g. Cohee 2008; Bacchus 2004; Petersmann 2004: 588–93), its transparency, and its cultural acceptability and foundations (e.g. Picker 2011; Footer and Graber 2000; Hahn 2006). Perhaps, as international law addressing relations between states increasingly blends with transnational regulation addressing relations of individuals, organisations and groups (e.g. Berman 2005; Berman 2006; Domingo 2011), the question of how far regulated populations are able to confer legitimacy on this law becomes steadily more pressing.

If transnational law is taken to be, as Philip Jessup (1956: 45) wrote, in establishing the term in the modern legal literature, 'law which regulates actions or events that transcend national frontiers', much of it comes from nation state (municipal) sources or from international agencies whose jurisdiction is ultimately guaranteed by states' approval. But some of it lacks the kinds of sources of public authority that municipal law relies on. How far can it find firm foundations by rooting itself in the aspirations and expectations of the populations whose general welfare it purports – directly or indirectly – to serve? For IEL these roots would surely have to be sought in interpersonal and intergroup economic relations (where corporations are also included as specially important persons and members of groups for this purpose). These are, in orthodox legal terms, private relations and so it seems necessary to descend from the 'public' to the 'private' or, indeed, to query how useful the public–private distinction may ultimately be in looking for the foundations of IEL.

In fact it is in the area of what is now often called *transnational private law* (law governing the transnational relations of private actors) that legal scholarship on the law-creating potential of economic networks of community has progressed furthest. In what follows, the wide-ranging recent analysis of this law by Gralf-Peter Calliess and Peer Zumbansen (2010) will serve as a partial basis for discussion. The relevant question is how far the character of transnational private law can be explained theoretically by reference to the nature of the communal networks it addresses.

The word 'private' is at first puzzling, as used by Calliess and Zumbansen, because they insist that any conception of transnational private law must recognise vital public elements in it. State law and public international law often support or frame emerging transnational regulation and where private actors create this regulation it will necessarily have a public element that makes it more than a compromise of particular private interests; in fact, any divide between private and public law is ultimately artificial, merely historical and conventional (2010: 63–4, 73–6; see also e.g. Bartley 2011). For Calliess and Zumbansen the interplay of different kinds of current regulation of transnational consumer contracts and of transnational corporate governance illustrates this blurring (2010: Chapters 3 and 4). But the focus on 'private' rather than 'public' signals that transnational private law imports a newly indeterminate, variable, shifting relationship between law and state, so that the nature of the involvement of state agencies in this kind of law in general cannot easily be theoretically specified.

Most fundamentally, 'private' in transnational private law seems to indicate the *social sources* of the regulation under consideration. Private law in the national context addresses social relationships developed in civil society and the market, rather than those focused on citizenship, government, administrative bureaucracy and the state. Transnational private law seems to get its identity from the idea that, as transnational regulation, it has its social sources in those relationships that, in a national context, would be the focus of private law if they were legally regulated at all. In Calliess' and Zumbansen's account, the manner in which transnational private law can emerge is typified by the new *lex mercatoria*, by codes of corporate social responsibility (sometimes partly statute-based, but especially developed in corporate practice; see Wheeler and Voiculescu in this volume), by dispute resolution and norm generation in e-commerce (especially in business to consumer relations) and by standardisation processes, norm development and dispute resolution among internet providers, experts, technical developers and interest groups.

What is of most interest about their discussion is that it focuses directly on the two major issues about transnational economic regulation that are likely to occupy legal theory. First, *how is it possible to decide what is 'law' in transnational private law* (how can this law be convincingly distinguished – as clearly 'law' – from numerous other kinds of standards, guidelines, directives, codes, 'soft law', best practice recommendations, membership rules, collective normative understandings, etc. that also populate the realm of economic regulation)? Second, *how is the legal authority of transnational private law to be recognised and guaranteed* if neither states nor international law regimes necessarily do this adequately?

Conceptualising law beyond the state

Calliess and Zumbansen address these two questions in a single analysis that enables us to see how they envisage regulation being, in a sense, 'distilled' out of social relations and acquiring legal character. It is necessary, they argue, to study transnational law *regimes* – that is, the whole procedure of creation, interpretation and enforcement of norms insofar as such a procedure exists for each variety of transnational private law (2010: 111).

Thus, this regulation is seen as in an uneven, unsystematic, contingent process of formation – observed dynamically in stages of emergence in various contexts as it takes shape almost organically, not statically as a finished set of norms. In this process of development, norms emerge over time from communal understandings and gradually take on a degree of authoritativeness (i.e. are increasingly recognised as binding on participants). Stages in this progress towards law can be identified but will vary greatly for different kinds and circumstances of regulation.

Law as such is identified in *functional* terms. Following Niklas Luhmann, its general function seems to be seen as that of stabilising normative expectations (Calliess and Renner 2009). Law is recognisable insofar as the carrying out of this function is observed. A relevant marker on the way to dispute processing becoming law is the 'verbalisation of conflict' in court-like procedures of some kind and the publishing of precedents of past decisions on disputes (a major step towards stabilising normative expectations by emphasising continuity and regularity in dealing with conflict cases). But no single process is always followed. Different kinds of 'economic governance' are appropriate to different kinds of transactions.

Building on Oliver Williamson's work on the 'economics of governance' Calliess and Zumbansen (2010) identify no less than 12 private governance mechanisms (that is, mechanisms of regulation that can be invoked by private actors in private transactions), combinable in 'tailor-made' fashion to deal with specific kinds of socio-economic relations. They include legislation, courts, legal sanctions, social norms, social sanctions, arbitration, negotiation, and internal corporate norms and board decisions. It seems that, again following Luhmann, there will be a 'thematisation threshold' when social communication becomes specifically *legal* – when the binary coding 'legal/non-legal' becomes appropriate and is used (Calliess and Zumbansen 2010: 51, 81–2).

The invocation of the binary legal coding as the mark of thematisation suffers, however, from admitted circularity: *legal* communications, for Luhmann, are those that mark out what is *legal* from what is *not legal*; his 'legal/non-legal' distinction has meaning only in terms of an already existing discourse of law. It would surely be more useful to think in terms of elements of doctrine (rules, principles, standards, guidelines, codes, directives, concepts) that can *potentially* amount to 'legal' communications, but at the same time to focus on how far these elements are themselves 'stabilised' as law through the actions of specific agencies. In national legal systems, legislatures, courts, police and enforcement agencies fulfil this function. In international and transnational law the range of agencies, and their character, will be different.

Thus, perhaps most useful is a general idea that to be 'law' transnational economic regulation needs to show the development of specific agencies or institutions tasked with creating, interpreting/adjudicating and/or enforcing doctrine. These could be of many different kinds and need not all be present in relation to any particular regulatory regime. Instead of the Luhmannian 'all-or-nothing' approach (suggesting that the thematisation threshold either has or has not been crossed) it is productive to see a regulatory continuum in which the legal character of regulation is a matter of *degree* (cf. Abbott *et al.* 2000). Transnational economic regulation can be more or less legal depending on how far its doctrine (rules, principles, codes, guidelines, standards, etc.) has been *institutionalised* – that is, how far it is created, interpreted and enforced by specific agencies of some kind.[4]

This would be a genuinely legal pluralist approach. One does not expect to see legal regimes all of the same kind (they could be very diverse), and some regimes will be *more legal than others*. Transnational private law can be thought of as law insofar as it can be seen as *institutionalised doctrine*. It is 'doctrine' in the sense that (even if some of it may seem very unlike municipal or international law) it may be capable of being expounded, organised or interpreted in comparable ways; and it is 'institutionalised' by recognised agencies managing at least some (not necessarily all) aspects of its creation, interpretation or enforcement. To the extent that transnational private law takes this form, it may attract ('internal') authority over the members of the communal networks it purports to regulate and ('external') legitimacy in the eyes of those who observe and take account of these networks (and perhaps seek to influence them through IEL).

A 'consensus' model of communal regulation

However, this is too quick a statement to make about authority and legitimacy. It begs the question of how transnational law regimes get sufficient stability, support and interest from their users to develop institutions and agencies to create, interpret and/or enforce their norms or standards. And it is here that Calliess' and Zumbansen's discussion is most illuminating. Throughout their book (but see especially 2010: 134–9) they use, as a model of an appropriate process for building legitimate and authoritative transnational regulation, the long established 'Request For Comments' mechanism for developing standards for internet operation among service providers, domain name authorities, IT experts, etc.

Simplified for present purposes, this involves (i) appointment of a chair of a working group that forms itself to address a perceived technical problem or disagreement; then (ii) an invitation to all interested parties (with no membership criteria laid down) to engage in online discussion; later (iii), after a period of free discussion in the group, the formulation by the chair of a 'rough consensus' (not a majority view but a distillation of prevailing understandings), either on the issue as a whole or some intermediate aspect of it; (iv) discussion and experimentation with the solution now proposed; (v) further stages of tentative proposals and circulation of a 'draft standard'; ultimately (vi), if the participant community's prevailing views support this, the stating of a 'full standard'. The standard thus becomes established as (in internet jargon) 'running code' – practically effective and authoritative.

Is this a model for anything other than the operations of the very special network of internet developers to which it relates? 'We reject kings, presidents and voting. We believe in Rough Consensus and Running Code' (RCRC), runs a mantra of this communal network (quoted in Calliess and Zumbansen 2010: 135). This suggests that the social organisation of norm-creation in this context might be treated as a model of communal participation in self-governance, more widely significant than its origin in a local IT context might suggest. The method of 'rough consensus' leading through many deliberative and experimental phases to the 'running code' of established doctrine could be claimed as a model of how to build the authority of norms 'from the bottom up'; not through voting or imposition but through negotiation, and without the need for any established hierarchy or political authority.

It may be easy to scorn the idea but Calliess, Zumbansen and others (e.g. Froomkin 2003) do, indeed, make this claim. What stands against it? First, RCRC addresses *technical* standards. A website introducing the working methods of the social network that uses it – the Internet Engineering Task Force (IETF) – states that: 'We try to avoid policy and business questions, as much as possible.'[5] Could such methods therefore be dismissed as not relevant to the formation of law, which necessarily deals with policy matters, values and interests? Calliess and Zumbansen (2010: 256–7) claim, however, that setting technical standards is not ultimately a policy-free matter divorced from wider normative considerations.

This seems right. The most productive way to view 'bottom-up' creation of transnational regulation may be as a process capable of moving through many kinds or gradations of standardisation – from establishing basic cognitive understandings through to policy-definition, value-clarification and imposed compromise of interests through binding norms. What seems purely 'technical' can be governed by decisions as to what kinds of technology are to be sought and why. Even technical requirements of accounting or financial transfer can embody moral and political choices and policies as to how particular socio-economic relations (e.g. in banking and investment practice) are to be arranged, and how 'efficiency', 'progress' and 'success' are to be measured in communal networks (Berman 2007: 1222–3). 'Pure' technique (or procedure) may ultimately be hard to isolate from its social uses.

A more fundamental critique, however, is surely that the network of community that internet technicians, experts, designers and enthusiasts make up is very different in its aims from most kinds of business networks in which transnational private law has been developed (e.g. through commercial arbitration practices, or commercial and corporate codes). There is a very strong collective interest, in the IETF and among the network of internet users more generally, in making the internet work effectively on a worldwide basis. It is in the interest of all users to have as much standardisation as possible and for the internet to be as inclusive and wide ranging in scope as it can be. To have to exclude potential parts of a relevant technical network from the internet would be an admission of collective failure, and at odds with its assumed purpose.

Thus, there is a strong incentive towards inclusiveness (of relevant participants in the technical network of community) and comprehensive standardisation of internet processes and protocols. But business networks need no such comprehensiveness. Their instrumental aims are focused on individual profit-making and the convergent projects of members. They can often benefit by excluding potential participants (e.g. through cartelisation, monopolisation, black-listing, pricing out). Thus, RCRC may be a special, limited case. There may, for example, be relatively few serious problems of reconciling the internally generated regulation of this particular network of community with that of other networks (because of its drive towards inclusiveness and comprehensiveness). The issue of where external coercive authority is to be found to police the production of internally generated regulation is not one that Calliess and Zumbansen find it necessary to discuss. But for much transnational economic regulation, the problem of co-ordinating regulatory regimes, and co-ordinating the networks of community to which they relate, is very important.

This is an aspect of the controlling, limiting function associated with the *voluntas* aspect of law – that is, law's coercive (as opposed to persuasive) authority. And while the discussion of RCRC in operation graphically depicts a process of developing *ratio* (reasoned principle) in regulatory doctrine through guided rough consensus and tentative drafting, there are surely questions to ask about the sources of *voluntas* in such a system if it is to be a model for law production (even if only of embryonic forms of law). In this connection, it is unfortunate that nothing is said in Calliess' and Zumbansen's discussion about power-relations in the RCRC process. It would be good to consider differential relations based on reputation and expertise. Perhaps coercive authority plays no part in RCRC; but if so, this is a reason why RCRC might not be a useful model for law-production in the rest of the world of communal networks. In most (if not all) such networks power and hierarchy are of vital significance, and law-like regulation is likely to have elements of coercive authority guaranteeing it, as well as elements of unfolding *ratio* that make it meaningful, at least to some degree, to those who must work with or are subject to it.

If RCRC relates to an atypical network of community, it is nevertheless worth considering. It illustrates how norms might arise in democratically organised networks of community.[6] In other networks, such as those of worldwide transnational industries (e.g. Snyder 1999a), the most powerful players (usually major corporate groups) have special power to set the rules. RCRC is interesting insofar as it shows an effort to avoid the dominance of particular power centres. But the communal network involved there may be structured as much by *shared ultimate values* (e.g. about the beneficial effects of the internet for knowledge diffusion and communication) as by common or convergent economic projects.

Also useful in the RCRC example is the idea of a gradual crystallisation of norms, which well illustrates the idea of transnational law regimes as *processes.* Above all it shows the importance of *mutual interpersonal trust* in the communal network, which makes possible the seemingly easy flow of deliberation, debate, experimentation, and consensus-emergence. At the same time, this trust is encouraged by transparency, open discussion and the universal sharing of knowledge in the network. The relationship may well be circular and cumulative – openness and knowledge sharing inspire trust; trust encourages openness and free flows of information.

Moral distance and communal 'embeddedness'

Yet the limitations of the RCRC model remain obvious. Calliess and Zumbansen use it to illustrate an ideal of consensus formation. But it can hardly represent the complexity of law's development. Ultimately the legal character of transnational economic regulation will be a *matter of degree*, to be judged by the extent of development of law-like *doctrine* (imperative standards, binding norms) and its *institutionalisation* by means of agencies dedicated to the creation, interpretation and/or enforcement of doctrine. A legal pluralist approach will expect to see many competing, overlapping, conflicting and mutually supporting regulatory regimes (Rosenau 2007), some more legal and more authoritative than others. The key to understanding the bases of their authority will lie in the nature of the networks of community they purport to serve and in which they have been created.

An analysis of transnational private law in terms of economic networks suggests that its strength derives in large part from its rootedness in these networks. Calliess and Zumbansen note that many norms and regulatory practices of transnational private law are developed by analogy with those of the private or public law of nation states, which are embedded in those national contexts. When transferred to the transnational sphere, they suggest, these norms and practices become 'disembedded', which establishes their autonomy as transnational private law (2010: 113, 123). Yet laws (like economic practices) acquire general acceptance by being seen as integrated with and an aspect of wider social relations. Karl Polanyi's

(1944) ambiguous insight about the importance of the 'embeddedness' of the economic in the social is directly paralleled by the claim (updating Ehrlich's view of living law) that law is part of the social – that is, it exists as an aspect or dimension of networks of community, as part of their regulatory structure.

Even state law (often thought of as remote from social life) is rooted in the networks of community that make up the nation state, and reflects the power structures present in them and the interplay of intra-national, nationwide and transnational networks. Durkheim expressed this differently, but to broadly similar effect, by suggesting that law that has no firm ties to the moral bases of social life has lost its 'soul' and can even seem 'a dead letter' (see Cotterrell 1999: 5, 54–5, 57–8). But state law's 'embeddedness' is surely often obscured because it reflects very complex interrelations (and often conflicts) between communal networks within the national society, as well as being influenced by other such networks extending beyond it.

Can international law be even more 'soulless' insofar as its links to networks of community are more indirect and potentially contradictory even than those of national law? With its vast, but abstract, potentially worldwide jurisdictional reach and its – so to speak – 'high altitude' trajectory in 'thin legal air' far above most of social life, could international law appear 'twice removed' from the conditions of existence of the regulated insofar as it regulates mainly the relations of states and their agencies *rather than* social relations among their populations? The issue is about *moral distance* between the regulators and the regulated – that is, about regulators' remoteness and isolation, and an inability (or unwillingness) to learn adequately about the conditions, expectations and motivations of the regulated; so that 'human scale' in regulation is in danger of getting lost.[7]

When the focus of analysis (as in Calliess' and Zumbansen's picture of transnational private law) is 'bottom-up' the emphasis is on how far and in what ways the regulated can influence the formulation of regulation, and how this input can interrelate with 'top-down' processes of legislation and decision-making by state and international agencies. Such an approach demands serious *sociological* inquiry about the kinds of regulatory needs that arise in communal relations. It requires a view of lawmaking as an endless process of observation, negotiation, compromise, influence and accommodation, rather than of policy formation, implementation and enforcement. This implies the need for very diverse sources of information about regulatory experience, expectations and aspirations in communal networks. How are lawmakers to acquire this information, to engage in communicative processes that can reveal it, to work within polycentric processes of law creation and application?

This complex project of what might be called embedded law creation cannot, for example, rely – as economic analysis of law often does – on abstract models of self-interested rational calculation as a satisfactory basis for understanding the environments to be regulated. Such models are inadequate substitutes for inquiring into the real understandings of regulated populations (Engelen 2010). The process of regulating, even for primarily economic relations, has to take account of varied *types* of motivations that are supports of social relations of community. These include not only instrumental cost-benefit calculations, but also emotional allegiances, rejections and resistances; as well as reliance on habit, customs, traditions and the attractions of the familiar, and also adherence to fundamental beliefs and ultimate values accepted for their own sake (Cotterrell 2006b: Ch. 4; Cotterrell 2008: Ch. 2). How far these varied motivations are 'rational' or 'irrational' is a question that can be left aside.

Voluntas and *ratio* in transnational regulation

Current thinking about international economic law clearly engages a wide range of political and cultural as well as economic and social variables (e.g. Jackson 2007: 8–10). Typically, trends, structural conditions, and socio-economic and political forces at work in national contexts are identified. The international actors who shape IEL can be assumed to have a wide appreciation of such matters and of world economic patterns and forces. But these may risk being – even where extensive consultation processes take place (Marceau and Pedersen 1999) – snapshots from 'on high' of the experience of socio-economic life 'on the ground' among individual citizens. One might speculate that much moral distance between regulators and regulated exists, insofar as the regulated economic actors are individual citizens or small firms; less so if they are large corporations or NGOs with much lobbying power.

Insofar as the idea of community focuses attention first on the participants in communal networks and then on the structures of power, organisation and interaction that the participants (or some of them) build, it directs initial attention to the 'atoms' (persons) that make up a regulated environment. It requires a descent from high-level abstraction to low-level accountability, reflexivity and participation.

The element of *ratio* (reasoned principle) in the norms needs to reflect their meaningfulness as guides to those participating in the relevant networks of community. Insofar as many such (overlapping, intersecting, conflicting) networks are involved, the scope for uniformity will be restricted – the acceptance of regulatory diversity and of merely piecemeal, provisional co-ordination of doctrine will surely be as important as the search for overarching regulatory principles (Cottier *et al.* 2011). The process has to be a dialogue between regulators seeking to understand typical regulatory problems of communal networks, and regulated populations asking how regulation can reflect their experience as members of such networks.

Sources of the *voluntas* (coercive authority) of transnational economic law are harder to identify in general terms than are those of *ratio*. Often they are 'external' from transnational networks of community – they lie in nation state law or international law providing ultimate guarantees of effectiveness in cases of otherwise irresolvable disputes or otherwise uncontrollable deviance. But no less important in practice may be organisational structures that economic networks produce for themselves – expressed through powers of blacklisting or exclusion from membership, insider-information control, management of members' reputations, and adjustment of trading conditions and privileges. Such structures inevitably reflect the power relations in communal networks (Snyder 1999a; Djelic and Quack 2010).

How far might the methods by which nation states have acquired their political mandate to make, manage and enforce law be somehow paralleled in transnational spheres? For example, how far is *democratic* legitimation of transnational economic law possible? Significantly, RCRC presents itself in opposition to representative democracy ('We reject kings, presidents and voting…'). RCRC adherents clearly view it as a system that can achieve acceptance through a process of ongoing deliberation, not through democratic representation (IETF has no fixed membership or qualifications for membership – thus no potential formally defined electorate; and no votes are taken). The idea of democracy might seem inappropriate to many economic networks of community, in which elites of major players lay down rules for newcomers and less powerful members in the market or industry. Yet, if deliberation and consensus can produce *ratio*, the problem of the source of *voluntas* available to end disputes over *ratio* remains to be solved.

In the context of the nation state, democratic or social contract theory presents the political basis of law's authority and legitimacy as deriving from the assumed consent of the governed, expressed through representative institutions entrusted with governing. What analogies might exist in non-state contexts of economic networks? Durkheim spoke of the state as a 'social brain' that 'thinks' for society – making evaluations related to but beyond those that individual citizens can establish, and geared to a collective interest (Cotterrell 1999: Ch. 10). Can transnational institutions that regulate economic networks operate authoritatively in any broadly comparable way? The most likely source of stable *voluntas* in transnational private law may come, perhaps, through the acceptance of *expertise* as the basis of a kind of authority to police and limit the proliferation of *ratio* produced through deliberation, negotiation and consensus. The numerous standard-setting agencies and authorities now coming into existence and flourishing in the transnational private law arena may depend ultimately for their claims to authority on perceptions of their expertise.

In this connection the *availability of knowledge*, referred to earlier for its significance in building mutual interpersonal trust, again assumes great importance. If the diffusion of knowledge may help the building of *ratio* out of a rough consensus in a network of community, its absence (perhaps impossibility) in many contexts reinforces the significance of *voluntas*. If people cannot know enough to contribute persuasively to debate, and if they cannot learn enough to be able to interpret other people's viewpoints and (assuming goodwill) to work towards consensus, the alternative is reliance on expertise (on the assumption that experts can close off debate by the superior authority of their knowledge).

Questions remain about the kind of expertise appropriate in transnational private law and how it is to be institutionalised (in the way that state legal systems institutionalise juristic expertise). The expert is not merely a contributor to debate but an authority able to impose a judgment, or terminate an argument. Under what conditions is expertise recognised and accepted; under what conditions will a 'social contract' to accept the expert's sovereign judgment be held to be in place? It is not obvious that in the case of transnational private law (and, indeed, of IEL) traditional *juristic* expertise is what is most required. The authority of the standard setter may come from claims to economic, managerial, political, technical, scientific or other expertise specifically related to the regulated field. The best hopes for legitimate and authoritative transnational regulation (and reliable processes for developing it) may well lie in variable combinations of (i) some sort of ostensible *egalitarianism* of rough consensus coupled with (ii) the institutionalised and accepted *elitism* of a more or less benevolent regulatory expertise.

By such means transnational private law may develop something to parallel the combinations of *voluntas* and *ratio* that are the key to law's effectiveness, authority and legitimacy. As such it can help to set in place building blocks for structures firmly grounded in communal networks yet capable of informing and meshing with the broadening legal doctrine of international economic law.[8]

IEL through a community lens

This chapter has emphasised the 'transnational' rather than the 'international', but not to suggest that the former is legally more significant than the latter. The focus on the transnational has been to highlight a 'bottom-up' approach to cross-national legal development that centres on networks of community rather than the treaty-making and convention-signing activity of states. A 'community lens'[9] applied to economic regulation across national borders raises issues rather than offering comprehensive theoretical formulations. But these issues may well be significant for the theoretical study of IEL.

First is an issue of defining *the constituencies that IEL serves*. Who are the regulated and how are they to be thought of as both sponsors and recipients of regulation? The idea of communal networks raises that issue. It refers to networks of social relations that are often fluctuating, overlapping, transient, variable in organisation or stability, tightly or loosely bonded, and almost always involving power-structures. Relations of community need some stability of expectations, and that depends on mutual interpersonal trust among participants. Different kinds of communal bonds often overlap; so, even networks of community primarily structured by economic interests may also embrace other aspects of community – not just members' common or convergent projects, but also perhaps their shared beliefs, customs, traditions or emotional commitments. It is important to distinguish these different aspects or types of community, which often present distinct regulatory needs and problems (Cotterrell 2006b: 116–25, 153–8).

Second, and following from the above, the community-focused approach indicates the need for *a sociology of IEL* to consider how it is and must be 'embedded' in networks of community, and to examine their nature. The focus would be on the typical regulatory needs and problems of different types of communal relations – whether primarily instrumental (especially economic), based in shared beliefs or ultimate values, or founded on purely emotional allegiances or rejections, or in the mere fact of co-existence in a shared environment. A guiding principle here would surely be that communal networks can hardly be expected to regulate themselves except to secure their own objectives. Constraints on them come from their interaction, conflict or overlap with or subordination to other such networks. Another guiding principle is that communal networks will seek to secure their objectives by trying to regulate beyond their own membership. Consequently, regulatory competition and conflict should be expected to be endemic and permanent in the transnational arena.

Third, new issues are raised about the *legitimacy of IEL* (its general acceptability as a regime or set of regimes). Insofar as IEL's sources are in municipal and international law this may seem to raise no issues different from those that bear on any other kinds of international law – the issues are traced back to those that relate to nation state law and state sovereignty. But, insofar as studies show a practical intertwining of bottom-up creation of transnational regulation with top-down production of state law and IEL,[10] it may be necessary to explore diverse sources of regulatory legitimacy – of international organisations and also transnational networks.

Fourth, a 'community lens' highlights the issue of *moral distance* that Ehrlich saw (although the term is mine, not his) as a founding concern of modern sociology of law. For him, working in the Bukovina lands at the remote eastern edge of the Austro-Hungarian Empire just before the outbreak of the First World War, moral distance was also geographical distance: his implicit warnings were addressed to imperial lawmakers, far away, purporting to regulate his ethnically diverse province. Today the moral distance that international law has to overcome, to address individuals and groups and not just states as legal actors, might seem even greater. It is hard to know what democratic lawmaking can mean as applied to the rule-making powers of many international institutions such as the World Trade Organization, except in the formal sense that these institutions are author-ised by states having, themselves, a more or less democratic character (Bacchus 2004: 669–70; Shaffer 2004; cf. Bronckers 1999).

Finally, the community approach warns of what might be called *regulatory hubris*. Few doubt the need for transnational economic co-ordination. The names of leading international economic institutions point to an ambition for 'world' regulation (the World Bank, the WTO). But ulti-mately economies exist for *local benefit* – for the wellbeing of individuals, mainly tied to particular environments, and increasingly affected by large forces labelled as globalisation. The main focus of IEL is on regulation of the economic policies and relations of states and, through that, the regula-tion of states' populations of economic actors. It presupposes as absolute virtues, economic growth (not just sustainability), formally uniform trading conditions, secure conditions for commercial enterprise, the ongoing extension of markets, and legal freedom of trade (see e.g. Khor 2000; for a radically alternative vision see IUC Group 2009).

How this law can reflect the complexity and diversity of economic and other aspirations of its innumerable regulated populations is often unclear. Indeed, it may be that the nature of these populations remains insufficiently studied in relation to economic regulation. They are some-times represented in world trade literature only through such abstract, aggregating measures as 'citizen welfare', 'market infrastructure', 'people attributes', 'culture and its impact', 'societal stress', 'labour antagonism', 'environmental costs' and 'population changes'.[11] The textures of com-munal experience are hard to capture in such categories.

Conclusion

The message of 'living law' in the context of transnational economic regu-lation is much the same as the message Ehrlich wished to convey by using this concept a century ago. His sociology of law, running against the main stream of socio-legal inquiry, warned against treating the state as an omnipotent legislator for which culture, like nature, presented no insur-mountable obstacles to progress. Today, more precise and nuanced con-cepts than that of living law are needed, and the idea of types and networks of community with their regulatory needs and problems can serve this need. A community lens focused on international law might offer a warning to transnational lawmakers, comparable to Ehrlich's warning to the lawmakers of the imperial state. Like the Hapsburg empire Ehrlich served, the current transnational realm is hardly to be seen as democratically structured. The realistic issue is not how to democratise economic regulation across national borders but how to maximise its responsiveness – its ability to recognise, reflect, organise and mediate between diverse communal demands through a continuum of regulatory responses: from facilitation or delegation, to guidance or advice, to pre-scription and enforcement.

Ehrlich thought that respect for cultural diversity, expressed in sensi-tive, flexible, carefully contextualised regulatory policies, might save the crumbling, unwieldy structure of the Austro-Hungarian state. Despite its ongoing crises, the international economic order is not crumbling. But its legitimacy needs strengthening in the face of political opposition to glo-balisation, perceptions of the remoteness of international regulatory pro-cesses and suspicion about their character. A way to direct research to these issues is in part through a socio-legal focus on the nature of networks of community and their significance for IEL. In this way Ehrlich's old vision for a critical sociology of law, which has inspired generations of scholars, finds an urgent new application in studying transnational eco-nomic relations.

Notes

1 Many thanks to Amanda Perry-Kessaris for valuable comments on a draft of this chapter.
2 The idea of transnational communities as sources of regulation has attracted valuable recent analysis: see especially Djelic and Quack 2010. But 'community' tends to be seen in this literature as an *object* (a social group united by a common project or identity) and difficult questions arise as to how com-munities are to be identified and where their boundaries lie. By contrast, 'com-munity' indicates, in this chapter, relatively stable trust-based social relations, with different types of these often combined in complex, fluid social networks. So, the issue is not to identify 'communities' but to study regulatory aspects of types and networks of communal relations. See Cotterrell 1995: 328–9; and for many illustrations and applications, Cotterrell 2006b, and Cotterrell 2008: Chapter s2 and Part 4.
3 A concept of living law in relation to transnational regulation is invoked in Hellum *et al.* 2010. But an analysis of different types of communal relations, with regard to their regulatory aspects, is needed to give precision to Ehrlich's idea.
4 In international trade regulation, the creation of the dispute settlement system of the World Trade Organization might be regarded as a striking illustration of 'institutionalisation towards legalisation'. But, in transnational regulation, such institutionalisation will often be incremental, embryonic, relatively localised (perhaps to a particular kind of economic activity or industry) and much less politically visible.
5 *Getting Started in the IETF.* Available at www.ietf.org/newcomers.html (accessed 11 October 2011).

6 See also Hachez and Wouters 2011, emphasising accountability to the regulated population as a basis of regulatory legitimacy.

7 On moral distance see Cotterrell 1995: 304–5, 330–1. I use the word 'moral' here in a Durkheimian sense to refer to the normative valuations and cognitive perceptions of regulators and regulated.

8 For an illustration of tensions between transnational private law and IEL regimes see Maher 2011.

9 Thanks to Amanda Perry-Kessaris for suggesting this term for the theoretical approach sketched here. See Perry-Kessaris 2011c.

10 See e.g. Levit 2008 on the Berne Union's 'private' regulation becoming a component of WTO regulation; Bartley 2011 on intersections of transnational regulation and state and international law.

11 See e.g. Jackson 2007: 9–10, using all of these terms. On social research in the World Bank context see e.g. Fine 2008.

Part III

Subtext

Chapter 10

A qui l'homme sauvage?

The text, context and subtext of agreements between mining corporations and indigenous communities

Deval Desai[1]

Introduction

> The subject of the present discourse, therefore, is more precisely this. To mark, in the progress of things, the moment at which right took the place of violence and nature became subject to law, and to explain by what sequence of miracles the strong came to submit to serve the weak, and the people to purchase imaginary repose at the expense of real felicity.
>
> (Rousseau 2006b: 82)

This chapter is a critical analysis of the 'text' of agreements between mining corporations and indigenous communities in the 'context' of the discourses by which they are framed. Using Jean-Jacques Rousseau's concept of the *homme sauvage* as an entry point, it examines the framing of the 'text' through discourses of *law*, *actors* and *the indigenous rights professional*. It examines each discourse through a close reading of Rousseau and reinterpretation of the *homme sauvage*, using these as organizing principles for the critical analysis of the text of the agreements. In so doing, it encourages those who advocate for legal empowerment of indigenous people to be reflexive, understanding themselves to be active participants in this process, rather than neutral tools to be deployed.

This chapter also offers a methodological intervention. The identification and analysis of literary narrative(s) underpinnings of legal text and legal practice is not new in the study of law (Thomas 1991; Bruner 2003). Yet its application to the role of law in development, and particularly notions of governance, is novel and allows for a broader range of source material and knowledge claims to be engaged in critiquing and shifting the discursive basis of the role of law in development.

Text

This chapter focuses on agreements between multinational enterprises (MNEs) and indigenous communities to share the benefits of mining on land subject to indigenous rights claims. These agreements are increasingly important tools for the governance of the mining sector and the construction of indigenity. They are rooted in international instruments,[2] valorized by the UN (UN 2007: 175) and emerging in the theory (Environmental Resources Management 2010; Otto 2010) and practice (International Finance Corporation 2012) of international financial institutions (IFIs). The 'texts' of these agreements also have significance in multiple national contexts. 'Mining agreements' are mandatory in the Northern Territory in Australia (Aboriginal Land Rights (Northern Territory) Act 1976 ss. 40–42); and provided for under the commonwealth-wide Native Title Act 1993 (ss. 24–44). Similarly, in Canada, 'impact and benefit agreements' (IBAs) are often drawn up to distribute mining benefits on land covered by settlements between Crown and Aboriginal groups, and are concluded voluntarily to avoid future litigation in relation to land claims not yet settled. Similar agreements (in different public law frameworks) exist, for example, in the Philippines, South Africa, Indonesia and Papua New Guinea. The details vary, but they are all negotiated agreements designed to formalize, with reference to public and private law, the sharing, between mining companies and indigenous communities who assert jural rights or claims over land, of risks and rewards associated with mining on that land (Llewellyn and Tehan 2004: 4).

Context

It is possible to identify two discursive frames in operation among national and transnational parties concerned with negotiated agreements and indigenous rights (IFIs, NGOs, MNEs, academics, and policy-makers). The first is rooted in Jean-Jacques Rousseau's *homme sauvage* (roughly translated as natural man and often used synonymously with the 'noble savage'). In *Discourse on Inequality* – a literary work as much as a political tract[3] – Rousseau sketched the social evolution of man from *l'homme sauvage* (Part I) through to his socialization (Part II), via the assertion and enforcement of (property) rights, a condition which leads to 'crimes, wars and murders' (Rousseau 2006b: 100). Presented in this Rousseaulian frame, natural man has two exalted characteristics. First, he is close to the land. Second, he is best placed to *know what to do with the land* in order to protect his lot in and way of life. Thus he operates in harmony with nature and is the reified signifier of natural balance (Rousseau 2006b: 83–84). He is unencumbered by the trappings of human society, sustained and nourished by nature (Rousseau 2006b: 83).

Literature at the juncture of nature and the indigenous, often drawing on (Rousseaulian) strands of art (Ellingson 2001: 11–20), ethnography (van der Ploeg 1993; Posey *et al.* 1984), environmentalism (Kramer *et al.* 1997; Terborgh 1999) and (non)governmental policy (Alcorn 2010; Waitt

1999), is the 'inheritor of the tendency ... to romanticize the indigenous as noble savages or primitives living in harmony with their environment ... corrupted by the problematic or ugly manifestations' of modern society (Horne 2001: 85, 89), such as mining.[4]

The second, rights-based, discursive frame takes these indigenous ties to land as its starting point. It conceives of land ties as rights or claims to be leveraged by indigenous communities (with some help) in order to obtain what they desire from mining companies, be it material benefit or simply to be left alone. A group that I shall refer to as 'indigenous rights professionals' (following David Kennedy's use of the 'human rights professional') is a central interlocutor in both of these discourses. These individuals and groups act out of a sense of 'compassion' (Kennedy 2002: 101) to further the wellbeing of indigenous communities against the interests of the state or other private parties.

Discourses of law

> Thus, as the most powerful or the most miserable considered their might or misery as a kind of right to the possessions of others, equivalent, in their opinion, to that of property, the destruction of equality was attended by the most terrible disorders. Usurpations by the rich, robbery by the poor, and the unbridled passions of both, suppressed the cries of natural compassion and the still feeble voice of justice, and filled men with avarice, ambition and vice. Between the title of the strongest and that of the first occupier, there arose perpetual conflicts, which never ended but in battles and bloodshed.
>
> (Rousseau 2006b: 107)

This section outlines the relevant legal and quasi-legal frameworks that 'fix[ ] the law of property' and 'destroy[ ] natural liberty.' They shape the operation of mining agreements at the international and national level. These simultaneously give content to and institutionalize the discourses to be discussed in the following sections.

Public–private law

Mining agreements sit at the boundary of private and public law. For example, the state is a party to negotiations in the Philippines (*Indigenous Peoples' Rights Act 1997* ss. 7(b), 12; Xanthaki 2003: 15), and must sign off on aspects of them in South Africa (*Mineral and Petroleum Resources Development Act* s. 104[5]), while Australia either requires or provides for privately negotiated agreements under public law (*Native Title Act* 1993 s. 25 onwards). Canada is more explicit in its application of a private law framework to these agreements, sometimes ensuring that impact and benefit agreements are governed 'in accordance with the common law of contract.'[6] Finally, Indonesia is at the private end of the spectrum. There is no public protection of or provision for mining agreements, meaning they will purely be private law instruments (Colchester *et al.* 2003: 135).

The agreements often adopt the features of private law. They have distinct private parties between whom the agreement is formed and who execute the document.[7] The parties negotiate terms and select governing law.[8] Adopting these features has implications for the ways in which parties are framed in law. The language of public law can distinguish between indigenous communities and ascribe to each specific characteristics (noting that this can differ from public law regime to public law regime). The language of private law individuates specific groups or parties to a contract, but rarely distinguishes between them beyond that save the characteristics that the parties themselves include through negotiation and consent (Kennedy 1982). For example, the language of the memorandum of agreement between Mindex Resources Development and the Mangyan community incorporates the language of parties agreeing on terms and includes sections delineating the 'rights and obligations of the parties' (at 5) and applicable law (at 2–3). The document takes on the characteristics of a privately executed agreement between parties establishing rights and duties. Framing the community in this way eschews a framing that highlights their specially-recognized political status in public law, downplaying the non-private avenues the community may take to engage with or resist the MNE.

Moreover, private law can oust public law solutions open to indigenous communities, for example by introducing presumptions in favor of arbitration,[9] as well as through stabilization and choice of law clauses. Although arbitration does not preclude access to public law remedies or appeals on matters of public law, it is the first port of call for disputes and may exhaust some or all of the resources of an indigenous community. Stabilization clauses 'freeze' or stabilize the law of the state over the life of the investment project and have proved controversial in the context of investor–state agreements as they restrict the effectiveness of state legislation designed to affect rights (Shemberg 2008); similar concerns can be raised as regards mining agreements and the rights of indigenous peoples. Likewise, choice of law clauses enable parties to specify the public and private law frameworks governing their agreement, so that mining companies may simply standardize their mining agreements, choosing the most expedient and favorable law to apply (as has been done with stabilization clauses: Shemberg 2008; Mann 2008).

Public and private law frameworks vary significantly from place to place. The choice to pursue private negotiations, public law reform, private remedy or judicial review is often strategic, having regard to resources, non-legal leverage in the public and private sphere, institutional access and cost, time constraints etc. This strategic role must be recognized by indigenous rights professionals: they must take heed of Rousseau's caveat, which saw 'might or misery as a kind of right to the possessions of others, equivalent, in their opinion, to that of property.' The choice of private or public law must account for the might or misery of the indigenous community, the MNE and the state when negotiating over the 'right [of] possession.'

Formality and informality

Godden *et al.* (2008), in a study of indigenous people, mining and law, aver that '[l]aw provides an important means of formalizing relationships that have been forged at an economic and policy level, but also as an instrument that defines what those relationships are, and how they are to be managed to achieve goals of economic empowerment and development' (Godden *et al.* 2008: 25). In line with the rights-based discursive frame outlined above, they view formal agreements not only as desirable, but as 'offer[ing] more scope to resolve longstanding issues of indigenous economic and cultural sustainability [than complex public-law processes]' (Godden *et al.* 2008: 24–25; citation omitted). The implication is that these agreements are more flexible than the byzantine processes of public law, while still encouraging virtuous behavior by MNEs:

> If corporations, whether strictly as part of their corporate social responsibility obligations or as more wide-ranging 'social licence to operate' seek to negotiate with indigenous and local communities ways to transform resource wealth into social and economic development, then, it is important to determine what provisions might be incorporated into agreements, and as well to ensure that there are measures for adequate evaluation of agreements and their implementation.
>
> (Godden *et al.* 2008: 28)

However, the value of this formalizing approach seems to be less certain than Godden *et al.* assert. It has been suggested that, in richer countries, 'it seems as if there is general consensus that CSR requires a business to voluntarily go beyond compliance,' while in poorer countries, it seems to be agreed that law – regulation and liability – must be used to 'encourage' the private sector to adhere to its social responsibilities' (Kloppers and du Plessis 2008: 95). Further, this approach may have an effect on the trust between indigenous community and MNE. *Pace* Weber, the very act of institutionalization *may* weaken the mutual quality of the trust. Informal CSR operations by MNEs can engage directly with individuals and groups in their own environments. In that sense, informal activity can build up trust between the parties (a scarce resource in relationships between MNEs and indigenous communities[10]), whereas formal dealings require trust to be placed in legal-economic institutions (Stiglitz 2000; Dixit 2007). Trust may be a more desirable good than formalization in certain circumstances (on the other hand, it may harm the community if the trust is misplaced). Whatever the outcome of formalization in a particular situation, it is clear that it is no panacea and may be undesirable in certain circumstances.

Formalization can also reduce the space available to the indigenous community to act. They are bound by arbitration clauses (which might restrict the avenues for political protest),[11] restricted in their political speech through confidentiality clauses,[12] hit with legal and negotiation costs (Sosa and Keenan 2001: 19–20) and often divided during difficult negotiations (Sosa and Keenan 2001: 3, 15). It is thus unclear whether formalization – the 'still feeble voice of justice' – will always institutionalize virtuous behavior and suppress '[u]surpations by the rich [and] robbery by the poor.'

Discourses of actors

> The body of a savage man being the only instrument he understands, he uses it for various purposes ... for our industry deprives us of that force and agility, which necessity obliges him to acquire ... Give civilised man time to gather all his machines about him, and he will no doubt easily beat the savage; but if you would see a still more unequal contest, set them together naked and unarmed, and you will soon see the advantage of ... carrying one's self, as it were, perpetually whole and entire about one.
>
> (Rousseau 2006b: 84)

This quotation, from the opening paragraphs of the *Discourse*, clearly established the oppositional relationship between civilized man (of machines and modernity) and natural man (of flesh and nature). This section argues that one can infer strong resonances between this relationship and the ways in which the parties are framed in the subtext of a mining agreement.

Indigenous communities

Mining agreements tend to portray indigenous communities as something akin to Rousseau's *homme sauvage*: they are close to the land and know what to do with it. It is on this basis that indigenous communities are afforded rights to land and benefit-sharing in international and domestic laws. Yet if the text of a formal mining agreement is read in light of the context of Rousseaulian natural man, one can see two tensions when considering the resultant discursive rendering of the indigenous community: cultural uniqueness I legal same-ness and naturalness I professionalization. Each tension reflects two opposing yet fundamental characteristics of this rendering of the community.

The cultural uniqueness I legal same-ness opposition is based on a tension between discourses of private law, which render indigenous actors the same as everyone else in the legal sphere (e.g., bound by the same rules of contract and the same microeconomic behavioral model that is applied to non-indigenous groups) and the special imaging of indigenous communities in international and national law that leads to the grant to them of rights over land. The naturalness I professionalization opposition is closely related. I argue that the natural aspect of the *homme sauvage* (his affinity to and peaceful co-existence with nature) can be in tension with the formalizing tendency of the legal discourses framing these agreements.

Such law is antithetical to the Rousseaulian construction of natural man: it is 'modern,' 'dominant,' 'alienated,' as opposed to a proprietary legal system of an indigenous community that forms part of their 'unique' culture (Cobo 1986: 30). Indigenous groups that see mining agreements as the most efficient tool to share the benefits from corporate activity on their land are in a double bind. Their indigenity is predicated on the image of their distinctive cultures and institutions, as understood by the non-indigenous community. However, the process of pursuing these agreements requires language, expertise and institutional structures borrowed from the non-indigenous community (Kingsbury 2002: 189–90). This would demystify the indigenous community and reduce the difference between the two. At worst, the indigenous community risks falling into that interim space sketched out by Rousseau in which 'the still feeble voice of justice' could be 'usurped' by the rich and powerful in the naked exercise of force and power (a notion that resonates with narratives about the corruption of the indigenous by the trappings of modernity: Gow 2008; Foster 2002).

I use a reading of Jacques Lacan to lay out some helpful insights into these tensions and the creation of identity inherent in negotiating and formalizing these mining agreements. I use as a starting-point Lacan's binary 'moi (ego) I autre' in the imaginary order and its transition to 'sujet I Autre' in the symbolic order. Identity is first created in the same way that a child forms its ego through its identification with an image of the self (an 'autre'), such as a reflection in a mirror (Lacan 1966: 90–95). In this reading, the ego emerges at the moment of concurrent identification and alienation, and is formed by and from this specular image. Identity is at once self-aware and contraposed against an other: Lacan sought to find out '[à] travers les identifications typiques du sujet, comment *se constitue le je*, où *il se* reconnaît?' (Lacan 1936: 86; emphasis added), the pronouns and verbal forms emphasizing the reflexive yet binary nature of self-identity. The other, by definition, is also non-identical to itself, as it is essentially bound to *its* 'autre' – the 'moi': 'l'autre … n'est pas un autre du tout, puisqu'il est essentiellement couplé avec le moi' (Lacan and Miller 1978: 370). Thus in this reading, if the act of negotiation of mining agreements begins from the first conscious contact between the indigenous community and MNE, or from the first contact between indigenous rights groups and the indigenous community in preparation for discussions with the MNE, both parties mutually constitute identities with this act by conceiving of themselves in opposition to the other.

However, this 'moi' and 'autre' themselves can only be fully conceived in terms of *difference* to the symbolic order's 'sujet' and 'Autre'. The 'Autre' designates a radical alterity, constructed by language, which cannot be assimilated by the self. The subject, 'made and remade in his encounter with th[is Autre]' (Bowie 1988: 117), imagines himself the way others perceive him. Crucially, then, the (difference in) unity of the 'moi' and 'autre' in the imaginary order leads to the essential distance between 'sujet' and 'Autre' in the symbolic order as transmutation between the orders occurs through the language of 'différences' that is central to Lacanian thought (Lacan 1973: 228). Again, looking at agreements, as soon as the parties' opposing identities are translated into language (which may be instantaneous), the symbolic order comes to bear. The parties become radically different, each constituted by their opponent's perception. For language, in the case of mining agreements, read discourses of law. This happens at the negotiation stage, when law is deployed by both parties and they begin the dynamic process of constituting the 'moi/sujet | autre/Autre' oppositions that define them. The act of negotiation produces the 'signifying chain of knowledge' (Schroeder 2008: 159) that codifies identity for the indigenous community and MNE.

Turning to the tensions outlined above, with regard to cultural uniqueness | legal same-ness, the law can now be seen as causing the creation of the 'sujet | Autre' and codifying in the symbolic order the essential difference between MNEs and indigenous communities. A similar argument can be made for the resolution of the naturalness | professionalization tension: the very language that can only be accessed by a professional creates and reinforces the Rousseaulian identity of the indigenous community.

However, the use of (the language of) law to construct identity in this fashion generates an important political subtext. The symbolic 'sujet' of the indigenous community is a representation of the entire community. Indigenous rights professionals should be aware of the political implications this has for communities and their space for negotiation with MNEs. For example, a homogenous 'sujet' narrows the contours of the political space internal to indigenous groups, thereby denying expressions of multiple identities (Conklin and Graham 1995). In fact, 'relationships between mining companies and communities are complex … [, are] enacted in diverse ways, are experienced differently both within and across communities and companies' (Cheney *et al.* 2002: 8). A denial of internal politics makes it easier for an MNE to negotiate with any person(s) it believes to be 'representative' of the indigenous community; furthermore, it decreases the space available to the rest of the community to reject the illegitimate representation.[13] Indeed, such rejection often has to be presented as unnatural rather than politically illegitimate: members of the Siocon Subano Association framed their attempted rejection of purported representatives in terms of their not being indigenous or their past cooperation with (unnatural) mines.

MNEs

As the 'autre | Autre' to indigenous groups' 'moi | sujet' (and vice versa), the discourses around MNEs are closely tied to those of indigenous groups. The indigenous community is, when viewed through the Lacanian 'mirror': natural, in harmony with its environment, close to the land and a good manager of natural resources. The MNE as its negative is: unnatural, anti-environmental, not in symbiosis with the land and an exploiter of resources. MNEs are so unnatural that they respond to that Rousseaulian construct of social man, the law. The law thus plays a formative and institutional role, creating the identity of an MNE and motivating its behavior within the parameters of that identity.

If one takes seriously the importance placed on formalization by indigenous rights professionals, it would imply that MNEs do not respond sufficiently to informal stimuli or pressures. Homologous to this idea is a particular and long-established understanding of the firm as a social actor (Friedman 1970; Micklethwaite and Wooldridge 2005; Reich 2007): apolitical or amoral; a receptor of norms only if financially desirable; and fundamentally focused on profits and the bottom line. This understanding has a metapolitical dimension. It presumes that the desired norms transmitted by laws do not need to be internalized by a company: as long as they are expressed in monetary terms they will be followed. As a result, the only political space needed to influence corporate behavior is that which frames market institutions (a notion problematized in a growing body of literature such as Gneezy and Rustichini 2000; Strahilevitz 2000). The space for and tools available to other actors (indigenous groups, activists, policy-makers and others) to exploit non-financial points of leverage over an MNE (such as the ego or social reputation of a CEO: Mace 2004: 94; Clarke 2004: 24–30) may be diminished as a result.

Discourses of the indigenous rights professional

The passage from the state of nature to the civil state produces a very remarkable change in man, by substituting justice for instinct in his conduct, and giving his actions the morality they had formerly lacked.

(Rousseau 2006a: 10)

As for men like me, whose passions have destroyed their original simplicity, who can no longer subsist on plants or acorns, or live without laws and magistrates ... they will not therefore have less contempt for a constitution that cannot support itself without the aid of so many splendid characters, much oftener wished for than found; and from which, notwithstanding all their pains and solicitude, there always arise more real calamities than even apparent advantages.

(Rousseau 2006b: 123)

The indigenous rights professional strives to secure certain goods for the indigenous community through the vocabulary of the law. Yet here, the text of the agreement and the Rousseaulian context brings out a very different political subtext. The indigenous rights professional seeks to uphold rights that draw in part on a Rousseaulian image of the indigenous. However, bringing Rousseau's caveat on the non-natural influence of law – 'substituting justice for instinct' – to the foreground, I argue that by his very position *as* a professional, he simultaneously creates the space (moreover, the need) for a buffer between natural man and the institutions of social man, and fills it.

It is helpful to explore the role of the professional by imagining the impact of his absence on discourses framing the indigenous community. Indigenous rights *academics* have warned that in the absence of a mediating NGO, indigenous communities struggle to remain 'indigenous' when engaging with an MNE. As Kingsbury notes:

Th[e] transformation [in language, institution and organizational structure of an indigenous community] is usually toward the most successful organizational forms fostered in the law and practice of modern secular liberal societies, principally NGOs or corporations. These same organizational forms are also favored in the construction of international civil society and fostered by its practices.

(Kingsbury 2002: 190, citation omitted)

What, then, is the role of the professional? Rather than pursue an intellectual history (Ellingson 2001) or a study of the actors continuing to use the narrative of the *homme sauvage* (Hames 2007), the Lacanian approach outlined above directs attention towards identity creation *through* law, or more accurately through the professional identity that law requires. By deploying the *homme sauvage* and the law in all its forms, the indigenous rights professional is part of the Lacanian 'mirror' in which the indigenous community's reflection is seen. The professional is able to embed into indigenous identity the ideational regime of natural man and the institutional regime of legal agreements. The space of difference between natural and social (legal) man is accepted by us, and, importantly, it is a space that the professional fills.

This can cause real problems for the indigenous community. The professional becomes the receptor of the community's values and the conduit for its desires; the community, meanwhile, must rely on the professional-as-middleman to translate these into something intelligible to social man. The community's future might thus be determined by the professional's capacity, priorities and time, which may be in short supply. By using the language of empowerment, the professional can *disempower* the community by denying it access to that very language. In the context of a detailed study of the negotiation and implementation of mining agreements in Australia, O'Faircheallaigh (2003: 21) writes:

> [The] actual process of designing and drafting agreements is undertaken by non-Indigenous technical staff who typically work with specific Indigenous organisations for brief periods of time and indeed often move onto another negotiation as soon as one is completed. These individuals build a professional reputation by facilitating the conclusion of agreements (not their implementation over extended periods of time), and they are rarely still working with an Indigenous organisation by the time the consequences of implementation failure become apparent.

While O'Faircheallaigh here considers implementation, the same argument can be made for organizations that disengage from the negotiation process, leaving the community to fend for itself against a legally sophisticated and well-resourced MNE.

If the professional or NGO disengages from the community once negotiations or an agreement have been put in place, it is difficult for the indigenous community to express itself in non-legal languages as the space for expression no longer exists. (Dis)engaging with (from) the agreement requires a community to take a legal approach; confidentiality clauses, arbitration clauses and the like may impede protest or other avenues of expression. While the professional needs this discursive space to act, and he acts in good faith for the best interests of the community, he should consider *himself* to be part of the indigenous strategy and establish whether his very presence is a help or hindrance. To be or not to be, that should be the question.

Conclusion

The moderns, understanding, by the term law, merely a rule pre-
scribed to a moral being, that is to say intelligent, free and considered
in his relations to other beings, consequently confine the jurisdiction
of natural law to man, as the only animal endowed with reason. But,
defining this law, each after his own fashion, they have established it
on such metaphysical principles, that there are very few persons
among us capable of comprehending them, much less of discovering
them for themselves.

(Rousseau 2006b: 80)

Observations

Mining agreements may become the norm: mining agreements are mandated by
some countries and are becoming common practice in others, including
those without strong indigenous land rights. MNEs may begin using them
as standard practice to avoid the risk of future litigation. Their use by IFIs
will also be determinative of their popularity going forward.

Discourses around mining agreements have an embedded narrative of indigenity:
these agreements will be governed by, operate in and take on the characteristics of the international and national legal frameworks, including an
indigenous narrative of spiritual and temporal relationships to land. This
is, of course, a subject for further empirical study.

Agreements have a(n identity) politics: agreements conceive of the indigenous community and MNEs in ways that both limit and expand their
external political spaces (often through alterity). They also conceive of the
actors as unitary, limiting their internal political spaces.

*The politics of an agreement is not always desirable, giving rise to strategic im-
plications*: the politics of indigenity and corporate action is one of *passivity*.
Law is the active mechanism that regulates the parties' relationships. By
institutionalizing relationships, parties may find it difficult to follow alternative strategies to achieve their ends.

*The indigenous rights professional has a vested interest in deploying agreements,
perhaps to the detriment of the indigenous community*: given the tensions between
the *homme sauvage* and the language of law, the indigenous rights professional creates a space for himself *qua* professional to help (save? interfere
with?) the indigenous community and provide it with benefits. This can lead
to the indigenous community becoming dependent upon him.

Contrat *and* contract; *or,* Rousseau *and anti-legalism*

A close reading of the *Discours* allows us to emphasize the notion of law as
the enemy of natural man. It is highly specialized: 'very few persons ... are

capable of comprehending [it]' (Rousseau 2006b: 80). It is the first thing that social man sought and it is used to entrench power elites, 'eternally fix[ing] the law of property and inequality ... for the advantage of a few ambitious individuals' (Rousseau 2006b: 109). Although the indigenous rights professional positions himself as a buffer between the indigenous community and the depredations of modern society (i.e., the MNE), by supporting mining agreements he perpetuates this modern/indigenous opposition.

Law is not only the enemy of natural man but also one of the corrupting influences that induced his fall from the state of nature. Legally fortifying private property rights and deploying the law to manage individual or human behavior can corrupt the *homme sauvage*. Mining agreements must be reliant on the highly professional activist if the very notion of indigenity is not to be undermined. The indigenous rights professional, acting on a belief in the nobility of the *homme sauvage*, seeks to protect indigenous communities. Yet by supporting mining agreements as a tool of empowerment, he in fact risks harming those very communities.

The indigenous rights professional must always ask himself the titular question of this chapter: 'A qui l'homme sauvage?' He must think critically about using the narrative of the *homme sauvage*: how it corresponds to the indigenous community's actual situation, whether he is deploying it for the community or to serve his own ends and how it might harm the very people he seeks to help. He must also consider how it intersects with the discourses of law, and the inherent tension therein between natural and social. It is hoped that in doing so, he is required take a step back and think about his own role, asking the reflexive, essential meta-corollary: 'A qui le professionnel des droits indigènes?'

Notes

1 A version of this chapter focusing on the indigenous rights dimensions of mining agreements appears as Desai, D. (2012) 'Narrating indigenous rights, indigenous rights professionals, and agreements between mining corporations and indigenous communities: A qui l'homme sauvage?', in Topidi, K. and Fielder, L. (eds), *Transnational Legal Processes and Human Rights*. London & New York: Ashgate.

2 *ILO Convention 169*, June 27, 1989, 28 I.L.M. 1382, especially articles 13–15; *United Nations Declaration on the Rights of Indigenous Peoples*, September 13, 2007, adoption by General Assembly Resolution 61/295, especially the Preamble and articles 25–26.

3 The *Discourse* is found in undergraduate French literature syllabi as well as in political philosophy ones: the Universities of Oxford (at https://weblearn. ox.ac.uk/access/content/group/modlang/general/handbooks/11–12/Prelims/ French/Frenchprelimhb11–12.pdf), Houston (at http://gator.dt.uh.edu/~ hagen/hum3320.pdf) and Florida (www.leeannhunter.com/wp-content/ uploads/2010/07/LIT_2120.1464.pdf) are but three easily-accessible examples.

4 A significant body of literature critiques this tendency, including Stearman 1994; Conklin and Graham 1995; and Hames 2007.
5 Social and labor plans are governed by regulation 42 of MPRDA 2002 (GN R527 in GG 26275 of April 23, 2004). Environmental plans are governed by s. 39(3) MPRDA 2002.
6 Art. 26.9, Nunavut Land Claims Agreement (1993), at www.nucj.ca/library/bar_ads_mat/Nunavut_Land_Claims_Agreement.pdf.
7 The Raglan Agreement (1995) between Nunavimmiut and Falconbridge (Canada) for a nickel-mining project, 1, 2, at http://pubs.aina.ucalgary.ca/makivik/CI236.pdf; the Diavik Agreement (Canada, 2000) 1, 2, at www.mveirb.nt.ca/upload/project_document/1154722210_877.PDF; Argyle Diamond Mine Participation Agreement – Indigenous Land Use Agreement (Australia, 2004) 1, 2, at www.atns.net.au/objects/Agreements/Argyle%20ILUA.pdf.
8 The Raglan Agreement at 86.
9 See, for South Africa, the Deed of Settlement between the Richtersveldt Community and Alexkor, www.dpe.gov.za/home.asp?id=779, at 3; for the Philippines, the Mindex/Mangyan memorandum at 9; for Canada, the Raglan Agreement at 97–101 and the Diavik Agreement at 6; for Australia, the Argyle agreement at 27.
10 Indigenous communities in Myanmar had difficulty engaging with the oil company Total as there was little trust between the two parties: CDA Collaborative Learning Projects (2005: 6).
11 On the impact of legal relationships on violent and non-violent protests against mines in Papua New Guinea, *see* Filer (2008); Filer (1997: 102) (arguing that the subsequent institutionalized process of contest was 'moderate' and consumed other avenues of resistance). I do not argue that violence may be more effective or desirable as a means of resistance; I simply note the exclusionary aspects of legal formalism in resistance to mines.
12 See the Raglan Agreement at 115 and the Diavik Agreement at 6. See also Sosa and Keenan 2001: 19 for the effect confidentiality can have on inter-community knowledge transfers and solidarity.
13 See, for example, the controversy over the Siocon Council of Elders who signed a memorandum in the Philippines in the face of significant 'internal' opposition: Mines and Communities, *Pro-TVI Member of the Siocon Council of Elders Admits Misrepresentation and Pays Penalty to Legitimate Chieftain* (June 23, 2007), www.minesandcommunities.org/article.php?a=6073 and Siocon Subano Association Inc., Open Letter (February 20, 2005), www.dcmiphil.org/ssai_ngos_letter.pdf.

Chapter 11

Global legal transplants through the lens of community

Lessons for and from Chinese property law

Ting Xu[1]

Introduction

> Law may be more efficient if it is 'rationally planned and purposeful'. But it is perhaps more important that it be 'deeply rooted in' the 'everyday conditions of social interaction'. For only then can law act as 'the cement that gives moral meaning to social existence'.
>
> (Perry-Kessaris 2008 146 Quoting Cotterrell 1996)

Globalization is about increasing inter-connections without regard to national borders. Such inter-connections provoke borrowings, lessons and transplants in relation to all aspects of social life, including the 'text' of law. It is well established that the flow of transplants has often been from 'Western' to 'non-Western' countries – so much so that Western laws are often regarded as universal or neutral, and therefore easily received. It is also well established that this view ignores incongruities and conflicts between transplanted laws and indigenous social orders.

The effects of globalization of norms and practices are manifested in China's legal reforms, which are partly triggered by trends in international economic law. Such trends emphasize laws designed to privilege and promote the values and interests, actions and interactions that are characteristic of liberal economic societies. The making of Chinese property law is a particular example. It is modelled on laws from Japan and continental Europe, and, more recently, the characteristically American style of individualistic, market-oriented law that is exported by transnational business, multinational law firms and development projects of international organizations.

This chapter deploys the analytical 'lens of community' (see Cotterrell, this volume) to highlight both some of the effects of global legal transplants on Chinese law, and the possibility of an alternative approach to ownership in China, beyond the constraints of the binary left-right tug of war (cf. Cotterrell, 1995, 2002b, 2006b; Barzilai, 2003; Perry-Kessaris 2008, 2011c). First the debate over legal transplants in the context of globalization is reviewed and connected to debates regarding relationships between law and society. Next the lens of community is applied to legal transplants generally, and then specifically to the example of property law reforms in China. The chapter concludes with an endorsement of Roger Cotterrell's (2002b) observation that the contemporary 'global-local dynamic' is best approached via a commitment to 'seeking similarity' and 'appreciating difference'.

Global legal transplants

The term 'globalization' refers to 'an aggregate of multifaceted, uneven, often contradictory economic, political, social and cultural processes' (Snyder 1999b: 6). The processes are associated with the rise of new networks of political and economic actors such as multinational firms, nongovernmental organizations and social movements (Snyder 1999b: 7). The processes of globalization have also implied the emergence of a new global culture and, at the same time, the marginalization of many local cultures (Snyder 1999b: 7–8). And each of these developments has been associated with new, newly applied, or newly revised, laws – local, national, transnational and international.

The traditional comparative law approach of grouping the legal phenomena into various 'families' or 'systems' is unable to capture the complexity of law in the context of the processes of globalization, which witnesses a multiplicity of legal orders cutting across the boundaries of the nation-states.[2] The approach of 'legal pluralism',[3] which takes its lead from legal anthropologists, is better equipped to respond to globalization. Like other socio-legal approaches, legal pluralism understands law broadly to include not only formal, state-based legal institutions and processes, but also informal norms and regulatory processes generated within groups such as traditional communities, corporations and other forms of local or transnational networks. Inspired in part by Michel Foucault's work on power and governmentality, legal pluralism also pays attention to governance – that is, the distribution and regulation of power and public authority by formal and informal processes (Howell 2003: 2).[4] More recently, this attention has extended to the study of 'global legal pluralism' and 'global governance' (cf. Perez 2003; Snyder 2010), including 'the totality of sites embracing private, public and hybrid sources of norms' (Snyder 2010: 30, 32), and in particular contemporary shifts of power and decision-making from nation-states to regional, international or transnational sites of governance (Snyder 2010: 35).

When dealing with legal transplants, legal pluralists are especially conscious of what wider socio-legal scholarship has referred to as the 'gap problem' (Tamanaha 2001: 107). Adapting the typology developed by Brian Tamanaha (2001: 131) to the purposes of the present collection, we can say that this 'gap problem' encompasses three dimensions. The first gap is identified between 'law-in-the-books' (text) and 'law-in-action' (context); the second is the gap between the legal rules (text) and the social dimension including the actual practices of people and the morals and customs (context and subtext). Globalization adds a third dimension to this problem – a gap between global and the local norms and practices, which involves interactions between text, context, and subtext beyond the boundaries of the nation-states.

This pluralist interpretation of law has been criticized by Alan Watson, who coined the term 'legal transplants'.[5] Watson (1985: 118) sees law as a specialized realm of the lawyers, especially of lawmakers, who have control over the mechanisms of legal change. For him, social, economic and political factors can influence legal development only through the consciousness of lawyers. Therefore, he argues, legal borrowings and transplants can successfully be made across geographic, cultural and linguistic boundaries, without much knowledge of the political, social, economic context from/ to which the laws flow (Watson 1976: 79; 1985: 110). So, for Watson, there is no gap problem in relation to legal transplants. Watson's argument bears some similarities to Luhmann's (2004) and Teubner's autopoiesis (1993), but while Watson poses a fundamental disconnect between law and society, Luhmann and Teubner still see law as a deeply integrated aspect of society (Tamanaha 2001: 109).

Indeed, because Watson focuses on physical territories such as nation-states, his approach reveals little about interactions between global legal transplants and social life in local or transnational networks. Some, such as Pierre Legrand (1997, 2001), have gone so far as to argue that real legal transplants – that is, those that result in genuine harmonization – are impossible because the meaning of law in different cultures can never be the same.

Invoking the concept of community

Roger Cotterrell has integrated elements of these two seemingly incompatible approaches to law – legal pluralism on the one hand, and law as an autonomous sphere of lawyers on the other – in his law-and-community approach (1995 to present). Cotterrell (2001) agrees that it is important to study the professional communities of lawyers and law-makers at the centre of Watson's analyses. But he also proposes widening the frame to study law as an integral and constitutive part of – or, as economic sociologists have put it, 'embedded in' – wider social life (see Frerichs, this volume).

Cotterrell (1995; 2001: 79) suggests that the concept of community – as he terms it 'networks of relations of community' – offers a powerful unit of analysis in exploring 'the social determinants of success or failure in transfers of law'. Drawing on Weber's (1978: 23–6) four types of social action (traditional, affectual, instrumentally rational and value-rational), he proposes 'four pure types of community': instrumental community, traditional community, community of belief, and affective community as part of a conceptual framework for understanding legal transplants. Each of these communities can facilitate or deter the transplant of different kinds of law (Cotterrell 2001: 81).

Of the four communities, instrumental community is mainly driven by economic and utilitarian values and interests. Instrumental relations of community tend to seek laws – such as contract, corporate, and commercial law – that are ' "facilitative" of economic transactions' and directed towards the interests of 'a "minimisation of legal costs …" ' (Perry 2002: 28). Because these values and interests point in the same direction across jurisdictions, they have been described by law and economics specialist Antony Ogus (1999) as 'homogenous'. And because there are, 'by definition … no losers' from homogenous law products, it is expected that 'harmonisation … across national boundaries' will occur 'naturally' (Perry 2002: 28). So instrumental communities and their laws are relatively well suited to accommodating legal transplants. In this context, Watson's suggestion that legal transplants can be achieved easily without much knowledge of political, economic and social contexts seems partially plausible. However, the same cannot be said of the other three ideal types of community. For example, traditional communities are based on custom, which is deeply rooted in cultural and social tradition; affective communities are shaped by emotion or friendship, which is often significant when dealing with issues regarding marriage and divorce, succession, and elderly support; and communities of belief focus on aspects of social relationships defined by shared beliefs or commitment to certain value (ethical, aesthetic, religious, etc.) for their 'own sake' (Weber 1978: 25). Such communities are inherently less suited than instrumental communities to being the source of, or destination for, global legal transplants. Furthermore, and as we shall see below, a special kind of friction occurs when, in the course of attempting a legal transplant, the values, interests and laws that are central to instrumental relations of community are confused with, and privileged over, those that are central to non-instrumental communities (see Perry-Kessaris 2011c).

The application of the 'lens of community' brings human beings to the centre of the analytical frame. In relation to legal transplants, we become able to accommodate the roles played not only by elites, but also by lay people in legal reforms – in short, to consider legal transformation from below. Communities are not physical – they are 'the abstract types of bonds that inform social relationships; different kinds of links potentially creating a sense of identity, solidarity or co-operation between people' (Cotterrell 2001: 81). Indeed they are 'important sources and carriers of identities in legal and sociopolitical contexts' (Barzilai 2003: 24; cf. Etzioni

1991, 1993, 1995). In order to be effective, transplanted texts must be adapted to local contexts and must respond to, or trigger in retrospect, some form of internal demand for legal change (Nelken 2001b: 46–50).

Furthermore, because the lens of community is capable of contemplating social actions and interactions without reference to state boundaries, it offers an important opportunity to more accurately reveal interactions between globalization and localization beyond nation-states. This dimension is particularly relevant to the examination of Chinese property law, which is widely considered, like other domestic laws, to be determined by its own historical trajectory and local context. Yet Chinese property law is being increasingly influenced by legal transplants in the globalization of trade, investments, and services. Thus, it subjects itself to International Economic Law. Numerous international treatises and human rights regimes have tried to endow it with the values, interests, actions, and interactions that are characteristic of liberal economic societies. Chinese property law is expected to reform in order to secure foreign investments and to protect transnational transactions and intellectual property rights and so on. In the next section, the utility of the lens of community is demonstrated using the example of transplantation in Chinese property law reform.

Chinese property law and community

Throughout Chinese history instrumental community (delineated by the sphere of influence of central government) and non-instrumental communities (including self-governing organizations such as kinship-based and grassroots associations) have co-existed in a state of tension. They are also named as 'large' and 'small' community respectively in order to characterize the imbalance of power that exists between them.[6] Francis Fukuyama (1995: 29) has observed that 'strong community can emerge in the absence of a strong state'. In fact, examples from Chinese history suggest that strong non-instrumental community can emerge *because of a weak state*. For example, since the decline of the aristocracy in the Tang dynasty (AD 618–907), relations of community centred around common lineage appear to have been weaker in the North where state power was stronger, but strong in those parts of South China (such as the Pearl River Delta) where the state power was weaker. Within lineage-based communities, people experienced a sense of belonging based on shared values, interests and trust – the core components of Cotterrell's networks of relations of community. Lineage-based communities performed a number of economic and governance functions in rural areas such as managing land and raising funds for famine relief, social welfare and education. They also played important roles in dispute resolution within the lineage (Chen 2002: 65). Although lineage-based communities were exclusive, they also linked together to form larger communities (Siu 1989: 5). There were often interactions and tensions between lineages and the central government.

The co-existence of state (instrumental) and non-state (lineage-based) organizational units poses a question: How to govern society if not by law? (Durkheim 1984 [1893]). In China, the central government largely rules by providing good 'examples', which have moral force that can be imitated by ordinary members of society (Murphy 2006: 114). A Confucian way of rulership was characterized as 'being an inner sage so as to rule the outside world' (*neisheng waiwang*). The same pattern was followed under Mao (1949–1976) and has continued in post-Mao China (1978–present). Society is not so much governed by law from above, but through 'the three pillars of Chinese society', namely: 'discipline, education, and morality' (Bakken 1999: 86). In this respect, state law is not the most important mechanism to govern instrumental communities. It is even less important for non-instrumental communities, where local customs maintain social order and enforce moral values through concepts such as *guanxi* (the rule of relationships and networks) and *renqing* (affection). Nevertheless, legal reforms have been shaped mainly from the top down – created and used by elite instrumental communities of bureaucrats, politicians and legal professionals – for the purposes of revolutionary change and modernization.

The state and lineage-based communities also hold overlapping values, interests and, therefore, attitudes towards the nature, origins, and functions of law, in particular as relates to the perceptions of the division between public and private that took root in the Western, especially civil law, tradition. The nearest Chinese equivalent to the word 'private' is *si*, which could mean 'personal, individual, and independent' but could have other negative connotations such as 'secret, illegal, partial, small, and evil'. *Gong* is the equivalent in Chinese to 'public'. It could refer not only to 'the court, the state, and the emperor' but also to 'just, fair, common, collective'. The Chinese *locus classicus* of the distinction between 'public' and 'private' is found in the *Book of Poetry's* 'may it first rain on our public fields, and then upon our private', or in Mencius' 'and not till the public work is finished, may they presume to attend to their private affairs'. The moral ideal of Confucianism is 'great altruism without selfishness'. In these Confucian writings, *gong* is nearly equivalent to *guo*, the emperor's family and the throne, and with complex bureaucracy, while *si* is similar to *min*, the people.[7] Furthermore, the private (*si*) usually refers to kinship, not the individual (Liang 1986: 162–188). *Gong* is superior to *si*. Nevertheless, the boundaries between *gong* and *si* were vague in traditional China. As Elman (1990: 34) puts it, 'where gentry associations based on non-kinship ties were defined as "private" [*si*] ... social organizations based on descent were perceived as "public" [*gong*]'.

'Private'? 'ownership'?

There was a fragmentation of property-holding in land in late imperial China (1368–1911), which bears some relevance to an evolutionary and pragmatic common law model. For example, different people could claim 'ownership' over both the topsoil and the subsoil of the land. Land was alienable, subject to sale and purchase. Yet 'landlords' were not necessarily individuals; they were landowning 'corporations' embedded in complex lineages (Watson 1977). Many lineages held commonly owned lineage properties. In practice, half or more of the land in a village was tied up in indivisible lineage estates (Watson 1990: 241).

Before examining the development of property law in detail it is necessary to have a brief introduction to the transformation of Chinese law more generally. Our story begins with civil 'law' in Qing (1644–1911) and Republican China (1911–1949). The Great Qing Code was in the form of prohibitions and restrictions. There existed no distinction between 'civil' and 'criminal'. Rather a divide was drawn between 'minor things' (*xishi*) and 'serious matters' (*zhongqing*). The former included matters concerning *huhun* (household, marriage, family division and inheritance), *tiantu* (land and real estate), and *qianzhai* (money, contract and debt).[8] The notion of 'civil' (*minshi*, literally 'people's matters') was not available until the late Qing reform.

The opening in the 1980s of local Chinese archives to foreign scholars provided an opportunity for foreign and Chinese scholars alike to re-examine assumptions about civil law in Qing and Republican China.[9] For example, the contents of the Danshui-Xinzhu archive suggest that in fact 'civil cases formed a major part of the caseload of local courts' (Bernhardt and Huang 1994: 4). Yet these empirical findings seem to further complicate our understanding of civil 'law' and problematize the complex relationship between code and practice in the Qing and the Republic. Although civil matters did constitute much of the caseload in local courts, it was found that not all the case files included conclusive verdicts, namely, 'court verdicts' or 'court decisions' (*tangyu*) (Allee 1994: 124). This may suggest that many civil disputes were resolved by informal methods, and even if when they were dealt by the court, the judges had to combine 'three factors – written law, broad cultural norms, and local customs' when making their decisions (Allee 1994: 124). This may also suggest that to understand the civil 'law' in the Qing we must go beyond codified law to examine both litigation and the court's procedures, which were qualitatively different from those pertaining to penal cases.

The foundations of the Qing legal system began to be eroded through a series of voluntary and involuntary Western legal influences. For example, between 1843 and 1948 the concept of 'consular jurisdiction' (*lingshi caipanquan*) gave foreign citizens immunity from Qing courts.

Then when Japan defeated China in the war of 1894–1895 Chinese politicians and intellectuals came to believe that Japan's success was built on its adoption of the 'modern' legal and political institutions borrowed from the Continental West (Huang 2006: 145). Japan was a regarded as a model for China to emulate. Customs came to be regarded as backward and irrational, and the legal reforms in the late Qing dynasty (1840–1911) and Republican China (1911–1949) introduced many aspects of the German Civil Law system to China via Japan. It was during the late Qing and Republic periods that the concept of unitary and exclusive property rights eventually emerged in the Civil Codes formulated by the Chinese Nationalist Party (KMT) in 1929–1931.

Public and collective ownership

The Civil Code was abolished in 1949, and from then until 1978 the Chinese economy was increasingly centrally planned and property was increasingly publicly owned, whether by the state or collectively. The concept of ownership in China was overwhelmingly influenced by former Soviet jurisprudence: ownership was regarded as indivisible and absolute. Public and collective interests were superior to individual interests; acquisition and management of property was under an overarching administrative fiat (Potter 2003: 126–7). Although civil law-making in the post-1978 era returned to the German Civil Law framework, a clear boundary between public ownership and private ownership still existed in law, and a tri-ownership system including state ownership, collective ownership and private ownership has evolved and persisted.[10]

Collectivization (1956–1978) was intended to remove landlords and governance by gentry in rural China, to eliminate private ownership, and to create collective proprietorship by farmers. This was modelled on post-1917 Soviet collectivization but ignored the differences in natural conditions and governance between the countryside in China and in the USSR. Russian farmers traditionally worked in communes (the *mir* or *obshchina*) (Heinzen 2004: 11–46); whereas China had limited urbanization and a huge rural area, and farmers were governed by kinship especially in southeast China. The elimination of private ownership and gentry governance in rural China left an empty space to be filled by the central government. But geographical, social and economic variations made it impossible to develop and execute a comprehensive rural development plan. So collective ownership has never been more than a legal and political fiction.

Privatization?

Since Deng Xiaoping's economic reforms commenced in 1978, the trend in the transformation of the property regime has been towards de-collectivization. After almost three decades in which private property was abolished, 'a revival' of private property has been set in motion by market reform in three ownership sectors, conceptualized in the PRC as relatively distinct: through the processes of dismantling rural communes, the 'corporatization' of state-owned enterprises (SOEs), and the emergence of urban property markets based on the allocation of use rights to urban land by the central government to local governments (with or without payment of fees) and then by local governments to developers (with payment of fees). Along with these processes, the concept of private ownership has been gradually recognized by law. However, as will be seen, clear gaps remain between the concept of ownership as it appears in text and in (real life) context.

Absolute ownership has been fragmented into the 'contractual management rights' of collectively owned rural land, the 'enterprise management rights' of state-owned enterprises (SOEs), the 'land use rights' (LURs) of state-owned urban land and so on. De-collectivization has given rise to hybrid forms of property, so that it is now difficult to draw clear boundaries between the public and the private in property rights. What we are witnessing is a 'fragmentation of de facto ownership' in which rights of land are held by individuals, corporate bodies, local governments, the central government and its agencies and so on. Such 'fragmentation' has more in common with the indigenous pattern of landholding in the Qing and Republican China than with the notion of an absolute and indivisible right derived from the Civil Law tradition.

Focusing on rural land property rights, we can say that de-collectivization began in rural China in 1978. With the introduction of the household responsibility system, the 'private' was selectively granted to farmers, and farmers were given more autonomy. However, there are many limits to this revival of private property. For example, according to Article 39 of Property Law 2007, ownership refers to the rights to possess, use, benefit from and dispose of one's own property. But in terms of the collective ownership of rural land, controversies surround the appropriation and alienability of rural land. Land is the most important social security for farmers but collective ownership of rural land is an incomplete ownership, because farmers cannot dispose of rural land freely. Collective ownership over rural land is vulnerable to both compulsory acquisition by the state and illegal confiscation. Local governments and rent-seeking local officials become the de facto owners and farmers are excluded.

The ambiguity of property rights in China has been largely due to problems within its governance system, including an ignorance of the existence, and self-sufficiency, of non-instrumental communities. In terms of grassroots organizations and property management in rural China, Article 10 of the Land Administration Law (2004) and Article 60 of the Property Law (2007) provide that collectively owned land shall be managed and administered by the village collective economic organization (a term undefined in law) or the villagers' committee. But villagers' groups – farmers' self-governing organizations at the basic level of rural governance – do not hold much power. This situation has been shaped by the transformation of reorganizing rural China in the post-1978 era. In the early 1980s, when the communes were dismantled, the production teams at the lowest level of the communes diminished fastest. After the township replaced the commune, the administrative village took the place of the production brigade, and the villagers' group superseded the production team, the villagers' group was weak while power was diverted to the administrative village level and the township level (Ho 2001: 405). Farmers lacked the power of self-governance. This kind of governance has led collective ownership to a paradoxical situation: although the *de jure* owner of rural land is the collective, the de facto owners are multiple.

Under the Property Law (2007), land use rights (LURs) of collective rural land were put into the category of '*usufruct*' (*yongyi wuquan*), which refers to the right to use another's property. LURs of collective rural land include contractual management rights, LURs of rural residential plots, and LURs for construction purposes. Since ownership of agricultural collective land is not transferable, leaseable or mortgageable per se, alienability of rural land actually refers to the transfer of LURs of rural land between the state, legal persons and individuals. In terms of transferring contractual management rights, according to the 2002 Land Contracting Law,[11] contracts can be transferred but cannot be mortgaged. A more controversial question is whether or not residential plots and LURs for construction can be transferred or sold. According to the law, without approval from the government at the county level, farmers cannot assign cultivated land for residential purposes, and the LURs for residential purposes cannot be transferred.[12] In terms of selling LURs for both farming and residential uses, transactions directly with farmers are illegal and prohibited by a system of land use certificates. Developers must obtain land use certificates from land administrative bureaux at or above city or county level before proceeding with projects (Yeh 2005: 40). The use of agricultural land is unchangeable;[13] without approval from the people's government at or above county level, farmers cannot contribute LURs to joint enterprises or joint ventures as investments, or assign LURs to township enterprises.[14]

Somewhat ritualized debates continue over the direction of change in rural land ownership. Some favour nationalization of rural land in China, while others support privatization of rural land. The privatization proposal is a neoliberal project aiming to transform public property into private property, while the nationalization proposal is along the lines of the new left. The former regards free markets, individual liberty and private property rights protected by 'the rule of law' as the *sine qua non* for sustained economic growth. The latter cherishes 'new collectivism' and warns against the dangers of diminishing state-ownership and encroachments upon social equality. The new left stresses the role of the state. But as the following section explains, the lens of community reveals the possibility of a 'third way' (Giddens 1994, 1998) beyond the binary left–right tug of war.

Recollectivization?

The nationalization–privatization debate ignores the diversity of networks of community that exists in rural China, as everywhere else. As a result it also misses alternative sources of power – individual and communal initiatives at the grassroots level – that are not necessarily aligned with the power of elites that favour economic and legal reforms. Such grassroots initiatives always run into obstacles when they seek legal recognition, and so they often linger in the grey area between the 'legal' and 'illegal' or are suppressed altogether. They are also, consequently, rather weak.

Despite formal legal prohibitions, farmers have begun to pool resources and circulate land use rights since the early 1990s. One trend apparent in many places has been 'recollectivization'. For example, farmers at Xiaogang Village – the first village that distributed LURs to farmers – have now recollectivized their dispersed LURs for more efficient use and management of land. Farmers have transferred contractual use rights to one commercial company (not set up by farmers) which specializes in agricultural production and management in order to achieve intensive and cooperative farming and management of rural land by which farmers could gain more income. In the processes of recollectivization, different kinds of 'quasi-commons' are emerging (Xu 2010). Further local reforms of the rural LURs focus on allowing farmers to contribute rural land contractual management rights as shares to enterprises or joint ventures.[15] Despite the contradictory laws and regulations, on 1 July 2007 Chongqing allowed farmers to contribute LURs to joint enterprises or joint ventures as shares, provided that the use purpose of arable land is not changed. Yet these reforms are clearly against Articles 60 and 63 of the Land Administration Law (2004). The embedding/disembedding/reembedding processes (Perry-Kessaris 2011c) are identified in the farmers' re-collectivization movement that legal relations are re-embedded where they suit the specific needs of the farmers' economic motivations (instrumental community) and back up their communal arrangements based on shared values and trust (non-instrumental community). Neverthess, the re-embedding process in China has another layer of complexity – that is, contradictions between central legislation and local rules and regulations. But this will be a subject of a further paper.

A 'third way' approach to rural ownership might be to recognize the status of self-governed, voluntarily organized rural communities, and to allow them to manage their own resources for the communal benefit. Such a revival of tradition-based communities could generate a self-sustaining demand for legal change from the grassroots. It also appreciates 'difference' in socio-legal transformation.

Conclusion

An examination of Chinese property law reform reveals significant divergences over time between ownership as defined in law (text) and ownership as understood and practised in real, social, life (context). Indeed many questions about the nature of the property law itself remain unresolved – for example, whether ownership should be an economic institution or a social and political institution. Current property law defines ownership as an economic institution, because being regarded as a social institution is closely linked to the sensitive dichotomy of socialism versus capitalism. Property law subjects itself to, as Perry-Kessaris (2011c: 409) points out, 'the disembedding forces of economics'. The property law legislation prioritizes 'efficiency' and economic growth. Its major aim is to 'clarify' property rights and minimize the 'transaction costs' in order to attact foreign direct investment (FDI). As a result, Chinese property law has disembedded from wider social context.

Furthermore, the boundaries between public ownership and private ownership are blurred. The official vision, defined by political elites and backed by law, is of *unitary* and *exclusive* property rights with a clear distinction between the public and private. These conceptions and distinctions are manifested in the rhetoric of rulers in imperial China, Mao's revolutionary rhetoric and in Deng's reform programme, and they have long served the purposes of control and governance of the elite. But they bear little relation to the real world *fragmentation* of property rights, and are often resisted in social practice and popular thinking, leading to alienation and conflict. Furthermore, property law-making often lags behind social change. The long process of property law-making is a process to 'propertize' the fragmented rights that emerged in the process of economic reform; however, there are still residual categories that are difficult to define.

Reading law through a community lens contributes to the observation and interpretation of this 'gap problem'. State law does not mirror an undifferentiated society but only instrumental community. In order to have a comprehensive insight into legal transplants, diverse social orders in non-instrumental communities and their interactions with state law need to be considered. Where law develops endogenously with the participation and involvement of members of non-instrumental communities besides legal professionals, legal institutions tend to function effectively. By contrast, where legal reform is imposed and promoted by instrumental community without the support by non-instrumental communities, the transplanted law does not operate effectively. Perhaps instead of talking about legal transplants in general, we should examine different processes including borrowing, imposition (due to political change, wars, colonial rule or a condition of financial aid etc.), adaption and accommodation of law and reactions of different communities. Furthermore, reading law through a community lens allows us to extend communitarianism, which underscores the interplay between state domination and the politics of identities in a communal context (Barzilai 2003: 50).

Of course, the law-and-community approach does not have all the answers. Relationships between states and communities raises plenty of complex questions – to what extent might the connection between state and law really be loosened, ought local autonomy to be licensed and controlled by those at the centre, and so on. For example, Roberts (2005: 16) argues that this shift should not be exaggerated, and there is a need to distinguish law from negotiated communal orders. Furthermore, to what extent does community undermine law or vice versa? For example, 'modern' forms of property law came into being in China in the context of shrinking, disintegrating local communities, and of tension between law and non-instrumental communities.

Furthermore, in abandoning the traditional–modern dichotomy, we must acknowledge that the transplanted law is not necessarily rational simply because it is considered modern and, conversely, the community knowledge embraced by rural dwellers is not necessarily backward and irrational simply because it is traditional. Of course, this is not to suggest that community knowledge and customs are inherently superior, nor that it is unimportant to distinguish law from community knowledge and customs. Despite these cautions, there would be little difficulty in enlarging the community lens to socio-legal change, since what it argues is 'only that socio-economic developments within a society transform law, not that they themselves are always the origins of legal developments' (Nelken 2001b: 5).

Most of all, it is clear that the agenda of 'seeking similarity, while appreciating difference' (Cotterrell 2002b) that underlies the law and community perspective can only be honoured if, instead of simply emphasizing the importance of 'rule of law' to society, we explore the processes of embedding–disembedding–re-embedding that bind economic, social and legal phenomena (Perry-Kessaris 2011c). That is, we take a socio-legal approach.

Notes

1 Thanks to Amanda Perry-Kessaris for her deep and insightful comments.
2 For example, René David proposed three major legal families (Romanistic-German, common law and socialist) while Zweigert and Kötz proposed six (Romanistic, Germanic, Nordic, Anglo-American, Far East and religious).

3 See e.g., Pospisil 1971; Hooker 1975; Moore 1978; Griffiths 1986; Merry 1988; Teubner 1997d.
4 See, e.g, Foucualt 1980; Hunt and Wickham 1994.
5 See, e.g., Watson 1974, 1977, 1983, 1985, 2000.
6 These two concepts are coined by Professor Qin Hui of Tsinghua University. See Qin 2000. See also Tönnies 2001. Tönnies focuses on a contrast linked to a theory of modernization between small-scale, kinship and neighborhood-based 'communities' and large-scale competitive market 'societies'.
7 *Guo* does not deliver the same meanings as nation or state.
8 See Daqing lüli (The Great Qing Code), 332.11.
9 See e.g., Huang 1982; Zelin 1986; Yang 1988.
10 The Property Law (2007) provides equal protection for public property and private property for the first time since 1949, but there is much debate over whether private property should be given the same status as public property.
11 Promulgated by the Standing Committee of the NPC on 29 August 2002, implemented on 1 March 2003.
12 Article 62 of the LAL (2004): 'Reapplication for a house site by a villager in a rural area who has sold or rented out his/her house shall not be approved'.
13 The LAL (2004), Article 63.
14 The LAL (2004), Article 60.
15 The Land Contracting Law and the LAL conflict at this point. Article 42 of the Land Contracting Law allows farmers to contribute rural land contractual management rights as shares; according to article 60 of the LAL, farmers cannot contribute LURs to joint enterprises or joint ventures as investments, or assign LURs to township enterprises without approval from the government at or above county levels.

Chapter 12

Culture clash

Valuing heritage in investment disputes

Valentina Sara Vadi[1]

Introduction

The tension between cultural heritage and private property rights has come to the forefront of legal debate in recent times, not least because it has been adjudicated before different fora, including national courts, regional human rights courts and international courts and tribunals. This chapter focuses on the specific 'clash of cultures' between international investment law and international cultural law. An example may clarify the issues at stake. An indigenous tribe has performed spiritual pilgrimage throughout the Californian desert for centuries and deems certain areas to be sacred land. How can and ought the law respond to the claim of a foreign investor that the legal protection of such land might constitute an indirect expropriation of the property rights of the investor?

In the context of growing foreign direct investment (FDI) flows, the privileged regime created by international investment law within the boundaries of the host state has increasingly been called upon to define and coordinate tensions between investors' rights and cultural heritage protection. In disputes brought before investment treaty arbitral tribunals, foreign investors have argued that regulations designed to protect cultural heritage have the effect of violating the rights accorded to them under international investment law.

As adjudication plays a fundamental, bottom-up, role in the implementation of a given legal regime, this chapter analyses the adjudicative patterns of cultural disputes in order to test the effectiveness of international investment law and, indirectly, of international cultural law. Have arbitral tribunals paid any attention to cultural heritage and if so, how have they balanced investors' rights and the cultural policies of the host State? What values and interests are at the heart of arbitral thinking and practice?

One might expect the embryonic field of cultural heritage law to be overwhelmed by the long-established and sophisticated web of international investment treaties – not least given that arbitral tribunals have limited jurisdiction and so cannot adjudicate on the violation of other norms of international law outside the realm of international investment law. However, this chapter shows that arbitrators have increasingly taken cultural concerns into consideration in deciding cases brought before them, refusing to limit themselves to purely economic standards of valuation. Nonetheless, concerns remain that, unlike bodies with, for example, responsibilities for human rights, arbitral tribunals are ill-suited to the task of protecting cultural rights.

In order to address these key questions, this chapter defines the concept of cultural heritage disputes and illustrates the available dispute settlement mechanisms. Next, clashes of cultural and investment values and interests are illustrated with reference to the arbitral case law. Finally, the chapter critically assesses the relevance of alternative dispute resolution mechanisms in adjudicating cultural disputes.

Cultural heritage law

Cultural heritage may be defined as 'the totality of cultural objects, traditions, knowledge and skills that a given nation or community has inherited by way of learning processes from previous generations and which provides its sense of identity to be transmitted to subsequent generations' (Francioni 2008b: 6). Some authors have argued that an emerging legal principle, i.e. norm of customary law, requires states to protect cultural heritage (Dupuy 2007: 358–362; Francioni 2007). Although not all the existing legal instruments are formally binding on states, they may contribute to the formation of the *opinio juris ac necessitatis*.[2] However, the practice is far from uniform. While it may be held that *customary* international law is gradually emerging in the field, the question as to whether such a norm already exists in international law is far from settled.

As a matter of treaty law, the concept of cultural heritage was officially adopted by UNESCO in the World Heritage Convention of 1972.[3] Earlier treaties had occupied the narrower terrain of 'cultural property'. The shift from cultural property to cultural heritage was due to the conceptual necessity of bringing together natural sites and cultural properties of outstanding and universal value; the change, however, determined a further conceptual shift. Not only does the notion of cultural heritage include cultural and natural properties, but it also expresses a public interest to be protected irrespective of ownership (Francioni 2008b: 5).

The Convention has proven to be one of UNESCO's 'most successful and dynamic instrument', and it has played a fundamental role in the conservation of world heritage (Francioni and Lenzerini 2008: 409). Throughout the years, the Convention has progressively attained almost universal recognition by the international community,[4] aided in part by its 'soft character' – that is, 'the clear prevalence of rights and advantages over legal obligations that states parties derive from the Convention' (Francioni and Lenzerini 2008: 402). The Convention establishes a system for the identification, registration, protection and conservation of World Heritage sites – that is, cultural properties and natural sites of outstanding universal value.[5] This emphasis on conservation over preservation (Redgwell 2008: 380), ensures that the sites 'may support a variety of ... uses that are ecologically and culturally sustainable.'[6]

Although the Convention constitutes a significant step toward the international protection of cultural heritage, it does have drawbacks. A key concern is that only those sites expressly designated by Member States and selected by the World Heritage Committee are protected. The requirement for state designation means that whether a site is listed may depend on the political sensibility of governmental institutions to put a given area in for listing (Galis 2009). The requirement for Committee selection threatens to render the system elitist, because it draws artificial distinctions between local and universal value (Fowler 2001: 17). Article 12 of the Convention demands the protection of those cultural properties that, although not included in the List, objectively satisfy the criteria for being regarded as of outstanding and universal value, but the provision has been concretely ineffective. The Committee has rarely called upon states to respect their responsibilities to properties not inscribed in the List, and even then its action has been unproductive (Lenzerini 2008: 208).

The World Heritage Convention reinforces the traditional top-down regulation of culture, which is based on cultural sovereignty – that is, the freedom of any state to choose its cultural model, beyond its own political, economic and social system (Pineschi 2010). In so doing it imposes an apparently neutral agenda that is detached from the controversies related to cultural rights and their legal value (Morijn 2008). By contrast a rights-based approach suggests that 'cultural objects or places must be understood in the function and role they perform in a given society as indispensable tools for the exercise of certain fundamental rights and freedoms' (Francioni 2008b: 7). Accordingly, current cultural provisions in human rights treaties are interpreted so as to entail a negative obligation of all states to abstain from conduct aimed at the destruction, damage or alteration of cultural objects and spaces that are of importance for the practice and enactment of people's culture, as well as a positive obligation to take steps to protect cultural groups and communities against the risk of destruction or damage to cultural property that is indispensable for the cultural practices of those communities.

However, this traditional divide between the *cultural rights approach* and the *cultural policy approach* is being overcome by developments in law-making and practice.[7] With regard to law-making, the same UNESCO that seemed to prefer a cultural policy approach has started to make express reference to cultural rights.[8] In parallel, the jurisprudence of international tribunals has assimilated the serious violation of international cultural heritage law to grave violations of human rights (Benvenuti and Sapienza 2007).

The culture–investment tension

In a preliminary way, no two parties will agree that a dispute is essentially 'cultural' (Sands 2007). While the investor will contend that the dispute centres around a violation of investment treaty standard, the respondent state will attempt rebutting such arguments on the basis of cultural law. Indeed, merely describing a dispute as 'cultural' may have implications for a case. In any case, cultural heritage related claims are rarely, if ever, raised in isolation from other international legal arguments. Therefore, it seems more appropriate to talk about 'disputes that have a cultural component'.

International investment disputes with a cultural heritage component are generally characterized by the need to balance the legitimate interests of a state to adopt cultural policies on the one hand, and the legitimate interests of foreign investors to protect their property rights on the other. While environmental concerns have been somehow integrated in investment treaties, cultural considerations are generally not mentioned at all in bilateral investment treaties, or only in vaguely drafted clauses.[9]

It is not possible to identify a 'typical' sector in which disputes involving cultural elements tend to arise. Such disputes arise in relation to investments in *all sectors*, including mineral exploitation, tourism and the media (Peterson 2010). What is typical is the taxonomy of claims. Investors tend to claim that certain forms of regulation that have been introduced with reference to cultural considerations constitute an indirect expropriation or regulatory taking, and that compensation must be paid. If a direct expropriation has occurred, claims may concern the amount of compensation.

These disputes illustrate a potential culture clash between the neoliberalism embedded in contemporary international investment governance and the cultural policies of the host state. The very fact that the balancing process occurs in the context of investor–state arbitration could lead to the procedure being deemed biased in favour of the investors. Therefore, it is important to analyse recent arbitrations that have involved elements of cultural heritage, in order to verify whether these cases have adequately dealt with cultural values.

Valuing culture

A preliminary question is whether cultural properties should be valued and, therefore, regulated differently from other properties. Posner famously argued that cultural property is just another form of property and is not entitled to differential treatment: cultural considerations should not affect the regulation of goods (Posner 2006). Posner's analysis was driven by economic efficiency concerns. However, it is increasingly accepted among commentators that cultural goods have a double nature – both economic and cultural – and thus deserve special consideration by policy makers. Empirically, it is argued that it is inappropriate to attempt cost-benefit analyses, when deciding whether to protect, or not, cultural considerations over private property. The two interests are incommensurable, not least because the significance of cultural goods to society cannot be quantified in monetary terms (Ackermann and Heinzerling 2004). Normatively, it is argued that the World Heritage Convention goes further than creating a system for integrating cultural heritage considerations into policy making and adjudication. It also values 'good cultural governance' – that is, the exercise of state authority according to due process and the rule of law, including respect for human rights and fundamental freedoms (Du Plessis and Rautenbach 2010: 48–62). In this sense, cultural policies are not to be implemented solely at the discretion of the host state; but the Convention provides international standards that need to be complied with.

With regard to the interplay between the World Heritage Convention and norms of international economic law, there is no specific provision in the Convention that spells out how to balance the two sets of norms. Thus, there is no *a priori* hierarchical relation between international cultural law and international economic law, unless some components of international cultural law are deemed to belong to *jus cogens* (Vadi 2011). Thus, it will be up to the adjudicators to face the interplay between eventually conflicting norms.

Dispute settlement

Proposals to establish a World Heritage Court for the settlement of disputes with cultural elements have not been successful (Chechi 2009), and the World Heritage Convention makes no reference to dispute settlement. As one author points out, 'cultural heritage disputes are often multidimensional, involving not only complex legal issues, but also sensitive, not necessarily legal elements, of an emotional, ethical, historical, moral, political, religious, or spiritual nature' (Theurich 2009). So, it is likely that 'UNESCO members states wanted to give preference to diplomatic means of dispute settlement, as opposed to choosing a clear operational *modus vivendi*' (Von Schorlemer 2007: 78).

By contrast, international investment law is characterized by well-developed and sophisticated dispute settlement mechanisms. Investment treaty arbitration has become the most successful mechanism for settling investment-related disputes (Franck 2009). Investment treaties provide investors direct access to an international arbitral tribunal. This is a major novelty in international law, as customary international law does not provide for such a mechanism. The use of the arbitration model is aimed at depoliticizing disputes, avoiding potential national court bias and ensuring the advantages of confidentiality and effectiveness (Shihata 1986). Arbitral tribunals review state acts in the light of their investment treaties, and this review has been compared to a sort of administrative review. Authors postulate the existence of a global administrative space in which the strict dichotomy between domestic and international has largely broken down (Krisch and Kingsbury 2006). Under this theoretical framework, investor-state arbitration has been conceptualized as a form of global administrative law (Van Harten and Loughlin 2006: 121), which compels states to adopt principles of good governance.

In the absence of a dedicated mechanism for the settlement of cultural heritage disputes, such cases have tended to come before arbitral tribunals. Obviously, this does not mean that these are the only available *fora*, let alone the superior *fora* for this kind of dispute. Other *fora* are available such as national courts, human rights courts, regional economic courts and the traditional state-to-state *fora* such as the International Court of Justice or even inter-state arbitration. Some of these dispute settlement mechanisms may be more suitable than investor–state arbitration to address cultural concerns. Given space limits, this study shall only focus on the case law of arbitral tribunals.

Emergent jurisprudence

While international investment law has not developed any institutional machinery for the protection of cultural heritage through dispute settlement (after all, international investment law is not intended to protect cultural heritage), a recently emergent jurisprudential trend towards taking cultural heritage into consideration is clearly discernable (Vadi 2009a).

The case *Compañia del Desarrollo de Santa Elena S.A. v. Republic of Costa Rica*[10] involved an area of particular naturalistic beauty including over thirty kilometres of Pacific coastline, as well as numerous rivers, springs, forests and mountains. Costa Rica directly expropriated the property of American investors to enlarge the Guanacaste Conservation Area, which was subsequently added to the World Heritage List. An ICSID tribunal awarded compensation to the investors, based on the property's fair market value. In so doing, it restated that international law permits the host state to expropriate foreign-owned property for a public purpose and against prompt, adequate and effective compensation. However, it emphasized that 'the international source of the obligation' and, in particular, the nature of the public purpose for which the expropriation was made do 'not alter the legal character of the taking for which adequate compensation must be paid.'[11] Compensation was still due, however valuable the public purpose.[12]

The result was slightly different in *Southern Pacific Properties (Middle East) Limited v. Arab Republic of Egypt* (the *Pyramids* case),[13] which centred on the unearthing of artefacts of archaeological importance during the construction of a tourist village at the pyramids of Gyza. Notwithstanding the previous approval of the investment at stake, Egypt cancelled the contract and the area was added to the World Heritage List. The ICSID Tribunal noted that the inscription in the List had been requested *after* the cancellation of the project. Therefore, it found contractual liability and sustained the claimant's argument that the particular public purpose of the expropriation could not change the obligation to pay fair compensation. However, it reduced the amount of such compensation, stating that only the actual damage (*damnum emergens*) and not the loss of profit (*lucrum cessans*) could be compensated.[14] Indeed, it stated: 'sales in the areas registered with the World Heritage Committee under the UNESCO Convention would have been illegal under [...] international law [...]', therefore 'the allowance of *lucrum cessans* may only involve those profits which are legitimate'.[15]

Both cases show that states may lawfully regulate and/or expropriate private property in order to protect cultural heritage, especially if the cultural heritage in question has outstanding and universal value for mankind as a whole. The issue becomes whether the amount of compensation to be paid to the investor should be reduced in light of the public purpose of the measure. While in the *Santa Elena* case, the arbitral tribunal ultimately did not take cultural values into account, the tribunal in the *Pyramids* case adopted a more nuanced approach which has been further developed in the most recent cases.

The *Glamis Gold* case involved an area of the Californian desert deemed sacred by the Quechan tribe (Vadi 2011a). When Canadian company Glamis Gold planned to begin mining in the area, the tribe opposed the project. Initially, the Department of the Interior withdrew the Imperial Project from further mineral entry for twenty years to protect historic properties.[16] Yet in 2002 the relevant authorities granted permission for the project subject to the condition of that all open-pit mines must be backfilled at the project end to re-create the approximate contours of the land prior to mining.[17]

Glamis Gold filed an investor–state arbitration arguing that the failure of the relevant authorities to approve the project promptly, together with the requirement for backfilling of open-pit gold mines, had rendered the mining operation uneconomical, and constituting an indirect expropriation in violation of Article 1110 of NAFTA.[18] The claimant asserted that the federal and state actions constituted a 'continuum of facts' that deprived its property rights of their value.[19] Not only was backfilling uneconomical, it was also arbitrary because it could not rationally be related to the stated purpose of protecting cultural resources:[20] 'once you take the material out [of] the ground, if there are cultural resources on the surface, they are destroyed. Putting the dirt back in the pit actually does not protect those resources' and might even lead to the burial of more artefacts and greater environmental degradation.[21] The claimant argued that the California measures were in fact intended 'to stop the Imperial project from ever proceeding while seeking to avoid payment of compensation it knew to be required had it processed transparently and directly through eminent domain'.[22]

The arbitral tribunal found the claimant's argument to be without merit.[23] First, the tribunal found that the California backfilling measures 'did not cause a sufficient economic impact to the Imperial Project to effect an expropriation of the claimant's investment'.[24] Second, the tribunal deemed the measures to be rationally related to their stated purpose:[25] 'some cultural artefacts will indeed be disturbed, if not buried, in the process of excavating and backfilling',[26] but without such legislative measures, the landscape would be harmed by significant pits and waste piles in the near vicinity.[27] Remarkably, the arbitral tribunal also expressly referred to Article 12 of the World Heritage Convention, which requires states to protect their cultural heritage even if it is not listed in the World Heritage list. Cultural heritage experts have repeatedly stressed that this provision is often neglected (Lenzerini 2008; O'Keefe 1994).

In the *Parkerings* case,[28] Parkerings, a Norwegian enterprise, filed a claim before an ICSID Arbitral Tribunal, claiming that Lithuania breached the most favoured nation (MFN) clause as a result of allegedly preferential treatment granted to a Dutch competitor. Parkerings had stipulated an agreement with the Municipality of Vilnius (Lithuania) for the construction of parking facilities. Because of technical difficulties and the growing public opposition due to the cultural impact of the investor's project, the municipality terminated the agreement and subsequently signed another contract with a Dutch company for the completion of the project. The new project would not excavate under the Vilnius historic centre – the Old Town – which has been included in the UNESCO World Heritage List since 1994.

The Tribunal dismissed this claim, deeming that Parkerings and the Dutch competitor were not in 'like' circumstances. The project presented by the Norwegian investor was larger and included excavation works under the Cathedral. Notably, the Tribunal held that: 'The historical and archaeological preservation and environmental protection could be and in this case were a justification for the refusal of the [claimant's] project'.[29] The tribunal did not mention any hierarchy among different international law obligations, but it did balance the competing norms. Although the arbitral tribunal dismissed all the claims in their entirety, it required each party to bear its own costs. In so doing it admitted that: 'Even if no violation of the [bilateral investment treaty (BIT)] or international law occurred, the conduct of the city of Vilnius was far from being without criticism.'[30] While legislative changes may be seen as a normal business risk, this does not exempt states from a general duty of good faith and transparency.

Critical assessment

Having scrutinized a few relevant case studies, one may identify underlying processes that lead to consideration of cultural concerns within investor–state arbitration. In the *Glamis Gold* case, the arbitral tribunal adopted a high standard of review, according deference to the federal and state legislative measures. The arbitral tribunal recognized that: 'It is not the role of this Tribunal or any international tribunal, to supplant its own judgment of underlying factual material and support for that of qualified domestic agency' [31] and that 'governments must compromise between the interests of competing parties.'[32] The tribunal admitted that 'some cultural artefacts will indeed be disturbed, if not buried, in the process of excavating and backfilling',[33] but it held that 'the sole inquiry for the tribunal [...] is whether or not there was a manifest lack of reasons for the legislation'. The tribunal deemed that there was a reasonable connection between the harm and the proposed remedy and that the claimant was using too narrow a definition of artefacts: 'there are, in addition to pot shards, spirit circles, and the like, sight lines, teaching areas and view shields that must be protected and would be harmed by significant pits and waste piles in the near vicinity'.[34] In *Parkerings*, the arbitral tribunal did not consider the cultural heritage elements of the case as a justification of a breach of investment rules, but considered them as an integral part of the adjudicative process. The consideration of the cultural features determined the finding that the two projects were different and thus no discrimination was involved. A similar approach was taken in the Pyramids case, where *lucrum cessans* was not awarded because of the unlawfulness of the proposed economic activity under cultural heritage law.

From an investment law perspective, the integration of cultural concerns within international investment arbitration is a welcome move because it contributes to the harmonious development of international law. Nonetheless, from a cultural heritage law perspective, concerns remain (Vadi 2012). One may wonder whether these developments are enough to protect cultural heritage when foreign investments are at stake. At the end of the day, these cases represent an *ex post* remedy, that is, a remedy that is available only after an investor files an investor state claim. What if an investor did not file a claim, but cultural heritage concerns arose nonetheless? What about the other relevant stakeholders, that is, the affected communities, in the context of investment disputes? The institutional structure, the processes and the outcomes that arbitral tribunals sanction can be far from what would be required of a body to which significant human rights authority could be entrusted. Furthermore there is a risk of 'epistemological misappropriation', that is, declining cultural heritage and related cultural rights in a way that is discordant from the jurisprudential developments and interpretations of human rights courts and tribunals. For instance, excavation will take place in the 'Trail of dreams', the sacred route of the Quechan tribe. As the complainant sharply pointed out, backfilling does not avoid harm to the cultural artefacts. What weight is given to anthropological studies in legal discourse? What relevance, if any, do the narratives of indigenous peoples have in the context of investor–state arbitration? Much more study is needed to explore ways in which the two bodies of law can best be reconciled and rendered complementary to the greatest extent possible.

Negotiation

In addition to investor–state arbitration, negotiation and mediation represent alternative dispute resolution (ADR) methods (that is, alternative to judicial settlement) utilized to balance the different interests at stake. BITs typically include a three- to six-month 'cooling-off period' for consultation and negotiation before a claim may be brought.[35] The practical purpose of the 'cooling off period' is two-fold. On the one hand, the host State is granted the right to be informed about the dispute before it is submitted to arbitration, and 'an *opportunity* to redress the problem before the investor submits the dispute to arbitration'.[36] On the other hand, the cooling-off period[37] can facilitate settlement before positions become entrenched.[38] While the obligation to negotiate is an obligation of means, not of results,[39] failure to observe a treaty's cooling-off period results in a tribunal declining jurisdiction.

Negotiation and mediation allow parties to look behind their stated legal positions to their underlying interests. They may produce more successful outcomes than the adversarial 'winner takes all' approach (Fisher and Ury 1983). Scott Rau illustrates the point with the parable of two children, each of whom wants a single orange (Scott Rau 1999: 157). Three solutions are possible. The orange can be legalistically allocated to the child with 'greater rights' to it, as would a tribunal. Alternatively, one might simply divide the orange between the children. The third solution is to investigate the reasons why the children want the orange. After verifying that one wants the pulp of the orange for orange juice, and the other wants the orange skin for preparing a cake, the third solution proposes the appealing compromise of allocating the pulp to one child, while awarding the skin to the other. The satisfaction of both parties is maximized, as the settlement constitutes a more-than-zero-sum game.

ADR can be suited to disputes involving cultural heritage, due to the singular nature of cultural objects and the often sensitive – not necessarily legal – context and subtext of their ownership and management (Nafziger *et al.* 2010: 605). Negotiation has proven to be a strategic tool to enhance cultural heritage protection while allowing sustainable development. For instance, negotiation allowed the US government to preserve the Yellowstone National Park, which is a World Heritage site, while creatively swapping the investor's property rights (Vadi 2008). Similarly, in Germany, the local community was able to negotiate the relocation of a fortified ancient church as part of an investment deal. As a US investor acquired a concession over a coal mine close to a village, the conservation of the 750-year-old Emmaus Church was in danger. After negotiation, the American investor agreed to relocate the church in a town nearby (Vadi 2008). Although the case did not involve a cultural heritage site of universal value, it is worth mentioning because it was a win–win situation: the local inhabitants saved their church transplanting it in a new environment; and the foreign investor had the chance to exploit his investment, albeit ultimately paying the transplantation costs.[40]

Mediation may also play a useful role in this context. Where the degree of animosity between the parties is so great that direct negotiations are unlikely to lead to a dispute settlement, the intervention of a third party to reconcile the parties may be very practical (Collier and Lowe 2000). Mediation involves the good offices of a neutral third party, which facilitates communication between the discussants. Like negotiation, mediation is guided by the goal of finding a win–win situation for all parties through a creative process that focuses on the interests of the parties rather than on their positions, and searches for creative alternatives to solve the dispute (Knötzl and Zach 2007). As the mediator does not have the authority to make a binding decision and does not follow a fixed procedure, she may further flexible and dynamic dialogue. Furthermore, mediation might involve other stakeholders' participation (Crocker *et al.* 1999).

Successful negotiations and mediations may have a positive impact on subsequent cases also, providing a useful paradigm and creating confidence that conflicts may generate positive outcomes (Depoorter 2010). Time is another intrinsic advantage of these ADR methods, as these instruments usually achieve results in a short time frame. Importantly, these methods are not required to deal with the past: they ask the parties to look at their future and reshape their duties and responsibilities towards each other. Foreign investors thus participate in the decision-making process that will ultimately affect them, becoming aware of the local population interests. In these proceedings all the different interests concerned are disclosed and discussed. Experience shows that agreements entered into through a voluntary process stand out for their durability. The underlying reason is that the parties identify strongly with the result they perceive as fair.

However, the suitability of ADR methods should not be overstated. For example, they may not be effective where the contracting parties do not have equal or similar bargaining power. So they may not be suited to disputes involving developing and least developed countries, which may be relatively captivated by foreign investors. This is particularly the case when the cultural heritage in question is associated with indigenous peoples and national minorities, for these have often been disregarded in the race to attract foreign investment.

Conclusion

Economic globalization 'has in many ways decentralized decisions as to where the proper balance between public and private interests lies' (Perry-Kessaris 2010: 1–2). The World Heritage Convention does not include a dispute settlement clause, so cultural heritage related investment disputes have gravitated towards a number of national, regional and international courts and tribunals, including investment treaty arbitral tribunals. So key stages of the balancing act between (public) cultural heritage and (private) investors' rights have been shifted to ad hoc arbitration tribunals established under the auspices international investment law, and the investor-centric values and interests that underpin it. The above snapshot of rhetoric and argumentative patterns emerging in these disputes suggests that the magnetism of arbitral tribunals offers mixed blessings (Vadi 2012).

On the one hand, arbitral tribunals constituted under BITs have become nodes of global governance. The resulting global administrative review of substantive domestic regulations can improve good cultural governance and the transparent pursuit of legitimate cultural policies. And those who fear the fragmentation of international law will be reassured that arbitrators in such cases often support a unitarian vision of international law by referring to international cultural law (Vadi 2009a).

On the other hand, from a cultural heritage perspective, concerns have arisen that investment arbitration tribunals come with an inbuilt institutional bias and that arbitral awards may limit the cultural sovereignty of the host state. In the end, arbitral tribunals have limited jurisdiction and cannot adjudicate on the eventual violation of cultural heritage norms. The mechanism is mostly triggered by foreign investors; the affected communities are represented by the host state, but have no procedural rights in the context of the proceedings. ADR mechanisms could enrich the discussion, if they were shaped so as to ensure the participation of the relevant stakeholders, bringing the cultural values of the affected communities to the table. More likely, however, is the risk that cultural considerations will be diluted in the context of highly differentiated bargaining power (Vadi 2012). Certainly there is no doubt that, in this field of limited text and unequal context, the delicate and urgent subtext of cultural heritage remains dangerously exposed.

Notes

1 Marie Curie Postdoctoral Fellow (Maastricht University). I wish to thank Judy Carter and Amanda Perry-Kessaris for helpful comments on an earlier draft. The usual disclaimer applies.
2 A custom is made up by two elements: a consistent practice (*usus* or *diuturnitas*) and the understanding that such a practice reflects existing international law (*opinio juris*) or it is made compulsory by impelling social, economic or political needs (*opinio necessitatis*).
3 UNESCO Convention concerning the Protection of World Cultural and Natural Heritage, 15511 U.N.T.S. 1037, 151.
4 At the time of writing, the states party to the WHC are 188. Available at http://whc.unesco.org/en/statesparties/ (accessed 10 October 2011).
5 WHC, Article 13.
6 Operational Guidelines for the Implementation of the World Heritage Convention, WHC 05/2, 2 February 2005, Para. 119. Available at http://whc.unesco.org/archive/opguide05-en.pdf (accessed 17 October 2011).
7 The two approaches can partially overlap, as state obligations under human rights law can, but do not necessarily coincide with the content of the cultural policy approach. See *General Comment No. 21*, § 48.
8 See, for instance, Universal Declaration on Cultural Diversity, Article 5.
9 In a previous study, I scrutinized the question as to whether the same 'institutional bias' is present in investor–state arbitration and whether and how adjudicators have an important role to play in adjudicating these disputes; due to the limited number of awards, it was not possible to reach definitive answers and I concluded that more studies on the sociological features of the arbitral community are needed (Vadi 2011b).
10 *Compañia del Desarrollo de Santa Elena S.A. v Republic of Costa Rica*, Award of 17 February 2000, ICSID Case NoARB/96/1. Available at www.worldbank.org/icsid/cases/santaelena-award.pdf (accessed 23 April 2011).
11 *Compañia del Desarrollo de Santa Elena*, § 71.
12 This award is often criticized as supporting the 'sole effect doctrine' according to which the existence of an indirect expropriation is determined by impacts on the economic value of an investment. But such criticism is irrelevant because this award related to direct, not indirect, expropriation (Stern 2008).
13 *Southern Pacific Properties (Middle East) Limited v Arab Republic of Egypt*, ICSID Case No. ARB/84/3, Award on the Merits, 20 May 1992, reprinted in 8 ICSID Rev-FILJ (1993) p. 328.
14 *Southern Pacific Properties*, § 157.
15 Ibid., §190.
16 *Glamis Gold Ldt v. United States of America* Award, 8 June 2009, available at www.state.gov/s/l/c10986.htm, last visited 17 October 2011, § 152.
17 *Glamis Gold v. US* § 183.
18 The North American Free Trade Agreement (NAFTA) was entered into by the United States, Canada and Mexico to establish a regional trade area for the free movement of goods and services among the three nations. Signed by the leaders of all three countries in December of 1992, it took effect on 1 January 1994. I.L.M. 32 I.L.M.289 (Parts 1–3) and 32 I.L.M. 612 (Parts 4–8).

19 *Glamis Gold v. US* § 358.
20 Ibid., § 321.
21 Ibid., § 687.
22 Ibid., § 703.
23 Ibid., § 360.
24 Ibid., § 536.
25 Ibid., § 803.
26 Ibid., § 805.
27 Ibid.
28 *Parkerings-Compagniet AS v. Republic of Lithuania*, ICSID Case No. ARB/05/08, Award of 11 September 2007, available at icsid.worldbank.org/ICSID/Index. jsp.
29 Ibid., § 392.
30 Ibid., § 464.
31 *Glamis Gold* Award, § 779.
32 Ibid., § 803.
33 Ibid., § 805.
34 Ibid., § 805.
35 See, for instance, Hong Kong Australia BIT, Article 10. See, US-Ecuador BIT, Article VI. The period runs from the date in which the dispute arose or was formally notified by the investor to the host state.
36 *Burlington Resources Inc. v. Republic of Ecuador* (ICSID Case No. ARB/08/5), Decision on Jurisdiction of 2 June 2010 para. 315.
37 *Murphy Exploration and Production Company International v Republic of Ecuador*, ICSID Case No. ARB/08/4 – award on jurisdiction, December 15, 2010. Available at http://icsid.worldbank.org/ICSID/FrontServlet?requestType=Case sRH&actionVal=showDoc&docId=DC1811_En&caseId=C267, at § 151.
38 Ibid., at § 154.
39 Ibid., § 135.
40 'A Holy Journey', Spiegel Online, 24 October 2007. Available atwww.spiegel. de/international/germany/0,1518,513286,00.html (accessed on 17 October 2011).

Chapter 13

'You are on my property'

Economic, legal and moral objections to regulation from a banker's perspective

Ioannis Glinavos

Introduction

High payments, usually in the form of end-of-year bonuses, have created an unprecedented gulf between the average earnings of employees and the remuneration of top-tier executives. For example, while the Chief Executive Officer (CEO) of General Motors took home roughly 66 times the earnings of his average employee in 1968, the CEO of Wal-Mart earns today 900 times as much (Judt 2010: 14). This bonus culture has been identified as a contributing factor in the financial crisis. It is said to have distorted the incentives of those working in the financial sector by rewarding short-term success without penalising failure. Ominously, it appears to have survived the economic and political turmoil of the intervening years: the bonus culture is still with us.

This chapter explores the assertion that the compensation of those who work in the financial sector is a matter for self-regulation, and the resulting tolerance for the 'bonus culture'. Put another way, it confronts the socio-economic context and moral subtext of an absence of legal text. It argues that any effort to re-envisage post-financial-crisis compensation structures, and financial regulation more generally, must take a socio-legal approach. That is, we must re-establish connections between text, context and subtext if we are to achieve suitably nuanced understanding of both the behaviour of markets, and their proper regulation.

The chapter begins with recent legislative initiatives, taking as its central example the European Union Committee of European Banking Supervisors (CEBS) Guidelines of December 2010, and the negative reactions of the industry to them. It is suggested that at the heart of these objections is a distinctive normative approach to private property rights and economic efficiency. Extensive reference is made to contemporary commentary by practitioners and journalists in order to demonstrate the immediate real-world significance of these debates over text, context and subtext.

Struggling towards text

A wide range of institutions informing the actions of regulators, including the European Union, the G-20 and the Committee of European Banking Supervisors, are agreed that 'excessive and imprudent risk-taking in the banking sector' are to blame for 'the failure of individual financial institutions and systemic problems ... globally'. They also agree that 'inappropriate remuneration structures of some financial institutions have been a contributory factor' in that they 'give incentives to take risks that exceed the general level of risk tolerated by the institution' and thereby 'undermine sound and effective risk management and exacerbate excessive risk-taking behaviour' (Recital 1, Capital Requirements Directive-CRD-III).

The colossal mismatch between performance and rewards in the financial services industry is well illustrated by the 2007 sale by Goldman Sachs to its clients of a product known as Abacus. This collateralised debt obligation (CDO) was specifically built to fail so that its creator, investment firm Paulson and Co., could collect on a related insurance policy. Goldman knew, but did not disclose to its clients, that the product had been designed to be 'shorted' in this way and was duly charged with fraud by the US Securities and Exchange Commission (SEC) in 2010. The firm settled for a $300 million fine and $250 million restitution payment to its clients (SEC 2010a, 2010b). The following year, Goldman set aside $15.3bn for its January bonus pool, and declared itself to be exercising 'restraint' (Treanor 2011).

One body that has been charged by the European Union (under the legal framework established by the Capital Requirements Directives) with offering regulatory responses to controlling compensation structures in the financial sector is the Committee of European Banking Supervisors (CEBS).[1] Its Guidelines on Remuneration Policies and Practices were issued in December 2010 (CEBS 2010). What follows is a short summary of this initiative that will allow us to put the industry's responses and attitudes in context.

The Guidelines consider as 'remuneration' all forms of payments or benefits made directly or indirectly by institutions in exchange for professional services rendered by their staff. The Capital Requirements Directive (2006/48/EC and 2006/49/EC) as amended in 2010 (by 2010/76/EU) seeks to link bonus payments to longer-term firm performance by establishing that at least 40 to 60 per cent of remuneration should be deferred. The criteria used to determine remuneration include a requirement that bonus payments should be delayed for three to five years and that at least 50 per cent of remuneration should be paid in shares rather than cash. Firms should not be able to evade these restrictions by claiming particular special circumstances. The regulator's aim is that institutions should not be able to create special group structures or offshore entities in order to circumvent the application of the remuneration policies to staff to which the remuneration principles should otherwise apply.

The aims of legislative actions in this area are well illustrated in the Recitals to the Directives. On the basis of Recital 15 of the Capital Requirements Directive (2010/76/EU) firms are obliged to maintain remuneration policies that are consistent with sound and effective risk management and, in order to ensure fast and effective enforcement, the Directive gives national authorities the power to impose financial penalties for breaches of its requirements. It is hoped that those measures and penalties will be effective, proportionate and most of all dissuasive. As Recital 20 recognises, since poorly designed remuneration policies and incentive schemes are capable of increasing the risks to which credit institutions and investment firms are exposed to an unacceptable extent, prompt remedial action and, if necessary, appropriate corrective measures should be taken by firms. Consequently, national authorities must have the power to impose qualitative or quantitative measures on the relevant entities that are designed to address problems that are identified in relation to remuneration policies.

What, however, are quantitative and qualitative measures? Broadly, qualitative measures available to the national regulators include requiring the firms to reduce the risk inherent in their activities, products or systems. Firms can achieve this by adjusting their structures of remuneration, or freezing the variable parts of remuneration to the extent that they are found to be inconsistent with effective risk management. Quantitative measures may include a requirement that firms hold additional own funds as a capital cushion against possible losses, including the possibility of regulator intervention where the awarding of bonuses is detrimental to the maintenance of a sound capital base. The idea is that requiring firms to hold more cash for security reduces the pool of funds they can invest and thus decreases the firm's ability to use its funds profitably. In order to avoid having to do this, it is hoped firms will structure compensation packages that promote sensible risk-taking, rather than develop avoidance techniques. It is worth remembering at this point that the whole derivatives market was created as an attempt to evade capital adequacy requirements introduced by the Basel I accord in 1988. In fact, if the capital base of an institution is, or risks being, unsound, the supervisor can require the institution to reduce (or apply a cap to) the bonus pool or require the institution not to pay out the overall pool of variable remuneration determined in the year where capital adequacy is affected (and potentially for subsequent years) until the capital adequacy situation improves. As one would expect, Recital 12 provides that in entities that benefit from exceptional government intervention, priority should be given to building up their capital base and providing for recovery of taxpayer assistance.

Throughout, the Guidelines reveal that EU institutions regard markets as having lost a sense of social context and moral subtext. For example, the Guidelines even suggest that remuneration should be aligned with the financial sector's role as the mechanism through which financial resources are efficiently allocated in the economy, and that performance-based components of remuneration should be directed towards enhancing fairness within remuneration structures. The fact that these statements are considered necessary shows the degree to which EU institutions fear that markets have lost a sense of their role in the greater social structure. This is a theme to which we will return to later in this chapter.

The CEBS Guidelines may strike the reader as timid, given the strength of feeling about payments of bonuses in times of severe hardship. It is difficult to read the Guidelines without concluding that they represent a very complicated way to convey a very simple concept: That managers of firms ought not to pay themselves lavishly when their firm is doing badly. That this simple truth needs to be dressed in law in order to be digested by the financial industry shows starkly two things. First, managers are disconnected from their legal duties to promote the success of the company (rather than feathering their own nests), and from the requirement to take into account interests of stakeholders.[2] Second, shareholders have abandoned any pretence of meaningful involvement in the firms they own, including involvement in decisions over remuneration. This second observation is interesting considering the UK government's proposed solution to the problem of excessive bonuses: to give shareholders more power. The government, despite a flurry of rhetoric in the beginning of 2012 (Parker 2012), has failed to offer a convincing explanation as to why those very shareholders who failed to act in the past on their existing powers, will be keen to act if given additional ones.

Mild as they are, the Guidelines have been rejected as excessive by the industry. Even industry representatives who participated in the consultation process were not wildly enthusiastic about the resulting recommendations. This is an issue of importance. How can the industry consider any attempt to temper its excesses unacceptable? How can Goldman Sachs, as discussed earlier, consider a bonus pool of $15.3bn a sign of restraint? Why does the financial industry pay out bonuses in the midst of the worst crisis since the Great Depression? The following section attempts to shed some light on these issues by presenting the main arguments behind the industry's objections to regulatory reform.

...despite the subtext?

Many objections to regulation centre on the contention that inhibiting financial innovation jeopardises future growth. For example, the European Private Equity and Venture Capital Association noted that under the circumstances of the current financial crisis, capital gains incentives are necessary to encourage long-term risk-taking in fledgling companies that stimulate the economy. Regulation of compensation is seen as a danger-ous constraint and, indeed, unnecessary when the private equity and hedge fund industry is, in its own estimation, without equal in guarantee-ing alignment of remuneration to performance (EVCA 2010). In fact, as Wolfgang Munchau (2009) explains so accessibly, most of the 'innova-tions' of which the financial section is so proud were devised to evade the Basel capital adequacy rules, and were not in fact an organic process of evolution towards financial products that offer better value to customers and investors.

Far more difficult to excavate and dislodge are those anti-regulation arguments that are founded in deeply rooted liberal economic subtext. A common subtext is provided by the normative assumptions that the market is fundamentally better than the state, and that inequalities in compensation, and consequently wealth, are justified.

Market before state

Friedrich von Hayek (1944) argued that economic planning is fundament-ally contrary to the rule of law because it requires that state actors have ad hoc decision-making power. If the state wishes to abide by the rule of law it should confine itself to establishing general rules, leaving individuals free to determine their actions in anything that depends on the circum-stances of time and place (Hayek, 1944: 80). Industry's vehement dislike of regulatory intervention is not only based on assumptions about the value of innovation to future economic performance, but also on past ex-perience of what it regards as excessive, poorly targeted regulation. History, we are told, is brimming with examples of state failure and cata-strophic regulatory assaults that are imprecise and catch unintended targets. The fault with intervention therefore is not that it is not needed, but that it is directed at the wrong parties. For example, the European Fund Asset Management Association welcomed the inclusion of principles on remuneration in the Guidelines, but objected to the suggestion that their remuneration structures should be primarily directed towards the promotion of effective risk taking. To do so would, they argued, go against the obligation of asset managers to manage portfolios in accordance with detailed rules agreed with their clients (EFAMA 2010).

In the same vein, commercial banks claim that they are prudent and point the finger at hedge funds as being responsible for share price fluctu-ations. Investment banks and hedge funds argue that they are only facili-tating the operations of their clients, so they ought not to be regulated. Giant consolidated financial institutions, such as insurance firm AIG, claim that their integrated structures promote efficiencies. Everyone claims that the state can only intervene where negative externalities are clearly identified, and where instances of market failure are acute, not least because regulators do not comprehend the market and are likely to make matters worse.

What does the past teach us about regulation? According to the industry, the lesson is that no matter how the market deals with things, it is still better than involving the state. The nationalisation of Northern Rock and the effective nationalisation of the Royal Bank of Scotland in 2008 in the UK prompted claims that the government of Prime Minister Gordon Brown had developed an appetite for nationalisation. The government retorted that it had no such intentions, as it would not be able to find the expertise to run the firms it was bailing out. In so doing the government implied a wider objection to financial regulation: complexity.[3] As one journalist has observed, the financial crisis was nurtured by a toxic combination of complacency – our willingness to depend on 'all knowing financial experts ... to run our system expertly' and ineptitude – the experts depended on other experts. 'Until, finally, the last expert down the line turned out to be just another greater fool, and the system crashed' (Anderson 2009).

Admitting complexity, however, does not solve our key problem as to what to do about it. If the experts are outwitted by the complexity then what hope is there for regulators? Is it better to leave these things to the experts, despite the fact that self- or light-touch regulation seems to have failed? Does one regulate before fully understanding or does one let the market 'innovate' and then mop up the consequences? These are the kinds of questions that prompted the FSA to oscillate between principles-based regulation, to law-backed enforcement, and back to principles-based regulation. Wondering, however, when to legislate as presented above is a false dilemma, as the key issue of the necessity of regulation lays still unresolved for policy makers. We do know, however, why financialized capitalism is unstable and how it can be brought under control.[4] The work of institutional economists like Douglass North (1990) and Oliver Williamson (2000) shows how misguided this view that the market always knows best is, and offers a framework based on understanding the interactions between economic institutions that explains how state action and a foundation of law are complementary to a successful market.[5]

Property rights and the rule of law

The bonus culture is not, contrary to so much commentary on the matter, the unexpected by-product of some new, distinctive version of capitalism. A commitment to a right to wealth – no matter how extreme – is central to capitalism, and it is realised through legal concepts such as private property rights. So bonus schemes are not aberrations, but an inevitable consequence of the philosophical bases of laissez-faire capitalism. Unwavering support for wealth accumulation was perfectly illustrated by David Willetts, now UK Minister for Universities and Science, when he stated in 2004 that:

> if you really want to experience a vicious Hobbesian war of all against all, then look to a non-market economy where resources are wasted, where power and influence are all that matters, and where a contract cannot be trusted. What a contrast with ... the scope for personal fulfilment ... of a modern market economy.
>
> (Cited in O'Keeffe 2004: 18)

So a further touchstone for arguments that compensation structures ought to be determined by private, contractual negotiation, free from the constraints of state regulation, is that private property rights are unassailable, and therefore, redistribution of wealth is a violation of personal freedom. That individuals are morally entitled to such wealth as they are given, or create, has underpinned mainstream economic theory since the days of Adam Smith's *The Wealth of Nations* (1776). This idea of justly deserved property is solidified – given legal (textual, analytical) and moral (subtextual, normative) weight – in the form of private property rights. The point of this section is not to question the overall capitalist settlement that accepts some inequalities of wealth. It is rather to challenge the legal and philosophical underpinnings of *extreme* inequalities of wealth and the *extreme* rewards that characterise the bonus culture. For before Smith and Hayek there was the ancient Aristotelian notion of a good society, defined mostly as a society in which moderation is a key moral virtue – one starkly absent today.

To the extent that they do legislate, mainstream economic theory argues, states must ensure the predictability, and strict application, of 'the rules of the game'. So, for Hayek (1960) individual entitlements are to be protected from all kinds of interference, including from the state, regardless of any substantive injustice caused by gross inequalities of those entitlements. This rationale is consistent with the contention of mainstream economists that factors of production, including labour, receive their true worth – what they actually contribute to production – so any distribution of wealth generated by markets is inherently just (Glinavos 2010: 20).

So, it would seem that to require firms to change their compensation structures is a violation of Hayek's rule of law; and to query the resulting distribution of wealth is a violation of mainstream economics. This is the mindset of many modern capitalists, such as those quoted above, who tend to assume (however subconsciously) that history is simply a process of removing impediments to the operation of markets, by which man's natural tendencies are released (Glinavos 2010: 146–7). To paraphrase

Francis Fukuyama (1992) then, history comes to an end when all market impediments are lifted. It is almost inconceivable, therefore, for capitalists to envisage regulation in anything other than negative terms. Indeed for the more liberal of mainstream economists, the failure of financial capitalism that we are currently experiencing is due to politically inspired impediments to market operations imposed by the state (Glinavos 2010: 147). The claim is that the government either made firms behave in ways that were risky (for example by encouraging them to offer loans to risky borrowers in order to increase home-ownership) and/or failed to stop them from making unwise investments when credit was becoming over-extended (Davies 2010). The idea that regulation necessarily impairs markets is a constant obstacle to reforms such as those recommended in the CEBS Guidelines.

Other critics reject both the economic determinism and economic isolationism inherent in the work of Hayek and Smith. For example, Karl Polanyi (1944) argued that the dynamics of history are produced not so much by certain natural human tendencies, but by the pressures exerted by prevailing property relations. This view remains unorthodox in part due to the economist's traditional refusal to address differences between theoretical models and empirical evidence (Krugman 2008: 182) – not least the fact that an economic man, especially the economic man of finance, is nearly always presented in theory as rational and (personally and generally) wealth maximising, despite his empirical irrationality and destruction of (general) wealth (Roubini and Mihm 2011: 54).

A key step towards escaping from this neoclassical logic is the realisation that property rights are not independent or natural phenomena, but rather legal constructs, preceded by political interventions that allocate rights. Property rights are nothing more than social relations of constraint (Cohen 1994: 16), and by extension money is nothing more than a legal fiction or construct. Markets are, to use Chang's (2002) phrase, premised upon 'rights-obligation structures' that are politically constituted. 'The market', and its rationality, is not apolitical or 'purely economic'. Karl Polanyi famously rebelled against the 'fictitious commodities' of capitalism, observing that:

> Labour is only another name for a human activity which goes with life itself, which in its turn is not produced for sale but for entirely different reasons, nor can that activity be detached from the rest of life, be stored or mobilized; land is only another name for nature, which is not produced by man; actual money, finally, is merely a token of purchasing power which, as a rule, is not produced at all, but comes into being through the mechanism of banking or state finance. None of them is produced for sale.
>
> (Polanyi 1944: 76)

In sum, it is a political decision to respect property rights and contractual agreements that rests at the basis of the legal system, not some God-given or naturally determined law. A temporal legal entitlement does not equate to moral right and, despite what the orators of the Institute of Economic Affairs try to tell us, redistributing wealth is not equivalent to theft. What makes property rights and contractual expectations unassailable is the political power of those who hold them. This is not, of course, a radical new revelation: it is the cornerstone of Marxist critique that has animated responses to the myths of capitalism since the nineteenth century.[6] Moreover, all capitalist legal systems contain rules, such as the English rules of Equity, which can help ameliorate the consequences of private bargains when they are socially harmful. None of this is to suggest that one should disrespect property and confiscate wealth. It is meant rather to reveal that an appreciation of the 'synthetic', legally constituted nature of our political economy allows us to debate, and democratically choose between, different forms of economic organisation.

Blackmail

A further set of objections to regulation posed by the industry suggest that the only solution is a global solution. So Simon Lewis, Chief Executive of the Association for Financial Markets in Europe (AFME), reported that his members 'support measures that will reduce risk in the financial system' but that 'unless there is recognition of the need for a global agreement on compensation practice' such measures will place 'banks operating in Europe, and European banks operating elsewhere in the world ... at a competitive disadvantage' (AFME 2010). Similarly respondents to a UK Financial Services Authority (FSA) consultation suggested that restrictions on employee-retention bonuses would place UK employers at a disadvantage, producing a 'poacher's paradise' that pushes firms towards external hiring over developing in-house talent (FSA 2010: 18–19).

A parallel mindset can be found in the 'regulate/tax us and we'll leave' discourse. This favourite of banking executives has been elaborated by Jon Terry, Reward Partner at PricewaterhouseCoopers, who declared it 'a huge disappointment to the European Banking industry' that the CEBS chose to propose the 'most stringent' guidance in the world. 'Unfortunately this deviation ... could make it more likely that banks move operations, or at least expand, outside of the European Union.' Why, one might ask, would 'a globally mobile bank employee ... continue to work for a European institution'? The industry 'had hoped for a more pragmatic' solution (PWC 2010). Similarly, HSBC Chief Executive Stuart Gulliver has remarked 'You get to a $2.5 billion cost for being UK headquartered. This is a non-trivial decision, you don't move your head office on a regular basis' (Slater and Miedema 2011). The British Bankers Association expressed similar concerns (BBA 2010).

Not everyone has been taken in by these thinly veiled threats. For example, European Commissioner Michel Barnier reassured the UK Treasury Select Committee that there would be no 'flight of talent towards Asia or elsewhere' (Treanor 2010). And there are, of course, those industrialists who appreciate that the threats themselves may be counterproductive. For instance, Andrew Witty, CEO of pharmaceutical giant GlaxoSmithKline, is reported to have warned that:

> it is 'completely wrong' for businesses to view themselves as 'mid-Atlantic floating entities' with no connection to society ... One of the reasons why we've seen an erosion of trust broadly in big companies is they've allowed themselves to be seen as being detached from society and they will float in and out of societies according to what the tax regime is ... While the chief executive of the company could move, maybe the top 20 directors could move, what about the 16,000 people who work for us? It's completely wrong, I think, to play fast and loose with your connections with society in that way.
>
> (Clark 2011)

But the fact remains that since a global consensus on any level other than grand rhetoric is nigh on impossible in the field of market regulation, the dilemma of global regulation or no regulation is a wonderful recipe for inaction.

One way to expose the dubious moral subtext of this argument against regulation is to adapt Cohen's kidnapper parable (Cohen 1991: 276). If someone kidnaps a child and contacts the parents to ask for ransom, then the following considerations play out: children should be with their parents; unless the kidnapper is paid, the child is not going to be returned to her parents; therefore parents ought to pay. The question of how to proceed can be resolved without reference to morality by what economists call utility maximising cost-benefit analysis: the child is worth more than any ransom, so the parents should pay. Now, consider the same situation played out in the first person. If the kidnapper calls the parents and says: 'Children ought to be with their parents; I will not return the child unless you pay; so you should pay me', a strong moral subtext emerges. While the argument is the same as before, and rational calculus still dictates that payment will be made, the moral subtext is entirely altered when such a statement is made in an interpersonal setting. Is the kidnapper merely explaining the likely consequences of different options, or blackmailing us?

Now reconsider the proposition, substituting banker for kidnapper. The argument goes like this: unregulated compensation offers incentives to higher production; controlling compensation will reduce production; therefore compensation arrangements should remain unregulated. Rational calculus points to acceptance of this position, assuming we accept the link between compensation and incentives. But let us again rework the argument in the first person: 'Unregulated compensation offers me incentives to higher production; controlling compensation means I will produce less; therefore the compensation structure must remain unregulated.' The ethical balance of the debate is skewed by bankers' expressed desire to accumulate limitless wealth. They are not describing a natural phenomenon, they do not present a situation independent of them. In fact, they create the dilemma.

What makes for an economic argument in the abstract, makes for blackmail in the first person. A real life example can be found in research by David De Cremer (Desmet *et al.* 2011), which suggests that Dutch executives favour self-regulation not for the purposes of their own enrichment, but as a recruitment tool. So the first person proposition 'I expect something' is elided in favour of the more palatable, abstract contention that the 'market expects something'. The moral subtext is now less discernible, but it remains a real and present accomplice to the "tax us and we'll leave" mantra (*The Economist* 2010). Are bankers merely explaining the likely consequences of different options, or are they blackmailing us? Are we really accepting the argument that 'I will only do my job properly if you agree to let me have whatever rewards I choose'? Would we accept it from a doctor, teacher or policeman? If not, why do we choose to accept it from finance executives?

Fishing for sport

A further set of objections to regulation rest on the claim that inequalities of wealth are morally defensible, even useful, because they both act as an incentive to increase productivity ('incentives argument'), and because the resulting wealth 'trickles down' from the very privileged to the less so (Hayek 1978: 44–9). This oft-repeated (yet empirically misplaced) argument of Thatcherite conservatism and of Reganomics has been resurrected by bankers. For example, Lord Griffiths of Fforestfach has, in his capacity as its vice-chairman, defended lavish bonuses in Goldman Sachs in 2009 by suggesting that the general public should 'tolerate the inequality as a way to achieve greater prosperity for all', and that 'we should not … be ashamed of offering compensation in an internationally competitive market which ensures the bank businesses here and employs British people' (Quinn and Hall 2009).

And, the argument goes, if wealth is legally right, and inequalities are economically beneficial to all, so wealth must also be morally justified. So, elsewhere Lord Griffiths has argued that the corporation is a crucial 'moral community' in economic life. Morality is rarely high on the agenda because, he acknowledged, its impact is difficult to measure; however, the explicit establishment of a moral standard within a company can bring significant benefits to everyone associated with it (Griffiths *et al.* 2001: 40).

It is difficult to ascribe moral content to legal fictions, such as the corporation-as-legal-person. It is perhaps easier to construct an ethical argument supporting the maintenance of inequalities of wealth in society, without paying particular attention to whether wealth is in the hands of real persons or legal persons. An influential illustration of the argument in favour of inequality was put forward by John Rawls in the form of his 'difference principle', which suggests that inequalities of wealth are acceptable so long as they improve overall social welfare, or do not make the relatively poorer even less well off.[7]

One might extend Rawls's argument to suggest that it is petty to complain about high earners when their rewards do not reduce the size of the overall pool of funds available for everyone else. However, such an analysis falls flat in the context of the current crisis, for the money that supported the banks through the credit crunch has came from the public. All too often the gap between performance and reward has been bridged by the taxpayer. States have socialised the losses of banks and then been penalised, by the same market forces, for having taken on too much debt. For example, the Republic of Ireland sought to shore up its financial sector by guaranteeing an estimated 400bn of liabilities in 2008, but by 2010 it found itself unsupported by the markets, and forced to accept an IMF/EU bailout, with associated austerity measures (Murray-Brown and Dennis 2008). Bonuses, whether paid before or after the crisis, have come at the expense of the relatively poor, who are now faced with the prospect of dramatic cuts to public services. So, high payments to bankers cannot be defended on a Rawlsian normative approach based on the 'difference principle'.

Furthermore, the very notion of using wealth inequality as a production incentive entails a denial of community that is at once stark, yet commonplace. We are so used to capitalist incentive structures that they do not immediately strike us as odd. While the presence and acceptance of inequality are not unique to capitalism, only in capitalist societies is inequality elevated to a virtue. For all the shameless divisions in communist societies, at least the rhetoric aspired to an equal society, rather than explicitly placing some entirely beyond it. In any case, the incentives argument is fundamentally cruel, which should make it unacceptable in any society that aspires to a balance of interests.

On what basis ought we to keep listening to arguments that extraordinary rewards must not be regulated because they are necessary to incentivise bankers to do their jobs? In a society that fulfils Rawls's 'difference principle', the poor are only as well off as the selfishness of the rich allows them to be (Cohen 1991: 320). Is this vision of society – where the super-rich refuse to improve the lot of the less fortunate unless they receive kickbacks for doing so – one to which we aspire? Are we always to prefer to conceptualise social relationships as bargains, rather than as relations of community? To draw on another of Cohen's parables, consider someone who goes fishing for sport. He derives satisfaction from fishing, but does not need to eat the fish to survive. If the fisherman meets another person who needs to eat, but does not have a fishing rod, would it be acceptable for the fisherman to say: my satisfaction from fishing exceeds your need to eat? Is it acceptable for bank executives to say: 'Our satisfaction in having multi-million-pound bonuses exceeds poor people's need for basic services'? Are we always to prefer a bargaining conception of social relationships over a community one?

Conclusion

Speaking on the BBC television programme *Newsnight*, presenter Jeremy Paxman expressed amazement at the brilliance of bankers in 'making the taxpayer liable for their own greed and stupidity' such that 'the law of 21st century capitalism is that the banking crisis is not a problem for the banks, it is a problem for the nation' (22 November 2010).

This chapter has demonstrated that even fairly mild proposals for reform, such as the CEBS Guidelines of December 2010, are met with vicious opposition by the financial sector. This is an industry that neither wants reform, nor feels responsibility for the catastrophe they have brought to bear on the rest of society. The reason lies less in a belief in propaganda about constraints on competitiveness and innovation, and more in a belief in the moral subtext that excessive wealth is legally unassailable, morally and economically justified, that interference with property rights is a violation of freedom that undermines the very basis of democratic capitalism, and that gross inequalities of wealth are good for everyone. It is these beliefs that this chapter seeks to bring to light.

If anything, the crisis that became global in 2008 has unearthed the near total inadequacy of self-regulation as a strategy. Yet the CEBS Guidelines propose business as usual, albeit with a greater degree of oversight, rather than a break from the traditions of the past. Discussions on reform will not make significant progress without a realisation that the balance between regulation and market freedom is a question for political consensus, not a matter of economic 'science', jurisprudence, or moral entitlement. If change is truly desired, then politics needs to reoccupy the space that we now consider the preserve of 'technical' scientific enquiry, and we need to refuse, politically, to accept the current structures and operation of financial capitalism. We must question the moral subtext of our decisions to allow bankers to determine their compensation structures, not as supplicants (citizens in a state at the mercy of market forces) but as masters of the legislative process in a democratic polity. As Wilhelm Röpke has observed:

> the market, competition and the play of supply and demand do not create ethical reserves; they presuppose and consume them. These reserves must come from outside the market.... Self-discipline, a sense of justice, honesty, fairness, chivalry, moderation, respect for human dignity, firm ethical norms. All of these are things which people must possess before they go to market and compete with each other.
>
> (Röpke 1960: 125)

The current crisis has proved that all these are qualities in short supply in the financial sector. We must demonstrate that they persist outside it.

Notes

1 As of 1.1.2011 the functions of the CEBS have passed to the European Banking Authority (EBA).
2 Enshrined in the UK in s.172 Companies Act 2006.
3 For an entertaining account of how complexity reached levels at which not even the financial industry fully understood the 'products' it was creating, see Michael Lewis (2011).
4 See for example Hyman Minsky's work (2008).
5 Joseph Stiglitz in his latest work (2010) also offers a wonderful dissection of the flaws of contemporary economic orthodoxy.
6 See for example David Harvey (2007), who suggests that economic distaste for regulation arises from personal self-interest, and is pandered to by a conspiracy of powerful political and market interests.
7 While there are many philosophers and political scientists who have attempted to construct justifications for inequality, Rawls is particularly suited to our analysis in this chapter as he has exerted considerable influence on legal scholars and offers the most identifiable point of opposition to the egalitarian message of G.A. Cohen discussed below.

Useful websites

Study resources linked to the documentary *Inside Job*: www.sonyclassics.com/inside-job/
Financial Services Authority: www.fsa.gov.uk
For information on principles based regulation see www.fsa.gov.uk/pubs/other/principles.pdf
European Commission Regulatory Capital: http://ec.europa.eu/internal_market/bank/regcapital/index_en.htm

Chapter 14

Corporate respect for human rights

As good as it gets?

Sally Wheeler

Introduction

In this contribution I want to look at what has become known as the Ruggie Principles (Ruggie 2006, 2007a, 2008, 2010, 2011a) and the position of trans-national corporations (TNCs) in relation to human rights and the question of corporate recognition of and support for human rights within their operations. The Principles have been endorsed by the UN and adopted by the OECD and so are the most recent and most authoritative statement on the relationship between TNCs and human rights. The examination is not one that looks either at the implications of the Ruggie principles for international law or at how corporations are affected by extant international law; those accounts abound elsewhere (Joseph 2004, 2008; McCorquodale and Simons 2007). Nor is it a detailed account of the specifics of the Ruggie framework. Rather it sets the Ruggie framework in the context of global business and considers the positive relationship that Ruggie posits between human rights and contemporary practices of corporate social responsibility (CSR). Given that CSR exists as a mechanism that allows TNCs, if they so choose as a strategic priority, to engage in wider purview of the appropriate field for business than in previous eras, the chapter suggests that linking responsibility for human rights observance to a voluntary corporate strategy is a flawed and reductionist step. In the first section, I sketch out the landscape of global business activity into which Ruggie has to fit the principles he put forward. In a longer section that follows I explain the immediate political context in which Ruggie was operating and some of the compromises that he felt obliged to make as the principles were formulated, adopted and subsequent illuminated in the Guidelines/Guiding Principles of 2011. In a final section I comment on the link between the Principles and the language and practices of CSR that have been designed by TNCs themselves either individually or as a collective endeavor through overarching trade and business organisations.

The landscape

Stories of what appears to be flagrant disregard by corporate actors of the human rights of individuals appear in the mainstream media on almost a weekly basis. Examples from the recent past would be the technology corporation Apple (Duhigg and Barboza 2012) and the mineral extractive corporation Glencore (Silverstein 2012), which were accused of benefiting from labour practices that abused the rights of workers in China and the Democratic Republic of the Congo respectively. These two states possess very different political and institutional structures from each other, and from the corporations' home countries. Apple and Glencore fit the classic model of foreign direct investment (FDI) into low-cost labour economies, but Apple's investment also illustrates the development of this paradigm as it was made via a locally based firm. I say more about this non-equity mode of corporate activity below. A further recent shift in the contours of globalization is that global business is much more complex and granular than traditional accounts would suggest. It is no longer the case that capital flows from the global north to the global south in the form of FDI (Rugman 2008). New or emerging economies now host TNCs, which in turn invest into other new or emerging economies across the global South. This creates a new, subtler, geopolitical dimension to TNC activities, and to the question of who will win and who will lose should there be any change of regulatory focus between home and host state.

The examples of Apple and Glencore are illustrative of the complex relationship that exists between states and corporations in the control of global production activity. It is trite to express this relationship merely in terms of a comparison between a state's GDP and a corporation's turnover. In the past this has been a popular methodology, but economists now criticise both the accuracy and utility of this comparison (Kinley 2009: 164) and furthermore it does not capture the 'the qualitative nature' of the exercise of corporate power in terms of its impact on the economic and social lives of individuals in particular geographic locations (Dicken 2003). Corporate power may be more usefully differentiated in terms of its effect across developed and developing states. Shankar powerfully explains, for example, how the desire for Coca-Cola in developed states has deprived the inhabitants of parts of India of the basic necessity that is water of drinking quality (Shankar 2010). Corporate power is a totemic force in terms of its impact upon the environment, contribution to taxation revenue through profit generation and wealth creation through employment end educative opportunities and the potential for redistribution of material wealth (Grant 1997).

The growth of corporations does not necessarily signal a decline of state, in favour of corporate, power; nor a conflict between corporate power and state power, but rather the shifting sands of economic globalisation (Scherer and Palazzo 2011). Industrialisation through FDI has changed some parts of some states significantly very quickly, and this brings new problems for host nations. The effects of global production produce for some states problems that are not of their making, for example environmental degradation. The proliferation of bilateral investment treaties (Ruggie 2008: 12) might restrict the space for host countries to develop their domestic policy in relation to the regulation of corporations but as these are interstate arrangements, in theory and subject to the point made at the end of this paragraph about the nature of international law, they do not directly lead to a leeching of power between state and inward investing corporation (Sheffer 2011). Corporations sometimes act in support of strong governments and sometimes against them. Corporations might, in a weak state, offer a form of stability that the state cannot. States in the neo-liberal era opened up new service markets for corporations by privatising state monopolies and now in the age of austerity have been increasingly devolving functions to the corporate sector that were previously the province of the state. The relationship between these two actors is fluid and constantly changing but it is the case that individuals are probably more exposed to the exercise of corporate power than ever before. If we pursue this narrative of power then states create institutions of law and government that offer justice and redress to individuals against the state. Even authoritarian states recognise the rule of law and states, even weak or failed states can be held accountable through the forces of democracy internally or, *in extremis*, externally by bodies such as the UN. States are required to recognise and uphold international obligations to other states. In relation to individuals, the recognition of human rights by the state is the ultimate bulwark against the capricious exercise by the state of its power. In theory at least, there are a series of checks and balances in relation to state power (Sinden 2007: 510–514).

Without wishing to rehearse in detail all the ways in which states and corporations are different it is clearly relevant that states are fixed entities while corporations are a fluid and collective response to markets and the laws and social norms that regulate markets. As such corporations can slip in and out of geographical locations, avoiding state sanction (and there will be many instances where a cost benefit analysis by a state mitigates against sanction in order to avoid corporate relocation); TNCs can offer infrastructure development in exchange for exemption from regulation and, as I explain below, they can use structures such as franchises and contracts to eliminate the need for an incorporated presence in a particular state. The same slippery presence manifests itself at the level of business lobby groups that pressure national governments to take particular positions in interstate trade negotiation forums such as the WTO while standing outside the official dialogue processes. Corporations have no official presence in international law so are able to exist in its margins, intervening when they wish (Simons 2012). There is no obvious brake on the accumulation of power by corporations in a trans-national sense.

In the second section I explain that Ruggie concluded that it would not be viable to seek to control and direct corporate power by imposing direct obligations on TNCs under international law. However, even if this is accepted as the non-negotiable reality of the political context in which Ruggie is operating, to describe, as he did, 'the permissive environment for wrongful acts by companies of all kinds without adequate sanctioning or reparation' as a result of 'governance gaps' created by globalisation was, at best, an unfortunate choice of words (Ruggie 2008: para 3 and 11; Ruggie 2011b: 132). For it suggests that the often negative interaction between corporate power and the observance of human rights is all an unfortunate mistake that can be remedied by looking at the 'gaps' rather than an as the result of a conscious strategy to increase corporate profits. As such it is a remarkably unambitious and conservative attempt at creating a context within which corporate behaviour may change. This observation is the heart of my critique of Ruggie. The absence of any aspirational sentiment that, while the global legal and regulatory environment for business does not offer a solution, a solution may nevertheless be possible, is damming. It sets the tone of compromise and low-level expectation. The recent accumulation of corporate power and influence is deserving of a more dynamic explanation than mere 'gaps'.

What is needed is a much less anaemic, more forceful, account of globalisation that identifies corporations as the dynamic possessors of power that they are, and both challenges and inspires them to channel that power towards invigorating the observance and protection of human rights. As long ago as 1996, Boutros Boutros-Ghali was talking of the need to provide an 'agreed means of participation' for 'new actors on the international scene' in areas 'heretofore primarily the province of states' (Boutros-Ghali 1996: 25). As I explain in the second section, the appropriate 'means of participation' is neither the top-down application of direct obligations in international law nor the bottom-up signing of the UN Global Compact. It is more constructive to follow O'Neill's suggestion (O'Neill 2001) that corporations be considered as 'agents of justice', alongside (and, in the case of failed or weak states, instead of) states, albeit with different capabilities than states.

Somewhat ironically, O'Neill's starting point for this proposition is also the notion of a 'gap'. For her the gap is the absence of designated agents responsible for delivering to individuals the rights they have been promised by the United Nations Declaration on Human Rights (UNDHR). While she recognises that states are considered to be the key agent of justice in delivering rights she problematises this by pointing out that it is not clear whether 'universal rights are matched and secured by universal obligations or by obligations held by some, but not by all, agents and agencies' (O'Neill 2001: 183). So states need to both construct and co-ordinate a variety of different agents and agencies to fulfill the promise of rights. That need for co-ordination between these actors is also recognised by Ruggie (2011a), but more as a device for alerting corporations to the absence of state policy or authority in particular areas. It is impossible here to do justice to the subtlety of O'Neill's argument on this point but she goes on to explain that it is not only in the context of weak states and failed states that her argument applies (Matten and Crane 2005: 171) but also in the context of the proliferation of rights discourses that focus on the position of recipients without considering the location of the counter-part obligation. She would not be alone in pondering the utility of this (Baxi 2001).

To close the 'gap', as she sees it, O'Neill draws on Sen's capabilities approach (O'Neill 2001: 189), which relates to the potential for action rather than simply the possession of power. This is where the dynamism of her proposal comes from – TNCs are in the position to choose whether they act as agents of justice, or contribute to injustice (Lee 2005). If TNCs could not choose – if they were completely constrained by regulators, investors and/or their own constitutions, there would be no clamour for them to do so. Their frequent failure to act as agents of justice attracts news coverage because of the existence of choice. TNCs do not have the same range of capabilities as states. Nor are they likely to have the same overview of needs and priorities as states. But they do have capabilities that can be complimentary to those of states, or of NGOs that sometimes take the place of states for whatever reason.

TNCs are not conducting business in a 'gap in governance'. They are potential agents of justice that must be inspired to recognize as much and to perform accordingly. Such inspiration need not be based on claims of legal or moral liability, merely on a recognition that a TNC might be the agent most capable agent of delivering justice in a given location (Kuper 2004: 15).

Beginning with compromise

Ruggie was appointed as the UN Special Representative for Business and Human Rights (UNSRBHR) in 2005. His appointment followed the 2003 announcement by the UN Sub-Commission for the Promotion and Protection of Human Rights, of the Draft Norms on the Responsibilities of Transnational Corporations and other Business Enterprises with Regard to Human Rights (Norms 2003). These Norms were expressly not adopted by the Commission on Human Rights in 2004, but are a useful point of comparison for the Ruggie framework.[1] Their fate tells us much about the acknowledged pragmatism (Ames 2011) of the recommendations presented by Ruggie and his disavowal of the Norms (Ruggie 2006), even if his retreat on some of their central tenets has been greeted with dismay by some scholars and activists (Weissbrodt 2006).

The Norms pertained to a basket of rights broadly mapped onto the UDHR and subsequent international covenants and customary law.[2] They advocated imposing on corporations and other enterprises a positive obligation to observe human rights, rather than a negative demand not to infringe them, while still casting states as bearing the primary responsibility for protecting human rights. This marked a considerable ratcheting up of corporate responsibility from previous attempts to link business to human rights (McCrudden 1999; Meyer 1998; Voiculescu 2011: 12–16). In addition to the revolutionary step of imposing liability on non-state actors, the Norms (at para 15) required TNCs to institute internal structures and monitoring mechanisms to ensure that they, and those with whom they enjoyed business relationships, complied with the requirements of the Norms. This compliance was to be externally monitored at either national or UN level with states also establishing a legal framework to ensure that there was compliance with the Norms.

For the following discussion on the Ruggie Principles, the most important point about the Norms is the assertion by their drafters that this was not a new obligation for TNCs, but was one already imposed by existing arrangements within international law; in other words that there was no distinction between direct and indirect duties. One part of the Norms that Ruggie did retain was the reparation principle that required TNCs to have in place mechanisms for those the bringing of grievances to TNCs and their swift resolution. Debate on the Norms quickly became polarised into those supporting them and those not, so they could not be revised or reformulated. Interestingly, as Kinley points, this was more sophisticated than business on one side and human rights activists on others (Kinley et al. 2007:33). In a manifestation of the competitive social conscience identified by Smith, trhere were those in the business community who volunteered to trial the monitoring suggested by the Norms (BLIHR 2004, 2006; Smith 1994). States, too, were divided by the Norms, with France, for example, supporting them, and developing states such as Pakistan and Malaysia taking the view that they might make them an uncompetitive location for TNC business (Jerbi 2009: 309). Criticisms ranged from substantive concerns around the interpretation placed on existing treaty arrangements and the breadth of liability ascribed to corporations and the meaning of previously unused phrases such as 'respective spheres of activity and influence' to more, albeit disputed (Kinley and Zerial 2007), procedural concerns with perceived lack of consultation of relevant, ultimately opposing, stakeholder groups. The validity of these criticisms was acknowledged by Ruggie in successive reports (Ruggie 2007b, 2008, 2010), foreshadowed by his describing of the Norms as a 'train wreck' full of exaggerated legal claims and conceptual and procedural ambiguities (Ruggie 2006).

Ruggie began his tenure as UN Special Representative by ameliorating two of the most contentious parts of the Norms: he set up multi-stakeholder consultations on five continents (Ruggie 2007a), a practice that he has continued throughout his mandate; and he abandoned attempts to base TNC liability on direct obligation, focusing instead on obligations flowing through states for violations of international criminal and humanitarian law (Ruggie 2006, para 7). In relation to corporations, he set out non-binding responsibilities intended to be a basis for the monitoring and, if necessary, remediation of corporate conduct. Through successive reports and drafts, always with extensive consultation, Ruggie created a framework resting on the three pillars of 'protect', 'respect' and 'remedy'. Protection of human rights is the role of the state; respect for human rights is the role given to corporations; remedying the infringement of rights is something that corporations should do or co-operate in legitimate processes that are advanced to effect a remedy. TNCs might be liable for committing international crimes and can be complicit in state violations of human rights if they have knowingly assisted in these violations even if they did not intend the violation to occur. A state's duty to protect does not extend extraterritorially but states should encourage TNCs to respect human rights when operating outside their home country (Ruggie 2011a: GP 2).

Thus the framework appears to be far more preoccupied with the position of states and their (non)enforcement of human rights obligations against corporations than with placing corporations under serious pressure to recognise and fulfil their obligations to the bearers of human rights. The responsibility of TNCs is strictly impact-based. There is no suggestion that that they should use their substantial power as leverage for an enhanced human rights policy from states (MacDonald 2011; Wood 2012). Those impacts are seen as micro-level breaches in relation to defined individuals or groups of individuals. There is no attempt to suggest that corporations should have a wider conception of human rights that causes them to think in a global sense what the effect particular business activities might have (Dowell-Jones and Kinley 2011). There is no mention of liability or responsibility attaching to corporate office holders for failing to ensure that there is corporate respect for human rights. Within this focus on states there appears to be more pressure on the host countries where TNC activity takes place than on home countries where TNCs locate their incorporated parent company. It is host countries that are expected to enact and enforce laws requiring TNCs to respect human rights, even though home states may have more bargaining power. And, while TNCs receive guidance on how to estimate human rights abuses that their operations might trigger, how to mainstream concern for, and protection of, human rights into their operations and how they might best tell the world that they have done so; there no instructions, or even clear suggestions, that these activities should be enhanced by the use of international monitoring standards and external validators.

None of the iterations through which the Principles have passed has occasioned the hostility that the Norms did. While this might be attributable in part to the change of tone and content from the Norms to the Principles that I indicated above, it might also be attributable in part to the changes in regulatory climate that businesses now operate in, as compared to 2003 when the Norms were first issued. The Ruggie principles sit atop a plethora of regulatory devices that impact on business practices. These devices fall into six distinct groups ranging from internationally promulgated and independent codes to codes created by particular TNCs. There are model business codes of general application supported by intergovernmental bodies such as the UN-backed Global Compact to which TNCs may become signatories; there are general codes of business operation agreed between governments such as the OECD Guidelines for Multinational Enterprise; multi-stakeholder codes drafted as a result of agreements between corporations, NGOs and governments such as the Ethical Trading Initiative; industry-wide codes such as the Sustainable Development Framework of the International Council on Mining and Metals; individual company codes which contain operating principles in relation to everything from bribery to environmental management to supply chain assurance; and independent reporting standards such as the ISO 14001 standard for environmental management. These reporting initiatives allow TNCs to benchmark their performance in certain areas against common standards.

These regulatory devices are much more invasive of the business space occupied by TNCs than they were in 2003. Some are more widely followed than others. For example, there are 6,000 business enterprises signed up to the Global Compact, not a particularly large figure when one considers that in 2007 there were estimated to be in excess of 77,000 TNCs in existence (UNCTD 2007: 3), but still a much higher number than were signatories in 2003 (Oppenheim *et al.* 2007). Virtually every listed corporation, regardless of whether it has a TNC structure or not, has a position, supported by policies and reports covering activities from providing healthcare to addressing homelessness that it makes publically available and by participation in reporting frameworks of some kind, on corporate social responsibility or, using the term that is fashionable currently, corporate sustainability (Scalet and Kelly 2010). The use of the descriptor 'corporate sustainability' signifies the absorption into everyday business practice of the risks posed by environmental and social issues to the business model (KPMG 2008; Carroll and Shabana 2010). Each corporation's approach to environmental and social risk is managed by using some or all of the regulatory devices listed above augmented by the creation of partnerships and agreements with NGOs and other community based stakeholders (Rajak

2011). This does not mean that these risks are always managed effectively or even responsibly through the use of these devices (Alves 2009; Delmas and Burbano 2011). The application of codes (Barrientos and Smith 2007; Wright and Madrid 2007), the reliability and independence of certification (Borial 2007; Boiral and Gendron 2011), the selection of the area of the business rendered up for scrutiny and the exclusion from view of illegal and or dangerous and damaging practices can all be questioned (Fonesca 2010) and regularly are by NGOs (see for example Global Witness 2012). Rather, the point being made here is that the Ruggie framework is simply one among many mechanisms, some of which are self-imposed, that exist to push TNC activity into the spotlight of greater scrutiny at the discretion of the individual TNC. Without the suggestion of duty or obligation on the part of TNCs within the framework, the Principles have no greater traction than any of these existing mechanisms. This is a point that I examine in more detail in the text that follows.

There appear to be several reasons, the explanatory power of which has increased considerably since the announcement of the Norms in 2003, for the corporate sector's apparent willingness to expose its business practices to this level of transparency (Vogel 2008). The most important of these is the exposure by campaigning NGOs of TNCs' environmental management and labour conditions. High-profile corporate targets have included GAP, Marks and Spencer and Nike, which were all criticized for the labour conditions involved in the production of their clothing products, and McDonalds for their support of intensive farming and their employment conditions. This rather gross simplification does not do justice to NGO activities, but it is sufficient for the point being made here. NGOs employ a range of often highly sophisticated tactics to attack the reputation and legitimacy (Hendry 2006) of the practices of corporations and of their positions as dominating economic institutions (Yaziji and Doh 2009: 93–109). They rely on consumer reactions (actual and feared) (Friedman 2007) – a tool which has more traction in some industries than others. The huge expansion in non-equity mode FDI (WIR 2011: 130–142) in the apparel industry (Vandenburgh 2007; Tokatli et al. 2008) in particular is closely linked to either a desire to avoid or respond to an attack (Suchman 1995). Non-equity mode FDI knits together areas of TNC operation for practical purposes, but it also enables the passing on – to an entirely independent, nationally based, business structure – of the burdens of costs and responsibility for, say, the observance of labour rights. Such use of supply chains, in combination with the adoption of TNC-specific or industry-wide voluntary codes, is seen as helping to forestall the possibility of any additional regulatory sanctions being imposed.

CSR is the perfect handmaiden to neoliberalism (Kinderman 2012) – a form of *chiaroscuro* by which certain practices are pushed forward for scrutiny, awards even, while others are held firmly back in the shade (Jackson and Carter 1995; Conley and Williams 2005–2006). On one level this is what corporate strategy is all about – the effective management of risk. For the recipients of course it is often rather less successful. The initial response of Coca-Cola to water shortages and water pollution caused by its production facilities was to embark upon a well-publicised school-building programme. Leaving aside the obvious question of why a TNC would set up a production plant requiring copious amounts of water in an area not famed for the abundance of water, the observation to be made is that schools, while needed, are not a substitute for drinking water (Shankar 2010). Policies of carbon reduction and other improving environmental measures may be adopted and put forward for certification in respect of certain areas of a corporation's activity in order to create a focus for attention away from a rather less environmentally friendly area of a corporation's operations (Takahashi and Nakamura 2010). It is then only a small step for the very public participation in CSR activities to become a ground of competition between TNCs. Cause-related marketing activities (Baghi *et al.* 2009) and the creation of 'ethical' product lines (Stanaland *et al.* 2011) are the two most obvious examples in this area. Self-exposure to scrutiny leads from CSR almost being used as a defence mechanism to it becoming an active part of profit accumulation.

The final factor behind this increased willingness to offer corporate policies and activities for scrutiny has considerable potential but is also the most speculative. It is that business values have genuinely changed. CSR policies are being adopted not just as the strategic interventions described above but also because business executives are confronting their own 'subtext'. They recognize, in a normative sense, that corporations do have a wider responsibility than mere profit-making. Ruggie certainly believed this as early as 2004 (Ruggie 2004: 512) but he does not offer any evidence of it beyond increased participation in CSR initiatives. It is almost impossible to disentangle changing norms from strategic intervention. One way perhaps of capturing this change in broad terms is to look at how business schools approach the teaching of business ethics – not because what they teach can be said to have a direct impact on the subsequent behaviour of business executives, but because their programmes are customer driven: they teach what the market place tells them business school graduates need to know. Research on the curriculum of business schools has shown that the teaching of ethics has moved from a marginal interest at the start of the 1990s (Ghorpade 1991) to a required subject at the majority of the top 50 business schools as ranked by the *Financial Times* (Christensen *et al.* 2007). If it is the case that business values are changing in a fundamental, normative sense – and especially if Ruggie believes this to be the case – then the Framework's emphasis on operating through states' obligations seems very much like a missed opportunity. I think we are entitled to wonder why he did not opt to suggest a much stronger pro human rights framework to an apparently receptive business world. These proposals would then at least have been discussed and re-negotiated against the background of an ambitious and aspirant framework. In the terminology of the present collection, the Framework would move beyond the constraints of the contemporary context, buoyed by a new, progressive subtext.

Ending with respect

The second core principle in Ruggie's framework is the corporate responsibility to respect human rights (Ruggie 2008: 9) which TNCs are to operationalise through due diligence (Ruggie 2008: 25). Respect is a 'baseline responsibility' of corporations, the scope of which 'is defined by social expectations as part of what is sometimes called a company's social license to operate', and the defiance of which might 'subject companies to the courts of public opinion' (Ruggie 2008: 54). This stands in sharp contrast to the language of 'obligation' used in relation to states. The language of respect, social expectation and public condemnation that Ruggie uses to explain corporate responsibilities for human rights is strikingly similar to that he used when talking of CSR in 2005. At that time he felt that NGO attention attracted by a corporation refusing to uphold the UNDHR was analogous to any social risk, and that social risks were 'not necessarily centred on independent judgements of corporate right and wrong doing' (Kytle and Ruggie 2005: 8). Indeed it is very much the language used to explain the advantages of corporate social responsibility for TNCs. It promotes CSR strategy as context-specific cost-benefit analysis: if the costs of CSR intervention are likely to be high, find something more beneficial to you; if failure to take a CSR intervention is likely to cost little, take the hit. But while CSR is about voluntary pursuit of enlightened self-interest, human rights are about *what it is to be human* and that ought not to be subject to corporate calculation (McCorquodale 2009: 391. See also Voiculescu in this volume). Respecting human rights is what should occur within corporate behaviour regardless of whether a CSR policy is in place. It is what is left in the absence of an economic case for CSR (Kinley 2009: 186).

Much depends on public opinion in the framework that Ruggie sets out. As Cragg explains, to the extent that the 'court of public opinion' in a given location does not expect that a given human right be respected, the business risk associated with failure to respect is low – unless and until there is a rise in 'public expectations about the standards that should have been respected in past transactions but were not' (Cragg 2012: 14). Public opinion is easier to mobilize in some 'contexts' than others: some industries and practices are more likely to be condemned, simply because the products are more or less familiar and the rights breached have more or less resonance. Why the observance of human rights should be reduced to something so specious is not explained.

A much more significant move on Ruggie's part would have been to create a new 'subtext': an expectation of what corporations 'should' do as morally responsible actors. Human rights are minimum standards primarily concerned with welfare. The cue for corporate managers, acting on behalf of an increasingly diversified shareholder body, is in the word 'minimum'. They could simply be asked to observe these minimum standards as an ethical imperative. Put in these terms this does not seem a very big step for them to take.

Respect is operationalised through a four-component 'due diligence' process. This requires a policy statement committing to respect human rights, an on-going assessment of actual and potential human rights impacts of corporate activities, an integration of the results of these assessments into corporate systems and a reporting on performance (Ruggie 2010: 83). As a process which moves from policy formulation through impact assessment to tracking performance, this will involve TNCs in a dialogue that is necessarily more open and less selective and defensive than perhaps previous dialogues have been (Mena *et al.* 2010). It will be a relational rather than a transactional process. Ruggie is right to recognize that human rights issues need to be mainstreamed throughout TNC policies (Ruggie 2011b: 131) but in using the concept of 'due diligence' to seek embed human rights in the discourse of business Ruggie once again missed an opportunity to shift to new discourse – to signal the novelty and fundamental nature of human rights.

Due diligence is a commonly used process for assessing and minimising corporate exposure to commercial risk (Muchlinski 2012: 156). Human rights are again tied to the entirely unsuited discourse of self-interested CSR. Ruggie defends his adoption of due diligence terminology as a way of demystifying human rights and framing them in terms that TNCs can understand (Ames 2011: 16). It is this very demystification that is objectionable; the very ordinariness – the banalising force – of due diligence, as it precipitates calculations around 'respect' for human rights in place of absolute observance. Human rights are genuinely 'minimum' standards once they are regularly delivered as part of 'business as usual'. Until then they should be treated as the 'gold standard' – a goal towards which we must actively strive. While Ruggie sees the inappropriateness of commercial calculation in relation to human rights, the Framework that bears his name does nothing to ensure that we move away from it.

Conclusion

The Ruggie Principles tell a story of globalisation without hope, aspiration or entitlement, which glosses the agency of corporations. The expressive force (text) and moral authority (subtext) of human rights deserve rather more than Ruggie gives them. 'Governance gaps', 'respect' and 'due diligence' are little more than placeholders – concepts imprisoned in their contemporary context, waiting for a time of moral commitment to give them the force of real intent. There is very little in the framework that would prompt corporate managers to arrange their business practices differently, or forecast downwards their expected profit figures. O'Neill (2005) warns that aspirations are empty and entitlements must be mirrored by obligations to deliver. But surely corporations are morally obliged both to deliver human rights and to care that they do so. As I have observed elsewhere (Wheeler 2002), the motivations of TNCs matter hugely if we seek a deep, normative change of corporate motivations, rather than superficial change in corporate strategy which will, after all, just play to the 'courts of public opinion'.

Notes

1 There are detailed accounts of the Norms available, many of which are contemporaneous to their promulgation (Kinley and Chambers 2006; Deva 2003–2004). Here the Norms are only briefly summarised to serve as a comparison with Ruggie's proposed framework.
2 Although the inclusion of economic and social rights as well civil and political rights marked a significant shift away from the anchoring effect of the UDHR in terms of expressing human rights obligations (de Feyter 2005: 28–30).

Chapter 15

Human rights, corporate social responsibility and international economic law

Strong answers to strong questions?

Aurora Voiculescu

Introduction

This chapter explores the intersection between two normative social discourses – market economy and human rights – at the micro level context of corporate social responsibility (CSR) and the macro level context of international economic law (IEL) discourses. Human rights have undergone a tremendous transformation in recent decades. From a purely aspirational 'nonsense on stilts' discourse, it has become an institutional discourse, acquiring a legal life of its own that influences a variety of other social discourses. Meanwhile, scholars began to question whether international trade policy had, or should have, a normative dimension rooted somewhere other than in classical economics (Brilmayer cited in Garcia 1998: 208). Today, the question is rather how such alternative normative dimensions – among which human rights dominate – should be gauged, incorporated and instrumentalised so that they complement each other rather than compromising their individual discursive integrity. It is in the context of such questions that human rights discourse underwent a profound transformation – moving beyond its traditional devotion to checking government powers, to interrogate dominant contemporary economic discourse from a social justice perspective. In this sense, corporate social responsibility (CSR) discourse emerged as a complement, as well as a reaction, to the slow development of human rights linkage at the institutional and infra-structural level reflected by international economic law (IEL) and international relations.

According to Santos, human rights are supposed to offer strong, universally valid, answers to the difficult problems and questions of the world. However, he argues, we live instead in a time of strong questions and weak answers (Santos 2009). The silver lining, Santos suggests, is that in the context of the present economic (and social) crisis, this combination of strong questions and weak answers could be sign of a paradigmatic change.

Economic regulation is defined broadly to include legal and non-legal regimes, whether internally generated or based on external interventions

(Picciotto 2002). Regulation that refers to the potential human rights dimensions of the economic activities is also seen as a means for embedding new social values into the market economy sphere and for socialising the economic actors (Zumbansen 2006; Voiculescu 2012). This chapter explores some of the parameters of such a potential paradigmatic transition at one specific human rights–market economy contact point: corporate social responsibility. It maps complementing CSR and IEL level regulatory attempts to embed in economic activity new human rights-based normative dimensions. First, the discourses of human rights and CSR are presented as complementary but potentially conflicting. CSR discourse is identified as the attempted 'answer' to the complex 'questions' of social justice. But it is an answer offered predominantly *via* the market, to problems that often originate *in* the market. When placed on the normative platform of CSR, human rights become an unfulfilling answer, an unlikely paradigm-challenger. The second half of the chapter examines how the IEL-level contact area between human rights and the market, as reflected in the IEL linkage debate, influences the CSR-level linkage; and the normative challenges posed by the concept of linkages, in particular to human rights. It exposes the resistance of IEL to expectations that it might shift away from its core market-based paradigm as a fundamental impediment to a CSR-level normative rethinking.

What the IEL and the CSR interface with human rights have in common is the attempt to 'i-patch' the neoliberal economic claim to universalism (and the resulting questions of social justice) with norms derived from human rights discourse (Castells 2000, p. 163ff).

Complementary, competing and conflicting discourses

Human rights discourse and market economy discourse meet in the corporate social responsibility debate, over how to respond to perceived dislocations of duties in relation to social justice parameters such as poverty, health, environmental protection, human development. Under complex pressures, corporations have rushed to introduce voluntary instruments into their business practices, often with rather vague reference to international human rights instruments. In this way, international human rights law has given birth to voluntary social norms that represent a practical *privatisation* of human rights (Voiculescu 2006), engendering a high level of normative promiscuity. At the same time, international organisations have endeavoured to create guidelines and frameworks that answer the social expectation for social justice whilst supporting business actors in their search for clearer normative coordinates.

While we may have some clarity about how and why CSR discourse evolved, there is less clarity regarding the concept of CSR itself. As early as three decades ago, Zenisek spoke of CSR as meaning 'something' but not always the same 'something' to everyone (Zenisek 1979). And yet, most definitions (Boeger *et al.* 2008: 2), present CSR as a way for business to engage with its own social environment by taking into consideration elements other than those strictly related to its own profit, including labour standards, human rights and environmental protection. Other issues or cross-cutting themes, are often included, such as philanthropy and responsible investment or 'alternative thematic frameworks' (Carroll 1999), such as social entrepreneurship, corporate ethics, corporate sustainability. Others still add colour and symbolism, advancing terms such as 'corporate citizenship' (Corkin 2008) or 'corporate consciousness' (Selznick 2002, p. 97).

Human rights discourse has added substantially to the ill-defined complexity with a long list of international initiatives – some more successful than others – such as the long-debated, then abandoned, United Nations Draft Code of Conduct for Transnational Corporations, the repeatedly revised OECD Guidelines for Multinational Enterprises, the UN Global Compact promoted as the flagship of the UN initiative aiming to build a bridge between business and society, the much maligned UN Draft Norms, or the recent UN Framework proposing the ultimate three-pillar instrument of 'protect, respect and remedy' (Voiculescu 2011). Through this complex set of initiatives, human rights discourse offers a distinctive and institutionally influential normative umbrella for CSR discourse. For instance, labour standards and environmental protection, both of which have distinct CSR dimensions, are increasingly couched in terms of human rights (Francioni 2010; Alston 2005). At the same time, due to its claim to universalism, human rights discourse has the potential to offer ethical and socialising subtextual normative parameters to the global market economy.

The roots of CSR are in voluntarism, but its includes the full spectrum of normativity (domestic, transnational, international) from voluntary corporate codes of conduct (with or without inbuilt implementation and control mechanisms) and ethical investment schemes to direct regulatory intervention, using a multitude of 'interactive', 'semi' and 'meta' regulatory mechanisms (Zumbansen 2011; Parker 2007).

Any meaningful register of responsibility ought, Carroll (1979) suggests, to encompass the full range of social expectations that are directed towards companies – economic, legal, ethical and philanthropic. This four-part categorisation is a useful tool for analysing the interface between existing and proposed corporate responsibilities on the one hand, and social expectations on the other (Griseri and Seppalla 2010). Economic expectations – to produce goods and services in a way that is profitable to owners – correspond most directly to the business self-perception of its scope and role in society. But that production must be done in compliance with regulations that express society's values and interests. These two types of expectations – economic and legal – were long seen as the only responsibilities of a business organisation. But the idea that business organisations are also expected to abide by ethical norms has gathered momentum as a solution to the failings of the neo-liberal market economy (Joyner and Payne 2002). Carroll argues that because these latter norms are not written in law, they are more ambiguous than legal requirements and therefore more difficult for companies to anticipate and follow. But ethical expectations underpin and predict the emergence of new laws and regulations; and law has its own insidious ways of cross-pollinating the domains of voluntarism and philanthropy (McBarnet 2007). Philanthropy, Carroll's fourth dimension of business responsibilities, involves discretionary activities that go beyond the expectations of society such as donations to public and non-profit organisations. It is quite common for companies to engage in such activities, even though failure to do so is not perceived as irresponsible (Kaptein and Wempe 2002).

Although reasonably comprehensive, not all of these possible normative expectations suggested by Carroll sit well with the public international law character of human rights norms. Most human rights initiatives taken on the CSR platform – whether in the public international or private sector – fall under Carroll's 'ethical norms of society' category of responsibility, rather than under the legal one. As such, these initiatives formally support the normative foundations of human rights while effectively undermining them by diluting – if not denying – the regulatory potential of international human rights law, as well as frustrating the legal imagination. To quote Santos, '[we] keep visiting the fairs of the industry of human rights with ever new products (*Global Compact, Millenium Goals, War on Poverty*, etc.), but, on the way, we have to go by an increasingly more ungraspable graveyard of betrayed promises' (Santos 2009, p. 4).

'Weak answers to strong questions'

Returning to Santos' idea of the potential of human rights discourse as signals of change of the dominant social paradigms, it is useful to note that he distinguishes within the category of weak answers between the weak-weak answers and the weak-strong answers. According to this distinction, a weak-weak answer fails to challenge the current 'horizon of possibilities', taking it as a given rather than as historically, culturally and politically determined (Santos 2009, p. 3). To suggest that there is no (or no better) solution than a neoliberal market economy to the threats to social justice – of homelessness, hunger and thirst, health, environmental devastation and so on – that are caused by, or at least remain unaddressed in, a neoliberal market economy is to, weakly, refuse to examine the roots and options related to existing, as well as potential, social paradigms. This is to a large extent precisely what the CSR discourse is conveying – a weak-weak answer to chronic social injustice. Some of the most striking lines in the normative portrait of the CSR are 'the business case' for CSR – that is, relying on market forces to correct failings of the market; the over-reliance on voluntary mechanisms – that is, rejecting regulation other than that which is designed to protect the market; the rejection of the potential for the corporate legal persona to do anything other than business – that is, refusing to acknowledge in law the increasing public role assumed by the business organisations and the market forces, thereby frustrating the normative and regulatory legal imagination required to address social injustice.

On the other hand, a weak-strong answer would conceive of the possibility of challenging the dominant paradigm, while acknowledging how the current horizon limits that possibility. This 'open[s] the space for social and political innovation'. The weak-strong answers are in the 'Not Yet' land of possibilities or, as Santos puts it, they emerge both as possibility and as risk. The distinction of weak-weak and weak-strong answers can be illustrated through the inconsistencies and contradictions of human rights on the CSR platform in relation to two of the last important UN initiatives addressing human rights in a business context: the UN Draft Norms on the Responsibility of Corporations and Other Business Enterprises with Regard to Human Rights (the Norms) and the UN Human Rights Framework that resulted from the Special Representative of the Secretary-General (SRSG) mandate. The UN Norms came out in 2003 as an initiative of the Sub-Commission on the Protection and Promotion of Human Rights within the UN Commission on Human Rights. The Norms addressed various points of tension that stemmed from the contradictory role that human rights plays in the CSR discourse. First of all, it addressed in succinct but clear terms the issue of the substantive list of human rights that are concerned; it stated in clear terms the requirement of a successful responsibility system for enforcement and monitoring mechanisms; it addressed the issue of stakeholder involvement. More importantly, however, it emphasised the anachronism and contradictions of human rights on the CSR platform by opening up the possibility of corporate legal responsibility for international human rights law violations 'within their sphere of activity and influence' while acknowledging the primary responsibility of the states. The lobbying that prevented the initiative from progressing towards a debate within the UN General Assembly is well documented. Among the Norms' most contentious elements, which brought the initiative to a standstill, was the attempt to more clearly define the normative and institutional bases for the business–human rights link. This was done primarily by relating the link to the internationally accepted human rights legal platform. By doing this, the Norms took in fact the business and human rights linkage largely *outside* the CSR platform, placing it on a possibly imperfect yet perfectible normative regulatory ground (Weissbrodt 2008; Kinley and Zerial 2007).

Some regarded the 2005 appointment of the SRSG to map out the human rights responsibilities of business organisations as a response to the standstill over the UN Norms (Mares 2012), others saw it as attempt to bring the Norms to a standstill (Kinley and Zerial 2007). The main report coming out of this initiative – *Protect, Respect and Remedy: A Framework for Business and Human Rights* (Ruggie 2008) – formed the basis of the UN Guiding Principles (Ruggie 2011a) adopted in 2011 by the UN Human Rights Council.

CSR experts and scholars are already putting this important and rich document under the microscope in order to extract its potential for change (Mares 2012, Wheeler in this volume). What answers does the Framework give to the strong question of social justice at the confluence of human rights and business? For the most part the document testifies, elaborately, to the status quo. While this is justified to a certain extent by the SRSG's mandate (Voiculescu 2011, p. 16), the lack of normative and institutional imagination is perhaps less justifiable. The SRSG's position on the voluntary–regulatory dichotomy, the setting aside of expert opinion that complementary state–private sector legal responsibilities were possible, the taking of business consensus as a sign of success rather than of a lack of regulatory imagination – these are just some of the indications that the Framework is a weak-weak, complacent response. The SRSG 'was supposed to develop standards, but has instead attempted to derail the standard-setting process and to bow to the corporate refusal to accept any standards except voluntary codes' (Weissbrodt 2008, p. 390).

Of course, the UN Framework and the Principles will take on a life of their own, and some of their most open-ended elements will be put to good use by NGOs, consumers, even courts and legislators – to challenge the dominant paradigm that emerges fundamentally unscathed from the SRSG process. But the weak-strong approach of the UN Norms, promising innovative but controversial legally binding obligations on business, was replaced with the weak-weak UN Principles that prided themselves on consensus. In the latter initiative, human rights discourse was grounded within CSR discourse, thus undermining its normative dimension, and ignoring that '[r]especting and protecting [human rights] was never meant to be an optional extra, a matter of choice', that it 'should be part of the mainstream of any company's strategy, not only seen as part of its corporate social responsibility strategy' (Irene Khan, Secretary-General of Amnesty International cited in Avery 2006).

IEL contributions to human rights answers

Not everybody sees CSR as a weak-weak answer to the questions of social justice. According to Cassel, for instance, in the past decade we have been

witnessing 'the stirrings of a second human rights revolution' that establishes the human rights responsibilities not of governments (as the first
human rights revolution did) but of business organisations (Cassel 1995).
With human rights at its heart, some also see CSR as part of the 'building
blocks' of a new economic order and 'the corporate governance of the
21st Century' (G. Brown 2005, p. 322f; Mullerat 2010). Are there conclusive signs of this new economic order, signs that show that human rights
offer a weak-strong position with respect to the questions of social justice
raised by the global market economy? This is an important question since
the normative and regulatory parameters at the IEL level support or
undermine the normative and regulatory approach at the business organisation level.

Often presented as a 'catalogue of stray topics' in search of consistency,
IEL is a relatively new field of practice and inquiry, covering a more or less
coherent set of domains. It includes public and private elements – economic relations between states as well as, to a certain extent, between
states, business organisations and individuals (Charnovitz 2011; Bunn and
Picker 2008; Perry-Kessaris in this volume). The discipline of economics,
in particular its neo-liberal variant, have been the dominant source of the
IEL's normative core. In the past years, however, this core was targeted by
processes of contestation aiming at the translation – if not transformation
– of IEL's normative core into a higher, more elevated normative language
that acknowledges the importance of democracy and legitimacy in international law (Franck 2006).

Contact between IEL and other so-called 'linkage' domains – such as
environmental protection, labour, human rights, (sustainable) development and, more generally, (global) social justice – has given birth to
normative tension points, and to new substantive areas policy regulation
and research, such as public health, environmental science, public services
and competition law. These all make a claim for the re-negotiation of the
public sphere in ways that are significant for the normative core of IEL.
The CSR discourse itself has made inroads into the IEL spheres. Moreover, from an epistemological point of view, the imagining of the new
normative survival kit for the neoliberal programme, including IEL, necessitates a re-engagement with disciplines such as anthropology, sociology,
moral philosophy and, of course, politics. Such a re-engagement may
inform the shaping of IEL's normativity beyond its now unsatisfactory economic normative paradigm.

This claim towards a new normative dimension is, of course, a challenging one. First of all, there is the need to justify the introduction of a
foreign normative corpus into a fairly discrete and independent discourse,
such as that of international trade or international investment dispute resolution. The subtext of the normative linkages may vary, and may be more
or less in tune with the social expectations surrounding them. For

instance, within both the IEL and the CSR discourses, existing normative parameters are sometimes re-interpreted through the same neoliberal economic lenses (Bagwell and Staiger 2001; Epps and Green 2010), incorporating rather than challenging the socially contested paradigm, and thereby remaining on the weak-weak scale of social reform. Parameters of democracy, environment, social justice are taken into account because, for instance, they are good for supporting long-term trade strategies or because they have been remodelled into a 'business case for...' (Deal 2008; D.K. Brown 2001). This allows the actual neoliberal normative paradigm to go fundamentally unchallenged. Most of the time, however, a sort of normative pragmatic indeterminacy is built into economic and business policy documents. While such indeterminacy can offer an opening for a common language and even accountability, it can also be normatively counterproductive.

Apart from justifying the formal and substantive normative changes, there is also the challenge of applying and operationalising the new normative parameters. A normative linkage brings various risks already manifest both within the IEL jurisprudence and the CSR discourse (Steinberg 1997). The strong, rule-based system of international trade, for instance, is unsettled by the idea of incorporating substantive external normative parameters beyond the level of declarative statements. On the other hand, social discourses such as environmental protection, labour standards, human development and so on, have a lot to lose from the outsourcing of decision-making and dispute resolution processes (that, ironically, it may not even possess yet) to the strong, market-oriented international trade regime. The linkage process, therefore, must be approached cautiously, allowing for an appropriate recognition of the epistemic and normative distinctiveness of the linked areas (Garcia 1998, p. 204).

One way of dealing with these risks on both sides of the normative coupling is by selecting the normative parameters that are to be lost, gained or shared. In principle, there are two approaches. The first aspires towards a certain level of normative universalism based on common roots between the linked social domains. The linkage between international trade or international investment domains and human rights often builds on the use by both sides of the notion of development, although with rather different meanings: development as a human right and as economic imperative. Similarly, at the CSR level, the concept of sustainable development has been increasingly used in order to integrate the new social responsibilities within the corporate agenda while re-enforcing the business case for CSR.

The second approach towards a normative understanding proposes a common normative basis that grows from consensus building processes (Garcia 2005). The WTO and labour standards debate is an example. Some authors, for instance, highlight the advantages of the 1998 ILO

Declaration on Fundamental Principles and Rights at Work for focusing on process-related standards, which have a greater chance to allow consensus to emerge, rather than outcome-related standards, which are much more difficult to negotiate and impose within the complex context of international trade (D. K. Brown 2001). The normative package, however, is often more complex, with the same linkage encountering both universalist and consensus dimensions. The practical – consensus building – approach to labour standards, for instance, will often be accompanied by universalist arguments for labour standards as natural rights or basic human rights (D. K. Brown 2001: 92f). In this process of normative balancing and negotiations, the neoliberal paradigm at both firm and international level appears in search of a soul for its *homo economicus*: corporate law tries to accommodate responsiveness to the public interest by tuning in to the CSR discourse (Corbett and Spender 2009: 148f), while IEL learns the language of 'linkage'.

The linkage between human rights and IEL is particularly complex due to their competing universalist claims. From a normative perspective, the human rights claim to universality is a problem in itself. As a now institutionalised discourse, it is generally accepted that human rights have precedence over any other values and – in the abstract – markets should not be allowed to harm, intentionally or otherwise, any individual's pursuit of welfare and happiness. However, the choice between competing courses of action is complicated considerably by the fact that the neoliberal underpinnings of IEL themselves build on a claim to universality. Put simply, this claim builds on the idea that the neoliberal model of market economy is uncontestably the best economic model for pursuing welfare and happiness. While the market itself does not 'care' directly about each individual, its individualism becomes its main virtue. Individual self-interest is put to work and, in the long run, it benefits society – hence the individual – more than in any other model. Borrowing a Habermasian expression, the market model is presented as 'subjectively anarchic', in the sense that it may produce random results for the individual expectations, but overall it is presented as 'objectively harmonious' – as the most efficient way of achieving almost any socially selected goals. In their turn, international and domestic regulatory instruments re-enforce the idea of social harmony achieved through the pursuit of self-interest within other social spheres (O'Connell 2007).

The neoliberal position on the trade–human rights link is associated with the idea of free, unfettered trade as a fundamental, economic, human right in itself. This position takes its roots from a variety of philosophical traditions and in particular from Mill's liberalism, which proposed economic freedom – based on private ownership – as the premise for liberty. The argument has been put forward that the economic relationships based on free enterprise and human rights share a common normative ground based on the common goal of human development and fulfilment (Aguirre 2008). Economic freedom has long been protected in domestic and international law, but only recently have business actors reached directly for human rights laws and institutions to protect their economic interests (Emberland 2006). Here the IEL normative proposition of trade and economic freedoms as basic freedoms (Petersmann 2002) is coupled with the business agency's aspiration to a citizenship status that entitles it to protection *under* human rights law (Grear 2007). The right to own property, freedom of speech and freedom of expression, the right to privacy, are some of the legally protected rights that have been used by corporations in order to curb the public authority's exercise of regulatory or enforcement powers. Human rights have been therefore converted and some would say diverted – often through courts – to the protection of the corporate entity (Emberland 2006; Grear 2007). The corporate duty to respect, protect and fulfil human rights becomes thus coupled with the corporate right to the human rights themselves.

IEL normative signals to CSR

Starting from such strained normative premises, it is unsurprising that the regulatory link between international economic domains such as trade, investment, and development on the one hand and the international human rights law on the other, has been rather feeble and has given only scant support to human rights on the CSR platform. Selective and inconsistent human rights causes have occasionally been met, for instance, with economic embargo measures imposed either unilaterally (Iglesias 1996, p. 371) or in the name of a fragmented international community via the UN Security Council (Reinisch 2001).

In the past years, however, various international organisations have come under pressure to value human rights in their decision-making processes. For example, when the World Bank was pressured to pay more attention to the risks to the environment that are posed by the major infrastructural projects that its supports (Abouharb and Cingranelli 2006; Clark 2002), it responded with social and environmental policy frameworks (Horta 2002; Bradlow 1996). Similarly, the International Monetary Fund (IMF) started applying human rights conditionalities (Bradlow 1996; Abouharb and Cingranelli 2006) associated with the various structural adjustment programmes it financed (Abouharb and Cingranelli 2007; Dreher 2009).

The GATT/WTO system is the site of further deep tensions between the international economic system and the human rights discourse. Institutionally, this is a linkage platform of great importance, with GATT/WTO being at the heart of the international trade system. The strong rule-based WTO system is oriented towards defining the international

trade-human rights interface as almost exclusively a matter of accommodating (or not) human rights within the WTO system, not the other way
round (see Flores Elizondo in this volume). So, although the first paragraph of the preamble to the 1994 WTO Agreement mentions the raising
of the standards of living, full employment, sustainable development and
environmental protection as guiding social values of the processes of international trade, these guiding values are not easily operationalized within
the system. The impression given by the Preamble and other such statements that international economic activity is a means to a noble, human,
end belies the very different, instrumental approach of the substantive
institutional provisions. In this approach, human rights are acceptable
normative elements only to the extent to which this can further the
achievement of the WTO objectives (Breining-Kaufmann 2005, p. 103).

WTO member states and NGOs have raised a number of arguments in
favour of introducing a human rights normative dimension into international trade practices. For example, in relation to Article III GATT on
'like' products they have unsuccessfully argued that a Member State
ought to be able to discriminate against an apparently like product based
on Process and Production Methods (PPMs) criteria – that is, on the fact
that the product is manufactured in a manner that violates labour or
human rights. Similar efforts are underway to ensure the validity under
the WTO rules of labelling programmes that facilitate discrimination
against products manufactured in conditions that violate labour and
human rights. Under WTO rules such programmes are more likely than
not to be classified as technical barriers to trade (Breining-Kaufmann
2005, p. 109).

One example of the instrumentalisation of human rights within the
international trade system is to be found in Article XX GATT (Marceau
2002) under which a contracting party may derogate from the most
favoured nation (MFN) principle *inter alia* for reasons of public morals
and the protection of human life and health (Article XX(a) and (b)). The
concept of 'public morals' remains rather ambiguous and the scope of its
application remains to e decided (Marceau 2002). Article XX(b) allows
room for a somewhat clearer linkage at least to the human rights related
to the protection of life and health, because the Appellate Body appears
to be taking a flexible approach to the interpretation of the notion of
'risk'. However, Article XX(b) appears limitative, the various economic
interactions under the WTO system having potentially a far broader
impact on human rights than what Article XX(b) allows to be understood
even when interpreted flexibly (O'Connell 2007).

Finally, the normative challenges identified earlier in the CSR discourse
appear to be largely reproducing the normative rigidities of IEL. If there
is a normative universalism that is active in this context, this is not the one
of human rights but rather the one of the market. Any 'consensus'

between the two discourses takes the form of compromise based on the smallest normative impact on the market ideology.

Human rights offers, the terms offered by Santos, a weak-weak answer to the questions of social justice posed at the CSR and IEL regulatory spheres. Neither sphere illustrates a significant change in paradigm, opting instead for a more or less openly the 'business case for...' as the proposed road to new horizons of justice. While it is not impossible to conceive some progress being achieved by following some of the mechanisms illustrated in this chapter at both CSR and IEL levels, these are far from challenging the *status quo*.

Conclusion

The normative underpinnings of global market economy have been contested in business organisations and international institutions, with international human rights norms increasingly used as an umbrella discourse. What happens to human rights when they are in conversation and competition to other normative systems? This chapter focused on one particular contact area, the one between human rights and the market economy discourse as the dominant economic model. It looked into the points of tension at both the micro, firm-based level that is predominantly reflected in the CSR debate, and the macro, international economic law level. Both levels were acknowledged in specific ways, as interplays of private–public regulatory networks.

The two discourses – the human rights and the market economy one – are brought into contact by a search for an answer to the challenge of social justice, a challenge to which both discourses otherwise appear to have their particular answer. The chapter is using the question of social justice as *the* strong question of our times and it takes Santos' distinction between weak-weak and weak-strong answers to a strong question as its main analytical framework in order to identify the extent to which the development of the human rights discourse on a CSR and IEL platform has the potential to enhance rather than postpone the pursuit of global justice. In this sense, the chapter emphasised the conflicts and normative incompatibilities of human rights and CSR, while highlighting the IEL's failure to provide conceptual support for a meaningful corporate responsibility.

The aim of the chapter was not to identify the minutia potential of one CSR initiative or another, not even of the latest one, the UN SRSG Principles. Rather, it attempts to capture the state of a discourse and of a dialogue together with the former's impoverished potential to enlarge the horizon of justice. In this sense, it looks not into what answer is given to the expectation for justice at the confluence between human rights and the market, but rather into how the two discourses interact. As Santos puts it candidly in his article, 'Whose side are they on? This is my basic criterion'.

Human rights on the CSR platform plays an important part in the normative re-negotiation of the link between the business and the economic spheres on the one hand and the social justice sphere on the other hand. The chapter emphasises that the controversial yet apparently strong development of the CSR linkages relates to the IEL's inadequate response to the new social expectations for a change in the socio-economic normative paradigm. However, CSR is itself revealed as an imperfect human rights channel. It is argued that a more substantial business and human rights linkage, that can bring a concrete impact on the realisation of human rights at the business organisation level, can only take shape if supported by a clearer, more focused and assertive IEL-level linkage that would recognise the human rights normativity, universality and ultimately imperative regulatory nature. In doing so, however, the very rationale of CSR – as a weak-weak answer, as an answer that does not challenge the hegemonic paradigms – would be itself challenged to the point of dissipation, allowing a human rights weak-strong answer to maybe take shape.

Chapter 16

Rewriting the centricity of the state in pursuit of global justice

Kirsteen Shields

Introduction

Whilst for Karl Polanyi it was the market, nowadays it is the corporation that is most often vilified as the source of global inequality. Yet the corporation is but a legal construct. It may be said, therefore, that the roots of global inequality lie within law. More specifically, these roots may be entangled within the boundaries, both conceptual and physical, that international law has constructed. Whilst our international institutions wrestle with the regulation of corporations, the underlying reality is that the state-centric structure at the centre of international law was intended for an entirely different world. Economic globalisation has diminished the importance of traditional boundaries of geography. Consequently, the fragmentation of geographically based communities and the construction of identity-based communities cast doubt over the utility and continued relevance of 'nationality' as a means of organising societies. The concept of state sovereignty, therefore, the cornerstone of international law, is based on geographical boundaries that no longer hold the significance they once did. In 'sovereignty' what was intended as a fortress may have become a prison.

Yet, the 'international community' continues to cling to the state as the *only* legitimate vehicle of international law. Only states are recognised as actors before the International Court of Justice (ICJ), only states are treated as full members of the United Nations (UN), and only states can sign international treaties. The supremacy of the state is further embedded in the principle of non-intervention – a principle that sits uncomfortably with the deepening of cosmopolitanism globally. Similarly, the doctrine of *pacta sunt servanda* endows treaty law with an almost sacred infallibility, enthroning the state as gatekeeper of international law.

Given the limitations of the modern state, this chapter is concerned with the extent to which international law, and specifically the exclusive nature of 'statehood', may serve as a 'root cause' of global inequality. Central to this critique is an understanding of the relationship between state sovereignty and 'fairness'. Here fairness (adapted from that of Thomas Franck, 1995) is understood as both procedural (global democracy) and substantive (distribution). It is argued that global inequality stems from an over-reliance on states as the bearers of both democracy and distribution. Given the economic and political restraints on state power, states simply are not effective procedural or substantive conduits.

This chapter is divided into two parts. It begins with an exploration of the dominant positivist narrative of international law, suggesting that the rise of positivism in the nineteenth century and the corresponding distancing from natural law principles has entrenched 'sovereignty', rather than, for example, 'peoples', as the cornerstone of international law. A troubling consequence of this metanarrative is that it encourages the unaccountability of corporations in certain legal contexts. This has served the rapacious growth of international economic law but has led to a certain disempowerment of human rights law as an instrument of change, or of justice.

The latter part of the chapter presents an alternative narrative that recognises the contribution of social movements in challenging inequality and in changing legal tradition. It is proposed that the success of these movements lies in their circumvention of the legal fiction of the state. It is hoped that through acknowledging the links between social movements and legal change, and then the link between legal change and distributive justice, we may achieve a critical distance from law that casts light on its ideological nature.

Metanarrative: state sovereignty in international law

In legal analyses of international law the state is its beating heart (Hall, 1880; Oppenheim et al. 1992; Brownlie, 2008; Oppenheim et al., 1905). By contrast, sociological interpretations of international law recognise the role of non-state actors in shaping international law (Weber et al., 1978; Hirsch, 2005; Cotterell, 2006). Had the natural law construction of international law not been dislodged by positivism in the nineteenth century we might now be living in an entirely different world. For a start, an understanding of legal personality might have evolved to relate to capacity rather than status. As it stands, however, corporate misdemeanours can be easily tucked away behind the thin veil of incorporation. The extent to which the 'modern state' benefits or suffers from this relationship depends on the extent of their alliances with said corporations. The reality is that the majority of corporations are domiciled and owned by developed states (Dunning and Lundan, 2008; Mayo, 2012). It is developed states, therefore, who stand to benefit most when corporations siphon profits of their foreign operations back to their home states.

From principles to rules

By supporting the unaccountability of corporations under human rights law and through the doctrines of legal personality and state sovereignty, law, and specifically legal positivism, has served the unfettered growth of corporate entities. On this basis, the dawn of corporate expansion may be traced to the detachment of natural law theories of international law in favour of positivist constructions of international law. Positivism was introduced as the basis of international law by European jurists in the nineteenth century and replaced the prevailing theory of natural law at the heart of international law. The rejection of natural law theories (Grotius, 1625; Bate *et al.*, Gentili *et al.*, 1933) in favour of more 'reason-based' law (Wheaton, 1846; Westlake, 1894; Hall, 1880) marked a critical junction in the evolution of international law. In particular, it marked the start of law's departure from foundations based on theories of morality and/or justice. As Anghie explains, '[P]ositivists rejected completely the naturalist notions that sovereign states were bound by an overarching natural law or that state action had to be guided by a higher morality' (Anghie, 1999: 12).

The dominance of positivism bore heavy symbolic consequences for those nations excluded from the elite group of 'sovereign states'. The underlying rationale of international law shifted from the naturalist notion of a 'single, universally applicable law' that 'governed a naturally constituted society of nations', to a positivist conception of international law as 'the exclusive province of civilised societies' (Anghie, 1999: 12). This shift signalled the subordination of principles of justice (fairness and equality being implicit therein) to principles of power (entailing exclusivity and inequality). Public international law's allusion to 'justice' provided a thin veneer on the cultural and economic imperialism of the West (Koskenniemi, 2001).

Castellino details the link between 'freezing' of boundaries and positivist doctrines of *terra nullius* and *uti possidetis juris* as follows:

> This broad definition of *terra nullius* served historically to legitimize the acquisition of large tracts of land throughout the nineteenth and early twentieth centuries and had a particularly adverse effect on indigenous communities. Once land was acquired, boundary lines were drawn to demarcate ownership between settlers. These boundaries were eventually recognized as territorial demarcations on the basis of which valid statehood – and its accompanying right of territorial integrity – could be awarded. The system was then buffered from change in a period of transition by the doctrine of *uti possidetis juris*, which sought to maintain order by freezing the boundaries.
>
> (Castellino, 2008: 507)

Subsequently, on establishing statehood, related concepts of 'recognition' and 'personality' became conceptual tools for exclusion of societies. Statehood brought privileges alongside responsibilities; the privilege of treaty-making acted as a gateway right to the subsequent privileges to resource trading and borrowing (Pogge, 2006: 737). That the mechanism of sovereignty, and related concepts such as recognition and personality, served to oppress non-European peoples is often omitted in modern edits of international law but has been widely acknowledged in counter movements within legal scholarship, such as that of Third World Approaches to International Law (TWAIL) (Anghie, 2003; Chimni, 2004; Rajagopal, 2000).

Subtext I: corporations have impunity

Meanwhile, processes of privatisation have stripped the state of one of its key raisons d'être: social welfare provision. Other key aspects of statehood are similarly no longer readily identifiable; the waters of state characteristics, traditionally thought to include jurisdiction, nationality and citizenship, have become steadily murkier throughout the twentieth century. The cross-border flow of persons and assets has triggered new understandings of jurisdiction, which present choice rather than exclusivity of jurisdiction. With similar elasticity, nationality and citizenship have further diminished the function of the state beyond regulating for its 'citizens' (Picciotto, 1999: 3). Yet, the ways and means of international law have not evolved in accordance with our understanding of citizenship and the state in order to serve society. Arguably, as per Polanyi, society has evolved instead to serve the market (Polanyi, 1944). International law has assisted this process.

For example, rather than evolve to adequately regulate business entities, international law has entrenched the legal fiction of the state with what Sol Picciotto has identified as 'another layer of legal fiction' – the legal personality of business entities (Picciotto, 1999). Picciotto explains that the concept of corporate personality in capitalist countries in the nineteenth century 'very quickly became a malleable form, in the hands of creative lawyers, to ... accommodate formal legal requirements to the strategies of capital accumulation' (Picciotto, 1999: 3). The removal of personal risk through legal personality endowed corporations with a unique feature that enabled them to take risks, both financial and social, which an individual simply could not routinely take.

The construction of law supporting the corporate entity has assisted their unprecedented growth. Legal regimes such as the international investment regime and international property rights, for instance, assign corporations with exclusive ownership and control over technology, territory and natural resources (Brownlie, 2008: 516–28; Beitz, 1999: 146). These regimes are constituted almost entirely of bilateral investment treaties or international investment agreements, many of which simply score out reference to prevailing principles of environmental or human rights law (Development, 2010). Ironically this entity endowed with personality within states is not recognised outside of the state – corporations are not recognised in international jurisdictions (Klabbers, 2003, Clapham, 2006).

The corporation therefore serves as an effective 'deflection device' (Dine, 2005: 43), serving to deflect responsibility away from that other legal fiction 'the sovereign state' – (and all the while keeping individuals out of the firing line). When, in the delivery of essential services leading to the provision of basic rights, the state passes the baton to corporations through a process of privatisation it effectively sends responsibility for these activities off the radar. Since the activity may be controlled by one state but operationalised in another, the responsibility of holding corporations responsible may require coordinated response by states that rarely occurs in practice. In instances where the hosting state prosecutes, the home state may refuse to enforce the judgement as has recently occurred in the case of Chevron in Ecuador (although subsequently overturned).[1]

This 'disappearing responsibility act' has transfigured traditional international law almost beyond recognition. The deployment of corporations as a second engine of states has accelerated the denunciation of natural law approaches to international law, in favour of more rule-driven, positivist approaches. In the case of states, consideration of general principles of international law may enter when states are held responsible for their obligations through adjudication before the Permanent Court of the International Court of Justice. Corporations, on the other hand, have been able to slip through the net of such jurisdictions and generally operate within an alternative reality of private mediation through international arbitration forums. Deepening the divide is a failure to identify, let alone resolve, gaps, overlaps and clashes between these two regimes (Shelton, 2006).

Subtext II: marginalisation of human rights law

This reading of the relationship between positivism and capitalism cannot be dissociated from the decline of international human rights law as an instrument of change. In *The Dark Side of Virtue* David Kennedy attempts a list of 'possible downsides, open risks, bad results which have sometimes occurred, which might well occur' when 'well-meaning people attempt to express their humanitarian yearnings on the global stage' (Kennedy and Mayhew, 2004: xv, 30). In a similar vein, Makau Mutua takes issue with the subtext of the human rights movement that 'depicts an epochal contest pitting savages, on the one hand, against victims and saviour, on the other' (Mutua, 2001: 201). Alex de Waal expresses a similar sentiment in his view of human rights as an exercise of power, in a world where ideals become commodities along with everything else: 'The global ethical enterprise,' he argues, 'begins in moral solipsism' (Waal, 2001: 1). Naomi Klein has made a strong case that the neutral, impartial and non-political nature of Amnesty International has encouraged the human rights movement to focus on crimes and not the causes behind human rights violations (Klein, 2007).

This critique has been countered by Susan Marks in her appraisal of Klein's *The Shock Doctrine*. Marks makes the point that the contemporary human rights movement has begun to focus on 'root causes' of human rights violations:

> The questions of the causes, indeed the 'root causes', of human rights violations has become a central and very conspicuous element of discussions within global civil society and, perhaps most strikingly, the United Nations.
>
> (Marks, 2011: 59)

In some instances, that 'root cause' can be found in the misapplication or non-application of law. In other contexts, inequality is rooted in legal lacunae – for example, the lack of adequate provisions for the protection and enforcement of economic, social and cultural rights. In yet more contexts, and this is the key contention here, it can be found in the precise application of law.

The latter instances have been facilitated by the growth of treaty law, which has pushed the 'general principles' as a source of international law into relative obscurity. When aired, the much maligned and neglected principle of equity has appeared only as 'corrective equity'– a shadow of its former, broader, self (Franck, 1995: 57). In *Fairness in International Law and Institutions* Thomas Franck calls for a return to considerations of procedural and substantive 'fairness' in international law. Procedural fairness is generally recognised as democracy. Substantively, Rawls refers to 'equity' as bearing the potential to channel what he describes as 'distributive justice' in law. 'Distributive justice' theory offers a theory for the best allocation of goods amongst societies and is generally accredited to Rawls egalitarian theory (Rawls and Kelly, 2001).

Yet the human rights framework, somewhat paralysed in its state-centricity, has little power to carry 'distributive justice'. It is unable to join the dots between extraterritorial obligations and international cooperation (Salomon *et al.*, 2007; Skogly and Gibney, 2010). Instead it clings to the idea that the best way to ensure human rights provision is by insisting upon states as the primary duty-bearers who should do a better job for *their* citizens on *their* territory.

To insist on the state as the vehicle for global justice (for example in the distribution of human rights) is to fail to acknowledge that state-centricity can be an exploitative structure. It encourages us to close our eyes to, or at least detach ourselves from, responsibility for the 'injustices' experienced by individuals within the black box of their own state (Føllesdal and Pogge, 2005: 121). But throughout history there have been those who have rejected such a state-centric world view – from the Abolitionist Movement to ethical trade movements and perhaps even the Occupy Movement.

Alterna(rra)tive: towards a more 'heroic' text

In the absence of any legal responsibility for global distribution, it is humanitarian missions and well-placed lawyers who have lead what Koskenniemi (2001: 511) terms the 'heroic period' of international law (to be distinguished from the 'colonising' mission[2]). It is possible to trace the humanitarian impulse, what Falk terms 'the law of humanity' (Falk, 1998), through legal developments prior to the human rights movement and up to the present day. Some of the greatest breakthroughs in legislation pertaining to global wealth distribution have been instigated by civil society, often driven by charismatic individuals and not our international institutions.[3] The Abolition Movement is a primary example. The Abolitionist Movement represents a triumph for the social movements in the construction of 'global distributive' law, the counter-wave it embodied has since extended to the labour rights movement (as in law which legislates for wealth distribution). This is the narrative that journeys between law and justice.

Distributive justice social movements have traditionally had the potential to restructure international relations by aligning themselves with the demands of developing states and humanitarianism (Della Porta and Diani, 2006), acting as redistributive 'counter-movements' and challenging hierarchies within and between states. In so doing they have challenged and transformed behaviour in areas beyond the reach of law, whilst simultaneously highlighting the failures of law.

Recent social movement action has driven important legal developments in the areas of environmental law (the establishment of the World Commission on Dams),[4] international humanitarian law (an advisory opinion of the International Court of Justice regarding the threat or use of nuclear weapons),[5] and also in international economic law.[6] With regard to this latter field, the following section focuses on the legal impact of social movements which triggered human rights realization by challenging the commodification of labour. Similar research can and has been undertaken on the impact of social movement on other commodities, for example, land (see Dangl, 2007; Petras and Veltmeyer, 2005).

Social movements can (much like a corporation) invoke change in both tangible and intangible ways. They can generate a change in the letter of the law by influencing law-makers and they can also influence social norms, for example by embodying certain principles (Cohen and Rai, 2000). Their impact is especially influential in areas that appear to be beyond the reach of regulation, such as the fields of human rights and the environment. These areas may be governed by regulation but have no effective means of ensuring compliance with regulation. Given the obstacles of enforcement within these fields, social movements can play an essential role in generating compliance with human rights and environmental norms.

Global distributive justice social movements have limited the power of corporations in international economic law by acting as a counter force in the realm of labour rights. The growth of this counter force can be traced through international legal normative developments in the advancement of labour standards and this chapter charts these developments up to present day developments in worker empowerment through co-ownership of the corporation. An interest in ownership and in alternative forms of ownership is emerging in all contexts of corporate activity and particularly in forestry regulation and ethical trade movements.[7] By contributing to legal changes in ownership, social movements offer a new method of challenging inequality beyond reliance on the inherently inadequate, state-centric, UN Economic, Social and Cultural Rights framework – could it be that therein lies its success?

The Abolitionist movement

One example of an alterna(rra)tive is provided by the Abolitionist movement, which stands as a landmark in the complex and reflexive evolution of the relationship between social movements and the law. Growing social awareness contributed to the contestation of slavery in various economic, social, political, philosophical, moral, religious contexts from the nineteenth century. The migration of social protest throughout Europe and the US ultimately led to changes in the law, which would in turn fundamentally impact on the structure of social relationships between individuals. The earliest recorded legal statements against slavery were concerned with the slave trade rather than use of slaves, and restricted to the nation states, namely Britain and the USA. In the UK, court judgments preceded the Act of Parliament 1807 outlawing the trade of slaves. In the US federal states starting abolishing slavery[8] and the Supreme Court judgments condemned slavery[9] ahead of the nationwide outlawing through the Thirteenth Amendment to the Constitution in 1865. This then spread to the British Colonies.[10]

Slowly but surely the migration of moral consensus achieved global consensus. The 1926 Slavery Convention sought to include slavery, the slave trade, forced labour and the slave trade at sea. Many states dragged their heels over 'forced labour'.[11] The overriding ethos of the negotiations of the 1926 Slavery Conventions is a continuation of the 'civilising' mission of the nineteenth century. The original seventy-seven signatories were later joined by states that had become party to the 1926 Slavery Convention by way of consenting to the 1953 Protocol amending the 1926 Slavery Convention. As of February 2010 ninety-nine states had signed the 1926 Slavery Convention and 123 states had signed the 1956 Supplementary Convention on the Abolition of Slavery, the Slave Trade, and Institutions and Practices Similar to Slavery.[12] This was later followed by the 1953 Protocol Amending the Slavery Convention and the 1956 Supplementary Convention. In this way mobilisation of public opinion achieved structural change that was codified in law.

The abolition of slavery had a significant impact on the distribution of wealth within states by setting legal limits on the exploitation of humans by humans. The codification of the moral consensus on slavery into an international covenant represents a landmark realisation of the impact of social movements on the law. Furthermore, by limiting the exploitation of labour, it generated a counter pressure to the hegemony of capitalism.

The labour movement

Labour law has the potential to act as an agent of distribution (of wealth) within states and, increasingly, between developed and developing states. Many advances in labour standards were born of individual struggles mobilised through national and international social movements such as the 1999 Battle of Seattle protests outside the WTO and the movement for a living wage in the US.[13] These developments within labour law have subsequently impacted on the structural relationships within and between states.

However, there are concerns that labour movements are not always beneficial to the relatively poor. For example, when they seek to retain industry within developed states they may prevent global wealth distribution; and when they pursue global labour standards, they may strip developing states of their comparative advantage in lower labour standards (Bhagwati, 1995) – and of those foreign investors who might otherwise have located there. Furthermore, some states were better resourced to enforce labour standards than others. Such critiques have contributed to lack of consensus on labour rights, and a considerable downshifting of ambition to a four 'core labour rights' at the International Labour Organization (ILO) (Alston, 2004).

One of the most significant features of the ILO in respect of distribution was that it formally recognised trade unions as stakeholders at the international level. This provided a platform for unions to express interests and convene internationally to circumvent the suppressive practices of multinational enterprises (Windmuller et al., 2010; Croucher and Cotton,

2011). The growth of international networks of labour movements has been incremental in enabling greater distribution processes from corporations. Peter Waterman and Jill Timms distil the growth of international labour movements into three periods of capitalism: Period 1, Early (largely European) craft and industrial capitalism, *c.* 1830s–1870s; Period 2, the mature industrial–national phase, *c.* 1880s–1970s, including the European periphery and parts of the (semi-) colonial world; and Period 3, the beginning of a globalised capitalism *c.* 1980s–today (Waterman, 2004–5).

As social movements have strengthened in their pursuit of distribution, the threat to this posed by globalisation has steadily increased. Gains made within the sphere of labour rights have come under persistent and direct attack from corporations. The sustained erosion of the right to freedom of assembly by corporations (in some instances with state support) provides an insight into the pressure point where demand for distribution can be suppressed. The ILO report also noted a decrease in allegations concerning the denial of civil liberties since 1995, yet noted that the largest single category of allegations, both globally and by region, concerns acts of anti-union discrimination (ILO, 2008: 10).

Counter-counter movements?

What is astonishing is that as globalisation has increased, protection of labour standards appears to have decreased. Tilly, for one, attributes this inverse relationship to the concomitant decline of the state in the process of globalisation, remarking that '[a]s states decline, so do workers' *rights*'; '[n]o individual state will have the power to enforce workers' rights in the fluid world that is emerging' (Tilly, 1995: 21).

Is the answer, then, a reinvigoration of the nation state? Ronaldo Munck points out the logic of Tilly's position would infer a 'defence of strengthening of the nation state if that is seen as the only way for workers' across the globe to retain or gain social economic and political rights' (Munck, 2000: 84). Yet, as the former part of this chapter suggested, insistence on state-sovereignty is what led us into this predicament in the first place. Besides, whilst many advocate a return to the safety of the nation state, changes in communication render a return as such somewhat implausible – indeed these changes were laid out as grounds for reform at the opening of this chapter.

What next then in the pursuit of global justice? This is admittedly a rather large question, yet a critical look at mechanisms of poverty alleviation would suggest that the greatest contribution to greater equality occurs not through human rights mechanisms but through the move towards co-ownership by employees within their organisations and employer corporations. Labour rights have only gone so far in advancing global distribution. Social movements have challenged corporate exploitation through influencing a chain of legal developments that ensure greater legislative protection of labour standards.

Yet the realisation of these standards internationally remains elusive. Whilst the statistics are rough and aggregate the International Labour Organization's (ILO) first global estimate on forced labour reported a *minimum* of 12.3 million (Belser *et al.*, 2005.), and some make higher estimates, such as Kevin Bales (Bales, 2005), who estimated 27 million in 2005. Overcoming the structural inequalities tied up in hierarchy requires rewiring the background rules that structure exploitation, principally, property law. The following section will present the case that social movements are beginning to reach out to these rules. Innovative systems of organisation are serving to enable workers to deconstruct the corporation from within through ownership, leading to greater democracy and distribution within those organisations. The aim is to democratise the organisations within the state from the bottom-up, rather than asking the state to regulate these organisations on behalf of its citizens.

Ownership movements

In his insightful analysis of labour law at century's end, D'Antona describes new and unforeseen demands advanced by workers as 'a vision of the worker not subaltern'. Central to the empowerment of workers is 'a new organisation of time to overcome rigid synchrony between production time and the time for life'. D'Antona also identifies that change will be catalysed by a 'new interest in worker participation as owners of the enterprise (really of anything on which one depends)' (D'Antona, 2002: 44). This new interest in workers as owners of the enterprise materialises in shareholding by employees. Increasingly employees are opting to trade the security of wage subordination for the control and risk involved in shareholding. As D'Antona identifies, 'Worker ownership of shares is a factor in the spread of economic power through the socialisation of property in favour of non-capitalist components of the firm. In this sense, it inserts into labour relations a previously unknown element' (D'Antona, 2002: 44).

Employee shareholding and other forms of distributed ownership facilitate the distribution of control necessary for the fulfilment of much of the international human rights framework. Rights are viewed in this respect as a mechanism for poverty alleviation, not as ends in themselves (UN Office of the High Commissioner for Human Rights, 2002). Where this fails – where labour is either unavailable or labour conditions are set so low as to inhibit escape from poverty – efforts may be made to seize ownership of capital in order to survive. This may occur on an individual basis or may become a popularised struggle in the form of a social movement, such as the land rights movement in Zimbabwe (see Moyo and Yeros, 2005).

Whilst not entirely conclusive, there is evidence to suggest that the Fairtrade movement is achieving good levels of compliance with international labour standards and also having some trickle-over impact on social economic and cultural rights in the labourer's communities (Nelson and Pound, 2009). Fairtrade has successfully fostered and linked several social enterprises together under the umbrella of Fairtrade certification. Collective decision-making processes replicating ownership in Fairtrade and collective ownership in forestry movements demonstrate the value of co-ownership as a mechanism for human rights in areas where the state, for whatever reason, does not provide. The successes of these movements in delivering labour standards whilst investing in communities serve to highlight the limits of the traditional human rights framework, constrained as it is by the state.

By operating through a network of social enterprises with smaller hierarchies, Fairtrade can be seen to be deconstructing the corporation from within. The evolution towards redistribution of ownership within the corporation finds a halfway house in social enterprises. Although definitions vary, Maria Granado defines social enterprises as occupying a unique space within the economy where, as businesses, they are driven by the need to be financially sustainable but, compared with a normal, for-profit organisation, they use economic surpluses to drive social and environmental growth. Additionally, social enterprises are distinguishable from other non-profit or charity organisations because they trade in the competitive marketplace (Granados et al., 2011; Horst, 2008; Kogut and Zander, 1992; Drucker, 1991).

Co-ownership and property rights

The right to property has repeatedly been identified as the bad apple of the human rights framework and, more recently, of new institutionalist development strategies. For example, Marx's exposé of the rights of man as the rights of the bourgeoisie was based on the claim that the right to property led to the universal extension of market principles to all of society.[14] More recently, David Kennedy has responded to development strategies that advocate clear and strong property rights (for example, North, 1973; Soto, 2000) with a warning that they are guilty of the:

> propagation of a serious misestimation of the allocative role of law. A property regime, like any other legal order, is all about choices. Small and large, these choices cannot be made by reasoning outward from the nature of property or general ideas about constitutions' 'good law'. They require economic, social and ethical analysis, and must be made and contested in those terms.
>
> (Kennedy, 2011: 55)

Arguably the problem is not the existence of property rights but rather their distribution. Particularly compelling is Polanyi's argument that it is the commodification of fictional commodities of labour, land and money that have led to society being controlled by the market, rather than the market controlled by society (Polanyi, 1944). On this note, the ongoing Occupy Movement[15] can be seen to represent the rejection of commodification of land (through its core strategy of occupying public space), whilst also offering a vision of community without the invisible boundaries of the market. Through the core aim of occupying public space, the Occupy Movement is using the physicality of occupation to manifest the re-acquisition of public space, creating the potential for its deconstruction, redistribution and redesign public space.

Critics have pointed out that the Occupy protesters lack a collective objective, yet there is much to learn from both the action of physically seizing public spaces and the subsequent non-hierarchical organisational structures employed in the Occupy 'camps'. 'Occupiers' are reclaiming the public space that has been squeezed to the margins by the 'city' – by the market. The Occupy Movement sees individuals bypassing the invisible boundaries of the market and constructing new communities (albeit transitory ones) without the commodities of labour and land, and, in some of the Occupy camps, without the commodity of money.

In rejecting these commodities, Occupiers have sought to free society from the market. Unified in their reaction to increased inequality amongst groups in society (local and global), they have identified the harmful impact of the market as global. What is more, by joining the dots globally, they have taken a bold step into that unknown territory – a distributive movement that does not necessitate nor call for a reinvigoration of the state, but which goes beyond the veil of state-sovereignty to ask for real remedies from global powers. One Occupier writes:

> There is only individual responsibility and accountability, with a counterweight of faith in the process of mutual aid. The empowering sense that we are all connected though commonality of work and all forms of survival – be they physical, mental, or spiritual – is embedded in our processes and our search for alternatives.
>
> (Suzahn, 2011: 1)

This manifests itself through communal spaces and property such as libraries and sanitation; through 'university tents' offering free education; through the provision of communal meals; through communal labour as a prerequisite to joining the camps.

Conclusion

This chapter has sought to critique the metanarrative of *sovereignty* in international law as an instrument of *inequality*. Both sovereignty and inequality are attached to certain *narratives*; sovereignty relates to that of positivism, inequality relates to that of capitalism. Within this paradigm, the relationship between the narratives of positivism and capitalism emerges – what is presented as cast-iron law crumbles into ideology. This is not to say an international order based on natural law would be any less ideological. Law, like all else, cannot escape ideology, yet it must recognise which ideology it serves. Tracing the successes of distributive justice social movements, as essentially doing the business of delivering on the principle of equity in international law, serves to highlight the shortcomings of a system of justice that insists on states as its messenger. As many international lawyers have already pointed out, addressing the many economic and environmental challenges facing the world today requires joined-up problem-solving and collective solutions. In so doing they might want to take their cue from social movements who have been doing just that for centuries.

Notes

1 See In re Application of Chevron Corp., No. 10–4699, 2011 WL 2023257, at *14 (3d Cir. May 25, 2011).
2 Koskennicmi uses this term to describe the efforts of French and German lawyers in the period between 1879 and 1939 throughout Koskenniemi, Marti. 2004. 'The Gentle Civilizer of Nations: The Rise and Fall of International Law 1870–1960', Hersh Lauterpacht Memorial Lectures, Cambridge (for example at 511).
3 For example, the first instance of prohibition on child labour in the UK is believed to have been instigated by an individual mill owner, Robert Owen. His vision was that New Lanark should act as a model for reform in labour conditions across Europe. This has been described as 'the real beginning of industrial legislation'. Follows, J. W. 1951. *Antecedents of the International Labour Organization*, Oxford, Clarendon Press.
4 The establishement of the World Commission on Dams as discussed in Kader, Asmal. 2001. 'Introduction: World Commission on Dams Report, Dams and Development', 16 *Am U INTK K REV* 1411.
5 See 'Legality of the Threat or Use of Nuclear Weapons', 1996, ICJ 95 (note, in particular, Justice Weeramantry's dissent). This advisory opinion was the result of a global movement against nuclear weapons.
6 For example see Bradlow, Daniel. 1994. 'International Organizations and Private Complaints: The Case of the World Bank Inspection Panel', 34, *VA J IINT L K* 553.
7 Paradoxically, this element of ownership is what is fundamentally missing from the social business model advocated by Nobel Peace prize winning 'Banker to the Poor', Mohammad Yunus. See Yunus, M. and Weber, K. 2007. *Creating a World Without Poverty: Social Business and the Future of Capitalism*, New York, PubliCAffairs; London: Perseus Running [distributor].

8 For example, the Vermont Constitution of 1777 in its Declaration of Rights of Inhabitants of Vermont; and Pennsylvania in 1780 and Rhode Island in 1784 enacted statutes for the 'gradual abolition of slavery'.

9 For a discussion of early decisions of the United States Supreme out relating to slavery, see Roper, D.M. 1969. 'In Quest of Juridicial Objectivity: The Marshall Court and the Legitimation of Slavery', 21 *Stanford Law Review* 532.

10 'An Act for the Abolition of Slavery Throughout the British Colonies; For Promoting the Industry of the Manumitted Slaves; and for Compensating the Persons Hitherto Entitled to the Services of Such Slaves', 3 & 4 Will. 4, c. 73 (1833).

11 See League of Nations. 1925. 'Questions of Slavery: Report of the Sixth Committee: Resolution', *League of Nations Official Journal* (Special Supplement 33) Records of the Sixth Assembly: Text of Debates, Nineteenth Plenary Meeting, 26 September 1925, pp. 156–157. Alain, Jean. 2008. *The Slavery Conventions: The Travaux Preparatoires of the 1926 League of Nations Convention and the 1956 United Nations Convention*, Martinus Nijhoff.

12 See the United Nations Treaty Collections online database on these treaties at http://treaties.un.org/pages/ViewDetails.aspx?src=TREATY&mtdsg_no=XVIII-3&chapter=18&lang=en and http://treaties.un.org/pages/ViewDetailsIII.aspx?&src=TREATY&mtdsg_no=XVIII~4&chapter=18&Temp=mtdsg3&lang=en.

13 Stephanie Luce details how new coalitions between labour unions and community groups have advanced the circumstances of working people by winning wage increases for workers. See in Luce, Stephanie. 2002. 'The Fight for Living Wages', in Shepard, B. H. and Hayduk, R. *From ACT UP to the WTO: Urban Protest and Community Building in the Era of Globalization*, London, Verso.

14 Marx's critique of rights is often sourced to passages from Marx, K. and McLellan, D. 2000. 'On the Jewish Question'. *Karl Marx: Selected Writings*. 2nd ed. Oxford: Oxford University Press. First published under the German title *Zur Judenfrage in the Deutsch–Französische Jahrbücher*, Paris 1844. Not all scholars agree that Marx was an ardent critic of rights, however. Robert Fine, for example, presents Marx's support for the rights to freedom of religion embodied within the Rights of Man as qualification of his much celebrated critique of rights in 'On the Jewish Question'. See Fine, R. 2009. 'An Unfinished Project: Marx's Critique of Hegel's Philosophy of Right', in Chitty, A. and McIvor, M. (eds) *Karl Marx and Contemporary Philosophy*. New York: Palgrave MacMillan, 105–120.

15 The Occupy Movement, which began as Occupy Wall Street on 17 September 2011 and spread to London (Occupy London Stock Exchange) on 15 October and to numerous other cities since (Occupy Nigeria, Occupy Dataran, Occupy Canada, etc.).

References

Abbott, A. (2005) 'Linked Ecologies: States and Universities as Environments for Professions', *Sociological Theory*, 23: 245–274.

Abbott, K. W., Keohane, R. O., Moravcsik, A., Slaughter, A.-M. and Snidal, D. (2000) 'The Concept of Legalization', *International Organization*, 54: 401–419.

Abolafia, M. (2010) 'The Institutional Embeddedness of Market Failure: Why Speculative Bubbles Still Occur', in M. Lounsbury and P. M. Hirsch (eds), *Markets on Trial: The Economic Sociology of the U.S. Financial Crisis. Part B*, Bingley: Emerald, pp. 177–200.

Abouharb, M. R. and Cingranelli, D. (2006) 'The Human Rights Effects of World Bank Structural Adjustment, 1981–2000', *International Studies Quarterly*, 50: 233–262.

Abouharb, M. R. and Cingranelli, D. (2007) *Human Rights and Structural Adjustment*, Cambridge: Cambridge University Press.

Ackermann, F. and Heinzerling, L. (2004) *Priceless: On Knowing the Price of Everything and the Value of Nothing*, New York: The New Press.

ACTSA (Action for Southern Africa) (2010) 'Economic Partnership Agreements – An Update', *ACTSA Briefing Paper*, May. Available at www.actsa.org/Pictures/UpImages/pdfs/EPAs%20Update%20-%20May%202010.pdf.

Adler, M. (2007) *Recognising the Problem: Socio-Legal Research Training in the UK*, London: Nuffield Foundation. Available at www.ucl.ac.uk/laws/socio-legal/empirical/docs/Adler_REPORT.pdf.

AFME (Association for Financial Markets in Europe) (2010) *AFME comment on CEBS guidelines*, 10 December. Available at www.afme.eu/WorkArea/DownloadAsset.aspx?id=5419 (accessed 28 January 2012).

Aguas del Tunari SA v. Bolivia (2005) Decision on Respondent's Objections to Jurisdiction, ICSID Case No ARB/02/3.

Aguirre, D. (2008) *The Human Right to Development in a Globalized World*, London: Ashgate.

Ahdieh, Robert B. (2006) 'Dialectical Regulation', *Connecticut Law Review*, 38: 863–927.

Akyüz, Yilmaz (2010) 'Multilateral Disciplines and the Question of Policy Space', in J. Faundez and C. Tan (eds), *International Economic Law, Globalization and Developing Countries*, Aldershot: Edward Elgar.

Albrow, M. (1996) *The Global Age: State and Society Beyond Modernity*, Cambridge: Polity Press.

Alcorn, J. (2010) 'Indigenous Peoples and Conservation', *MacArthur Foundation Conservation White Paper Series*. Available at: www.macfound.org/atf/

cf/%7Bb0386ce3–8b29–4162–8098–e466fb856794%7D/INDIGENOUS%20 PEOPLES%20WHITE%20PAPER.PDF (accessed 6 February 2012).

Alexander, Gregory (2000) *Commodity and Propriety: Competing Visions of Property in American Legal Thought, 1776–1970*, Chicago: Chicago University Press.

Allee, M. (1994) 'Code, Culture, and Custom: Foundations of Civil Case Verdicts in a Nineteenth-Century County Court', in K. Bernhardt and P. Huang (eds), *Civil Law in Qing and Republican China*, Stanford: Stanford University Press, 122–141.

Alston, P. (2002) 'Resisting the Merger and Acquisition of Human Rights by Trade Law: A Reply to Petersmann', *European Journal of International Law*, 13: 815–844.

Alston, P. (2004) 'Core Labour Standards and the Transformation of the International Labour Rights Regime', *European Journal of International Law*, 15: 457–521.

Alston, P. (ed.) (2005) *Labour Rights as Human Rights*, Oxford: Oxford University Press.

Alvarez, José E. (2009) 'Contemporary Foreign Investment Law: An "Empire of Law" or the "Law of Empire"?' *Alabama Law Review*, 60: 943–975.

Alves, I. (2009) 'Green Spin Everywhere: How Greenwashing Reveals the Limits of the CSR Paradigm', *Journal of Global Change and Governance*, 2(1).

Ames, J. (2011) 'Taking Responsibility', *European Lawyer* 103(15).

Amsden, Alice (2007) *Escape from Empire: The Developing World's Journey Through Heaven and Hell*, Cambridge: The MIT Press.

Andenas, M. and Ortino, F. (eds) (2005) *WTO Law and Process*, London: British Institute of International and Comparative Law.

Andersen, K. (2009) 'The Avenging Amateur', *Time Magazine*, 10 August. Available at www.time.com/time/magazine/article/0,9171,1913776,00.html (accessed 28 January 2012).

Anderson, Gavin W. (2005) *Constitutional Rights After Globalization*, Oxford: Hart Publishing.

Anderson, K. and Blackhurst, R. (eds) (1993) *Regional Integration in the Global Trading System*, London: Harvester Wheatsheaf.

Anghie, A. (1999) 'Finding the Peripheries: Sovereignty and Colonialism in Nineteenth-century International Law, *Harvard International Law Journal*, 40.

Anghie, Antony (2004) *Imperialism, Sovereignty and the Making of International Law*, Cambridge: Cambridge University Press.

ANSA (2009) Joint Demarche to the EU, 7 January. Available at www.acp-eu-trade. org/library/files/ANSA%20_EN_070109_Demarche-to-EU-MS.pdf.

Arthurs, H. W. (1985) *Without the Law: Administrative Justice and Legal Pluralism in mid 19th Century England*, Toronto: University of Toronto Press.

Ashiagbor, D., Kotiswaran, P. and Perry-Kessaris, A. (eds) (forthcoming 2013) *Towards an Economic Sociology of Law*, Oxford: Wiley-Blackwell.

Ashiagbor, Diamond (forthcoming) 'Ameliorating Globalization? European Union Approaches to the Social Dimension of Globalization', *Comparative Labor Law and Policy Journal*.

Asian Development Bank (2000) 'Report on Insolvency Law Reforms in the Asian and Pacific Region', *Law and Policy Reform Bulletin*, I: 10–86.

Avery, C. (2006) 'The Difference Between CSR and Human Rights', *Corporate Citizenship Briefing*, Aug/Sep, 89: 4.

Avineri, S. and de Shalit, A. (eds) (1992) *Communitarianism and Individualism*, Oxford: Oxford University Press.

Bacchus, J. (2004) 'A Few Thoughts on Legitimacy, Democracy, and the WTO', *Journal of International Economic Law*, 7: 667–673.

Baghi, I., Rubaltelli, E. and Tedeschi, M. (2009) 'A strategy to Communicate Corporate Social Responsibility: Cause Related Marketing and its Dark Side', *Corporate Social Responsibility and Environmental Management*, 16(1): 15–26.

Bagwell, K. and Staiger, R. W. (2001) 'The WTO as a Mechanism for Securing Market Access Property Rights: Implications for Global Labor and Environmental Issues', *Journal of Economic Perspectives*, 15: 69–88.

Bakken, B. (1999) *The Exemplary Society: Human Improvement, Social Control, and the Dangers of Modernity in China*, Oxford: Oxford University Press.

Balakrishnan, Rajagopal (2003) *International Law from Below: Development, Social Movements and Third World Resistance*, Cambridge: Cambridge University Press.

Bales, K. (2005) *Understanding Global Slavery: A Reader*, Berkeley, CA; London, University of California Press.

Balkin, J. (1990) 'Nested Oppositions', *The Yale Law Journal*, 99: 1669.

Balkin, J. (1994) 'Being Just with Deconstruction', *Social and Legal Studies*, 3: 393.

Barker, Ernest (1947) *Political Thought in England, 1848–1914*, London: Oxford University Press.

Barrientos, S. and Smith, S. (2007) 'Do Workers Benefit from Ethical Trade? Assessing Codes of Labour Practice in Global Production Systems', *Third World Quarterly*, 28: 7130.

Bartels, L. (2001) 'Applicable Law in the WTO Dispute Settlement Proceedings' *Journal of World Trade*, 35: 499–519.

Bartley, T. (2011) 'Transnational Governance as the Layering of Rules: Intersections of Public and Private Standards', *Theoretical Inquiries in Law*, 12: 517–542.

Barzilai, G. (2003) *Communities and Law: Politics and Culture of Legal Identities*, Ann Arbor, MI: University of Michigan Press.

Bate, J. P. *et al.* (1917) *Francisci de Victorie de Indis et de jure belli relections.* (Being parts of Relectiones Theologicæ. XII), Nys, E. (ed.). [Text revised by Herbert Francis Wright, and English translation by John Pawley Bate.] Oceana Publications.

Baxi, U. (2001) 'Too Many, or Too Few, Human Rights', *Human Rights Law Review*, 1(1): 1–10.

BBA (British Banker's Association) (2010) *BBA Response to CEBS CP42*, 8 November. Available at www.bankfacts.org.uk/download/6241 (accessed 28 January 2012).

Beck, A. (1994) 'Is Law an Autopoietic System?', *Oxford Journal of Legal Studies*, 14, 401–418.

Beckett, J. (2007) 'Conflicting Orders: How Peace is Waged' *Leiden Journal of International Law*, 20(2): 281.

Been, Vicki and Beauvais, Joel C. (2003) 'The Global Fifth Amendment? NAFTA's Investment Protections and the Misguided Quest for an International "Regulatory Takings" Doctrine', *New York University Law Review*, 78: 30–143.

Beitz, C. R. (1999) *Political Theory and International Relations*, Princeton, NJ: Princeton University Press.

Belser, P., de Cock, M. and Mehrab, F. (2005) *ILO minimum estimate of forced labour in the world*, Geneva: ILO.

Benvenuti, P. and Sapienza, R. (eds) (2007) *La tutela internazionale dei diritti culturali nei conflitti armati*, Milan: Giuffré.

Berman, H. J. (2005) 'The Historical Foundations of Law', *Emory Law Journal*, 54: s. 13–24.

Berman, P. S. (2002) 'The Globalization of Jurisdiction', *University of Pennsylvania Law Review*, 151: 311.

Berman, P. S. (2005) 'From International Law to Law and Globalization', *Columbia Journal of Transnational Law* 43(2): 485–556.

Berman, P. S. (ed.) (2006) *The Globalization of International Law*, Aldershot: Ashgate.

Berman, P. S. (2007) 'Global Legal Pluralism', *Southern California Law Review*, 80: 1155–1237.

Berman, P. S. (2009) 'The New Legal Pluralism', *Annual Review of Law and Social Science*, 6: 225–242.

Bernhardt, K. and Huang, P. (eds) (1994) *Civil Law in Qing and Republican China*, Stanford: Stanford University Press.

Bhagwati, J. (1995) 'Trade Liberalisation and "Fair Trade" Demands: Addressing the Environmental and Labour Standards Issues', *The World Economy*, 18.

Bierstecker, Thomas J. and Hall, Rodney Bruce (2002) 'Private Authority as Global Governance' in R. B. Hall and T. J. Bierstecker (eds), *The Emergence of Private Authority in Global Governance*, Cambridge: Cambridge University Press.

Black, J. (1996) 'Constitutionalising Self-Regulation', *Modern Law Review*, 59(1): 24–55.

Black, J. (2002) 'Critical Reflections on Regulation' *Australian Journal of Legal Philosophy*, 27: 1–35.

Blecher, M. (2009) 'Reclaiming the Common or On Beginning and End of the (Legal) System', in G. P. Calliess, A. Fischer-Lescano, D. Wielsch and P. Zumbansen (eds), *Soziologische Jurisprudenz Festschrift fur Gunther Teubner*, Berlin: De Gryter Recht.

BLIHR (2004) *Report 2: Work in Progress*. Available at: http://www.globalgovernancewatch.org/resources/blihr-report-2-work-in-progress.

BLIHR (2006) *Report 3: Towards a Common Framework on Business and Human Rights: Identifying Components*. Available at: www.realizingrights.org/pdf/BLIHR3Report.pdf.

Block, Fred (1987) 'Beyond Relative Autonomy: State Managers as Historical Subjects' in Fred Block, *Revising State Theory: Essays in Politics and Postindustrialism*, Philadelphia: Temple University Press.

Block-Lieb, Susan and Halliday, Terence C. (2006) 'Legitimacy and Global Lawmaking', *Fordham Law Legal Studies Research Paper No 952492*: SSRN.

Block-Lieb, Susan and Halliday, Terence C. (2007a) 'Incrementalisms in Global Lawmaking', *Brooklyn Journal of International Law*, XXXII: 851–903.

Block-Lieb, Susan and Halliday, Terence C. (2007b) 'Harmonization and Modernization in UNCITRAL's Legislative Guide on Insolvency Law', *Texas International Law Journal*, 42: 475.

Block-Lieb, Susan and Halliday, Terence C. (2011) 'Social Ecology, Recursivity and Temporality: A Sociology of Global Law-Making', *American Sociological Association Annual Meeting*, Las Vegas, NV.

Boeger, N., Murray, R. and Villiers, C. (eds) (2008) *Perspectives on Corporate Social Responsibility: Corporations, Globalisation and the Law*, London: Edward Elgar Publishing.

Boiral, O. and Gendron, Y. (2011) 'Sustainable Development and Certification Practices: Lessons Learned and Prospects', *Business Strategy and the Environment*, 20: 331.

Borgen, C. J. (2005) 'Resolving treaty conflicts', *George Washington Law Review*, 37: 603.

Borial, O. (2007) 'Corporate Greening Through ISO 14001: A Rational Myth?' *Organization Science*, 18: 127.

Boudon, R. (1991) 'Review: What Middle-Range Theories Are', *Contemporary Sociology*, 20(4): 519–522.

Bourdieu, Pierre (1998) *Acts of Resistance: Against the Tyranny of the Market*, New York: The New Press.

Bourdieu, Pierre (2000) *Pascalian Meditations*, Stanford: Stanford University Press.

Bourdieu, Pierre and Wacquant, Loïc (2005) 'The Cunning of Imperial Reason', in Loïc Wacquant (ed.), *Pierre Bourdieu and Democratic Politics*, Cambridge: Polity Press, pp. 178–198.

Boutros-Ghali, B. (1996) *An Agenda for Democratization*, United Nations Department of Public Information New York.

Bowie, M. (1988) *Freud, Proust and Lacan: Theory as Fiction*, Cambridge and New York: Cambridge University Press.

Boyle, Alan and Chinkin, Christine (2007) *The Making of International Law*, Oxford: Oxford University Press.

Bradlow, D. D. (1996) 'The World Bank, the IMF, and Human Rights', *Transnational Law and Contemporary Problems*, 6: 47–90.

Braithwaite, J. and Drahos, P. (2000) *Global Business Regulation*. Cambridge: Cambridge University Press.

Braithwaite, John (2002) 'Rules and Principles: A Theory of Legal Certainty', *Australian Journal of Legal Philosophy*, 27: 47–82.

Breining-Kaufmann, C. (2005) 'The Legal Matrix of Human Rights and Trade Law: State Obligations versus Private Rigths and Obligations', in T. Cottier, J. Pauwelyn and E. Bürgi (eds), *Human Rights and International Trade*, Oxford; New York: Oxford University Press.

Bronckers, M. C. E. J. (1999) 'Better Rules for a New Millennium: A Warning Against Undemocratic Developments in the WTO', *Journal of International Economic Law*, 2: 547–566.

Brown, D. K. (2001) 'Labor Standards: Where Do They Belong on the International Trade Agenda?', *Journal of Economic Perspectives*, 15: 89–112.

Brown, G. (2005) 'Governments and Supranational Agencies: A New Consensus?', in J. H. Dunning (ed.), *Making Globalization Good: The Moral Challenges of Global Capitalism*, Oxford: Oxford University Press.

Brownlie, I. (2008) *Principles of Public International Law*, Oxford; New York: Oxford University Press.

Bruner, J. (2003) *Making Stories: Law, Literature, Life*, Cambridge, MA: Harvard University Press.

Bunn, I. D. and Picker, C. (2008) 'The State and Future of International Economic Law', in C. Picker, I. D. Bunn and D. W. Arner (eds), *International Economic Law: The State and Future of the Discipline*, Oxford: Hart Publishing.

Calliess, G. P and Zumbansen, P. (2010) *Rough Consensus and Running Code A Theory of Transnational Private Law*, in C. Scott (ed.), Hart Monographs in Transnational and International Law; Oxford and Portland, Oregon: Hart Publishing.

Calliess, G.-P. (2002) 'Reflexive Transnational Law: The Privatisation of Civil Law and the Civilisation of Private Law', *Zeitschrift fur Rechtssoziologie* (June 2010 edn, 23), 185–216.

Calliess, G.-P. and Renner, M. (2009) 'Between Law and Social Norms: The Evolution of Global Governance', *Ratio Juris*, 22: 260–280.

Calliess, G.-P. and Zumbansen, P. (2010) *Rough Consensus and Running Code: A Theory of Transnational Private Law*, Oxford: Hart.

Calvino, I. (1997) *Invisible Cities*, trans. W. Weaver [Originally published in Italian as *Le città invisibili*, 1972], London: Vintage.

Campbell, C. M. and Wiles, P. (1976) 'The Study of Law in Society in Britain' *Law and Society Review* 10: 547–578.

Canan, P. and Reichman, N. (2001) *Ozone Connections: Expert Networks in Global Environmental Governance*, New York: Greenleaf Publications.

Carroll, A and Shabana, K. (2010) 'The Business Case for Corporate Social Responsibility: A Review of Concepts, Research and Practice', *International Journal of Management Reviews*, 12(1): 85.

Carroll, A. B. (1979) 'A Three-Dimensional Conceptual Model of Corporate Social Performance', *Academy of Management Review*, 4: 497–505.

Carroll, A. B. (1999) 'Corporate Social Responsibility: Evolution of a Definitional Construct', *Business and Society*, 38: 268–295.

Carruthers, B. G. and Halliday, T. C. (1998) *Rescuing Business: The Making of Corporate Bankruptcy Law in England and the United States*, Oxford: Oxford University Press.

Cassel, D. (1995) 'Corporate Initiatives: A Second Human Rights Revolution', *Fordham International Law Journal*, 19: 1963–1984.

Castellino, J. (2008) 'Territorial Integrity and the "Right" to Self-Determination: An Examination of the Conceptual Tools', *Brooklyn Journal of International Law*, 33.

Castells, M. (2000) *The Rise of the Network Society: Economy, Society and Culture: The Information Age: Economy, Society and Culture Vol 1* 2nd ed., Oxford: Wiley-Blackwell.

CDA Collaborative Learning Projects (2005) *Corporate Engagement Project: Report of Fourth CDA/CEP Visit to the Yadana Pipeline*. Online. Available at: www.cdainc.com/cdawww/pdf/casestudy/cep_myanmar__fourth_visit_field_visit_report_Pdf.pdf (accessed 6 February 2012).

CEBS (Committee of European Banking Supervisors) (2010) *Guidelines on Remuneration Policies and Practices*, 10 December. Available at www.eba.europa.eu/cebs/media/Publications/Standards%20and%20Guidelines/2010/Remuneration/Guidelines.pdf (accessed 28 January 2012).

Cerny, Philip G. (1997) 'Paradoxes of the Competition State: The Dynamics of Political Globalization', *Government and Opposition*, 32: 251–274.

Cerny, Philip G. (2008) 'The Governmentalization of World Politics', in Eleanore Kofman and Gillian Youngs (eds), *Globalization: Theory and Practice*, 3rd edn., New York: Continuum, pp. 221–236.

Chang, Ha-Joon (2002) *Kicking Away the Ladder: Development Strategy in Historical Perspective*, London: Anthem Press.

Chang, Ha-Joon (2005) 'Policy Space in Historical Perspective: With Reference to

Trade and Industrial Policies', Talk Presented at Tufts University, 27 October 2005 on the Occasion of the Award of the 2005 Leontief Prize.

Chanock, Martin (1985) *Law, Custom and Social Order: The Colonial Experience in Malawi and Zambia*, Cambridge: Cambridge University Press.

Charnovitz, S. (2011) 'What Is International Economic Law?', *Journal of International Economic Law*, 14: 3–22.

Chechi, A. (2009) 'The Settlement of International Cultural Heritage Disputes'. Paper presented at the Workshop *Legal Aspects of the Protection of Cultural Heritage in International Law*, held at the Law Department, European University Institute, 8 May 2009.

Chen, G. B. (2002) *Law without Lawyers, Justice without Courts: on Traditional Chinese Mediation*, Aldershot: Ashgate.

Cheney, H., Lovel, R. and Solomon, F. (2002) 'People, Power, Participation: A Study of Mining–Community Relations,' *Mining, Minerals and Sustainable Development/Ameef Working Paper*. Online. Available at: www.isf.uts.edu.au/publications/HC_RL_FS_2002.pdf (accessed 6 February 2012).

Chimni, B. S. (2004) 'An outline of a Marxist course on public international law', *Leiden Journal of International Law*, 17, 1–30.

Chinkin, Christine (2003) 'Normative Development in the International Legal System', in Dinah Shelton (ed.), *Commitment and Compliance: The Role of Non-binding Norms in the International Legal System*, Oxford: Oxford University Press.

Christensen, I., Peirce, E., Hartman, L., Hoffman, W. and Carrier, J. (2007) 'Ethics, CSR and Sustainability Education in the *Financial Times* Top 50 Global Business Schools: Baseline Data and Future Research Directions', *Journal of Business Ethics*, 73: 347.

Clapham, A. (2006) *Human Rights Obligations of Non-state Actors*, Oxford: Oxford University Press.

Clark, A. (2011) 'GSK Chief Executive Andrew Witty Warns That Drive For Profits is Undermining Public Trust in Big Companies', *Observer*, 20 March. Available at www.guardian.co.uk/environment/2011/mar/20/firms-quit-britain-tax-reasons (accessed 28 January 2012).

Clark, D. L. (2002) 'The World Bank and Human Rights: The Need for Greater Accountability', *Harvard Human Rights Journal*, 15: 205–226.

Clarke, T. (2004) 'Theories of Governance: Reconceptualizing Corporate Governance Theory After the Enron Experience,' in T. Clarke (ed.), *Theories of Corporate Governance: The Philosophical Foundations of Corporate Governance*, London and New York: Routledge.

Cloatre, E. (2008) 'Trips [Trade-related aspects of intellectual property rights] and pharamaceutical patents in Djibouti: an ANT [actor network theory] analysis of socio-legal objects', *Social and Legal Studies*, 17(2): 263–281.

Coase, R. (1960) 'The Problem of Social Cost', *Journal of Law and Economics*, 3: 1–44.

Cobo, J. M. (1986) *Study of the Problem of Discrimination Against Indigenous Populations*, UN Doc. E/Cn.4/Sub.2/1986/7Add.4.

Cohee, James R. (2008) 'The WTO and Domestic Political Disquiet: Has Legalization of the Global Trade Regime Gone Too Far?', *Indiana Journal of Global Legal Studies*, 15: 351–374.

Cohen, Benjamin J. (2008) *International Political Economy: An Intellectual History*, Princeton: Princeton University Press.

Cohen, G. A. (1991) 'Incentives, Inequality, and Community', The Tanner

Lectures on Human Values, 21 May. Available atwww.tannerlectures.utah.edu/lectures/documents/cohen92.pdf (accessed 28 January 2012).

Cohen, G. A. (1994) 'Back to Socialist Basics', *New Left Review*, 207: 3–16.

Cohen, R. and Rai, S. (2000) *Global Social Movements*, London; New Brunswick, NJ: Athlone Press.

Colchester, M., Sirait, M. and Wijardjo, B. (2003) *The Applications of FSC Principles 2 and 3 in Indonesia: Obstacles and Possibilities*. Online. Available at: www.forestpeoples.org/region/indonesia/publication/2010/application-fsc-principles-2-3-indonesia-obstacles-and-possibiliti (accessed 6 February 2012).

Cole, G. D. H. (1920a) *Social Theory*, New York: Frederick A. Stokes Company.

Cole, G. D. H. (1920b) *Guild Socialism Re-Stated*, London: Parsons.

Collier, J. and Lowe, V. (2000) *The Settlement of Disputes in International Law*, Oxford: OUP.

Conklin, B. A. and Graham, L. R. (1995) 'The Shifting Middle Ground: Amazonian Indians and Eco-Politics,' *American Anthropologist*, 97: 695–710.

Conley, J. and Williams, C. (2005–2006) 'Engage, Embed and Embellish: Theory versus Practice in the Corporate Social Responsibility Movement', *Journal of Corporation Law*, 31(1).

Corbett, A. and Spender, P. (2009) 'Review Essay: Corporate Constitutionalism', *Sydney Law Review*, 31: 147–162.

Corkin, J. (2008) 'Misappropriating Citizenship: The Limits of Corporate Social Responsibility', in N. Boeger, R. Murray and C. Villiers (eds), *Perspectives on Corporate Social Responsibility: Corporations, Globalisation and the Law*, London: Edward Elgar Publishing.

Corporate Observatory Europe (2009) 'Pulling the Strings of African Business: How the EU Commission Orchestrated Support from African Business for EPAs', *Corporate Observatory Europe*, 23 March. Available at http://archive.corporateeurope.org/docs/pulling-the-strings-of-african-business.pdf.

COSATU (2009) 'COSATU is Against the Break Up of SACU', Briefing Statement, 1 July. Available at www.cosatu.org.za/docs/pr/2009/pr0701a.html.

Cotterrell, R. (1992) *The Sociology of Law: An Introduction*, 2nd edition, London: Butterworths.

Cotterrell, R. (1995) *Law's Community: Legal Theory in Sociological Perspective*, Oxford: Clarendon Press.

Cotterrell, R. (1997) 'A Legal Concept of Community', *Canadian Journal of Law and Society*, 12(2): 75–91.

Cotterrell, R. (1998) 'Why must Legal Ideas be Interpreted Sociologically?' *Journal of Law and Society*, 25: 171–192.

Cotterrell, R. (1999) *Emile Durkheim: Law in a Moral Domain*, Edinburgh: Edinburgh University Press.

Cotterrell, R. (2001) 'Is There a Logic of Legal Transplants?', in D. Nelken and J. Feest (eds), *Adapting Legal Cultures*, Oxford: Hart Publishing, 69–98.

Cotterrell, Roger (2002a) 'Subverting Orthodoxy, Making Law Central: A View of Sociolegal Studies', *Journal of Law and Society*, 29(4): 632–644.

Cotterrell, R. (2002b) 'Seeking Similarity, Appreciating Difference: Comparative Law and Communities', in A. Harding and E. Örücü (eds), *Comparative Law in the 21st Century*, London: Kluwer Law International, 21–34.

Cotterrell, R. (2006a) *Law in Social Theory*, Aldershot Ashgate.

Cotterrell, R. (2006b) *Law, Culture and Society: Legal Ideas in the Mirror of Social Theory*, Aldershot: Ashgate.

Cotterrell, R. (2008) *Living Law: Studies in Legal and Social Theory*, Aldershot: Ashgate.

Cotterrell, R. (2010) 'Durkheim on Justice, Morals and Politics', in R. Cotterrell (ed.) *Emile Durkheim: Justice, Morality and Politics*, Farnham: Ashgate.

Cottier, T., Delimatsis, P., Gehne K. and Payosova, T. (2011) 'Fragmentation and Coherence in International Trade Regulation: Analysis and Conceptual Foundations', in T. Cottier and P. Delimatsis (eds), *The Prospects for International Trade Regulation*, Cambridge: Cambridge University Press, 1–65.

Cover, Robert M. (1983–84) 'Foreword: *Nomos* and Narrative', *Harvard Law Review*, 97: 4–68.

Cox, Robert W. (1976) 'On Thinking About Future World Order', in Cox with Sinclair, *Approaches to World Order*, Cambridge: Cambridge University Press, pp. 60–84.

Cox, Robert W. (1981) 'Social Forces, States, and World Orders: Beyond International Relations Theory' in Cox with Sinclair, *Approaches to World Order*, Cambridge: Cambridge University Press, pp. 85–123.

Cox, Robert W. (1987) *Production, Power and World Order: Social Forces in the Making of History*, New York: Columbia University Press.

Cox, Robert W. (1991) 'The Global Political Economy and Social Choice' in Robert W. Cox with Timothy J. Sinclair, *Approaches to World Order*, Cambridge: Cambridge University Press, pp. 191–208.

Cox, Robert W. (1992a) ' "Take Six Eggs": Theory, Finance, and the Real Economy in thee Work of Susan Strange' in Robert W. Cox with Timothy J. Sinclair, *Approaches to World Order*, Cambridge: Cambridge University Press, pp. 174–188.

Cox, Robert W. (1992b) 'Global Perestroika', in Robert W. Cox with Timothy J. Sinclair, *Approaches to World Order*, Cambridge: Cambridge University Press, pp. 296–313.

Cox, Robert W. (1992c) 'Multilateralism and World Order', in Robert W. Cox with Timothy J. Sinclair, *Approaches to World Order*, Cambridge: Cambridge University Press, pp. 494–523.

Cox, Robert W. (1996) 'Influences and Commitments', in Robert W. Cox with Timothy J. Sinclair, *Approaches to World Order*, Cambridge: Cambridge University Press, pp. 19–38.

Cox, Robert W. (2002a) 'Civilizations and the Twenty-First Century: Some Theoretical Considerations', in Mehdi Mozaffari (ed.), *Globalization and Civilizations*, London: Routledge, pp. 1–23.

Cox, Robert W. (2002b) *The Political Economy of a Plural World: Critical Reflections on Power, Morals and Civilization*, London: Routledge.

Cox, Robert W. with Michael G. Schechter (2008) *The Political Economy of the Plural World: Critical Reflections on Power, Morals and Civilization*, London: Routledge.

Cox, Robert W. with Timothy J. Sinclair (1996) *Approaches to World Order*, Cambridge: Cambridge University Press.

Cragg, W. (2012) 'Ethics, Enlightened Self-Interest, and the Corporate Responsibility to Respect Human Rights: A Critical Look at the Justificatory Foundations of the UN Framework', *Business Ethics Quarterly*, 22(1): 9.

Crawford, J. (2002) *The International Law Commission's Articles on State Responsibility: Introduction, Text and Commentaries*, Cambridge: Cambridge University Press.

Crocker, C. A., Osler Hampson, F. and Aall, P. (1999) *Herding Cats: Multiparty Mediation in a Complex World*, Washington, DC: United States Institute of Peace.

Croucher, R. and Cotton, E. (2011) *Global unions, global business: global union federations and international business*, Faringdon: Libri Pub.

Cutler, A. Claire (2000) 'Theorizing the "No-Man's Land" Between Politics and Economics' in Thomas C. Lawton, James N. Rosenau and Amy C. Verdun (eds), *Strange Power: Shaping the Parameters of International Relations and International Political Economy*, Aldershot: Ashgate, 159–74.

Cutler, A. Claire (2003) *Private Power and Global Authority: Transnational Merchant Law in the Global Political Economy*, Cambridge: Cambridge University Press.

D'Antona, M. (2002) 'Labour Law at the Century's End: An Identity Crisis?' In J. Conaghan, R. M. Fischl, and K. Klare (eds), *Labour Law in an Era of Globalization*, Oxford: Oxford University Press.

Dahl, Robert A. (1961) *Who Governs? Democracy and Power in an American City*, New Haven: Yale University Press.

Dana, David A. and Merrill, Thomas W. (2002) *Property: Takings*, New York: Foundation Press.

Dangl, B. (2007) *The Price of Fire: Resource Wars and Social Movements in Bolivia*, Oakland, CA; Edinburgh: AK Press.

Das, D. (2004) *Regionalism in Global Trade*, Cheltenham: Edward Elgar.

David, R. and Brierley, J. E. C. (1978) *Major Legal Systems in the World Today: An Introduction to the Comparative Study of Law*, 2nd edn., London: Stevens.

Davies, H. (2010) *The Financial Crisis*, Cambridge: Polity.

de Feyter, K. (2005) *Human Rights*, London: Zed.

Deal, T.E. (2008) *WTO Rules and Procedures and Their Implication for the Kyoto Protocol.* Available at: www.uscib.org/docs/wto_and_kyoto_2008.pdf (accessed 28 April 2012).

Dean, Jodi (2009) *Democracy and Other Neoliberal Fantasies*, Durham: Duke University Press.

Deflem, M. (2008) *Sociology of Law: Visions of a Scholarly Tradition*, Cambridge, MA: Cambridge University Press.

Della Porta, D. and Diani, M. (2006) *Social Movements: An Introduction*, Malden, MA: Blackwell Publishing.

Delmas, M. and Burbano, C. (2011) 'The Drivers of Greenwashing', *California Management Review*, 54: 64.

Depoorter, B. (2010) 'Law in the Shadow of Bargaining: The Feedback Effect of Civil Settlements', *Cornell Law Review*, 95: 101.

Desmet, P., de Cremer, D. and Dijk, E. (2011) 'In Money we Trust? The Use of Financial Compensations to Repair Trust in the Aftermath of Distributive Harm', *Organizational Behaviour and Human Decision Processes*, 114(2): 75–86.

Deva, S. (2003–2004) 'UN's Human Rights Norms for Transnational Corporations and Other Business Enterprises: An Imperfect Step in the Right Direction?' *Journal of International and Comparative Law*, 10: 493.

Development, UCOTA (2010) World investment report 2010: investing in a low-carbon economy, July 22 2010. U.N. Doc UNCTAD/WIR/2010 ed.

Dezalay, Y. and Garth, B. G. (2002) *The Internationalization of Palace Wars: Lawyers, Economists, and the Contest to Transform Latin American States*, Chicago and London: University of Chicago Press.

Dicken, P. (2003) ' "Placing" Firms: Grounding the Debate on the "Global" Corporation' in J. Peck and H. Young (eds), *Remaking the Global Economy: Economic-Geographic Perspectives*, London: Sage, 27.

Dine, J. (2005) *Companies, international trade, and human rights*, Cambridge: Cambridge University Press.

Dixit, A. (2007) *Lawlessness and Economics: Alternative Modes of Governance*, Princeton, NJ: Princeton University Press.

Dixon, M. and McCorquodale, R. (2003) *Cases and Materials on International Economic Law*, 4th edn; Oxford: Oxford University Press.

Djelic, M.-L. and Quack, S. (2010) 'Transnational Communities and Their Impact on the Governance of Business and Economic Activity', in M.-L. Djelic and S. Quack (eds), *Transnational Communities: Shaping Global Economic Governance*, Cambridge: Cambridge University Press, 377–413.

Djelic, Marie-Laure and Sahlin-Andersson, Kerstin (2008) *Transnational Governance: Institutional Dynamics of Regulation*, Cambridge: Cambridge University Press.

Domingo, R. (2011) 'Gaius, Vattel, and the New Global Law Paradigm', *European Journal of International Law*, 22: 627–647.

Dowell-Jones, M. and Kinley, D. (2011) 'Minding the Gap: Global Finance and Human Rights', *Ethics and International Affairs*, 25(2): 183.

Draper, P. (2007) 'EU–Africa Trade Relations: The Political Economy of Economic Partnership Agreements', ECIPE Jan Tumlir Policy Essays, No. 02/2007.

Dreher, A. (2009) 'IMF Conditionality: Theory and Evidence', *Public Choice*, 141: 233–267.

Drucker, P. F. (1991) The New Productivity Challenge, *Harvard Business Review*, 6, 69–79.

Du Plessis, A. A. and Rautenbach, C. (2010) 'Legal Perspectives on the Role of Culture in Sustainable Development', *Potchefstroom Electronic L. J.* 13: 27–46.

Duddy, J. (2009) 'Namibia: Geingob Lays into EU', *The Namibian*, 1 June.

Duhigg, C. and Barboza, D. (2012) 'In China, Human Costs are Built into an iPad' www.nytimes.com/2012/01/26/business/ieconomy-apples-ipad-and-the-human-costs-for-workers-in-china.html?_r=2&pagewanted=1 (accessed 1 May 2012).

Dunning, J. H. and Lundan, S. M. (2008) *Multinational enterprises and the global economy*, Cheltenham, Edward Elgar.

Dunoff (2001) 'The WTO in Transition: Of Constituents, Competence and Coherence', *George Washington International Law Review*, 33: 979.

Dupuy, P. M. (2007) 'The Impact of Legal Instruments Adopted by UNESCO on General International Law', in A. A. Yusuf (ed.), *Normative Action in Education, Science and Culture*, Paris: UNESCO, 351–364.

Durkheim, E. (1893) *De la division du travail social:* livre I. Online. Available at: http://classiques.uqac.ca/classiques/Durkheim_emile/division_du_travail/division_travail_1.pdf (accessed 28 January 2012).

Durkheim, E. (1984 [1893]) *The Division of Labour in Society*, W. D. Halls (trans.) 2nd edn., Basingstoke: Macmillan.

Dutfield, Graham and Suthersanen, Uma (2008) *Global Intellectual Property Law*, Aldershot: Edward Elgar.

Edelman, L. B. (2004) 'Rivers of Law and Contested Terrain: A Law and Society Approach to Economic Rationality', *Law and Society Review*, 38(2): 181–197.

EFAMA (European Fund and Asset Management Association) (2010) *Response to CEBS Consultation Paper on Guidelines on Remuneration Policies and Practices (CP42)*, 12 November. Available at www.efama.org/index2.php?option=com_docman&task=doc_view&gid=1389&Itemid=-99 (accessed 28 January 2012).

Ehrlich, E. (1936) *Fundamental Principles of the Sociology of Law*, transl. By W. L. Moll, New Brunswick: Transaction reprint, 2002.

Eisel, U. (1992) 'About Dealing with the Impossible: An Account of Experience in Landscape Planning Courses', *European Journal of Education*, 27(3): 239.

Ellingson, T. J. (2001) *The Myth of the Noble Savage*, Berkeley and Los Angeles, CA: University of California Press.

Elman, B. (1990) *Classicism, Politics, and Kinship: The Ch'ang-Chou School of New Text Confucianism in Late Imperial China*, Berkeley: University of California Press.

Emberland, M. (2006) *The Human Rights of Companies: Exploring the Structure of ECHR Protection*, Oxford: Oxford University Press.

Engelen, B. (2010) 'Beyond Markets and States: The Importance of Communities', *International Social Science Journal*, 61: 489–500.

Environmental Resources Management (2010) *Mining Community Development Agreements – Practical Experiences and Field Studies. Final Report for the World Bank*, Washington, DC: Environmental Resources Management. Online. Available at: www.sdsg.org/wp-content/uploads/2011/06/CDA-Report-FINAL.pdf (accessed 6 February 2012).

Epps, T. and Green, A. (2010) *Reconciling Trade and Climate: How the WTO Can Help Address Climate Change*, London: Edward Elgar Publishing.

ESRC (Economic and Social Research Council) (2005) *Postgraduate Training Guidelines*, 4th edition. Available at www.esrc.ac.uk/_images/Postgraduate_Training_Guidelines_2005_tcm8-4449.pdf.

Etzioni, A. (1991) *A Responsive Society: Collected Essays on Deliberate Social Change*, San Francisco: Jossey-Bass.

Etzioni, A. (1993) *The Spirit of Community: Rights, Responsibilities, and the Communitarian Agenda*, New York: Crown Publishers.

Etzioni, A. (ed.) (1995) *Rights and the Common Good: The Communitarian Perspective*, New York: St. Martins.

European Commission (2005) 'Trade for Development: EU–SADC Economic Partnership Agreement', Trade Report, European Commission. Available at http://trade.ec.europa.eu/doclib/html/127350.htm.

European Commission (2009) 'Fact Sheet on the Interim Economic Partnership Agreements: SADC Group', European Commission. Available at http://trade.ec.europa.eu/doclib/docs/2009/january/tradoc_142189.pdf.

European Union (2001) Measures Affecting Asbestos and Asbestos Containing Products, Reports of the Appellate Body, WT/DS135/AB/R, 12 March.

EVCA (European Private Equity and Venture Capital Association) (2010) *Industry Response to the CEBS Consultation on the Guidelines on Remuneration Policies and Practices*, 8 November. Available on www.evca.eu/WorkArea/linkit.aspx?LinkIdentifier=id&ItemID=6030 (accessed 28 January 2012).

Everson, Michelle (2011) 'The Limits of the "Conflicts Approach": Law in Times of Political Turmoil', *Transnational Legal Theory*, 2: 271–285.

Falk, R. A. (1998) *Law in an Emerging Global Village: A Post-Westphalian Perspective*, Ardsley, NY, Transnational Publishers.

Fama, E. F. (1970) 'Efficient Capital Markets: A Review of Theory and Empirical Work', *Journal of Finance*, 25: 383–341.

Faundez, Julio (2010) 'International Economic Law and Development: Before and After Neoliberalism', in Julio Faundez and Celine Tan (eds), *International Economic Law, Globalization and Developing Countries*, Aldershot: Edward Elgar.

Faundez, Julio and Tan, Celine (2010) 'Introduction', in Julio Faundez and Celine Tan (eds), *International Economic Law, Globalization and Developing Countries*, Aldershot: Edward Elgar.

Figgis, J. N. (1913) *Churches in the Modern State*, London: Longmans Green.

Filer, C. (1997) 'The Melanesian Way of Menacing the Mining Industry,' in B. Burt and C. Clerk (eds), *Environment and Development in the Pacific Islands*, Canberra: National Centre for Development Studies, Australian National University; Port Moresby: University of Papua New Guinea Press.

Filer, C. (2008) 'Development Forum in Papua New Guinea: Upsides and Downsides,' *Journal of Energy and Natural Resources Law*, 26: 120–149.

Financial Services Authority (2010b) *FSA Publishes Revised Remuneration Code*, 17 December. Available at www.fsa.gov.uk/library/communication/pr/2010/180.shtml (accessed 28 January 2012).

Fine, B. (2008) 'Social Capital in Wonderland: The World Bank Behind the Looking Glass', *Progress in Development Studies*, 8: 261–269.

Fine, B. (2010) *Theories of Social Capital: Researchers Behaving Badly*, London: Pluto Books and IIPPE.

Fine, R. (2009) An unfinished project: Marx's Critique of Hegel's Philosophy of Right. In Chitty, A. and McIvor, M. (eds), *Karl Marx and Contemporary Philosophy*. New York: Palgrave MacMillan.

Fiorentino, R., Crawford, J. and Toqueboeuf, C. (2009) 'The landscape of regional trade agreements and WTO surveillance', in R. Baldwin and P. Low (eds), *Multilateralizing Regionalism: Challenges for the Global Trading System*, Cambridge: Cambridge University Press.

Fisher, R. and Ury, W. (1983) *Getting to Yes: Negotiating Agreement Without Giving In*, New York: Penguin Books.

Fisher-Lescano, Andreas and Teubner, Gunther (2004) 'Regime Collisions: The Vain Search for Legal Unity in the Fragmentation of Global Law', *Michigan Journal of International Law*, 25, 999–1046.

Fitzpatrick, Peter (1992) *The Mythology of Modern Law*, London: Routledge.

Føllesdal, A. and Pogge, T. W. M. (2005) *Real World Justice: Grounds, Principles, Human Rights, and Social Institutions*, Dordrecht, Springer.

Follows, J. W. (1951) *Antecedents of the International Labour Organization*, Oxford, Clarendon Press.

Fonesca, A. (2010) 'How Credible are Mining Corporations' Sustainability Reports? A Critical Analysis of External Assurance under the Requirements of the International Council on Mining and Metals', *Corporate Social Responsibility and Environmental Management*, 17: 355.

Footer, M. E. and Graber, C. B. (2000) 'Trade Liberalization and Cultural Policy', *Journal of International Economic Law*, 3: 115–144.

Foster, R. J. (2002) 'Bargains with Modernity in Papua New Guinea and Elsewhere,' *Anthropological Theory*, 2: 233–251.

Foucault, Michel (1980) *Power-Knowledge: Selected Interviews and Other Writings*,

1972–1977, C. Gordon (ed.), C. Gordon *et al.* (trans.), Brighton: Harvester Press.

Foucault, Michel (1991) *The Foucault Reader: An Introduction to Foucault's Thought*, Paul Rabinow (ed.), London: Penguin.

Foucault, Michel (1994) *Power: Essential Works of Foucault 1954–1984, Volume 3*, James D. Faubion/trans. Robert Hurley and others (ed.), London: Penguin.

Foucault, Michel (2008) *The Birth of Biopolitics: Lectures at the College de France, 1978–79*, Trans. Graham Burchell, Houndmills: Palgrave Macmillan.

Fowler, P. (2001) 'Cultural Landscape: Great Concept, Pity about the Phrase', in R. Kelly, L. Macinnes, D. Thackray and P. Whitbourne (eds), *The Cultural Landscape: Planning for a Sustainable Partnership between People and Place*, London: ICOMOS UK.

Francioni, F. (2007) 'Au-delà des traités: l'émergence d'un nouveau droit coutumier pour la protection du patrimoine culturel', *Revue générale de droit international public* 19–42.

Francioni, F. (2008a) 'The World Heritage Convention: An Introduction', in F. Francioni and F. Lenzerini (eds), *The 1972 World Heritage Convention A Commentary*, Oxford: Oxford University Press.

Francioni, F. (2008b) 'Culture, Heritage and Human Rights: An Introduction', in F. Francioni and M. Scheinin (eds), *Cultural Human Rights*, Leiden/Boston: Brill.

Francioni, F. (2010) 'International Human Rights in an Environmental Horizon', *European Journal of International Law*, 21(1): 41–55.

Francioni, F. and Lenzerini, F. (2008) 'The Future of the World Heritage Convention: Problems and Prospects' in F. Francioni (ed.), *The 1972 World Heritage Convention: A Commentary*, Oxford: Oxford University Press, 401–410.

Franck, S. (2009) 'Development and Outcomes of Investor-State Arbitration', *Harvard Journal of International Law*, 9(2): 435–489.

Franck, T. M. (1995) *Fairness in International Law and Institutions*, New York, Clarendon Press.

Franck, T. M. (2006) 'The Power of Legitimacy and the Legitimacy of Power: International Law in an Age of Power Disequilibrium', *American Journal of International Law*, 100: 88–106.

Freidrichs, Jörg (2008) 'Global Governance as the Hegemonic Project of Transatlantic Civil Society' in Markus Lederer and Phillip S. Müller (eds), *Criticizing Global Governance*, Houndmills, Basingstoke: Palgrave Macmillan, pp. 45–68.

Frerichs, S. (2009) 'The Legal Constitution of Market Society: Probing the Economic Sociology of Law', *Economic Sociology – European Electronic Newsletter*, 10(3): 20–25.

Frerichs, S. (2011a) 'False promises? A sociological critique of the behavioural turn in law and economics', *Journal of Consumer Policy*, 34(3): 289–314.

Frerichs, S. (2011b) 'Re-embedding Neo-liberal Constitutionalism: A Polanyian Case for the Economic Sociology of Law', in C. Joerges and J. Falke (eds), *Karl Polanyi, Globalisation and the Potential of Law in Transnational Markets*, Oxford: Hart Publishing, pp. 65–84.

Frerichs, S. (2012) 'Studying Law, Economy, and Society: A Short History of Socio-Legal Thinking', Helsinki Legal Studies Research Paper No. 19 (University of Helsinki). Online. Available at: http://papers.ssrn.com/sol3/papers. cfm?abstract_ id=2022891 (accessed 15 March 2012).

Frerichs, S. (forthcoming) 'The Law of the Market Society: Conflicts and Dynamics' [prepared for publication in C. Joerges and J. Falke (eds), *The Conflicts-Law Approach on Trial*, Oxford: Hart Publishing].

Friedman, L. M. (2005) 'Coming of Age: Law and Society Enters an Exclusive Club', *Annual Review of Law and Social Science*, 1: 1–16.

Friedman, M. (1970) 'The Social Responsibility of Business is to Increase its Profits,' *The New York Times Magazine*, September 13.

Friedman, M. (2007) 'Using Consumer Boycotts to Stimulate Corporate Policy Changes: Marketplace, Media and Moral Considerations' in M. Micheletti, A. Follesdal and D. Stolle (eds), *Politics, Products, and Markets*, Transaction New Jersey 45.

Froomkin, A. M. (2003) 'Habermas@Discourse.Net: Toward a Critical Theory of Cyberspace', *Harvard Law Review*, 116: 749–873.

FSA (Financial Services Authority) (2010a) *Policy Statement 10/20: Feedback on CP10/19*. Available at www.fsa.gov.uk/pubs/policy/ps10_20.pdf (accessed 28 January 2012).

Fukuyama, F. (1992) *The End of History*, Harmondsworth: Penguin Books.

Fukuyama, F. (1995) *Trust: The Social Virtues and the Creation of Prosperity*, London: Hamish Hamilton.

G-22 (1998a) 'Key Principles and Features of Effective Insolvency Regimes'. Washington DC: G-22 Working Group on International Financial Crises.

G-22 (1998b) 'Summary of Reports on the International Financial Architecture'. Washington DC: G22.

Galanter, M. and Edwards, M. A. (1997) 'Introduction: The Path of the Law *Ands*', *Wisconsin Law Review*, 72(3): 375–387.

Galis, A. (2009) 'UNESCO Documents and Procedure: The Need to Account for Political Conflict When designating World Heritage Sites', *Georgia Journal of International and Comparative Law*, 38: 205–235.

Garcia, F. J. (1998) 'The Trade Linkage Phenomenon: Pointing the Way to the Trade Law and Global Social Policy of the 21st Century', *University of Pennsylvania Journal of International Economic Law*, 19: 201–208.

Garcia, F. J. (2005) 'Globalization and the Theory of International Law', *International Theory*, 11: 9–22.

Genn, H., M. Partington and Wheeler, S. (2006) *The Nuffield Inquiry on Empirical Legal Research*, London: Nuffield Foundation. Available at www.ucl.ac.uk/laws/socio-legal/empirical/docs/inquiry_report.pdf.

Gentili, A., *et al.* (1933) *De iure belli libri tres ... Vol. I. A photographic reproduction of the edition of 1612 ... Vol. II. A translation of the text*, by John C. Rolfe, with an introduction by Coleman Phillipson, Oxford, Clarendon Press.

Ghorpade, J. (1991) 'Ethics in MBA Programs: The Rhetoric, the Reality and a Plan of Action', *Journal of Business Ethics*, 10(12): 891.

Giddens, A. (1994) *Beyond Right and Left*, Cambridge: Polity.

Giddens, A. (1998) *The Third Way*, Cambridge: Polity.

Gierke, Otto (1900) *Political Theories of the Middle Age*, Trans. F. W. Maitland, Cambridge: Cambridge University Press.

Gill, Stephen (2008) *Power and Resistance in the New World Order*, 2nd edn., Houndmills, Basingstoke: Palgrave Macmillan.

Gill, Stephen and Law, David (1988) *The Global Political Economy: Perspectives, Problems and Policies*, Baltimore: The Johns Hopkins University Press.

Glinavos, I. (2010) *Neoliberalism and the Law in Post Communist Transition*, Abingdon: Routledge.

Global Witness (2012) Oil, gas and mining website www.globalwitness.org/campaigns/corruption/oil-gas-and-mining (accessed 1 May 2012).

Gneezy, U. and Rustichini, A. (2000) 'A Fine is a Price,' *Journal of Legal Studies*, 29: 1–18.

Godden, L., Langton, M., Mazel, O. and Tehan, M. (2008) 'Accommodating Interests in Resource Extraction: Indigenous Peoples, Local Communities and the Role of Law in Economic and Social Sustainability,' *Journal of Energy and Natural Resources Law*, 26: 1–30.

Goodison, P. (2007) 'EU Trade Policy and the Future of Africa's Trade Relationship with the EU', *Review of African Political Economy*, 34(112): 247–266.

Gow, D. D. (2008) *Countering Development: Indigenous Modernity and the Moral Imagination*, Durham, NC: Duke University Press.

Granados, M. L., Hlupic, V., Coakes, E. and Souad, M. (2011) 'Social enterprise and social entrepreneurship research and theory: A bibliometric analysis from 1991 to 2010', *Social Enterprise Journal*, 7, 198–218.

Granovetter, M. (1985) 'Economic Action and Social Structure: The Problem of Embeddedness', *American Journal of Sociology*, 91(3): 481–510.

Granovetter, M. (1992) 'Economic Institutions as Social Constructions: A Framework for Analysis', *Acta Sociologica* 35(1): 3–11.

Granovetter, M. (2005) 'The Impact of Social Structure on Economic Outcomes', *The Journal of Economic Perspectives*, 19(1): 33–50.

Grant, R. (1997) 'Measuring Corporate Power: Assessing the Options' *Journal of Economic Issues*, 31(2): 453.

Grear, A. (2007) 'Challenging Corporate Humanity: Legal Disembodiment, Embodiment and Human Rights', *Human Rights Law Review*, 7: 511–543.

Griffiths, B., Sirico, R.A., Barry, N. and Field, F. (2001) *Capitalism, Morality and Markets*, London: Institute of Economic Affairs.

Griffiths, J. (1986) 'What is Legal Pluralism?', *Journal of Legal Pluralism*, 24: 1–50.

Griseri, P. and Seppala, N. (2010) *Business Ethics and Corporate Social Responsibility First*, Andover: Cengage Learning Press.

Grossman, G. M. and Helpman, E. (1999) 'The Politics of Free-Trade Agreements', in J. Bhagwati, P. Krishna and A. Panagariya (eds), *Trading Blocs: Alternative Approaches to Analysing Preferential Trade Agreements*, MIT Press.

Grotius, H. (1625) *De Jure Belli ac Pacis libri tres*, Apud Nicolaum Buon Publications.

Guzman, A. (2004) 'Global Governance and the WTO', *Harvard International Law Journal*, 45: 313.

Hachez, N. and Wouters, J. (2011) 'A Glimpse at the Democratic Legitimacy of Private Standards: Assessing the Public Accountability of GlobalG.A.P.', *Journal of International Economic Law*, 14: 677–710.

Hahn, M. (2006) 'A Clash of Cultures? The UNESCO Diversity Convention and International Trade Law', *Journal of International Economic Law*, 9: 515–552.

Hall, W. E. (1880) *International Law*, Oxford, Clarendon Press.

Halliday, T. and Carruthers, B. (2009) *Bankrupt: Global Lawmaking and Systemic Financial Crisis*, Stanford: Stanford University Press.

Halliday, T. C. (2009) 'Recursivity of Global Normmaking: A Sociolegal Agenda', *Annual Review of Law and Social Science*, 5: 263–290.

Halliday, T. C. (2011) 'Architects of the State: International Financial Institutions and the Reconstruction of States in East Asia'. *Law & Social Inquiry*, 37: 265–296.

Halliday, T. C. (forthcoming) 'Why the Legal Complex is Integral to Theories of Judicial Power'. In *How Courts Evolve: Judicial Roles in Comparative Perspective*, edited by Gordon Silverstein, Robert A. Kagan and Diana Kapiszewski: Under submission.

Halliday, T. C. and Carruthers, B. G. (2007) 'The Recursivity of Law: Global Norm-making and National Lawmaking in the Globalization of Bankruptcy Regimes'. *American Journal of Sociology*, 112: 1135–1202.

Halliday, T. C. and Carruthers, B. G. (2009) *Bankrupt: Global Lawmaking and Systemic Financial Crisis*. Palo Alto: Stanford University Press.

Halliday, T. C., Pacewicz, J. and Block-Lieb, S. (2011) 'Delegations: The Micro-Politics of Influence in International Organizations'. in *SSRN eLibrary*. Available at http://papers.ssrn.com/sol3/papers.cfm?abstract_id=1928801 (accessed 5 October 2012)

Halliday, T. C., Block-Lieb, S. and Carruthers, B. G. (2009) 'Rhetorical Legitimation: Global Scripts as Strategic Devices of International Organizations'. *European Socio-Economic Review*, 2009: 1–36.

Hames, R. (2007) 'The Ecologically Noble Savage Debate,' *Annual Review of Anthropology* 36: 177–190.

Hammersley, M. and Atkinson, P. (1997) *Ethnography: Principles in Practice*, London: Sage.

Hannan, M. T. (2005) 'Ecologies of Organizations: Diversity and Identity'. *Journal of Economic Perspectives* 19: 51–70.

Hardt, Michael and Antonio Negri (2009) *Commonwealth*, Cambridge: Harvard University Press.

Harvey, D. (2007) *A Brief History of Neoliberalism*, Oxford: Oxford University Press.

Hayek, F. (1944) *The Road to Serfdom*, London: G. Routledge & Sons.

Hayek, F. (1960) *The Constitution of Liberty*, London: Routledge and Kegan Paul.

Hayek, F. A. (1978) *The Constitution of Liberty*, Chicago: University of Chicago Press.

Hee-jin, Kim (2012) 'Second Facebook Judge Disciplined' *Korean Joongang Daily* (15 February). Available at http://koreajoongangdaily.joinsmsn.com/news/article/article.aspx?aid=2948487&cloc=joongangdaily%7Chome%7Cnewslist1 (accessed 16 February 2012).

Heinzen, J. W. (2004) *Inventing a Soviet Countryside: State Power and the Transformation of Rural Russia, 1917–1929*, Pittsburgh: University of Pittsburgh Press.

Hellum, A., Sardar Ali, S. and Griffiths, A. (eds) (2010) *From Transnational Relations to Transnational Laws: Northern European Laws at the Crossroads*, Farnham: Ashgate.

Hendry, J. (2006) 'Taking Aim at Business: What Factors Lead Non Governmental Organizations to Target Particular Firms?', *Business and Society*, 45: 47.

Hettne, B. (2005) 'Regionalism and World Order', in M. Farrell, B. Hettne and L. van Langenhove (eds), *Global Politics of Regionalism: Theory and Practice*, Pluto Press.

Hettne, B. and Söderbaum, F. (2000) 'Theorising the Rise of Regions', *New Political Economy*, 5(3): 457–473.

Hillyard, P. (2002) 'Invoking indignation: reflections on future directions of socio-legal studies', *Journal of Law and Society*, 29(4): 645–656.

Hinkle, L. and Schiff, M. (2004) 'Economic Partnership Agreements Between Sub-Saharan Africa and the EU: A Development Perspective', *World Economy*, 27(9): 1321–1333.

Hirsch, M. (2005) 'The Sociology of International Law: Invitation to Study International Rules in Their Social Context', *University of Law Journal*, 55.

Hirsch, M. (2008) 'The Sociology of International Economic: Sociological Analysis of the Regulation of Regional Trade Agreements in the World Trading System', *European Journal of International Law*, 19(2): 277–299.

Ho, P. (2001) 'Who Owns China's Land? Policies, Property Rights and Deliberate Institutional Ambiguity', *The China Quarterly*, 166: 394–421.

Hooker, M. B. (1975) *Legal Pluralism: An Introduction to Colonial and Neo-Colonial Laws*, Oxford: Clarendon Press.

Horne, W. C. (2001) 'Samuel Johnson Discovers the Arctic: A Reading of a "Greenland Tale" as Arctic Literature,' in K. Armbruster and K. R. Wallace (eds), *Beyond Nature Writing: Expanding the Boundaries of Ecocriticism*, Charlottesville and London: University Press of Virginia.

Horst, D. V. D. (2008) 'Social enterprise and renewable energy: emerging initiatives and communities of practice', *Social Enterprise Journal*, 4: 171–185.

Horta, K. (2002) 'Rhetoric and Reality: Human Rights and the World Bank', *Harvard Human Rights Journal*, 15: 227–243.

Hovenkamp, H. J. (2009) 'Knowledge About Welfare: Legal Realism and the Separation of Law and Economics', *Minnesota Law Review*, 84(4): 805–862.

Howell, J. (2003) 'Governance Matters: Key Challenges and Emerging Tendencies', in J. Howell (ed.), *Governance in China*, Lanham, MD: Rowman & Littlefield Publishers, 1–18.

Howse, R. (2002) 'From Politics to Technocracy – and back again: the fate of the multilateral trading regime', *The American Journal of International Law*, 96(1): 94–117.

Huang, P. (1982) 'County Archives and the Study of Local Social History: Report on a Year's Research in China', *Modern China*, 8(I): 133–143.

Huang, P. (2006) 'Court Mediation in China, Past and Present', *Modern China*, 32(3): 275–314.

Hunt, A. (1976) 'Problems of the State: Law, State and Class Struggle', *Marxism Today*, 178–187.

Hunt, A. and Wickham G. (1994) *Foucault and Law: Towards a Sociology of Law as Governance*, London: Pluto Press.

Hurt, S. R. (2003) 'Cooperation and Coercion? The Cotonou Agreement Between the EU and ACP States and the end of the Lomé Convention', *Third World Quarterly* 24(1): 161–176.

Hyo-sik, Lee (2011) 'Judge Criticizes President Lee on Facebook Over US FTA' *The Korea Times* (25 December). Available at www.koreatimes.co.kr/www/news/nation/2011/11/113_99555.html (accessed 16 February 2012).

Iglesias, E. M. (1996) 'Human Rights in International Economic Law: Locating Latinas/os in the Linkage Debates', *University of Miami Inter-American Law Review*, 28: 361.

ILO (International Labour Organization) (2008) Freedom of association in practice: lessons learned, global report under the follow-up to the ILO-Declaration on Fundamental Principles and Rights at Work, International Labour Conference, 97th Session 2008 Report I (B). International Labour Organization.

IMF (International Monetary Fund) (1999) *Orderly and Effective Insolvency Procedures: Key Issues*, Washington, DC: International Monetary Fund.

International Finance Corporation (2012) *Performance Standard 7: Indigenous Peoples*. Online. Available at: http://www1.ifc.org/wps/wcm/connect/1ee703804

9a79139b845faa8c6a8312a/PS7_English_2012.pdf?MOD=AJPERES (accessed 6 February 2012).

International Monetary Fund (2011) 'Articles of Agreement of the International Monetary Fund'. Available at www.imf.org/external/pubs/ft/aa/aa10.htm (accessed 20 December 2011).

IUC Group (IUC Global Legal Standards Research Group) (2009) 'IUC Independent Policy Report: At the End of the End of History – Global Legal Standards: Part of the Solution or Part of the Problem', *Global Jurist*, 9: issue 3, art 2. Available at www.bepress.com/gj/vol. 9/iss3/art2 (accessed 9 October 2011).

Jackson, J. H. (1995) 'International economic law: reflections on the "boiler room" of international relations', *American University Journal of International Law and Policy*, 10: 595.

Jackson, J. H. (2007) 'International Economic Law: Complexity and Puzzles', *Journal of International Economic Law*, 10: 3–12.

Jackson, N. and Carter, P. (1995) 'Organizational Chiaroscuro: Throwing Light on the Concept of Corporate Governance', *Human Relations*, 48: 875.

James, C. P. (1982) 'Seriality and narrativity in Calvino's *Le cittá invisibili*', 97(1) *Modern Language Notes* (Italian Issue), 144–161.

Jensen, J. and De Sousa Santos, B. (eds) (2000) *Globalizing Institutions: Case Studies in Renovation and Innovation*, Aldershot; Burlington: Ashgate.

Jeong-pil, Kim (2011) 'Support for Judge Lambasted for Facebook Post' *The Hankyoreh* (29 November). Available at http://english.hani.co.kr/arti/english_edition/e_national/507657.html (accessed 16 February 2012).

Jerbi, S. (2009) 'Business and Human Rights at the UN: What Might Happen Next?', *Human Rights Quarterly*, 31: 299.

Jessop, Bob (1982) *The Capitalist State*, New York: New York University Press.

Jessop, Bob (1990) *State Theory: Putting Capitalist States in the Their Place*, University Park, PA: University of Pennsylvania Press.

Jessup, P. C. (1956) 'Transnational Law', extracts reprinted in Tietje, Brouder and Nowrot (eds) (2006) *Philip C. Jessup's* Transnational Law *Revisited. Beiträge zum Transnationalen Wirtschaftsrecht no. 50*, Halle-Wittenberg: Martin-Luther-Universität, 45–55. Available at www.wirtschaftsrecht.uni-halle.de/sites/default/files/altbestand/Heft50.pdf (accessed 9 October 2011).

Joerges, C. and Falke, J. (eds) (2011) *Karl Polanyi, Globalisation and the Potential of Law in Transnational Markets*, Oxford: Hart Publishing.

Joerges, Christian (2010) 'The Idea of a Three-Dimensional Conflicts Law as Constitutional Form,' RECON Online Working Paper 2010/05. Available at www.reconproject.eu/main.php/RECON_wp_1005.pdf?fileitem=5456171 (accessed 1 June 2010).

Joerges, Christian and Rödl, Florian (2012) 'Reconceptualizing the Constitution of Europe's Postnational Constellation – by Dint of Conflict of Laws', in Ioannis Lianos and Okeoghene Odudu, *Regulating Trade in Services in the EU and the WTO: Trust, Distrust and Economic Integration*, Cambridge: Cambridge University Press, pp. 381–399.

Johnson, Simon and Kwak, James (2010) *13 Bankers: The Wall Street Takeover and the Next Financial Meltdown*, New York: Pantheon Books.

Joseph, S. (2004) *Corporations and Transnational Human Rights Litigation*, Oxford: Hart Publishing.

Joseph, S. (2008) 'Liability of Multinational Corporations', in M. Langford (ed.), *Social Rights Jurisprudence: Emerging Trends in International and Comparative Law*, New York Cambridge University Press 613.

Joyner, B. E. and Payne, D. (2002) 'Evolution and Implementation: A Study of Values, Business Ethics and Corporate Social Responsibility', *Journal of Business Ethics*, 41: 297–311.

Judt, T. (2010) *Ill Fares the Land*, London: Allen Lane.

Julian, M. (2010) 'EPA Update', *Trade Negotatiation Insights*, 9(3), March. Available at http://ictsd.org/i/news/tni/72888/.

Kadens, Emily (2012) 'The Myth of Customary Law Merchant', *Texas Law Review*, 90: 1153–1206.

Kamidza, R. (2007) 'SADC EPA Information Seminar Failed Civil Society', *SEATINI Bulletin* 10: 7 (16 July). Available at www.seatini.org/bulletins/pdf/2007/10.07.pdf.

Kaptein, M. and Wempe, J. (2002) *The Balanced Company: A Theory of Corporate Integrity*, Oxford: Oxford University Press.

Karpik, L. and Halliday, T. C. (2011) 'The Legal Complex', *Annual Review of Law and Social Science*, 7: 217–236.

Kelly, C. (2006) 'Power, Linkage and Accommodation: The WTO as an International Actor and its Influence over other Actors and Regimes', *Berkeley Journal of International Law*, 24: 79.

Kennealy, P. (1988) 'Talking about Autopoiesis – Order from Noise', in Teubner (ed.) *Autopoietic Law: A New Approach to Law and Society*, Berlin: Walter de Gruyte.

Kennedy, David (1994) 'The International Style in Postwar Law and Policy', *Utah Law Review*, 7–103.

Kennedy, David (1999) 'The Disciplines of International Law and Policy', *Leiden Journal of International Law*, 12(1): 9–133.

Kennedy, David (2000) 'Challenging Expert Rule: The Politics of Global Governance,' *Sydney Law Review*, 27: 5–28.

Kennedy, David (2006) 'Three Globalizations of Law and Legal Thought: 1850–2000', in D. M. Trubek and A. Santos (eds) *The New Law and Economic Development*, Cambridge: Cambridge University Press, pp. 19–73.

Kennedy, David (2011) Some Caution about Property Rights as a Recipe for Economic Development, *Accounting, Economics, and Law*, 1.

Kennedy, D. and Mayhew, D. (2004) *The Dark Sides of Virtue: Reassessing International Humanitarianism*, Princeton, NJ; Oxford, Princeton University Press.

Kennedy, Duncan (1982) 'Distributive and Paternalist Motives in Contract and Tort Law, with Special Reference to Compulsory Terms and Unequal Bargaining Power', *Maryland Law Review*, 4: 563–658.

Khor, M. (2000) 'Rethinking Liberalization and Reforming the WTO', reprinted in J. Kelsey (ed.) *International Economic Regulation*, Aldershot: Ashgate, 2002, 257–262.

Kinderman, D. (2012) ' "Free Us Up So We Can Be Responsible!" The Co-evolution of Corporate Social Responsibility and Neo-liberalism in the UK, 1977–2010', *Socio-Economic Review*, 10: 29.

Kingsbury, B. (2002) 'First Amendment Liberalism as Global Legal Architecture: Ascriptive Groups and the Problems of the Liberal NGO model of International Civil Society,' *Chicago Journal of International Law*, 3: 183–195.

Kinley, D. (2009) *Civilising Globalisation*, Cambridge: Cambridge University Press.

Kinley, D. and Chambers, R. (2006) 'The UN Human Rights Norms for Corporations: The Private Implications of Public International Law' 6 *Human Rights L Rev* 447.

Kinley, D. and Zerial, N. (2007) '"The Norms are Dead! Long Live the Norms!" The Politics Behind the UN Human Rights Norms for Corporations' in D. McBarnet, A. Voiculescu and T. Campbell (eds), *The New Corporate Accountability*, CUP Cambridge 459.

Kinley, D., Nolan, J. and Zerial, N. (2007) 'The Politics of Corporate Social Responsibility: Reflections on the United Nations Human Rights Norms for Corporations,' *Company and Securities Law Journal*, 25(1): 30.

Kiobel v. Royal Dutch Petroleum, Co. (Shell) (Esther Kiobel, individually and on behalf of her late husband, Dr. Barinem Kiobel, et al., petitioners v. Royal Dutch Petroleum co. et al.) US Supreme Court Case 10–1491.

Klabbers, J. (2003) '(I Can't Get No) Recognition: Subjects Doctrine and the Emergence of Non-state Actors,' in Petman, J. and Klabbers, J. (eds), *Nordic Cosmopolitanism: Essays in International Law for Martti Koskenniemi.*

Klein, J. T. (1996) *Crossing Boundaries: Knowledge, Disciplinarities and Interdisciplinarities*, London: University Press of Virginia.

Klein, N. (2007) *The Shock Doctrine: The Rise of Disaster Capitalism*, New York, Metropolitan Books/Henry Holt.

Kloppers, H. and du Plessis, W. (2008) 'Corporate Social Responsibility, Legislative Reforms and Mining in South Africa', *Journal of Energy and Natural Resources Law*, 26: 91–119.

Knötzl, B. and Zach, E. (2007) 'Taking the Best from Mediation Regulations', *Arbitration International*, 23(4): 665.

Kogut, B. and Zander, U. (1992) 'Knowledge of the firm, combinative capabilities, and the replication of technology', *Organization Science*, 383–397.

Koh, Harold H. (1996) 'Transnational Legal Process', *Nebraska Law Review*, 75: 181–207.

Koh, Harold H. (2006) 'Why Transnational Law Matters', *Pennsylvania State International Law Review*, 24: 745–753.

Koskenniemi, M. (1989) *From Apology to Utopia: The Structure of International Legal Argument*, Helsinki: Finnish Lawyer's Publishing Company.

Koskenniemi, M. (2001) *The Gentle Civilizer of Nations: The Rise and Fall of International Law, 1870–1960*, New York: Cambridge University Press.

Koskenniemi, M. (2006) 'Fragmentation of International Law: Difficulties Arising from the Diversification and Expansion of International Law' UN Doc. *International Law Commission* A/CN.4/L.682, 13 April.

Koskenniemi, M. (2007) 'The Fate of Public International Law: Between Technique and Politics', *The Modern Law Review*, 70(1), 1–30.

Koskenniemi, M. (2011) *The Politics of International Law*, Oxford: Hart.

Koskenniemi, M. and Leino, P. (2002) 'Fragmentation of International Law? Postmodern Anxieties', *Leiden Journal of International Law*, 15: 553–579.

KPMG (2008) *Climate Changes Your Business*, London: KPMG International.

Krajewski, M. (2011) 'Commodifying and Embedding Services of General Interests in Transnational Contexts: The Example of Healthcare Liberalisation in the EU and the WTO', in C. Joerges and J. Falke (eds), *Karl Polanyi, Globalisation and the Potential of Law in Transnational Markets*, Oxford: Hart Publishing, pp. 232–254.

Kramer, R.A., van Schaik, C.P. and Johnson, J. (eds) (1997) *Last Stand: Protected Areas and the Defense of Tropical Biodiversity*, New York: Oxford University Press.

Krippner, G. (2010) 'The Political Economy of Financial Exuberance', in M. Lounsbury and P. M. Hirsch (eds), *Markets on Trial: the economic sociology of the U.S. financial crisis. Part B*, Bingley: Emerald, pp. 141–175.

Krippner, G., Granovetter, M., Block, F., Biggart, N., Beamish, T., Hsing, Y., Hart, G., Arrighi, G., Mendell, M., Hall, J., Burawoy, M., Vogel, S. and O'Riain, S. (2004) 'Polanyi Symposium: A Conversation on Embeddedness', *Socioeconomic Review*, 109–135.

Krisch, N. and Kingsbury, B. (2006) 'Introduction: Global Governance and Global Administrative Law in the International Legal Order', *European Journal of International Law*, 17(1): 1.

Krisch, Nico (2010) *Beyond Constitutionalism: The Pluralist Structure of Postnational Law*, Oxford: Oxford University Press.

Krücken, G. and Drori, G. S. (eds) (2009) *World Society: The writings of John W. Meyer*, Oxford: Oxford University Press.

Krugman, P. (2007) 'Regionalism versus Multilateralism: Analytical Notes', in C. Freund (ed.), *The WTO and Reciprocal Preferential Trade Agreements*, Cheltenham: Edward Elgar.

Krugman, P. (2008) *The Return of Depression Economics*, Harmondsworth: Penguin.

Krygier, M. (2012) *Philip Selznick: Ideals in the World*, Stanford: Stanford University Press.

Kuper, A. (2004) 'Harnessing Corporate Power: Lessons from the UN Global Compact', *Development*, 47: 9.

Kuyper, P. J. (1994) 'The Law of GATT as a Special Field of International Law', *Netherlands Yearbook of International Law*, 25: 140.

Kwarteng, C. (1993) 'Africa and the European Challenge after 1992', *International Social Science Journal*, 45(3): 405–413.

Kwarteng, C. (1997) *Africa and the European Challenge: Survival in a Changing World*, Avebury.

Kytle, B. and Ruggie, J. (2005) 'Corporate Social Responsibility as Risk Management: A Model for Multinationals' Corporate Social Responsibility Initiative Working Paper No. 10, John F Kennedy School of Government, Harvard University.

Lacan, J. (1936) 'Au-delà du principe de réalité,' *L'Evolution Psychiatrique* 3: 67–86.

Lacan, J. (1966) *Ecrits*, Paris: Seuil.

Lacan, J. (1973) *Les Quatre Concepts Fondamentaux de la Psychanalyse*, Paris: Seuil.

Lacan, J. and Miller, J.-A. (1978) *Le séminaire de Jacques Lacan: Le moi dans la théorie de Freud et dans la technique de la psychanalyse*, Paris: Seuil.

Lang, A. (2007) 'Reflecting on Linkage: Cognitive and Institutional Change in the International Trading System', *The Modern Law Review*, 70(4): 523–549.

Lang, A. (2011) *World Trade Law After Neoliberalism: Reimagining the Global Economic Order*, Oxford: Oxford University Press.

Laski, Harold J. (1919) *Authority in the Modern State*, New Haven: Yale University Press.

Laski, Harold J. (1922) 'The State in the New Social Order,' Fabian Tract No. 200, London: Fabian Society.

Laski, Harold J. (1948) *A Grammar of Politics*, 5th edn., London, UK: George Allen & Unwin.

Lasser, M., Kennedy, D., Kennedy, D. and Berman, N. (1999) 'Critical Legal Theory,' in S. Tiefenbrun (ed.) *Law and the Arts*, Westport, CT: Greenwood Press.

Latour, B. and Lépinay, V. (2009) *The Science of Passionate Interests: an introduction to Gabriel Tarde's economic anthropology*, Chicago: Prickly Paradigm Press.

Lee, I. (2005) 'Is there a Cure for Corporate "Psychopathy"?', *American Business Law Journal*, 42(1–6): 65–90.

Leebron, D. (2002) 'Linkages', *American Journal of International Law*, 96(5): 5–27.

Legrand, P. (1997) 'The Impossibility of Legal Transplants', *Maastricht Journal of European and Comparative Law* 4: 111–124.

Legrand, P. (2001) 'What "Legal Transplants"?', in D. Nelken and J. Feest (eds), *Adapting Legal Cultures*, Oxford: Hart Publishing, 53–69.

Lenzerini, F. (2008) 'Article 12', in F. Francioni (ed.), *The 1972 World Heritage Convention: A Commentary*, Oxford: OUP.

Levit, J. K. (2008) 'Bottom-Up Lawmaking: The Private Origins of Transnational Law', *Indiana Journal of Global Legal Studies* 15: 49–74.

Lewis, M. (2011) *The Big Short*, Harmondsworth: Penguin.

Liang, S. M. (1986) *Zhongguo Wenhua Yaoyi [Gist of Chinese Culture]*, Shanghai: Xuelin Chubanche, 162–188.

Lindross, A. and Mehling, M. (2005) 'Dispelling the chimera of "self-contained regimes": international law and the WTO' 16(5) *EJIL* 857.

Lipshaw, J. (2010) 'The Epistemology of the Financial Crisis', *Southern California Interdisciplinary Law Journal*, 19: 299.

Llewellyn, D. and Tehan, M. (2004) '"Treaties," "Agreements," "Contracts and Commitments" – What's in a Name? The Legal Force and Meaning of Different Forms of Agreement Making,' *Melbourne Law School Legal Studies Research Paper* No. 134.

Llwellyn, Karl M. and Adamson Hoebel, E. (1941) *The Cheyenne Way: Conflict and Case Law in Primitive Jurisprudence*, Norman: University of Oklahoma Press.

Loibl, Gerhard (2006) 'International Economic Law', in Malcolm Evans (ed.), *International Law*, 2nd edition, Oxford: OUP.

Lowenfeld, A. F. (2010) 'The international monetary system: a look back over seven decades' 13:3 *Journal of International Economic Law* 575–595.

Luhmann, N. (1977) 'Differentiation of Society', *Canadian Journal of Sociology*, 2(1): 29–53.

Luhmann, N. (1985) *A Sociological Theory of Law*, M. Albrow (ed.), trans. E. King-Utz and M. Albrow (London, Boston, Melbourne, Henley: Routledge & Keagan Paul).

Luhmann, N. (1992) 'Operational Closure and Structural Coupling: The Differentiation of the Legal System', *Cardozo Law Review*, 13, 1419–1441.

Luhmann, N. (2004) *Law as a Social System*, trans. K. Ziegert, Oxford: Oxford University Press.

MacCormick, Neil (1993) 'Beyond the Sovereign State', *The Modern Law Review*, 56: 1–18.

MacDonald, K. (2011) 'Re-thinking "Spheres of Responsibility": Business Responsibility for Indirect Harm', *Journal of Business Ethics*, 99(4): 549.

Mace, M. (2004) 'Directors: Myth and Reality,' in T. Clarke (ed.), *Theories of Corporate Governance: The Philosophical Foundations of Corporate Governance*, London and New York: Routledge.

MacLeod, G. (2001) 'New Regionalism Reconsidered: Globalization and the Remaking of Political Economic Space', *International Journal of Urban and Regional Research*, 25(4): 804–829.

Maher, I. (2011) 'Competition Law and Transnational Private Regulatory Regimes: Marking the Cartel Boundary', *Journal of Law and Society*, 38: 119–137.

Maine, H. J. Sumner (1983 [1861]) *Ancient Law: Its Connection with the Early History of Society, and its Relation to Modern Ideas*, Buffalo: W. S. Hein.

Maitland, F. W. (1900) 'Translator's Introduction' in Otto Gierke, *Political Theories of the Middle Age*, Trans. F. W. Maitland, Cambridge: Cambridge University Press, pp. vii–xlv.

Maitland, F. W. (1911) 'Trust and Corporation', in *The Collected Paper of Frederick W. Maitland*, Vol. III, H. A. L. Fisher (ed.), Cambridge: Cambridge University Press, pp. 320–404.

Mambara, J. (2007) *An Evaluation of Involvement of Southern Africa's Civil Society in EPA Negotiations to Date*, Trades Centre Report: Zimbabwe.

Mann, H. (2008) *International Investment Agreements, Business and Human Rights: Key Issues and Opportunities*, IISD Research Paper. Online. Available at: www.iisd.org/pdf/2008/iia_business_human_rights.pdf (accessed 6 February 2012).

Mansfield, E. D. and Milner, H. V. (1999) 'The New Wave of Regionalism', *International Organization*, 53(3): 589–627.

Mansfield, E. D. and Reinhardt, E. (2003) 'Multilateral Determinants of Regionalism: The Effects of GATT/WTO on the Formation of Preferential Trade Agreements', *International Organisation*, 57(4): 829–862.

Marceau, G. (1999) 'A Call to Coherence in International Law', *Journal of World Trade*, 33(5): 87.

Marceau, G. (2002) 'WTO Dispute Settlement and Human Rights', *European Journal of International Law*, 13: 753–814.

Marceau, G. and Pedersen, P. N. (1999) 'Is the WTO Open and Transparent?', *Journal of World Trade*, 33: 5–49.

Mares, R. (2012) 'Business and Human Rights After Ruggie: Foundations, the Art of Simplification and the Imperative of Cumulative Progress', in R. Mares (ed.), *The UN Guiding Principles on Business and Human Rights: Foundations and Implementation*, Leiden/Boston: Martinus Nijhoff Publishers.

Marks, S. (2011) 'Human rights and root causes', *Modern Law Review*, 74, 57–78.

Marrakesh Agreement (nd) Establishing the World Trade Organization Article IV (Structure of the WTO) para 1. Available at: www.wto.org.

Marx, K. (1842) 'Debates on the Law on Thefts of Wood', *Rheinische Zeitung, Supplement*. Online. Available at: www.marxists.org/archive/marx/works/1842/10/25.htm (accessed 28 January 2012).

Marx, K. (1859) 'A Contribution to the Critique of Political Economy' [preface]. Online. Available at: www.marxists.org/archive/marx/works/1859/critique-pol-economy/preface.htm (accessed 28 January 2012).

Marx, K. and McLellan, D. (2000) 'On the Jewish Question', *Karl Marx: selected writings*. 2nd ed, Oxford: Oxford University Press.

Masters, Brooke and Braithwaite, Tom (2011) 'Bankers versus Basel', *Financial Times*, (3 October) 9.

Matten, D. and Crane, A. (2005) 'Corporate Citizenship: Toward An Extended Theoretical Conceptualization', *Academy of Management Review*, 30(1): 166.

Mavrodis, P. (2003) 'The trade disputes concerning health policy between the EC and the US' in E. Petersmann and M. Pollack (eds), *Transatlantic Economic Disputes: The EU, the US and the WTO*, Oxford: Oxford University Press, pp. 233–245.

Mayo, E. (2012) Co-operatives UK–global Business Ownership Report 2012. Co-operatives UK.

McBarnet, D. and Whelan, C. (1997) 'Creative Compliance and the Defeat of Legal Control: The Magic of the Orphan Subsidiary', in *The Human Face of Law*, K. Hawkins (ed.) Oxford: Oxford University Press.

McBarnet, D. J. (2007) 'Corporate Social Responsibility Beyond Law, Through Law, for Law: The New Corporate Accountability', in D. J. McBarnet, A. Voiculescu, and T. Campbell (eds), *The New Corporate Accountability: Corporate Social Responsibility and the Law*, Cambridge: Cambridge University Press.

McCloskey, D. (2002) *The Secret Sins of Economics*, Chicago: Prickly Paradigm Press.

McCorquodale, R. (2009) 'Corporate Social Responsibility and International Human Rights Law', *Journal of Business Ethics*, 87: 385.

McCorquodale, R. and Simons, P. (2007) 'Responsibility Beyond Borders: State Responsibility for Extraterritorial Violations by Corporations of International Human Rights Law', *Modern Law Review*, 70(4): 598.

McCrudden, C. (1999) 'Human Rights Codes for Transnational Corporations: What can the Sullivan and MacBride Principles Tell Us?', *Oxford Journal of Legal Studies*, 19(2): 167.

McMillan, J. (1993) 'Does Regional Integration Foster Open Trade? Economic Theory and GATT's Article XXIV', in K. Anderson and R. Blackhurst (eds), *Regional Integration in the Global Trading System*, Harvester Wheatsheaf.

Melissaris, Emmanuel (2009) *Ubiquitous Law: Legal Theory and the Space for Legal Pluralism*, Surrey: Ashgate.

Mena, S., Leede, M., Baumann, D., Black, N., Lindeman, S. and McShane, L. (2010) 'Advancing the Business and Human Rights Agenda: Dialogue, Empowerment, and Constructive Engagement', *Journal of Business Ethics*, 93(1): 167.

Merry, S. E. (1988) 'Legal Pluralism', *Law and Society Review*, 22: 869–896.

Merry, Sally Engle (1992) 'Anthropology, Law and Transnational Processes', *Annual Review of Anthropology*, 21: 357–377.

Merton, R. K. (1957) *Social Theory and Social Structure*, Glencoe, IL: FreePress.

Meyer, W. (1998) *Human Rights and International Political Economy in Third World Nations: Multinational Corporations, Foreign Aid and Repression* Westport Conneticut: Praeger.

Michaels, R. (2009) 'Global legal pluralism', *Annual Review of Law and Social Science*, 5: 243–262.

Michelman, Frank I. (1967) 'Property, Utility, and Fairness: Comments on the Ethical Foundations of "Just Compensation" Law', *Harvard Law Review*, 80: 1165–1258.

Michelman, Frank I. (1988) 'Law's Republic', *Yale Law Journal*, 97: 1493.

Micklethwaite, J. and Wooldridge, A. (2005) *The Company*, New York: Random House.

Minsky, H. (2008) *Stabilizing an Unstable Economy*, New York: McGraw Hill.

Mold, A. (ed.) (2007) *EU Development Policy in a Changing World: Challenges for the 21st Century*, Amsterdam: Amsterdam University Press.

Moloney, N. (2010) 'EU Financial Market Regulation After the Global Financial Crisis: "More Europe" or More Risks?' *Common Market Law Review*, 47: 1317.

Moore, Sally Falk (1978) *Law as Process: An Anthropological Approach*, London: Routledge & Kegan Paul.

Moore, Sally Falk (1973) 'Law and Social Change: The Semi-Autonomous Social Field as an Appropriate Subject of Study', *Law & Society Review*, 7(4): 719–746.

Moore, Sally Falk (2000) *Law as Process: An Anthropological Approach*, Introduction by Martin Channock, Hamburg: LIT Verlag & James Curry.

Morijn, J. (2008) 'The Place of Cultural Rights in the WTO System', in F. Francioni and M. Scheinin (eds), *Cultural Human Rights*, Leiden: Martinus Nijhoff Publishers, 285–316.

Moyo, D. (2009) *Dead Aid: Why Aid is Not Working and How There is Another Way For Africa*, Allen Lane/Penguin.

Moyo, S. and Yeros, P. (2005) 'Land occupations and Land Reform in Zimbabwe: Towards the National Democratic Revolution', S. Moyoto and P. Yeros (eds), *Reclaiming the Land: the Resurgence of Rural Movements in Africa, Asia and Latin America*. Zed Books.

Muchlinski, P. (2012) 'Implementing the New UN Corporate Human Rights Framework: Implications for Corporate Law, Governance, and Regulation' 22 *Bus Eth Quart* 145.

Muchlinski, P. (2003) 'Globalisation and Legal Research', *The International Lawyer*, 37(1): 221–240.

Mullerat, R. (2010) *International Corporate Social Responsibility: The Role of Corporations in the Economic Order of the 21st Century*, The Netherlands: Kluwer Law International.

Munchau, W. (2009) *The Meltdown Years*, New York: McGraw Hill.

Munck, R. (2000) 'Labour in the global: challenges and prospects', in R. Cohen and S. Rai (eds), *Global Social Movements*. London; New Brunswick, NJ, Athlone Press.

Murphy, W. T. (2006) 'Durkheim in China', in M. Freeman (ed.), *Law and Sociology*, Oxford: Oxford University Press, 107–118.

Murray-Brown, J. and Dennis, N. (2008) 'Ireland Guarantees Six Banks' Deposits', *Financial Times* 30 September. Available at www.ft.com/cms/s/0/2124f8 f4–8eb9–11dd-946c-0000779fd18c.html#ixzz1VNFj9OTG (accessed 28 January 2012).

Mus, J. B. (1998) 'Conflicts between treaties in international law', XLV *Netherlands International Law Review*, 219–220.

Mutua, M. (2001) Savages, Victims, and Saviors: the Metaphor of Human Rights, *Harvard International Law Journal*, 42, 201.

Nafziger, J. A. R., Kirkwood Paterson, R. and Dundes Renteln, A. (2010) *Cultural Law: International, Comparative and Indigenous*, Cambridge: Cambridge University Press.

Nelken, D. (1998) 'Blinding Insights? The Limits of a Reflexive Sociology of Law', *Journal of Law and Society*, 25: 407–426.

Nelken, D. (2001a) 'Can Law Learn from Social Science?', *Israeli Law Review*, 35: 205.

Nelken, D. (2001b) 'Towards a Sociology of Legal Adaptation', in D. Nelken and J. Feest (eds), *Adapting Legal Cultures*, Oxford: Hart Publishing, 5–53.

Nelken, D. (2010) 'Human Trafficking and Legal Culture', *Israel Law Review*, 43: 479–513.

Nelson, V. and Pound, B. (2009) The Last Ten Years: A Comprehensive Review of the Literature on the Impact of Fairtrade. Natural Resources Institute, University of Greenwich.

Nicholas, P. (1996) 'Trade without values', *Northwestern University Law Review*, 701.

Nicholls, David (1994) *The Pluralist State: The Political Ideas of J.N. Figgis and His Contemporaries*, 2nd edn., Houndmills: The Macmillan Press.

Nocera, Joe (2010) 'U.S. Bills Just Scratch the Surface' *The New York Times* [Global Ed.] (5–6 June) 15.

Norms on the Responsibilities of Transnational Corporations and Other Business Enterprises with Regard to Human Rights, 26 August 2003, E/CN.4/Sub.2/2003/12/Rev.2. Available at: http://www.unhchr.ch/huridocda/huridoca.nsf/%28Symbol%29/ E.CN.4.Sub.2.2003.12.Rev.2.En.

North, D. (1990) *Institutions, Institutional Change and Economic Performance*, Cambridge: Cambridge University Press.

North, D. C. (1973) *The Rise of the Western World: A New Economic History* [S.l.], Cambridge, Cambridge University Press.

Nourse, V. and Shaffer, G. (2009) 'Varieties of new legal realism: can a new world order prompt a new legal theory?', *Cornell Law Review*, 95(1): 61–137.

O'Connell, P. (2007) 'On Reconciling Irreconcilables: Neo-Liberal Globalisation and Human Rights', *Human Rights Law Review*, 7: 483–509.

O'Faircheallaigh, C. (2003) 'Implementing Agreements between Indigenous Peoples and Resource Developers in Australia and Canada,' *Griffith University School of Politics and Public Policy Research Paper* No 13. Online. Available at: www. griffith.edu.au/business-commerce/griffith-business-school/pdf/research-paper-2003-implementing-agreements.pdf (accessed February 6, 2012).

O'Hara, E. and Ribstein, L. E. (2009) *The Law Market*, Oxford: Oxford University Press.

O'Keefe, P. (1994) 'Case Note: Foreign Investment and the World Heritage Convention', *International Journal of Cultural Property* 3: 259–265.

O'Keeffe, D. (2004) *Economy and Virtue Essays on the Theme of Markets and Morality*, London: Institute of Economic Affairs.

O'Neill, O. (2001) 'Agents of Justice', *Metaphilosophy*, 32: 180.

O'Neil, O. (2005) 'The Darkside of Human Rights', *International Affairs*, 81: 427.

Ogus, A. (1999) 'Competition between National Legal Systems: A Contribution of Economic Analysis to Comparative Law', *International and Comparative Law Quarterly*, 48: 405–418.

Oh, A. and Halliday, T. C. (2009) 'Rehabilitating Korea's corporate insolvency regime, 1992–2007', in *Pushing Back against Globalisation*, J. Gillespie and R. Peerenboom (eds). London: RoutledgeCurzon, pp. 238–269.

Oh, S. (2003) 'Insolvency Law Reform of Korea: A Continuing Learning Process', presentation at the conference *Forum on Insolvency Risk Management*. Washington, DC.

Oppenheim, J., Bonini, S., Bielak, D., Kehm, T. and Lacy, P. (2007) *Shaping the New Rules of Competition: UN Global Compact Participant Mirror*, McKinsey & Company London.

Oppenheim, L. F. L., Jennings, R. S. and Watts, A. (1905) *Oppenheim's International Law. vol. 1, peace*, OUP Oxford.

Oppenheim, L. F. L., Jennings, R. S., Watts, A. and Oppenheim, L. F. L. I. L. (1992) *Oppenheim's international law. vol. 1, peace.*

Ortino, Federico and Ortino, Matteo (2008) 'Law of the Global Economy: In Need of A New Methodological Approach?', in Colin Picker, Isabella D. Bunn and Douglas Warner (eds), *International Economic Law: The State and Future of the Discipline*, Oxford and Portland, Oregon: Hart Publishing.

Otto, J. (2010) *Community Development Agreement Model Regulations and Example Guidelines*, World Bank Report No. 61482. Online. Available at: www.eisourcebook.org/cms/files/attachments/worldbank/9point6-COMMUNITY-DEVELOPMENT-AGREEMENT-MODEL-REGULATIONS-&-EXAMPLE-GUIDELINES.pdf (accessed 6 February 2012).

Pahuja, Sundhya (2011) 'Decolonizing International Law: Development, Economic Growth and the Politics of Universality', *Melbourne Law School Legal Studies Research Paper*, No 520.

Panagariya, A. (2000) 'Preferential Trade Liberalisation: The Traditional Theory and New Developments', *Journal of Economic Literature*, 38: 287–331.

Parker, C. (2007) 'Meta-Regulation: Legal Accountability for Corporate Social Responsibility', in D. J. McBarnet, A. Voiculescu and T. Campbell (eds), *The New Corporate Accountability: Corporate Social Responsibility and the Law*, Cambridge: Cambridge University Press.

Parker, G. (2012) 'Cameron Vows Executive Pay Crackdown', *Financial Times* 9 January. Available at www.ft.com/cms/s/0/088b69ae-39e7-11e1-8707-00144 feabdc0.html (accessed 28 January 2012).

Paterson, J. (1995) 'Who is Zenon Bankowski Talking To? The Person in the Sight of Autopoiesis', *Ratio Juris*, 8(2), 212–229.

Paterson, J. (2003) 'Trans-Science, Trans-Law and Proceduralization', *Social & Legal Studies*, 12(4), 525–545.

Paulsson, Jan (2005) *Denial of Justice in International Law*, Cambridge: Cambridge University Press.

Pauwelyn, J. (2001) 'The role of public international law in the WTO: how far can we go?', *American Journal of International Law*, 95(3): 535–78R.

Pauwelyn, J. (2003) *Conflict of Norms in Public International Law: How WTO Law Relates to Other Rules of International Law*, Cambridge: Cambridge University Press.

Pauwelyn, J. (2008) 'New trade politics for the 21st century' 11:3 *Journal of International Economic*, 11(3): *Law* 559–573.

Pauwelyn, J. (2009) 'Legal Avenues to Multilateralising Regionalism: Beyond Article XXIV', in R. Baldwin and P. Low (eds), *Multilateralising Regionalism: Challenges for the Global Trading System*, Cambridge: Cambridge University Press.

Peck, Jamie (2010) *Constructions of Neoliberal Reason*, Oxford: Oxford University Press.

Peel, Quentin (2012) 'A Very Federal Formula' *Financial Times* (10 February) 7.

Penn Central Transportation Co. v. *City of New York*, 438 U.S. 104 (1978) (U.S. Sup. Ct).

Perez, O. (2003) *Ecological Sensitivity and Global Pluralism: Rethinking the Trade and Environment Conflict*, Oxford: Hart Publishing.

Perry, A. J. (2002) 'Multinational Enterprises, International Economic Organizations and Convergence among Legal Systems', *Non-State Actors and International Law*, 2: 23–39.

Perry-Kessaris, A. (2008) *Global Business, Local Law: the Indian legal system as a communal resource in foreign investment relations*, Aldershot: Ashgate.

Perry-Kessaris, A. (2010) 'Introduction', in A. Perry-Kessaris (ed.), *Law in the Pursuit of Development – Principles into Practice?* Abingdon, Oxon: Routledge.

Perry-Kessaris, A. (2011a) 'Reading the Story of Law and Embeddedness Through a Community Lens: A Polanyi-Meets-Cotterrell Economic Sociology Of Law?', *Northern Ireland Legal Quarterly*, 62(3): 401–413.

Perry-Kessaris, A. (2011b) 'Prepare your Indicators: Economics Imperialism on the Shores of Law and Development', *International Journal of Law in Context*, 7(4): 401–421.

Petersmann, E. (2002) 'Taking Human Dignity, Poverty and Empowerment of Individuals More Seriously: Rejoinder to Alston', *European Journal of International Law*, 13: 845–851.

Petersmann, E.-U. (2004) 'Challenges to the Legitimacy and Efficiency of the World Trading System: Democratic Governance and Competition Culture in the WTO: Introduction and Summary', *Journal of International Economic Law*, 7: 585–603.

Peterson, L. E. (2010) 'International Investment Law and Media Disputes: A Complement to WTO Law', *Columbia FDI Perspectives*, 17, 27 January.

Petras, J. F. and Veltmeyer, H. (2005) *Social Movements and State Power: Argentina, Brazil, Bolivia, Ecuador*, London: Pluto Press.

Picciotto, S. (2002) 'Reconceptualizing Regulation in the Era of Globalization', *Journal of Law and Society*, 29: 1–11.

Picciotto, S. (1999) 'Offshore: The State as Legal Fiction, in Hampton, M. and Abbott, J. P. (eds), *Offshore Finance Centres and Tax Havens: the Rise of Global Capital*, Basingstoke: Macmillan.

Picciotto, Sol (1998) 'Globalisation, Liberalisation, Regulation', paper presented at the Conference on Globalisation, the Nation State and Violence, organised by the Review of International Political Economy, University of Sussex, 16 April.

Picciotto, Sol (2006) 'Regulatory Networks and Global Governance', paper presented at the W. G. Hart Legal Workshop 2006, 'The Retreat of the State: Challenges to Law and Lawyers', Institute of Advanced Legal Studies, University of London, 27–29 June.

Picciotto, Sol (2011) *Regulating Global Corporate Capitalism*, Cambridge: Cambridge University Press.

Picker, C. (2011) 'International Trade and Development Law: A Legal Cultural Critique', *Law and Development Review*, 4: no. 2, art 4. Available at www.bepress.com/ldr/vol. 4/iss2/art4 (accessed 9 October 2011).

Pineschi, L. (2010) 'Cultural Diversity as a Human Right? General Comment No. 21 of the Committee on Economic, Social and Cultural Rights', paper presented at the conference The Human Dimension of Culture, University of Siena, 8 October 2010, on file with the author.

Pogge, T. (2006) 'Recognised and Violated by International Law: The Human Rights of the Global Poor', *Leiden Journal of International Law*, 18: 717–745.

Pogge, T. W. M. and Moellendorf, D. (2008) *Global Justice: Seminal Essays. Global Responsibilities. Vol. 1*, St. Paul, MN, Paragon House.

Poirier, Marc (2002) 'The Virtue of Vagueness in Takings Doctrine', *Cardozo Law Review*, 24: 93–191.

Poirier, Marc (2003) 'The NAFTA Chapter 11 Expropriation Debate Through the Eyes of a Property Theorist', *Environmental Law*, 33: 851–928.

Polanyi, K. (1944) *The Great Transformation: The Political and Economic Origins of Our Time*, Boston: Beacon Press, reprint, 2001.

Popielarz, P. A. and Neal, Z. P. (2007) 'The Niche as a Theoretical Tool', *Annual Review of Sociology*, 33: 65–84.

Posey, D. A., Frechione, J., Eddins, J., Da Silva, L. F., Myers, D., Case, D. and Macbeath, P. (1984) 'Ethnoecology as Applied Anthropology in Amazonian Development,' *Human Organization* 43: 95–107.

Posner, E. A. (2006) 'The International Protection of Cultural Property: Some Sceptical Observations', *University of Chicago, Public Law and Legal Theory Working Paper* 141, available from www.law.uchicago.edu/academics/publiclaw/141.pdf (accessed 12 October 2011).

Posner, R. A. (1995) 'The Sociology of the Sociology of Law: a View from Economics', *European Journal of Law and Economics*, 2(4): 265–284.

Pospisil, Leopold (1967) 'Legal Levels and Multiplicity of Legal Systems in Human Societies', *The Journal of Conflict Resolution*, 11: 2–26.

Pospisil, Leopold (1971) *Anthropology of Law: A Comparative Theory*, New York: Harper & Row.

Potter, P. (2003) 'Globalization and Economic Regulation in China: Selective Adaptation of Globalized Norms and Practices', *Washington University Global Studies Law Review*, 2(119): 126–127.

Poulsen, Lauge Skvorgaard (2010) 'Learning About BITs' [unpublished].

PwC (PriceWaterhouseCoopers) (2010) 'Committee of European Banking Supervisors Guidelines on Remuneration Policies and Practices: PWC Comment', 8 October. Available at www.ukmediacentre.pwc.com/content/Detail.aspx?ReleaseID=3890&NewsAreaID=2 (accessed 28 January 2012).

Qin, H. (2000). 'Ping Tengnisi "Gongtongti yu shehui" [Comments on Tonnies' "Community and Civil Society"]' *Shuwu* 2. Available at: www.gongfa.com/gongtongtiqh.htm (accessed 12 June 2012).

Quinn, J. and Hall, J. (2009) 'Goldman Sachs Vice-Chairman Says: "Learn to Tolerate Inequality"' *Telegraph*, 21 October. Available at www.telegraph.co.uk/finance/financetopics/recession/6392127/Goldman-Sachs-vice-chairman-says-Learn-to-tolerate-inequality.html (accessed 28 January 2012).

Rafael, R. (2011) 'Gaius, Vattel, and the New Global Law Paradigm', *European Journal of International Law*, 22: 627–647.

Rahaman, M. (2010) 'Agrobiotechnology, right to food and food sovereignty: emancipation and regulation in an age of risk', paper presented at the conference 'Socializing economic relationships – new perspectives and methods for analysing transnational risk regulation', 15–16 April 2010, Centre for Socio-Legal Studies, University of Oxford.

Rahn, Kim (2011) 'Judges Revolt Against FTA Gaining Momentum' *The Korea Times*. Available at http://english.hani.co.kr/arti/english_edition/e_national/507657.html (accessed 16 February 2012).

Rajagopal, B. (2003) *International law from below: development, social movements, and Third World resistance*, Cambridge: Cambridge University Press.

Rajak, D. (2011) 'Theatres of Virtue: Collaboration, Consensus, and the Social Life of Corporate Social Responsibility' *Focaal – Journal of Global and Historical Anthropology*, 60: 9.

Ramasastry, A., Slavova, S. and Vandenhoeck, L. (2002) 'EDRB Legal Indicator Survey: Assessing Insolvency Laws after Ten Years of Transition', *Law in Transition*, 34–43.

Randles, S. (2003) 'Issues for a Neo-Polanyian Research Agenda in Economic Sociology', *International Review of Sociology*, 13(2): 409–434.

Rasulov, A. (2006) 'International law and the Poststructuralist Challenge', *Leiden Journal of International Law*, 19: 799.

Ratner, Steven R. (2008) 'Regulatory Takings in Institutional Context: Beyond the Fear of Fragmented International Law', *The American Journal of International Law*, 102: 475–528.

Raustiala, Kal (2002) 'The Architecture of International Cooperation: Transgovernmental Networks and the Future of International Law', *Virginia Journal of International Law*, 43(1): 5–92.

Ravenhill, John (2008) 'In Search of the Missing Middle', *Review of International Political Economy*, 15: 18–29.

Rawls, J. and Kelly, E. (2001) *Justice as Fairness: A Restatement*, Cambridge, MA; London: Belknap.

Recital 1, Capital Requirements Directive (2010/76/EU, CRD-III).

Redgwell, C. (2008) 'The World Heritage Convention and Other Conventions Relating to the Protection of Natural Heritage', in F. Francioni (ed.), *1972 World Heritage Convention*, Oxford: Oxford University Press.

Reich, R. (2007) *Supercapitalism*, New York: Knopf.

Reinisch, A. (2001) 'Developing Human Rights and Humanitarian Law Accountability of the Security Council for the Imposition of Economic Sanctions', *American Journal of International Law*, 95: 851.

Richardson, M. (2007) 'Endogenous Protection and Trade Diversion', in C. Freund (ed.), *The WTO and Reciprocal Preferential Trade Agreements*, Cheltenham: Edward Elgar.

Rittich, Kerry (2006) 'The Future of Law and Development', in David M. Trubek and Alvaro Santos (eds), *The New Law and Economic Development: A Critical Appraisal*, Cambridge: Cambridge University Press.

Roberts, Anthea (2010) 'Power and Persuasion in Investment Treaty Interpretation: The Dual Role of States', *American Journal of International Law*, 104: 179.

Roberts, S. (2005) 'After Government? On Representing Law Without the State', *Modern Law Review*, 68(1): 1–24.

Robinson, William I. (2008) *Latin America and Global Capitalism: A Critical Globalization Perspective*, Baltimore: The Johns Hopkins University Press.

Root, Elihu (1910) 'The Basis of Protection to Citizen's Residing Abroad', *Proceedings of the American Society of International Law*, 7: 16–27.

Röpke, W. (1960) *A Humane Economy*, London: Wolff.

Rose, Carol (2000) 'Property and Expropriations: Themes and Variations in American Law', *Utah Law Review*, 1: 1–38.

Rosenau, James N. (2007) 'Governing the Ungovernable: The Challenge of a Global Disaggregation of Authority', *Regulation and Governance*, 1: 88–97.

Roubini, N. and Mihm, S. (2011) *Crisis Economics*, Harmondsworth: Penguin.

Rousseau, J.-J. (2006a) 'The Social Contract,' in *The Social Contract, a Discourse on the Origin of Inequality, and a Discourse on Political Economy*, trans. G. D. H. Cole, Stilwell, KS: Digireads.com.

Rousseau, J.-J. (2006b) 'A Discourse on the Origin of Inequality,' in *The Social Contract, a Discourse on the Origin of Inequality, and a Discourse on Political Economy*, trans. G. D. H. Cole, Stilwell, KS: Digireads.com.

Ruggie, J. (2004) 'Reconstituting the Global Public Domain: Issues, Actors and Practices', *European Journal of International Relations*, 10(4): 499.

Ruggie, J. (2006) *PPHR (Promotion and Protection of Human Rights)*, Interim Report of the Special Representative of the Secretary-General on the Issue of Human Rights and Transnational Corporations and Other Business Enterprises, U.N. ESCOR, Commission on Human Rights, 62d Sess, Provisional Agenda Item 17, UN Doc./CN.4/2006/97 (2006). Available at: http://www.ohchr.org/EN/Issues/TransnationalCorporations/Pages/Reports.aspx.

Ruggie, J. (2007a) *Business and Human Rights: Mapping International Standards of Responsibility and Accountability for Corporate Acts* Report of the Special Representative of the Secretary-General on the Issue of Human Rights and Transnational Corporations and Other Business Enterprises, John Ruggie, 44, UN Doc. A/HRC/4/35 (Feb. 19, 2007). Available at: http://www.business-humanrights.org/Documents/RuggieHRC2007.

Ruggie, J. (2007b) *Prepared Remarks at Clifford Chance*, London (19 February 2007) www.reportsand-materials.org/Ruggie-remarks-Clifford-Chance-19-Feb-2007.pdf (accessed 1 August 2012).

Ruggie, J. (2007c) 'Business and Human Rights: The Evolving International Agenda', *American Journal of International Law*, 101: 819.

Ruggie, J. (2008) *Protect, Respect and Remedy: A Framework for Business and Human Rights*, Report of the Special Representative of the Secretary-General, John Ruggie, UN GAOR, Human Rights Council, 8th Sess., Agenda Item 3, UN Doc. A/HRC/8/5 (2008). Available at: 198.170.85.29/Ruggie-protect-respect-remedy-framework.pdf.

Ruggie, J. (2010) *Business and Human Rights: Further Steps Toward the Operationalization Of The 'Protect, Respect And Remedy' Framework*, Report of the Special Representative of the Secretary-General on the issue of human rights and transnational corporations and other business enterprises, John Ruggie, Human Rights Council Fourteenth session Agenda item 3, UN Doc A/HRC/14/27 (2010). Available at: 198.170.85.29/Ruggie-report-2010.pdf

Ruggie, J. (2011a) *Guiding Principles on Business and Human Rights: Implementing the United Nations 'Protect, Respect and Remedy' Framework*, Report of the Special Representative of the Secretary-General on the issue of human rights and transnational corporations and other business enterprises, John Ruggie, UN Doc. A/HRC/17/31 (2011). Available at: http://www.ohchr.org/EN/Issues/TransnationalCorporations/Pages/Reports.aspx.

Ruggie, J. (2011b) 'The Construction of the UN "Protect, Respect and Remedy" Framework for Business and Human Rights: The True Confessions of a Principled Pragmatist' *EHRLR* 127.

Rugman, A. (2008) 'How Global are TNCs from Emerging Markets', in K. Sauvant (ed.), *The Rise of Transnational Corporations from Emerging Markets*, Cheltenham: Edward Elgar, 86.

Runciman, David (1997) *Pluralism and the Personality of the State*, Cambridge: Cambridge University Press.

Sacerdoti, G. (2005) 'The Role of Lawyers in the WTO Dispute Settlement System' in R. Yerxa and B. Wilson, *Key Issues in WTO Dispute Settlement: The First Ten Years*, Cambridge: Cambridge University Press, pp. 125–131.

Salomon, M. E., Tostensen, A. and Vandenhole, W. (2007) *Casting the Net Wider: Human Rights, Development and New Duty-bearers*, Antwerp; Oxford, Intersentia.

Sands, P. (2007) 'Litigating Environmental Disputes: Courts, Tribunals and the

Progressive Development of International Environmental Law', in T. Ndiaye and R. Wolfrum (eds), *Law of the Sea, Environmental Law and Settlement of Disputes: Liber Amicorum Judge Thomas Mensah*, Leiden: Brill.

Santos, B. de S. (2009) 'If God Were A Human Rights Activist: Human Rights and the Challenge of Political Theologies', *Law, Social Justice and Global Development*, 1: 1–42.

Santos, Boaventura de Sousa (2002) *Toward A New Legal Common Sense: Law, Globalization and Emancipation*, 2nd edition, London: Butterworths LexisNexis.

Sassen, Saskia (2002) *Territory, Authority, Rights: From Medieval to Global Assemblages*, Princeton: Princeton University Press.

Sax, Joseph L. (1964) 'Takings and the Police Power,' *Yale Law Journal*, 74: 36–76.

Scalet, S. and Kelly, T. (2010) 'CSR Rating Agencies: What is their Global Impact?', *Journal of Business Ethics*, 94(1): 69.

Scherer, A. and Palazzo, G. (2011) 'The New Political Role of Business in a Globalized World: A Review of a New Perspective on CSR and its Implications for the Firm, Governance, and Democracy', *Journal of Management Studies*, 48(4): 899.

Schneiderman, David (2006) 'Transnational Legality and the Immobilization of Local Agency', *Annual Review of Law and Social Science*, 2: 387–408.

Schneiderman, David (2008) *Constitutionalizing Economic Globalization: Investment Rules and Democracy's Promise*, Cambridge: Cambridge University Press.

Schneiderman, David (2009) 'Promoting Equality, Black Economic Empowerment, and the Future of Investment Rules', *South African Journal on Human Rights*, 25: 246–279.

Schneiderman, David (2010) 'Investing in Democracy? Political Process and International Investment Law', *University of Toronto Law Journal*, 60: 909–940.

Schneiderman, David (2011) 'Revisiting the Depoliticization of Investment Disputes', *Yearbook on International Investment Law and Policy, 2010–11*, Oxford: Oxford University Press, pp. 693–714.

Schroeder, J.-L. (2008) *The Four Lacanian Discourses: or Turning Law Inside-Out*, Abingdon and New York: Birkbeck Law Press and Routledge-Cavendish.

Schwartz, A. and R. E. Scott (1995) 'The Political Economy of Private Legislatures', *University of Pennsylvania Law Review*, 143: 595–653.

Schwarz, S. L. (1995) 'A Fundamental Inquiry into the Statutory Rulemaking Process of Private Legislatures', *Georgia Law Review*, 29: 909–989.

Scott Rau, A. (1999) 'Mediation in Art-Related Disputes', in Q. Byrne-Sutton and F. Geisinger-Mariéthoz (eds), *Resolution Methods for Art Related Disputes*, Zürich: Schultess Verlag.

Scott, R. E. (1994) 'The Politics of Article 9'. *Virginia Law Review*, 80: 1783–1851.

SEC (Securities and Exchange Commission) (2010a) 'SEC Charges Goldman Sachs With Fraud in Structuring and Marketing of CDO Tied to Subprime Mortgages', SEC #2010–59, Washington DC, 16 April. Available at www.sec.gov/news/press/2010/2010–59.htm (accessed 28 January 2012).

SEC (2010b) *Goldman Sachs to Pay Record $550 Million to Settle SEC Charges Related to Subprime Mortgage CDO* (15.7.2010) SEC #2010–123, Washington, DC. Available on www.sec.gov/news/press/2010/2010–123.htm (accessed 28 January 2012).

Sell, Susan K. (2003) *Private Power, Public Law: The Globalization of Intellectual Property Rights*, Cambridge: Cambridge University Press.

Selznick, P. (2002) *The Communitarian Persuasion*, Woodrow Wilson Center Press.

Shaffer, G. (2004) 'Parliamentary Oversight of WTO Rule-Making: The Political, Normative, and Practical Contexts', *Journal of International Economic Law*, 7: 629–654.

Shaffer, G. (2011) 'Transnational Recursivity Theory: A Review Essay of Halliday and Carruthers' Bankrupt', *Socio-Economic Review* 9: 371–394.

Shaffer, G. (forthcoming) 'Transnational Legal Process and State Change: Opportunities and Constraints', *Law & Social Inquiry*.

Shaffer, G. C. (2008) 'A new legal realism: method in international economic law' in C. Picker, I. Bunn and D. W. Arner (eds), *International Economic Law: the state and future of the discipline*, Oxford: Hart.

Shaffer, Gregory C. (2003) *Defending Interests: Public-Private Partnerships in WTO Litigation*, Washington, DC: Brookings Institution Press.

Shankar, S. (2010) 'Necessity and Desire: Water and Coca-Cola in India' in P. Bose and L. Lyons (eds), *Cultural Critique and the Global Corporation*, Bloomington, IN: Indiana University Press, 151.

Shavell, S. (2004) *Foundations of Economic Analysis of Law*, Cambridge, MA: Harvard University Press.

Sheffer, M. (2011) 'Bilateral Investment Treaties: A Friend or Foe to Human Rights', *Denver Journal of International Law and Policy*, 39(3): 483.

Shelton, D. (2006) Normative hierarchy in international law, *American Journal of International Law*, 100.

Shemberg, A. (2008) *Stabilization Clauses and Human Rights*, IFC/SRSG Research Paper. Online. Available at: www.ifc.org/ifcext/enviro.nsf/AttachmentsByTitle/p_StabilizationClausesandHumanRights/$FILE/Stabilization+Paper.pdf (accessed 6 February 2012).

Shepard, B. H. and Hayduk, R. (2002) *From ACT UP to the WTO: Urban Protest and Community Building in the Era of Globalization*, London: Verso.

Shihata, I. F. I. (1986) 'Towards a Greater Depoliticization of Investment Disputes: The Role of ICSID and MIGA', *ICSID Review Foreign Investment Law Journal*, 1(1): 1–25.

Shiller, R. J. (2000) *Irrational Exuberance*, Princeton, NJ: Princeton University Press.

Silbey, S. (2010) Keynote Address, Socio-Legal Studies Association Conference 'Exploring the "Socio" of socio-legal studies', Institute of Advanced Legal Studies, London, 3 November.

Siltala, R. (2011) *Law, Truth, and Reason: A Treatise on Legal Argumentation*, New York: Springer.

Silverstein, K. (2012) 'A Giant Among Giants', *Foreign Policy*, www.foreignpolicy.com/articles/2012/04/23/a_giant_among_giants (accessed 14 May 2012).

Simon, J. (1999) 'Law after society', *Law and Social Inquiry*, 24(1): 143–194.

Simons, P. (2012) 'International Law's Invisible Hand and the Future of Corporate Accountability for Violations of Human Rights', *Journal of Human Rights and the Environment*, 3.

Sinden, A. (2007) 'Power and Responsibility: Why Human Rights Should Address Corporate Environmental Wrongs' in D. McBarnet, A. Voiculescu and T. Campbell (eds), *The New Corporate Accountability*, Cambridge: Cambridge University Press, 501.

Siu, H. F. (1989) *Agents and Victims in South China: Accomplices in Rural Revolution*, London: Yale University Press.

Sklair, Leslie (2002) *Globalization: Capitalism and its Alternatives*, 3rd edn., Oxford: Oxford University Press.

Skogly, S. I. and Gibney, M. (2010) *Universal Human Rights and Extraterritorial Obligations*, Pennsylvania: University of Pennsylvania Publications.

Skordas, A. (2009) 'Is There Justice in International Law?', in G. P. Calliess, A. Fischer-Lescano, D. Wielsch and P. Zumbansen (eds), *Soziologische Jurisprudenz*, Berlin: De Gryter Recht.

Slater, S. and Miedema, D. (2011) HSBC Says May Leave UK, Hit by US Bad Debts', Reuters, 9 November. Available at www.reuters.com/article/2011/11/09/us-hsbc-idUSTRE7A829120111109 (accessed 28 January 2012).

Slaughter, A. M., Tulumello, A. S. and Wood, S. (1998) 'International law and international relations theory: a new generation of interdisciplinary scholarship', *The American Journal of International Law*, 92(3): 367–397.

Slaughter, Anne-Marie and Zaring, David (2006) 'Networking Goes International: An Update', *Annual Review of Law and Social Science*, 2: 211–229.

Smith, N. Craig (1994) 'The New Corporate Philanthropy', *Harvard Business Review*, 105.

Snape, R. (2007) 'History and Economics of GATT's Article XXIV', in C. Freund (ed.), *The WTO and Reciprocal Preferential Trade Agreements*, Cheltenham: Edward Elgar.

Snyder, F. (1999a) 'Governing Economic Globalization: Global Legal Pluralism and European Law', *European Law Journal*, 5: 334–374.

Snyder, F. (1999b) *Global Economic Networks and Global Legal Pluralism*, Florence: European University Institute.

Snyder, F. (2010) *The EU, the WTO and China: Legal Pluralism and International Trade Regulation*, Oxford: Hart Publishing.

Söderbaum, F. (2004) *The Political Economy of Regionalism: The Case of Southern Africa*, Palgrave.

Söderbaum, F. (2005) 'Exploring the Links Between Micro-Regionalism and Macro-Regionalism', in M. Farrell, B. Hettne and L. van Langenhove (eds), *Global Politics of Regionalism: Theory and Practice*, Pluto Press.

Sosa, I. and Keenan, K. (2001) 'Impact Benefit Agreements Between Aboriginal Communities and Mining Companies: Their Use In Canada.' Online. Available at: http://s.cela.ca/files/uploads/IBAeng.pdf (accessed 6 February 2012).

Soto, H. D. (2000) *The Mystery of Capital: Why Capitalism Triumphs in the West and Fails Everywhere Else*, London: Bantam.

South Africa, Department of Trade and Industry. (2009) 'Bilateral Investment Treaty Policy Framework Review: Government Position Paper' (June). Available at http://d2zmx6mlqh7g3a.cloudfront.net/cdn/farfuture/mtime:1248087345/files/docs/090626trade-bi-lateralpolicy.pdf (accessed 14 August 2012).

Springer, G. (1985) 'Textual geography: The Role of the Reader in *Invisible Cities*', *Modern Language Studies*, 15(4): 289.

Stanaland, A., Lwin, M. and Murphy, P. (2011) 'Consumer Perceptions of the Antecedents and Consequences of Corporate Social Responsibility', *Journal of Business Ethics*, 102(1): 47.

Stearman, A. M. (1994) 'Revisiting the Myth of the Ecologically Noble Savage in Amazonia: Implications for Indigenous Land Rights', *Culture and Agriculture*, 14: 2–6.

Steger, D. P. (2002a) 'Afterword: The "Trade and...." Conundrum – A Commentary', *The American Journal of International Law*, 96, 136–145.

Steger, D. P. (2002b) 'Book review', *Journal of International Economic Law*, 5: 565–570.

Steger, Manfred B. (2008) *The Rise of the Global Imaginary: Political Ideologies form the French Revolution to the Global War on Terror*, Oxford: Oxford University Press.

Stein, H. (2008) 'Balance of Payments', *The Concise Encyclopedia of Economics*, available at http://www.econlib.org/library/Enc/BalanceofPayments.html

Steinberg, R. H. (1997) 'Trade-Environment Negotiations in the EU, NAFTA, and WTO: Regional Trajectories of Rule Development', *American Journal of International Law*, 91: 231–267.

Stephan, Paul B. (2011) 'Privatising International Law', University of Virginia School of Law John M Olin Law and Economics Research Paper Series No 2011–02, March.

Stern, B. (2008) 'In Search of the Frontiers of Indirect Expropriation', in A. Rovine (ed.), *Contemporary Issues in International Arbitration and Mediation*, Leiden/Boston: Martinus Nijhoff.

Stevens, C. (2006) 'The EU, Africa and EPAs: Unintended Consequences of Policy Leverage', *Journal of Modern African Studies*, 44(3): 441–458.

Stiglitz, J. (2000) 'Formal and Informal Institutions,' in P. Dasgupta and I. Serageldin (eds), *Social Capital: A Multifaceted Perspective*, Washington, DC: World Bank.

Stiglitz, J. (2002) *Globalisation and its Discontents*, London: Penguin Group.

Stiglitz, J. (2010) *Freefall*, Harmondsworth: Penguin.

Stinchcombe, A. S. (2001) *When Formality Works: Authority and Abstraction in Law and Organizations*. Chicago: University of Chicago Press.

Stopford, John and Susan Strange with John S. Henley (1991) *Rival States, Rival Firms: Competition for World Market Shares*, Cambridge: Cambridge University Press.

Strahilevitz, L. (2000) 'How Changes in Property Regimes Influence Social Norms: Commodifying California's Carpool Lanes,' *Indiana Law Journal*, 75: 1231–1296.

Strange, Susan (1988) *States and Markets*, 2nd edn., London: Pinter Publishers.

Strange, Susan (1990) 'The Name of the Game' in Nicholas X. Rizopoulos (ed.), *Sea Changes: American Foreign Policy in a World Transformed*, New York: Council on Foreign Relations, pp. 238–273.

Strange, Susan (1995) 'Political Economy and International Relations' in Ken Booth and Steve Smith (eds), *International Relations Theory Today*, University Park: University of Pennsylvania Press, pp. 154–174.

Strange, Susan (1999) 'The Westfailure System', *Review of International Studies*, 25: 345–354.

Streeck, W. (2009) *Re-forming Capitalism: Institutional Change in the German Political Economy*, Oxford: Oxford University Press.

Streeck, Wolfgang (2011) 'The Crises of Democratic Capitalism', *The New Left Review*, 71: 5–29.

Suchman, M. (1995) 'Managing Legitimacy: Strategic and Institutional Approaches', *The Academy of Management Approaches*, 20(3): 571.

Sunstein, Cass (1993) *The Partial Constitution*, Cambridge: Harvard University Press.

Suzahn, E. (2011) 'An Occupier's Note', *Tidal: Occupy Theory, Occupy Strategy*, 1.

Swedberg, R. (2003) 'The Case for an Economic Sociology of Law', *Theory and Society*, 32(1): 1–37.

Swedberg, R. (2006) 'Max Weber's Contribution to the Economic Sociology of Law', *Annual Review of Law and Social Science*, 2: 61–81.

Sweet, Alec Stone (2006) 'The New *Lex Mercatoria* and Transnational Governance', *Journal of European Public Policy*, 13: 627–646.

Sykes, A. O. (1998) 'Comparative advantage and the normative economics of international trade policy', *Journal of International Economic Law*, 1(1): 49–82.

Takahashi, T. and Nakamura, M. (2010) 'The Impact of Operational Characteristics on Firms' EMS Decisions: Strategic Adoption of ISO 14001 Certifications', *Corporate Social Responsibility and Environmental Management*, 17: 213.

Tamanaha, B. Z. (2001) *A General Jurisprudence of Law and Society*, New York: Oxford University Press.

Tamanaha, B. Z. (2008) 'Understanding Legal Pluralism: Past to Present, Local to Global', *Sydney Law Review*, 30(3): 375–411.

Tamanaha, Brian Z. (2000) 'A Non-Essentialist Version of Legal Pluralism', *Journal of Law and Society*, 27: 296.

Tan, Celine (2011) *Governance through Development: Poverty Reduction Strategies, International Law and the Disciplining of Third World States*, London: Routledge-Cavendish.

Tarullo, Daniel K. (1985) 'Logic, Myth and the International Economic Order', *Harvard International Law Journal*, 26(2): 533–552.

Terborgh, J. (1999) *Requiem for Nature*, Washington, DC: Island Press.

Teubner, G. (1983) 'Substantive and Reflexive Elements in Modern Law', *Law & Society Review*, 17(2), 239–285.

Teubner, Gunther (1984) 'Autopoiesis in Law and Society: A Rejoinder to Blakenburg', *Law & Society Review*, 18(2), 291–301.

Teubner, Gunther (1986) 'After Legal Instrumentalism? Strategic Models of Postregulatory Law', in G. Teubner (ed.), *Dilemmas of Law in the Welfare State*, Series A-3; Berlin and New York: Walter de Gruyter, 299–325.

Teubner, Gunther (1987a) *Autopoietic Law: A New Approach to Law and Society*, Berlin: Walter de Gruyter.

Teubner, Gunther (1987b) 'Juridification: Concepts, Aspects, Limits, Solutions', in Gunther Teubner (ed.), *Juridification of Social Spheres: A Comparative Analysis in the Areas of Labour, Corporate, Antitrust and Social Welfare Law*, European University Institute, Florence; Berlin, New York: Walter de Gruyter, 3–48.

Teubner, Gunther. (1989) 'How the Law Thinks: Toward A Constructivist Epistemology of Law', *Law & Society Review*, 23(5): 727–757.

Teubner, Gunther (1992) 'The Two Faces of Janus: Rethinking Legal Pluralism', *Cardozo Law Review*, 13: 1443–1462.

Teubner, Gunther (1993) *Law as an Autopoietic System*, trans. R. Adler, A. Bankowska and Z. Bankoski, Oxford: Blackwell.

Teubner, Gunther (1997) '*Altera Pars Audiatur*: Law in the Collision of Discourses' in R. Rawlings (ed.), *Law, Society and Economy*, Oxford: OUP, pp. 149–176.

Teubner, Gunther (1997b) '"Global Bukowina": Legal Pluralism in a World Society' in Gunther Teubner (ed.), *Global Law Without a State*, Aldershot: Dartmouth.

Teubner, Gunther (1997c) 'Breaking Frames: The Global Interplay of Legal and Social Systems', *American Journal of Comparative Law*, 45, 149–169.

Teubner, Gunther (1997d) *Global Law without a State*, Dartmouth: Aldershot.

Teubner, Gunther (2001) 'Alienating Justice: On the Surplus Value of the Twelfth Camel', in J. Priban and D. Nelken (ed.), *Consequences of Legal Autopoiesis* (Aldershot: Ashgate), 21–24. Available at www.ssrn.com/abstract=876958 (accessed 25 July 2012).

Teubner, Gunther (2002) 'Idiosyncratic Production Regimes: Co-evolution of Economic and Legal Institutions in the Varieties of Capitalism', in M. Wheeler, J. Ziman and M. A. Boden (eds), *The Evolution of Cultural Entities* (Proceedings of the British Academy; Oxford, New York: Oxford University Press), 161–181.

Teubner, Gunther (2004a) 'Societal Constitutionalism: Alternatives to State-Centred Constitutional Theory?', in Christian Joerges, Inger Johanne Sand and Gunther Teubner (eds), *Transnational Governance and Constitutionalism*, Oxford: Hart Publishing.

Teubner, Gunther (2004b) 'Global Private Regimes: Neo-spontaneous Law and Dual Constitution of Autonomous Sectors in World Society?', in Karl-Heinz Ladeur (ed.), *Public Governance in the Age of Globalization*, Aldershot: Ashgate.

Teubner, Gunther (2006) 'The Autonomous Matrix: Human Rights Violations by "Private" Transnational Actors', *Modern Law Review*, 69(3), 327–346.

Teubner, Gunther (2007) 'The Private/Public Dichotomy: After the Critique?', Re-public: Re-imagining Democracy. Available at www.re-public.gr/en/?p=99 (accessed 25 July 2012).

Teubner, Gunther (2008) 'Justice under Global Capitalism?', *Law Critique*, 19, 329–334.

Teubner, Gunther (2009) 'Self-Subversive Justice: Contingency or Trascendence Formula of Justice?', *Modern Law Review*, 72(1), 1–23.

Teubner, Gunther (2010) 'Constitutionalising Polycontexturality', *Social & Legal Studies*, 19. Available at http://www.jura.uni-frankfurt.de/1_Personal/em_profs/teubner/dokumente/ConstitutionalisingPolicontexturality_eng.pdf.

Teubner, Gunther (2011a) 'A Constitutional Moment? The Logics of 'Hit the Bottom' (April 19, 2010)', in P. and Teubner Kjaer, G (ed.), *The Financial Crisis in Constitutional Perspective: The Dark Side of Functional Differentiation*, Oxford: Hart. Available at: http://www.jura.uni-frankfurt.de/1_Personal/em_profs/teubner/dokumente/constitutionalmoments_eng.pdf.

Teubner, Gunther (2011b) 'The Idea of the Commons: Liberation and Emergence of a Different World', *International University College, UniNomade 2.0, Antonio Negri and Gunther Teubner Workshop* (www.youtube.com/watch?v=k4a9Iqi7cZM).

Teubner, Gunther (2011c) 'Constitutionalizing Polycontextuality', *Social and Legal Studies*, 20: 210–229.

The Economist (2010) The Bonus Myth: Why Bankers May Believe Less in Their Colleagues' Integrity Than in Their Own – and How That's a Problem', *The Economist*, 23 March.

Theurich, S. (2009) 'Art and Cultural Heritage Dispute Resolution', *WIPO Magazine* 4. Available at: www.wipo.int/wipo_magazine/en/2009/04/article_0007.html (accessed 21 September 2011).

Thomas, B. (1991) *Cross-Examinations of Law and Literature: Cooper, Hawthorne, Stowe, and Melville*, Cambridge: Cambridge University Press.

Thomas, P. (ed.) (1997) *Socio-Legal Studies*, Aldershot: Ashgate.

Tietje, C. and Nowrot, K. (2006) 'Laying Conceptual Ghosts of the Past to Rest', in

Tietje, Brouder and Nowrot (eds) *Philip C. Jessup's* Transnational Law *Revisited. Beiträge zum Transnationalen Wirtschaftsrecht no. 50*, Halle-Wittenberg: Martin-Luther-Universität, 17–31. Available at www.wirtschaftsrecht.uni-halle.de/sites/default/files/altbestand/Heft50.pdf (accessed 9 October 2011).

Tietje, C., Brouder, A. and Nowrot, K. (eds) (2006) *Philip C. Jessup's* Transnational Law *Revisited. Beiträge zum Transnationalen Wirtschaftsrecht no. 50*, Halle-Wittenberg: Martin-Luther-Universität. Available at www.wirtschaftsrecht.uni-halle.de/sites/default/files/altbestand/Heft50.pdf (accessed 9 October 2011).

Tilly, C. (1995) 'Globalization Threatens Labor's Rights', *International Labor and Working Class History*, 47, 1–23.

Tokatli, N., Wrigley, N. and Kizilgün, Ö. (2008) 'Shifting Global Supply Networks and Fast Fashion: Made in Turkey for Marks and Spencer', *Global Networks*, 8: 261.

Tönnies, F. (2001) *Community and Civil Society*, J. Harris and M. Hollis (trans.), New York: Cambridge University Press.

Trachtman, J. (1999) 'The Domain of WTO Dispute Resolution', *Harvard International Law Journal*, 40: 333–377.

Trachtman, J. (2002) 'Institutional Linkage: Transcending "Trade and…"', *American Journal of International Law*, 96: 77–93.

Trachtman, J. (2004) 'The Jurisdiction of the WTO', *American Society of International Law Proceedings*, 98: 135–142.

Trachtman, J. (2008) 'International Economic Law Research', in C. Picker, I. Bunn and D. W. Arner (eds), *International Economic Law: The State and Future of the Discipline*, Oxford: Hart, pp. 43–52.

Travers, M. (2001) 'Sociology of law in Britain', *The American Sociologist*, 32(2): 26–40.

Treanor, J. (2010) 'Bankers' Threat to Quit City "Blackmail", says Michel Barnier', *Guardian*, 13 December. Available at www.guardian.co.uk/business/2010/dec/13/banking-bonuses-fsa-regulations (accessed 28 January 2012).

Treanor, J. (2011) 'Goldman Sachs Bankers to Receive $15.3bn in Pay and Bonuses', *Guardian* 19 January. Available on www.guardian.co.uk/business/2011/jan/19/goldman-sachs-bankers-pay-bonuses (accessed 28 January 2012).

Tully, James (2002) 'Public Philosophy as a Critical Activity' in James Tully (ed.), *Public Philosophy in a New Key*, Cambridge: Cambridge University Press, pp. 15–38.

Twining, W. (1973) *Karl Llewllyn and the Realist Movement*, reprinted with postscript 1985, London: George Weidenfeld and Nicolson.

Twining, William (2000) *Globalisation and Legal Theory*, London: Butterworths.

Twining, William (2009) *General Jurisprudence: Understanding Law from a Global Perspective*, Cambridge: Cambridge University Press.

UN (2007) *World Investment Report 2007*, U.N. Doc. UNCTAD/WIR/2007.

UN Office of the High Commissioner for Human Rights. 2002. Draft guidelines: a human rights approach to poverty reduction strategies, 10 September 2002, available at: http://www.unhcr.org/refworld/docid/3f8298544.html (accessed 8 August 2012).

UNCITRAL (1999) *UNCITRAL Model Law on Cross-Border Insolvency with Guide to Enactment*. New York: United Nations.

UNCITRAL (2004) *UNCITRAL Legislative Guide on Insolvency*. New York: United Nations.

UNCTAD (United Nations Commission on Trade and Development) (2011) *World Investment Report 2011: Non-Equity Modes of International Production and Development*, New York and Geneva: United Nations.

UNCTD (2007) *The Universe of the Largest Transnational Corporations* UN New York. Available at: unctad.org/en/docs/iteiia20072_en.pdf.

United States (1998) Import Prohibition of Certain Shrimp and Shrimp Products WT/DS58/AB/R, 12 October, paragraphs 156–157, 159, World Trade Organization, Report of the Appellate Body.

Vadi, V. (2008) 'Cultural Heritage and International Investment Law: A Stormy Relationship', *International Journal of Cultural Property*, 15: 1–23.

Vadi, V. (2009a) 'Fragmentation or Cohesion? Investment v. Cultural Protection Rules', *Journal of World Investment and Trade*, 10(4): 573–600.

Vadi, V. (2009b) 'Investing In Culture: Underwater Cultural Heritage and International Investment Law', *Vanderbilt Journal of Transnational Law*, 42: 853–904.

Vadi, V. (2011a) 'When Cultures Collide: Foreign Direct Investment, Natural Resources and Indigenous Heritage in International Investment Law', *Columbia Human Rights Law Review*, 42(3): 797–889.

Vadi, V. (2011b) *Cultural Diversity Disputes and the Judicial Function in International Economic Law*, Onati Institute for the Sociology of Law Working Papers vol. 1 No. 4 (2011) 1–24. Available at: http://opo.iisj.net/index.php/osls/issue/archive.

Vadi, V. (2012 forthcoming) 'The Protection of Cultural Landscapes and Indigenous Heritage in International Investment Law', in L. Westra, C. Soskolne and D. Spady (eds), *Human Health and Ecological Integrity: Ethics, Law and Human Rights*, London: Earthscan.

Vagts, D. (2006) 'International Economic Law and the *American Journal of International Law*', *American Journal of International Law*, 100(4): 769.

Van der Ploeg, J. D. (1993) 'Potatoes and Knowledge,' in M. Hobart (ed.), *An Anthropological Critique of Development: The Growth of Ignorance*, London: Routledge.

Van Harten, G. and Loughlin, M. (2006) 'Investment Treaty Arbitration as a Species of Global Administrative Law', *European Journal of International Law*, 17: 121–150.

Van Harten, Gus (2007) *Investment Treaty Arbitration and Public Law*, Oxford: Oxford University Press.

van Reisen, M. (2007) 'The Enlarged European Union and the Developing World: What Future?' in A. Mold (ed.), *EU Development Policy in a Changing World: Challenges for the 21st Century*, Amsterdam: Amsterdam University Press.

Vandenburgh, M. (2007) 'The New Wal-Mart Effect: The Role of Private Contracting in Global Governance', *University of California Law Review*, 54: 3.

Vandevelde, K. J. (1998) 'The Political Economy of a Bilateral Investment Treaty', *American Journal of International Law*, 92: 621.

Viner, J. (1950) *The Customs Union Issue*, Carnegie Endowment for International Peace.

Vogel, D. (2008) 'Private Global Business Regulation' 11 *Ann Rev Pol Sci* 261.

Voiculescu, A. (2006) 'Privatising Human Rights? The Role of Corporate Codes of Conduct', in L. Williams (ed.), *International Poverty Law: An Emerging Discourse*, London: Zed Books Ltd, pp. 176–209.

Voiculescu, A. (2011) 'Human Rights and the Normative Ordering of Global

Capitalism' in A. Voiculescu and H. Yanacopulos (eds), *The Business of Human Rights* London: Zed, 10.

Voiculescu, A. (2012) '"Etiquette and Magic": Between Embedded and Embedding Corporate Social Responsibility', in A. Sarat and B. Lange (eds), *Studies in Law, Politics, and Society* (forthcoming 2012).

Von Schorlemer, Sabine (2007) 'UNESCO Dispute Settlement', in A. A. Yusuf (ed.), Standard-Setting in UNESCO: Normative Action in Education, Science and Culture Essays in Commemoration of the Sixtieth Anniversary of UNESCO, Leiden/Boston: Martinus Nijhoff, 73–103.

Waal, A. D. (2001) The Moral Solipsism of Global Ethics Inc. *London Review of Books*.

Wai, R. (2003) 'Countering, Branding, Dealing: Using Economic and Social Rights in and Around the International Trade Regime', *European Journal of International Law*, 14: 59.

Wai, Robert (2005) 'Transnational Private Law and Private Ordering in a Contested Global Society', *Harvard International Law Journal*, 46(2): 471–486.

Wai, Robert (2008) 'The Interlegality of Transnational Private Law', *Law and Contemporary Problems*, 71: 107–127.

Waitt, G. (1999) 'Naturalizing the "Primitive": A Critique of Marketing Australia's Indigenous Peoples as "Hunter-Gatherers",' *Tourism Geographies*, 1: 142–163.

Walker, Neil (2002) 'The Idea of Constitutional Pluralism', *Modern Law Review*, 65: 317–359.

Walker, Neil (2008) 'Taking Constitutionalism Beyond the State', *Political Studies*, 56: 519–543.

Warleigh-Lack, A. (2006) 'Towards a Conceptual Framework for Regionalisation: Bridging "New Regionalism" and "Integration Theory"', *Review of International Political Economy*, 13(5): 750–771.

Waterman, P. and Timms, J. (2004–5) 'Trade Union Internationalism and a Global Civil Society in the Making', in H. Anheier, M. Glasius, and M. Kaldor, (eds), *Global Civil Society*, London: Sage.

Watson, A. (1974) *Legal Transplants: An Approach to Comparative Law*, Edinburgh: Scottish Academic Press.

Watson, A. (1977) *Social and Legal Change*, Edinburgh: Scottish Academic Press.

Watson, A. (1983) 'Legal Changes: Sources of Law and Legal Culture', *University of Pennsylvania Law Review*, 131(5): 1121–1157.

Watson, A. (1985) *The Evolution of Law*, Oxford: Blackwell.

Watson, A. (2000) *Law out of Context*, Athens, Georgia: University of Georgia Press.

Watson, J. (1977) 'Hereditary Tenancy and Corporate Landlordism in Traditional China: A Case Study', *Modern Asian Studies*, 11(2): 161–182.

Watson, R. S. (1990) 'Corporate Property and Local Leadership in Pearl River Delta, 1898–1941', in J. W. Esherick and M. B. Rankin (eds), *Chinese Local Elites and Patterns of Dominance*, Berkeley: Oxford University of California Press, 239–260.

Weber, M. (1978) *Economy and Society: An Outline of Interpretive Sociology*, E. Fischoff (trans.), Berkeley: University of California Press.

Weber, M., Roth, G. and Wittich, C. (1978) *Economy and Society: An Outline of Interpretive Sociology*, Berkeley: University of California Press.

Weiler, J. (2001) 'The Rule of Lawyers and the Ethos of Diplomats: Reflections on the Internal and External Legitimacy of the WTO Dispute Settlement', *Journal of World Trade*, 35(2): 191.

Weiler, J. H. H. (1999) *The Constitution of Europe: 'Do the New Clothes Have an Emperor' and Other Essays on European Integration*, Cambridge: Cambridge University Press.

Weissbrodt, D. (2006) 'UN Perspectives on Business and Humanitarian and Human Rights Obligations', *American Society of International Law*, 100: 135.

Weissbrodt, D. (2008) 'Keynote Address: International Standard-Setting on the Human. Rights Responsibilities of Businesses', *Berkeley Journal of International Law*, 26: 373–391.

Westlake, J. (1894) *Chapters on the Principles of International Law*, Cambridge: Cambridge University Press.

Wheaton, H. (1836) *Elements of International Law*, Lea and Blanchard Publications, 3rd ed. Windmuller, J. P., Pursey, S. K. and Baker, J. 2010. The international trade union movement. In R. Blanpain, (ed.), *Comparative Labour Law and Industrial Relations in Industrialised Market Economies*. 10th ed., New York: Kluwer International Law.

Wheeler, S. (2002) *Corporations and the Third Way*, Oxford: Hart Publishing.

White, J. Boyd (1985) *Heracles' Bow: Essays on the Rhetoric and Poetics of the Law*, Madison: University of Wisconsin Press.

Williamson, O. (2000) 'The New Institutional Economics: Taking Stock, Looking Ahead', *Journal of Economic Literature*, 38(3): 595–613.

WIR (World Investment Report) (2011) *Non-Equity Modes of International Production and Development*. Available at: www.unctad-docs.org/UNCTAD-WIR2011-Chapter-IV-en.pdf.

Wold, C. (1996) 'Multilateral Environmental Agreements and the GATT: Conflict and Resolution?', *Environmental Law*, 26(3): 843.

Wood, S. (2012) 'The Case for Leverage-Based Human Rights Responsibility', *Business Ethics Quarterly*, 22(1): 63.

World Bank (2000) *Trade Blocs: A World Bank Policy Research Report*, Oxford: Oxford University Press.

World Bank (2005) *Principles for Effective Insolvency and Creditor Rights Systems*. Washington, DC: World Bank.

World Bank/UNCITRAL (2005) 'Creditors' Rights and Insolvency Standard', Washington, DC: World Bank.

World Trade Organization (2009) *WTO Annual Report 2009*, WTO.

World Trade Organization (2010) 'Understanding on Rules and Procedures Governing the Settlement of Disputes', in World Trade Organization (ed.), The Legal Texts The Results of the Uruguay Round of Multilateral Trade Negotiations, Cambridge: Cambridge University Press.

Wright, C. and Madrid, G. (2007) 'Contesting Ethical Trade in Colombia's Cut-Flower Industry: A Case of Cultural and Economic Injustice', *Cultural Sociology*, 1: 255.

Xanthaki, A. (2003) 'Land Rights of Indigenous Peoples in South-East Asia,' *Melbourne Journal of International Law*, 4: 467–496.

Xu, T. (2010) 'The End of the Urban-Rural Divide? Emerging Quasi-Commons in Rural China', *Archiv für Rechts und Sozialphilosophie (the Archives for Philosophy of Law and Social Philosophy)*, 96(4) (October): 557–573.

Yang, G. Z. (1988) *Mingqing Tudi Qiyue Wenshu Yanjiu [The Research of Land Titles and Contracts in the Ming and Qing]*, Beijing: Renmin Chubanshe.

Yaziji, M. and Doh, J. (2009) *NGOs and Corporations*, Cambridge: Cambridge University Press.

Yearwood, R. (2011) *The Interaction between World Trade Organization (WTO) Law and External International Law: The Constrained Openness of WTO Law (a prologue to theory)*, London, New York: Routledge.

Yearwood, R. (2012) *The Interaction between World Trade Organisation (WTO) Law and External International Law*, Abingdon: Routledge.

Yeh, A. G. (2005) 'The Dual Land Market and Urban Development in China', in Ding Chengri and Song Yan (eds), *Emerging Land and Housing Markets in China*, Cambridge, Mass.: Lincoln Institute of Land Policy, 39–58.

Yunus, M. and Weber, K. (2007) *Creating a World Without Poverty: Social Business and the Future of Capitalism*, New York, PublicAffairs; London: Perseus Running [distributor].

Zelin, M. (1986) 'The Rights of Tenants in Mid-Qing Sichuan: A Study of Land-Related Lawsuits in the Baxian Archives', *Journal of Asian Studies*, 45(3): 499–526.

Zenisek, T. J. (1979) 'Corporate Social Responsibility: A Conceptualisation Based on Organisational Literature', *Academy of Management Review*, 4: 359–368.

Zumbansen, P. (2006) 'The Conundrum of Corporate Social Responsibility: Reflections on the Changing Nature of Firms and States', *CLPE Research Paper No. 01–3*. Available at: http://papers.ssrn.com/sol3/papers.cfm?abstract_id=885373 (accessed 3 July 2011).

Zumbansen, P. (2011) 'Neither "Public" Nor "Private", "National" Nor "International": Transnational Corporate Governance From a Legal Pluralist Perspective', *Journal of Law and Society*, 38: 50–75.

Zumbansen, Peer (2010) 'Transnational Legal Pluralism', *Transnational Legal Theory*, 1: 141–189.

Zweigert, K. and Kötz, H. (1987) *Introduction to Comparative Law*, T. Weir (trans.), 2nd edn., Oxford: Clarendon Press.

Index